JO-02

Readers of the manga version of Ceres will not be disappointed. In short, Ceres is beautiful, deep, and enjoyable—a topnotch supernatural work of art.
—John Robinson, NeedCoffee.com

Yû Watase's character designs are nothing short of spectacular. [She] is not only an amazing artist, but an amazing storyteller as well. Such depth is rarely found in any form of entertainment, but with Yû Watase at the helm of the project, it was guaranteed to be good.
—Louis Bedigian, DarkStation.com

The Ceres series is a great one, drama, action and suspense fill the plot and keep the pace moving while also keeping the continuing series interesting.
—John Stanley, DVDAnswerman.com

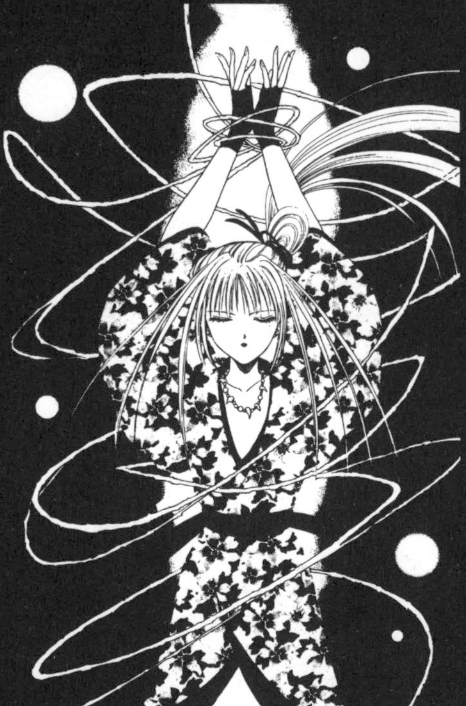

VIZ GRAPHIC NOVEL

Ceres™
Celestial Legend
VOL. 2 YUHI

Story and Art by
Yû Watase

CERES™
Celestial Legend
VOL. 2: Yūhi

This volume contains the CERES: CELESTIAL LEGEND installments from Part 2,
issue 1 through Part 2, issue 6 in their entirety.

STORY & ART BY YŪ WATASE

English Adaptation/Gary Leach

Translation/Lillian Olsen
Touch–Up Art & Lettering/Bill Schuch
Cover Design/Hidemi Sahara
Layout & Graphics/Carolina Ugalde
Editor/William Flanagan

Managing Editor/Annette Roman
Director of Sales & Marketing/Dallas Middaugh
Editor–in–Chief/Hyoe Narita
Publisher/Seiji Horibuchi

Printed in Canada

Published by Viz Communications, Inc.
P.O. Box 77010 • San Francisco, CA 94107

10 9 8 7 6 5 4 3 2 1
First printing, September 2002

Get your FREE Viz Shop-By-Mail catalog at store.viz.com!

· get your own vizmail.net email account
· register for the weekly email newsletter
· sign up for your free catalog

On the day of their sixteenth birthday, boisterous Aya Mikage and her twin brother Aki are required to attend a strange ceremony at the mansion of their grandfather. The two are shown a mummified hand which causes Aki's body to be lacerated with multiple wounds, and Aya to feel powers emerge—powers she doesn't understand. Aya's grandfather, the patriarch of the powerful Mikage family, announces that Aki is to be taken into seclusion, and Aya is to be killed!

With the aid of a handsome-but-mysterious man who ostensibly works for the Mikage family, Tôya, Aya manages to escape the clutches of the murderous Mikage household and is rushed into the arms of two odd allies: the beautiful traditional-dancing teacher Suzumi Aogiri and her stepbrother, the hapless martial-artist Yûhi Aogiri. Suzumi is an indirect descendant of a being called a "Celestial Maiden," a character out of a Japanese fairy tale, and Suzumi tells Aya that she is a direct descendant of a similar being with powers far surpassing Suzumi's telekinetic tricks.

With strangers making unbelievable claims, and her own family seemingly out to kill her, Aya makes her way back to the Mikage mansion to try to make sense of the world. But the Mikage's intent to murder Aya is all-too real, and Aya's father is killed trying to protect his daughter. Again with the aid of Tôya, Aya escapes.

Aya tries to live with the Aogiris, but her longing for her brother leads her back to her own home. There she finds her mother, but because of lies told her by Kagami, the CEO of the Mikage's corporation, Aya's mother is convinced that Aya murdered her father. Wielding a kitchen knife, Aya's mother chases Aya through the house, and before Yûhi and Tôya can rescue her, Aya suddenly transforms into the Celestial Maiden that Suzumi talked about—she changes into Ceres!

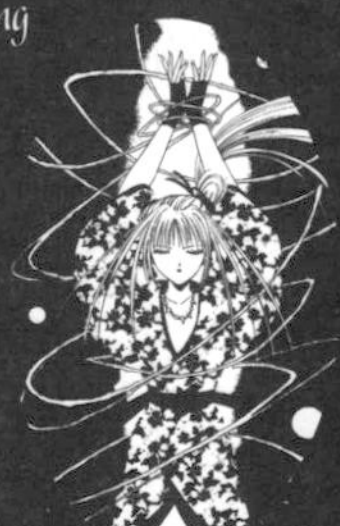

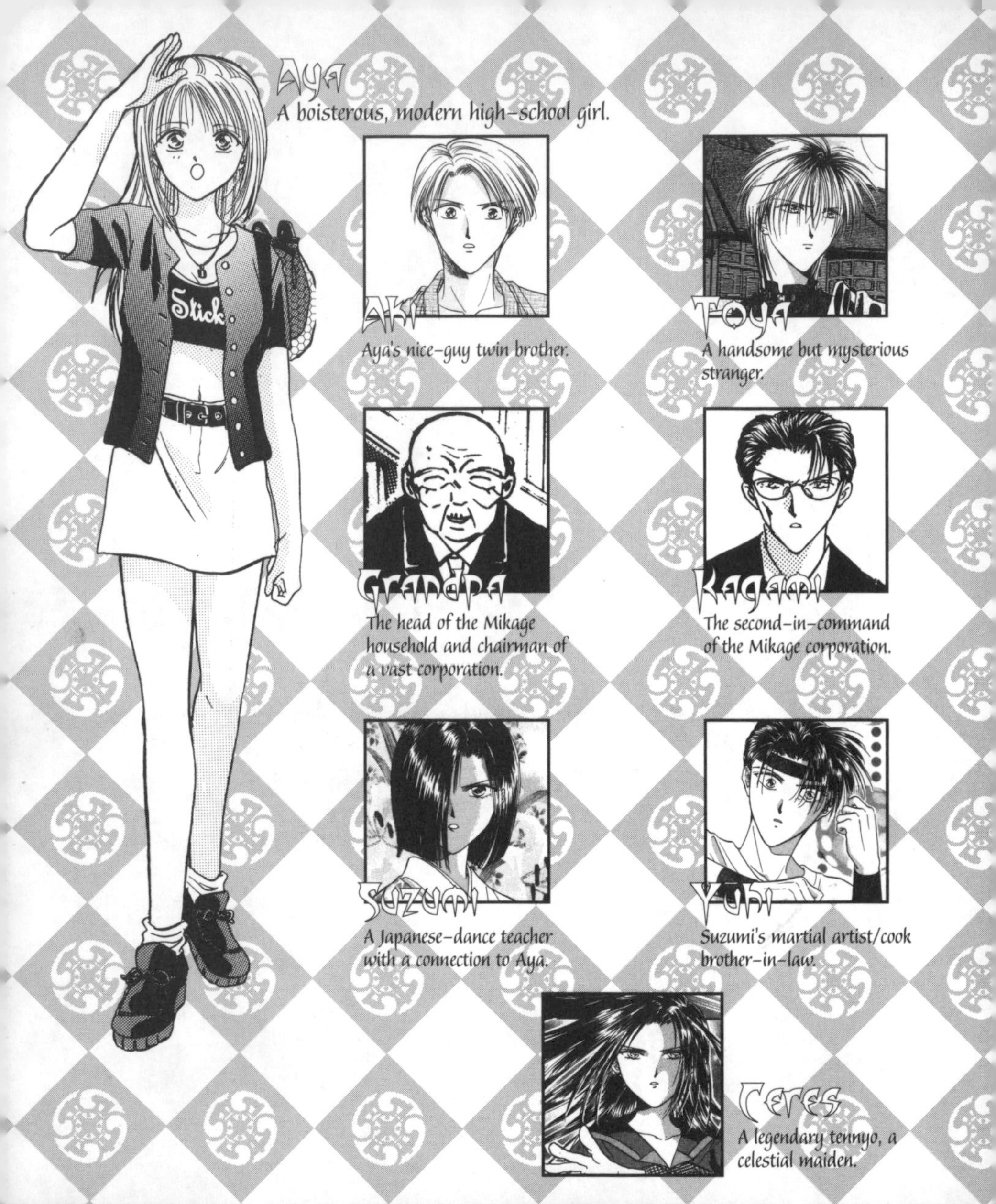
Aya
A boisterous, modern high-school girl.
Aki
Aya's nice-guy twin brother.
Toya
A handsome but mysterious stranger.
Grandpa
The head of the Mikage household and chairman of a vast corporation.
Kagami
The second-in-command of the Mikage corporation.
Suzumi
A Japanese-dance teacher with a connection to Aya.
Yuhi
Suzumi's martial artist/cook brother-in-law.
Ceres
A legendary tennyo, a celestial maiden.

With the author's support, this edition is translated to appeal to the tastes of American readers—meaning that some of the Japanese pop-culture references have been replaced with American equivalents. You may find below a list of the original references.

Page 27:	The beautiful, serious Natilie Merchant was originally the beautiful-but-frivolous Chisato Moritaka. Neither *really* looks like Mrs. Q.
Page 46:	The Abba Teens were actually the overly energetic Japanese band, the Ulfuls.

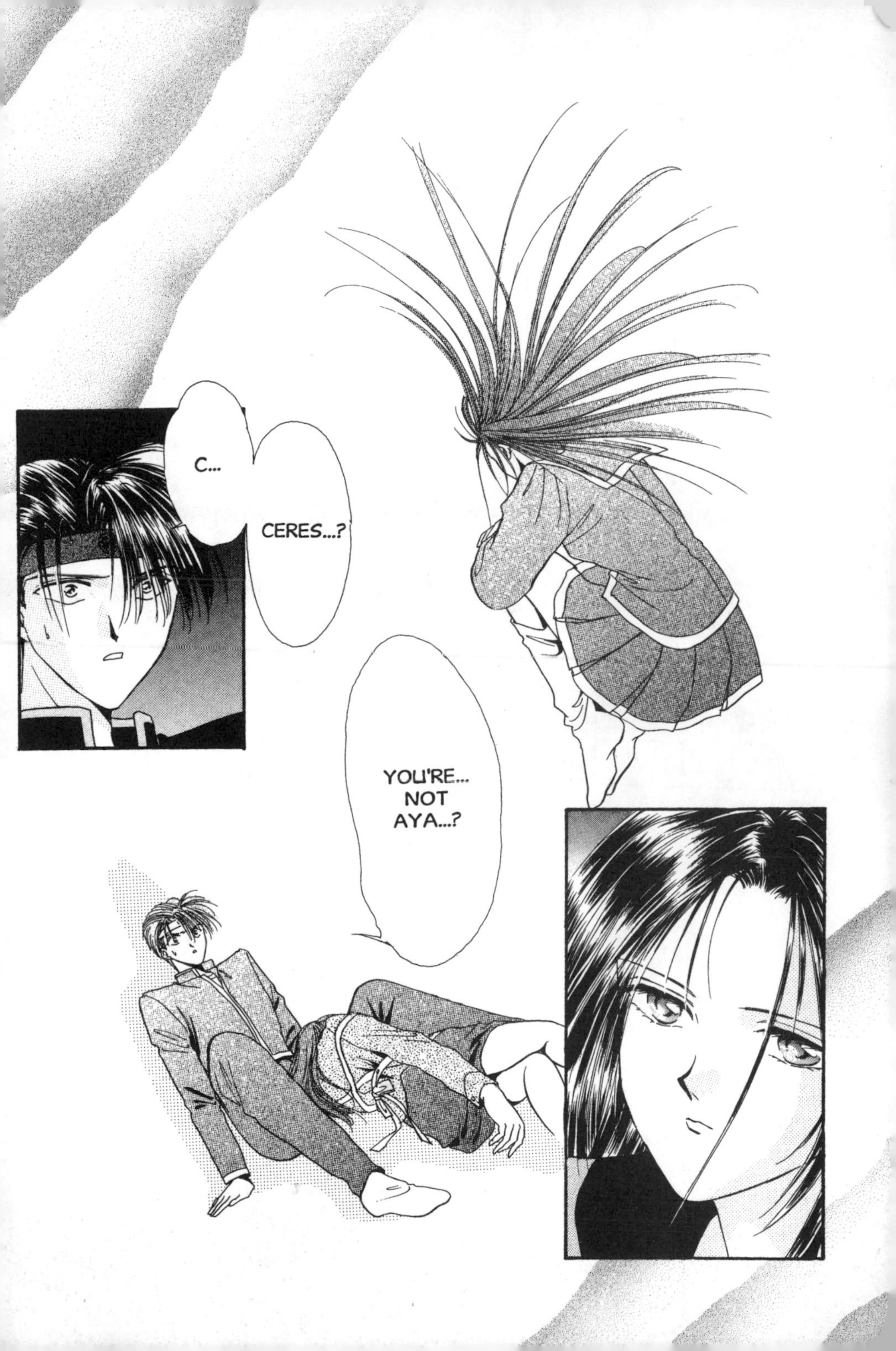
C...
CERES...?
YOU'RE... NOT AYA...?

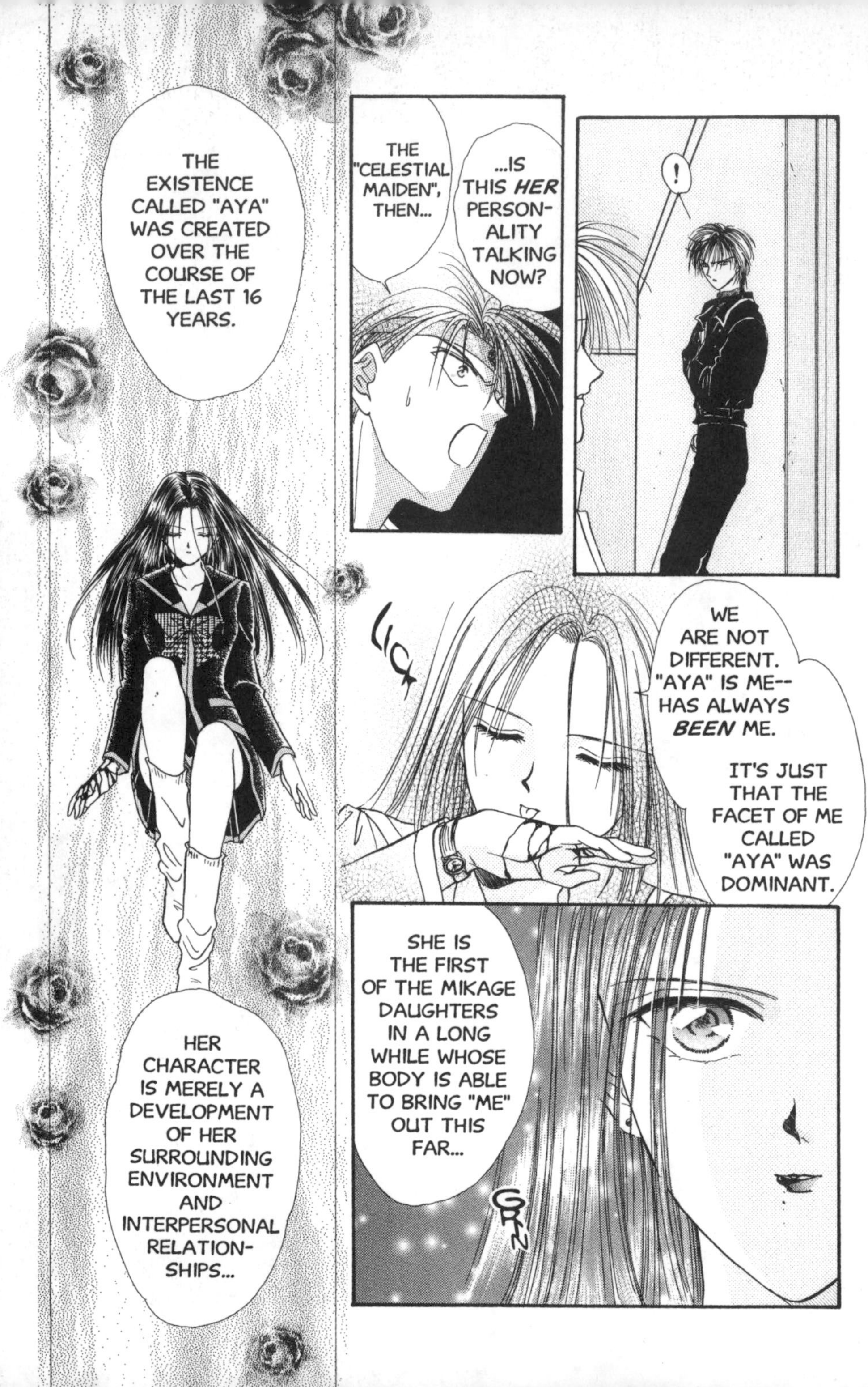
!
THE "CELESTIAL MAIDEN", THEN...
...IS THIS *HER* PERSONALITY TALKING NOW?
LICK
WE ARE NOT DIFFERENT. "AYA" IS ME-- HAS ALWAYS *BEEN* ME.
IT'S JUST THAT THE FACET OF ME CALLED "AYA" WAS DOMINANT.
SHE IS THE FIRST OF THE MIKAGE DAUGHTERS IN A LONG WHILE WHOSE BODY IS ABLE TO BRING "ME" OUT THIS FAR...
GRIN
THE EXISTENCE CALLED "AYA" WAS CREATED OVER THE COURSE OF THE LAST 16 YEARS.
HER CHARACTER IS MERELY A DEVELOPMENT OF HER SURROUNDING ENVIRONMENT AND INTERPERSONAL RELATION-SHIPS...

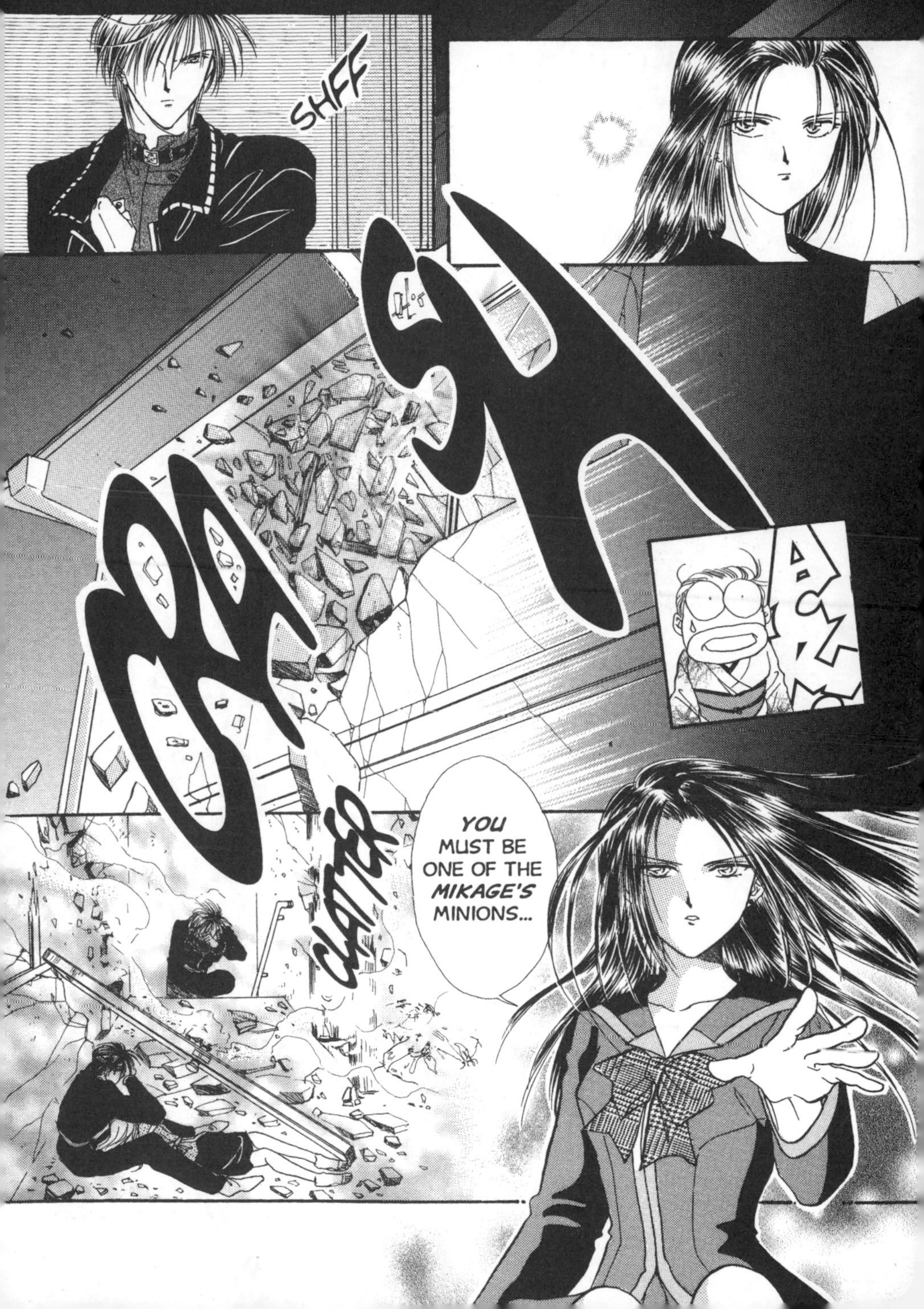
SHFF
AACK
YOU MUST BE ONE OF THE *MIKAGE'S* MINIONS...

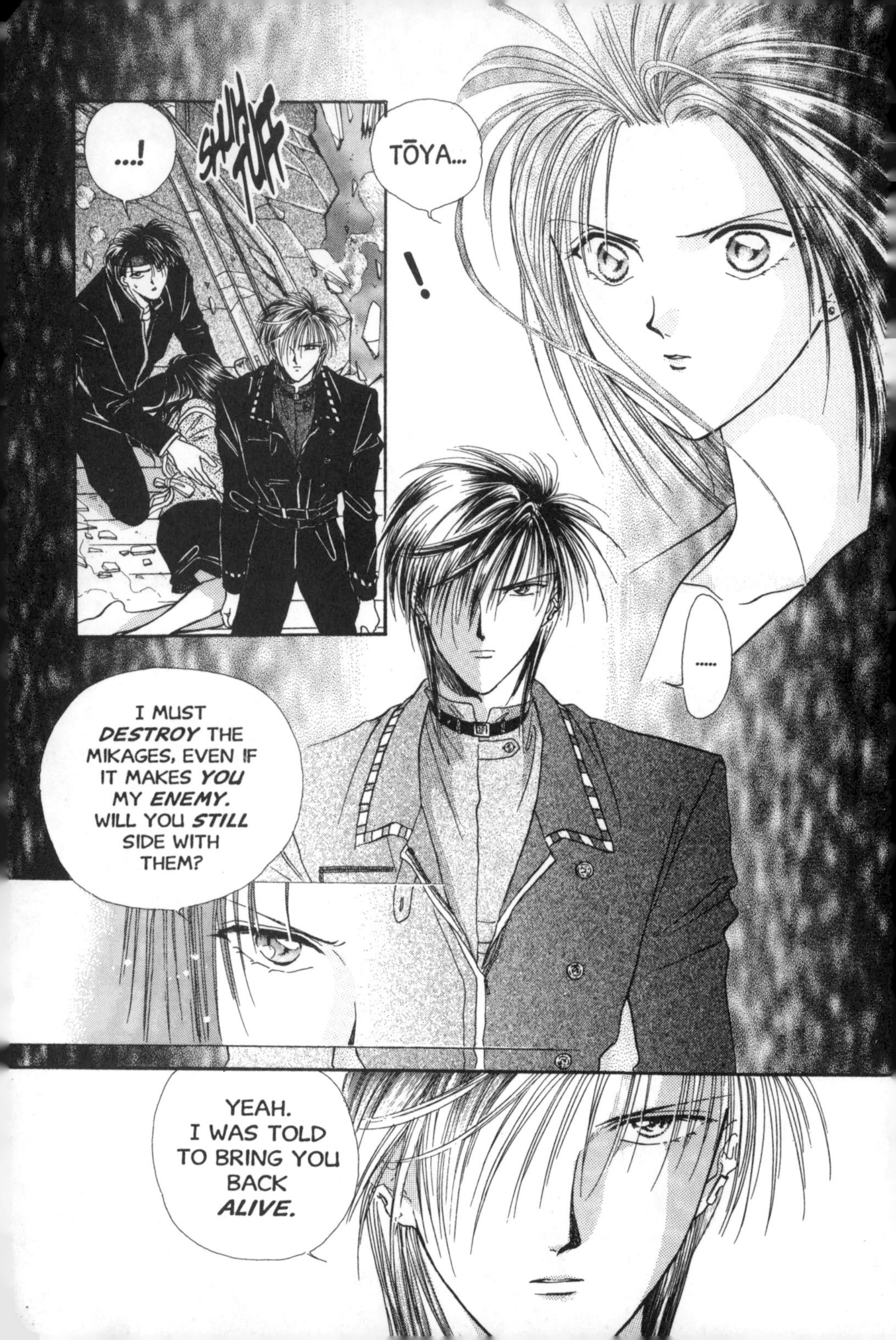
TŌYA...
!
...!
SHUH TUP
......
I MUST *DESTROY* THE MIKAGES, EVEN IF IT MAKES *YOU* MY *ENEMY.* WILL YOU *STILL* SIDE WITH THEM?
YEAH. I WAS TOLD TO BRING YOU BACK *ALIVE.*

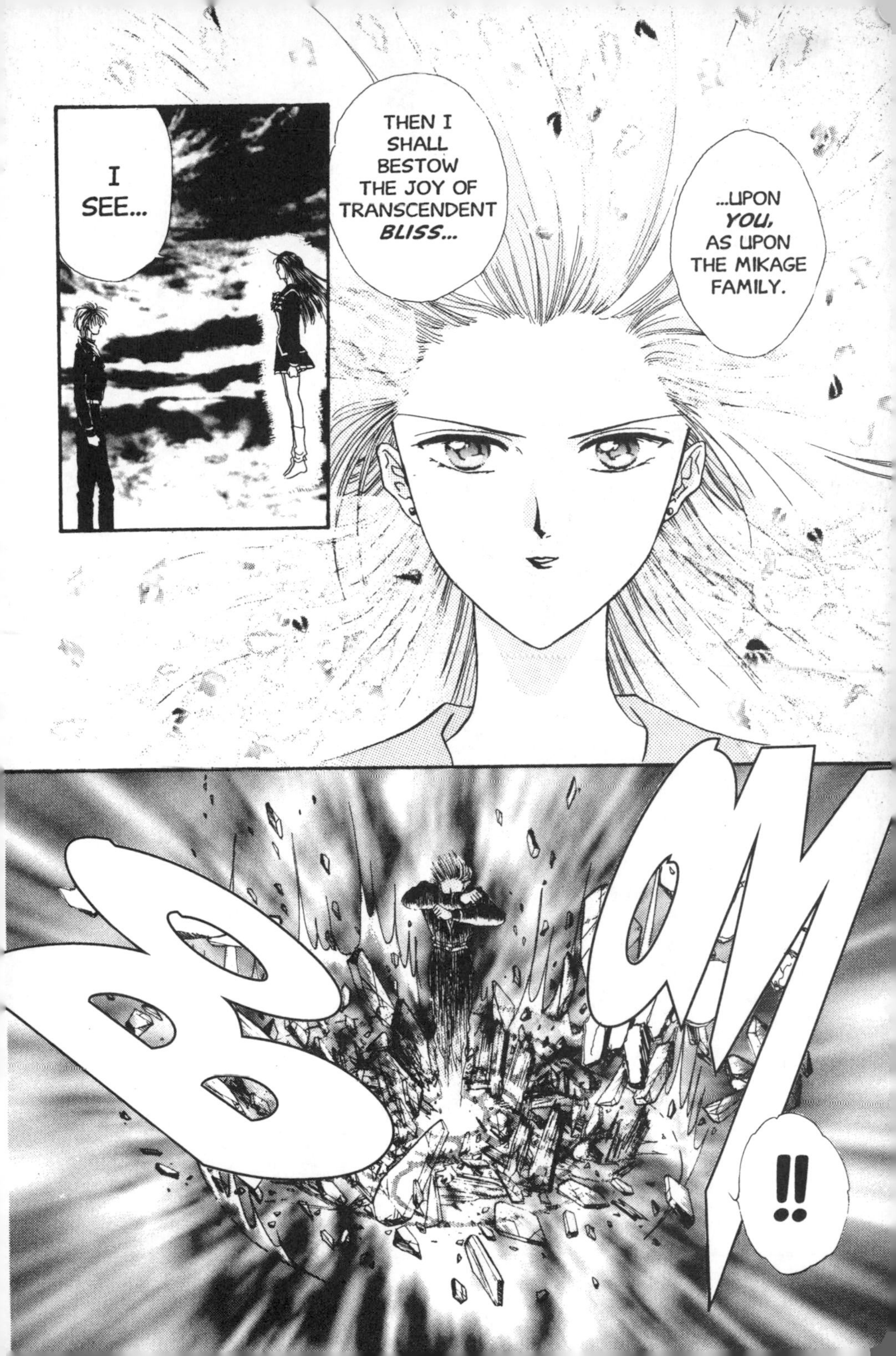
I SEE...
THEN I SHALL BESTOW THE JOY OF TRANSCENDENT *BLISS*...
...UPON *YOU,* AS UPON THE MIKAGE FAMILY.
BAM
!!

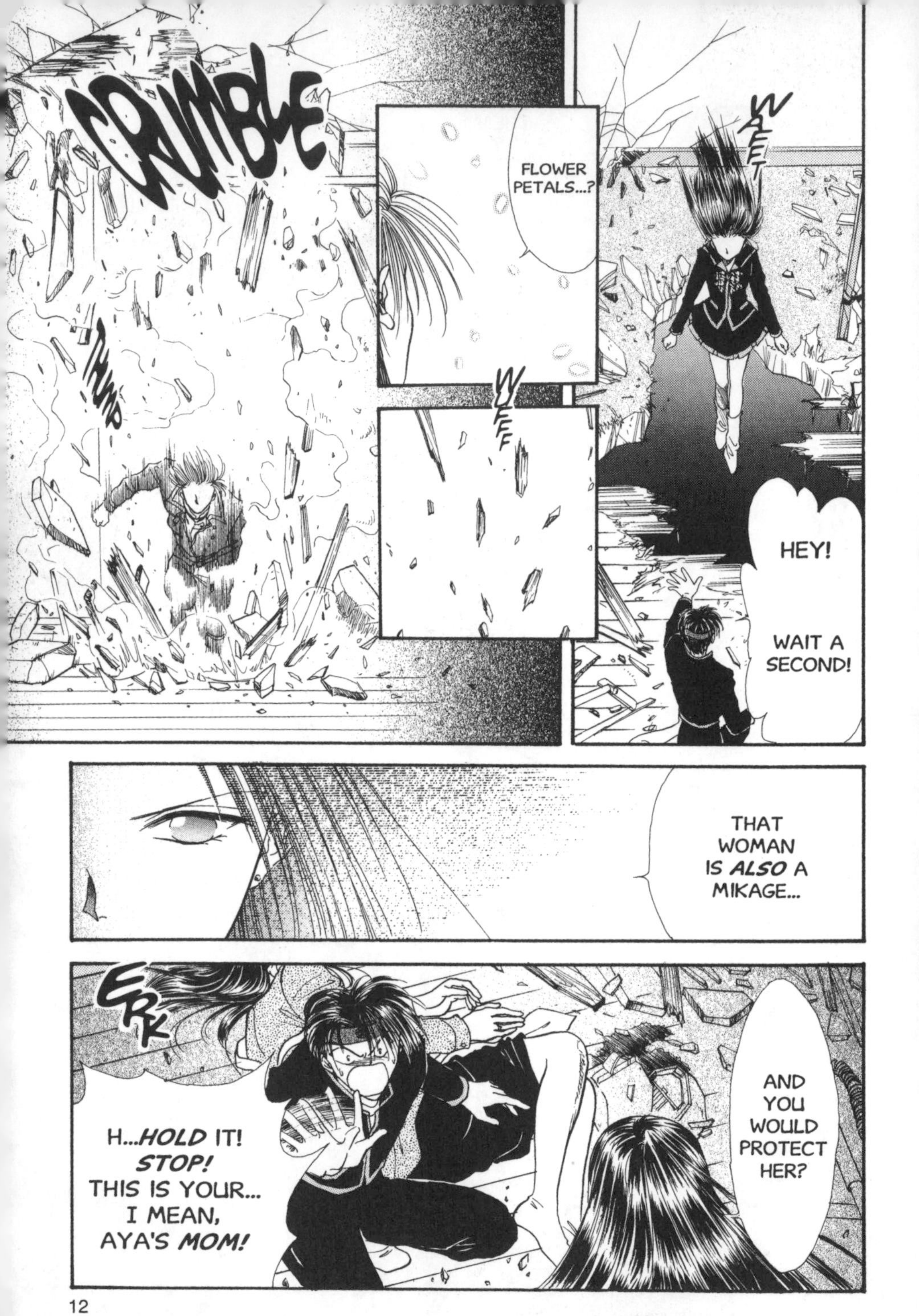
WAEET
HEY!
WAIT A SECOND!
FLOWER PETALS...?
WEFF
CRUMBLE
THUMP
THAT WOMAN IS *ALSO* A MIKAGE...
AND YOU WOULD PROTECT HER?
ERK
H...*HOLD* IT! *STOP!* THIS IS YOUR... I MEAN, AYA'S *MOM!*

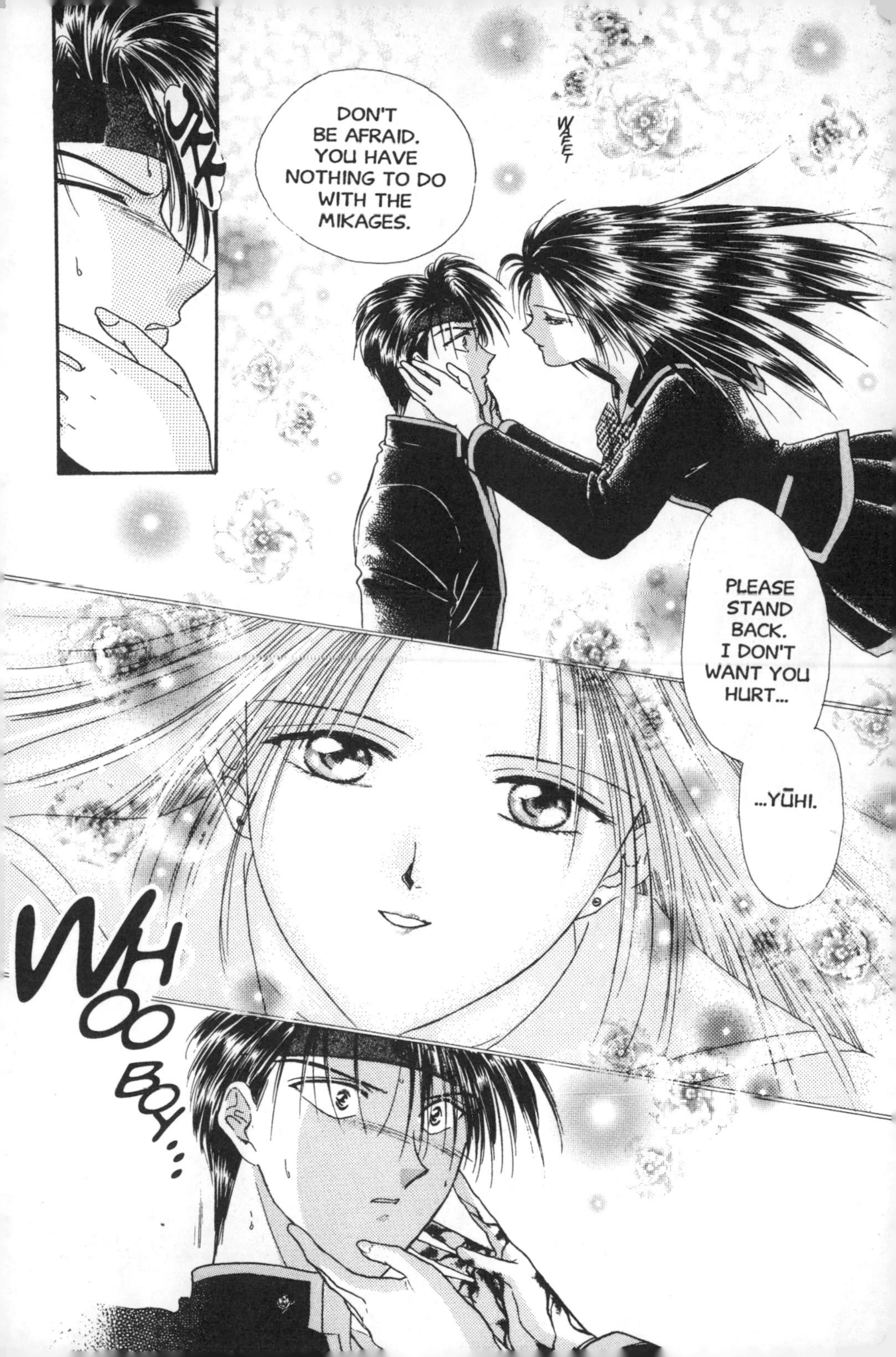
WAFT
DON'T BE AFRAID. YOU HAVE NOTHING TO DO WITH THE MIKAGES.
UKK
PLEASE STAND BACK. I DON'T WANT YOU HURT...
...YŪHI.
WHOO BOOH...

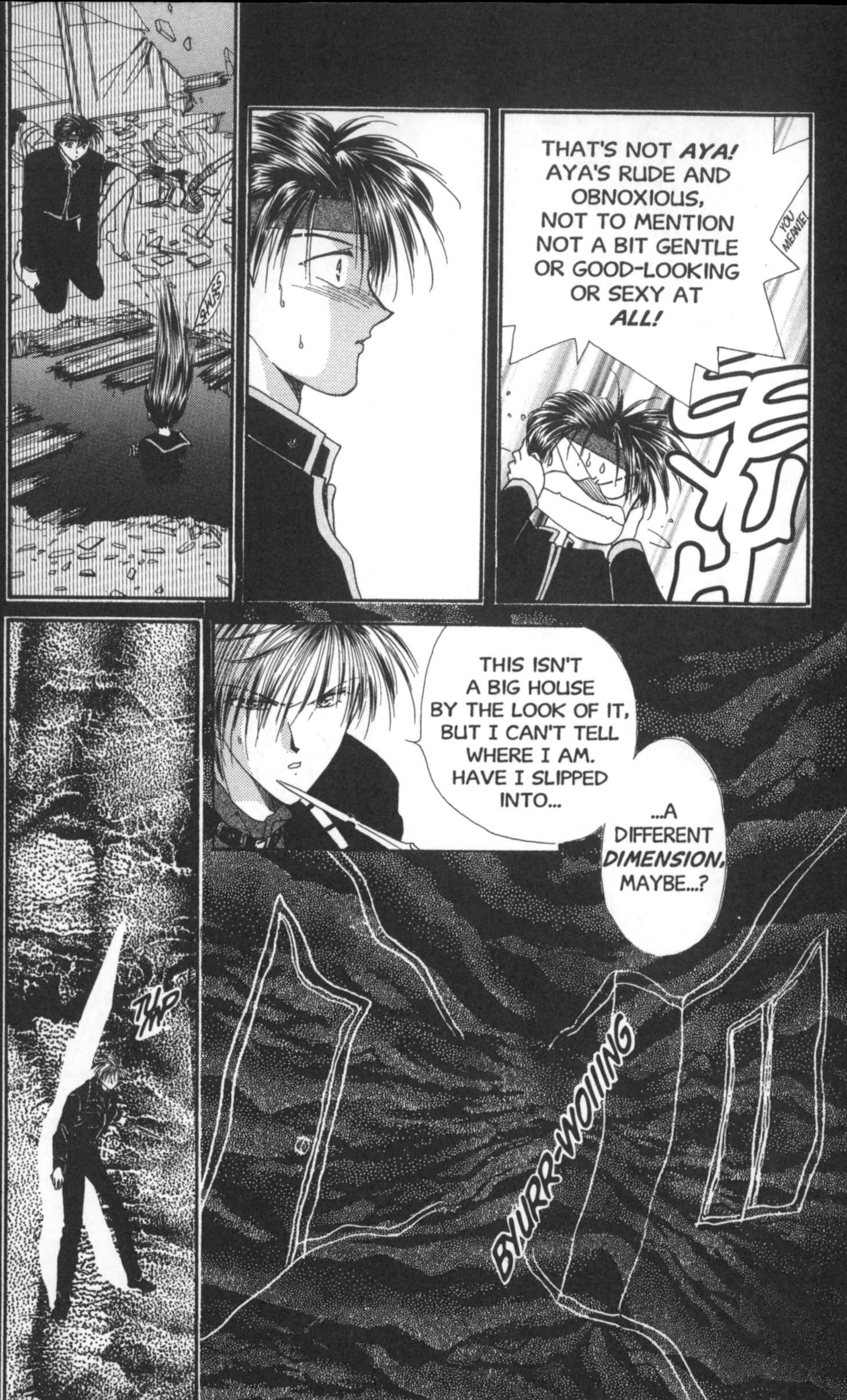
THAT'S NOT AYA! AYA'S RUDE AND OBNOXIOUS, NOT TO MENTION NOT A BIT GENTLE OR GOOD-LOOKING OR SEXY AT ALL!
YOU MEANIE!
SWISS
THIS ISN'T A BIG HOUSE BY THE LOOK OF IT, BUT I CAN'T TELL WHERE I AM. HAVE I SLIPPED INTO...
...A DIFFERENT DIMENSION, MAYBE...?
BYURR-WOIIING
THMP

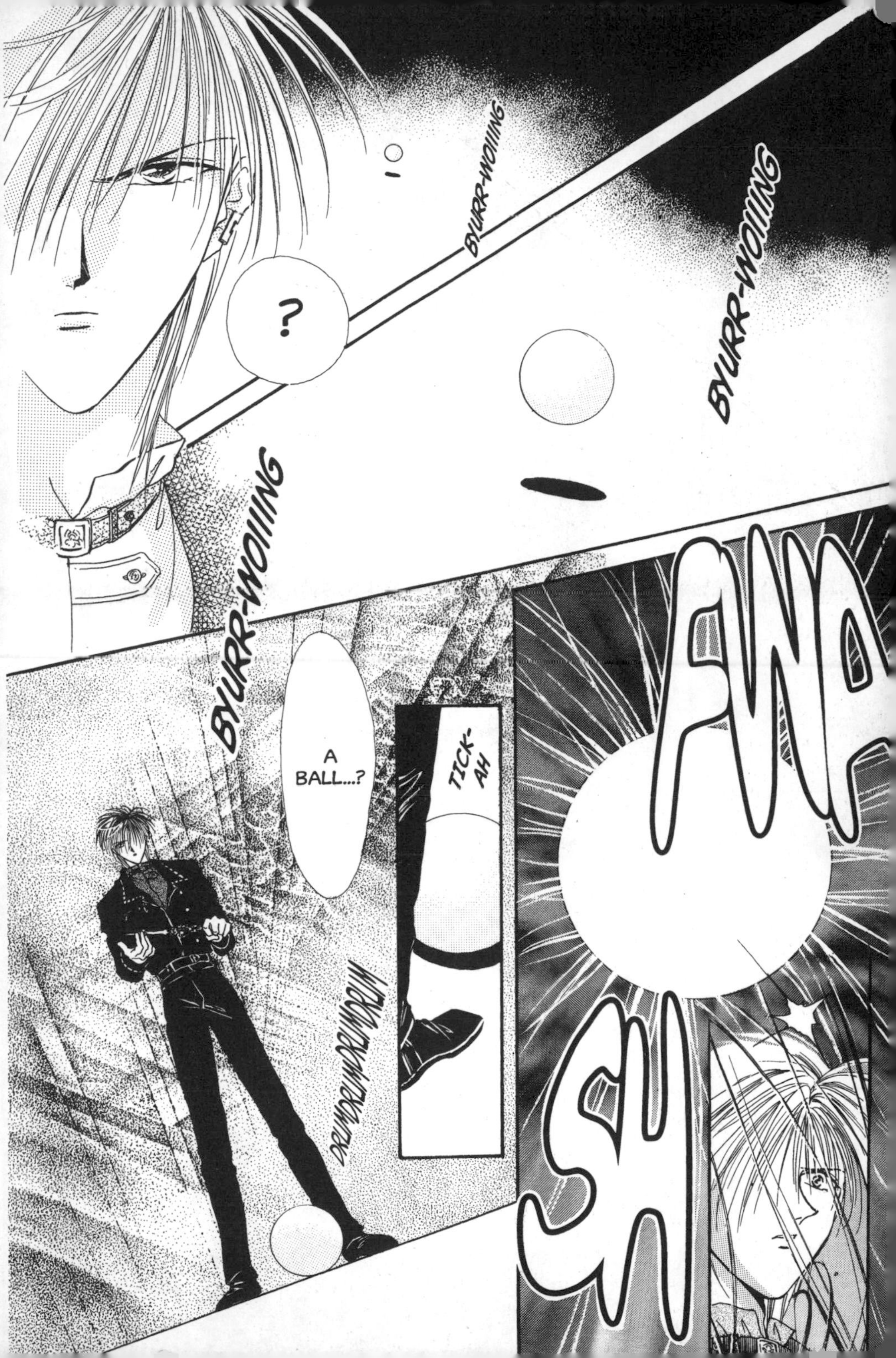
BYURR-WOIIING
BYURR-WOIIING
?
BYURR-WOIIING
BYURR-WOIIING
SHFWAP
TICK-AH
A BALL...?
DRUMDRUMDRUMDRUM

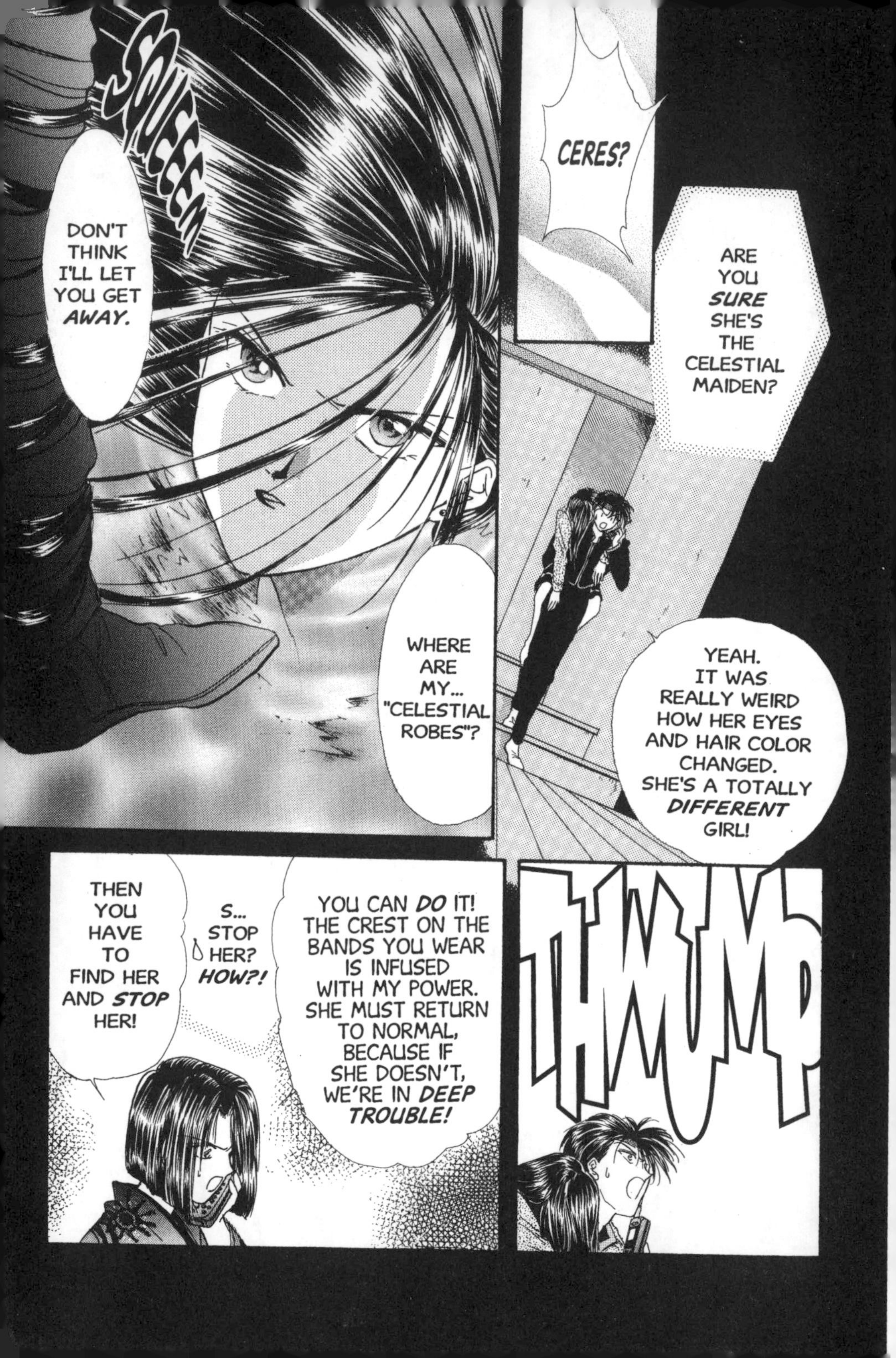
CERES?
ARE YOU *SURE* SHE'S THE CELESTIAL MAIDEN?
YEAH. IT WAS REALLY WEIRD HOW HER EYES AND HAIR COLOR CHANGED. SHE'S A TOTALLY *DIFFERENT* GIRL!
SQUEEEM
DON'T THINK I'LL LET YOU GET *AWAY.*
WHERE ARE MY... "CELESTIAL ROBES"?
THUMP
YOU CAN *DO* IT! THE CREST ON THE BANDS YOU WEAR IS INFUSED WITH MY POWER. SHE MUST RETURN TO NORMAL, BECAUSE IF SHE DOESN'T, WE'RE IN *DEEP TROUBLE!*
S... STOP HER? *HOW?!*
THEN YOU HAVE TO FIND HER AND *STOP* HER!

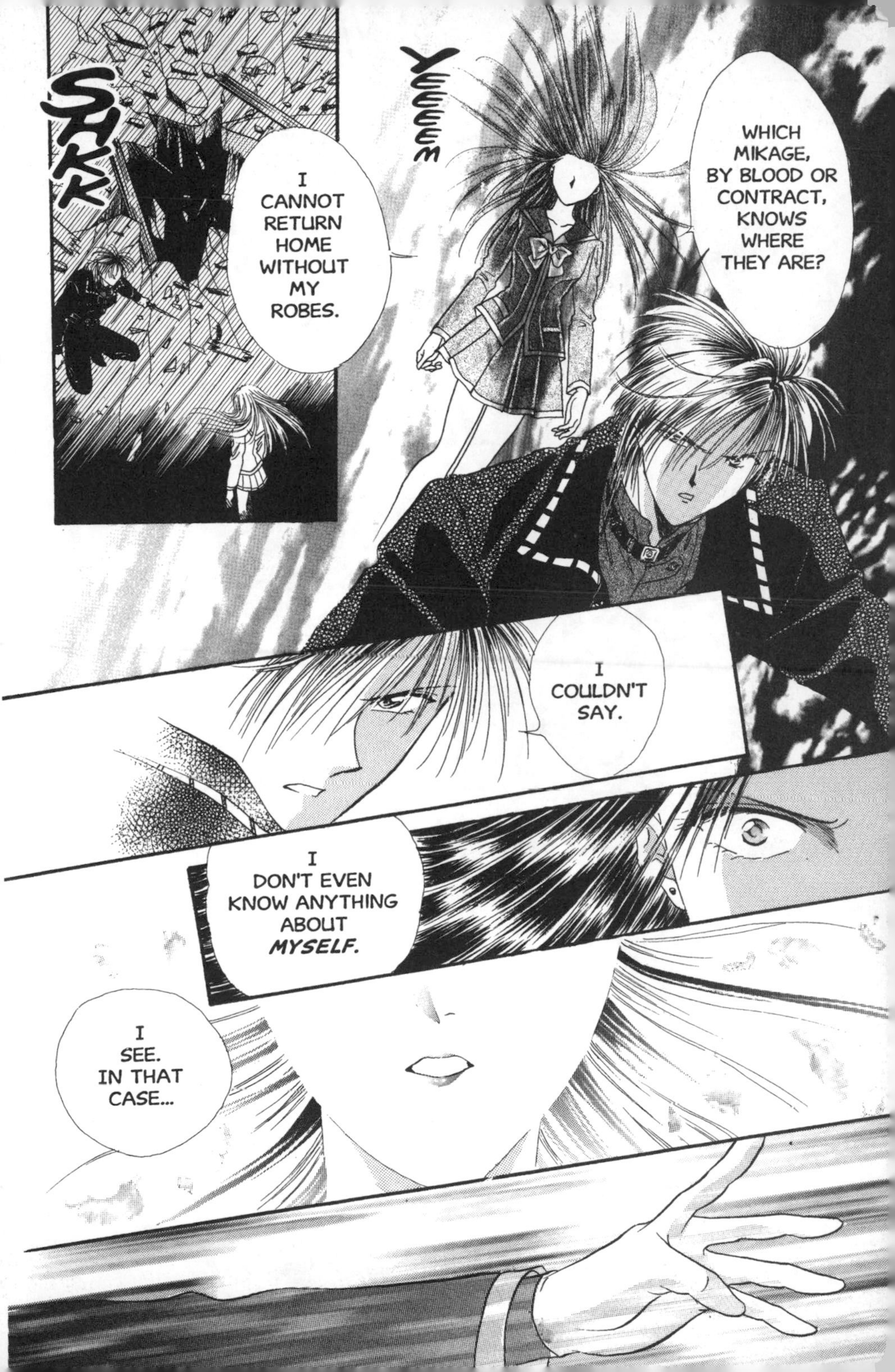
SHAKK
YEEEEM
I CANNOT RETURN HOME WITHOUT MY ROBES.
WHICH MIKAGE, BY BLOOD OR CONTRACT, KNOWS WHERE THEY ARE?
I COULDN'T SAY.
I DON'T EVEN KNOW ANYTHING ABOUT *MYSELF*.
I SEE. IN THAT CASE...

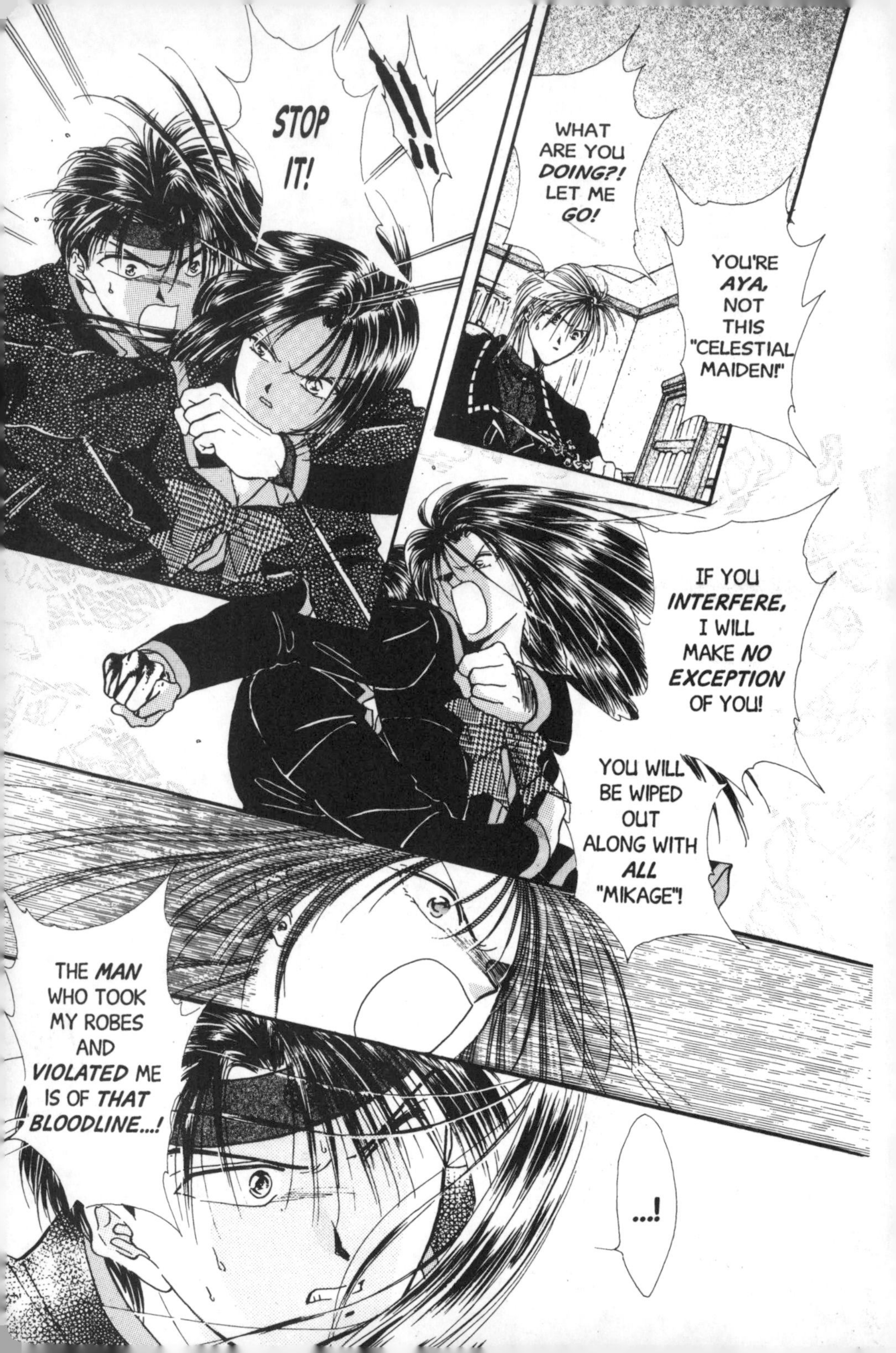
STOP IT!
WHAT ARE YOU DOING?! LET ME GO!
YOU'RE AYA, NOT THIS "CELESTIAL MAIDEN!"
IF YOU INTERFERE, I WILL MAKE NO EXCEPTION OF YOU!
YOU WILL BE WIPED OUT ALONG WITH ALL "MIKAGE"!
THE MAN WHO TOOK MY ROBES AND VIOLATED ME IS OF THAT BLOODLINE...!
...!

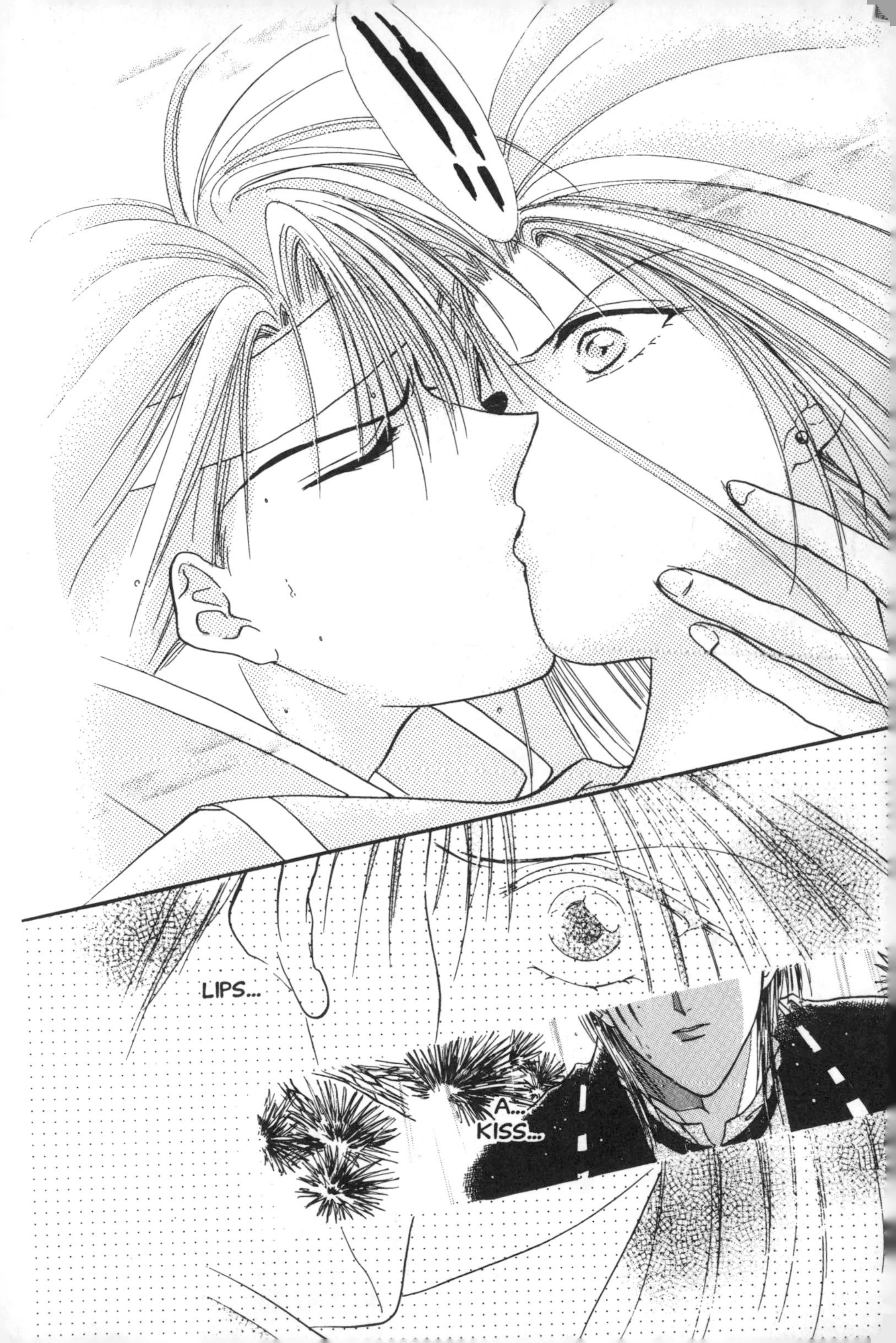
LIPS...
A...
KISS...

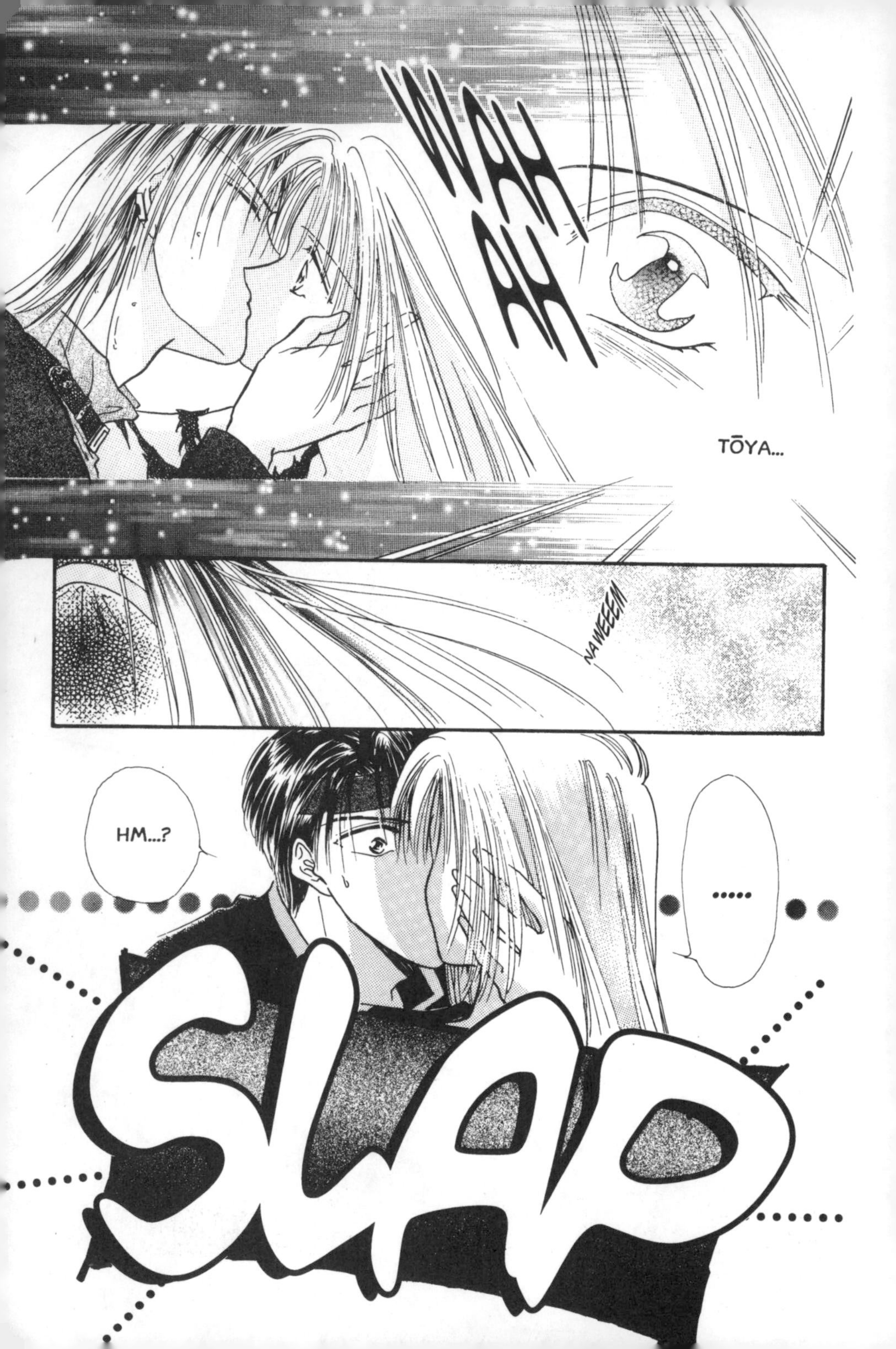
WAH AH
TŌYA...
NAWEEEM
.....
HM...?
SLAP

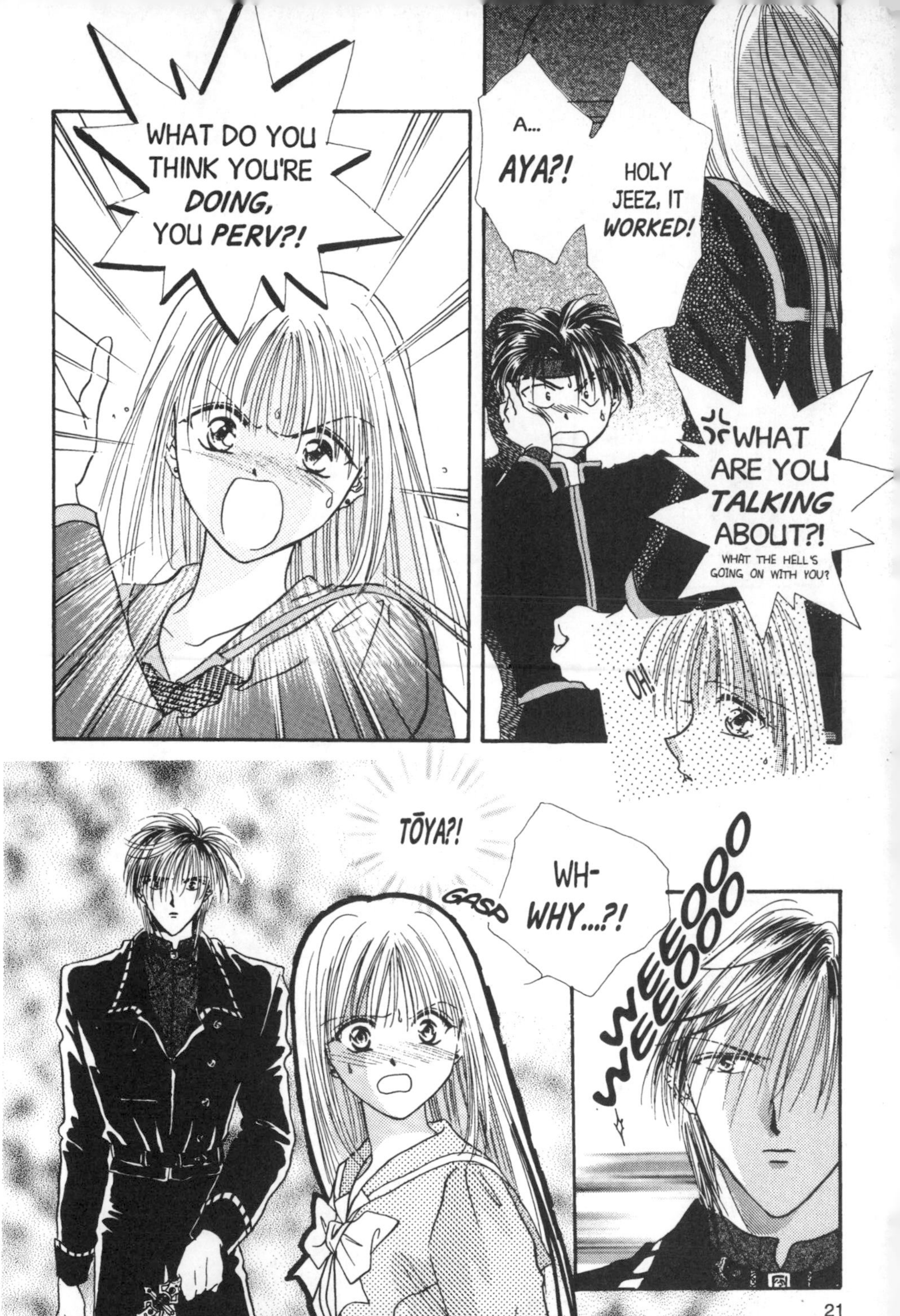
A... AYA?!
HOLY JEEZ, IT WORKED!
WHAT ARE YOU TALKING ABOUT?!
WHAT THE HELL'S GOING ON WITH YOU?
OH!
WHAT DO YOU THINK YOU'RE DOING, YOU PERV?!
WEEOOOO WEEOOOO
TŌYA?!
GASP
WH- WHY...?!

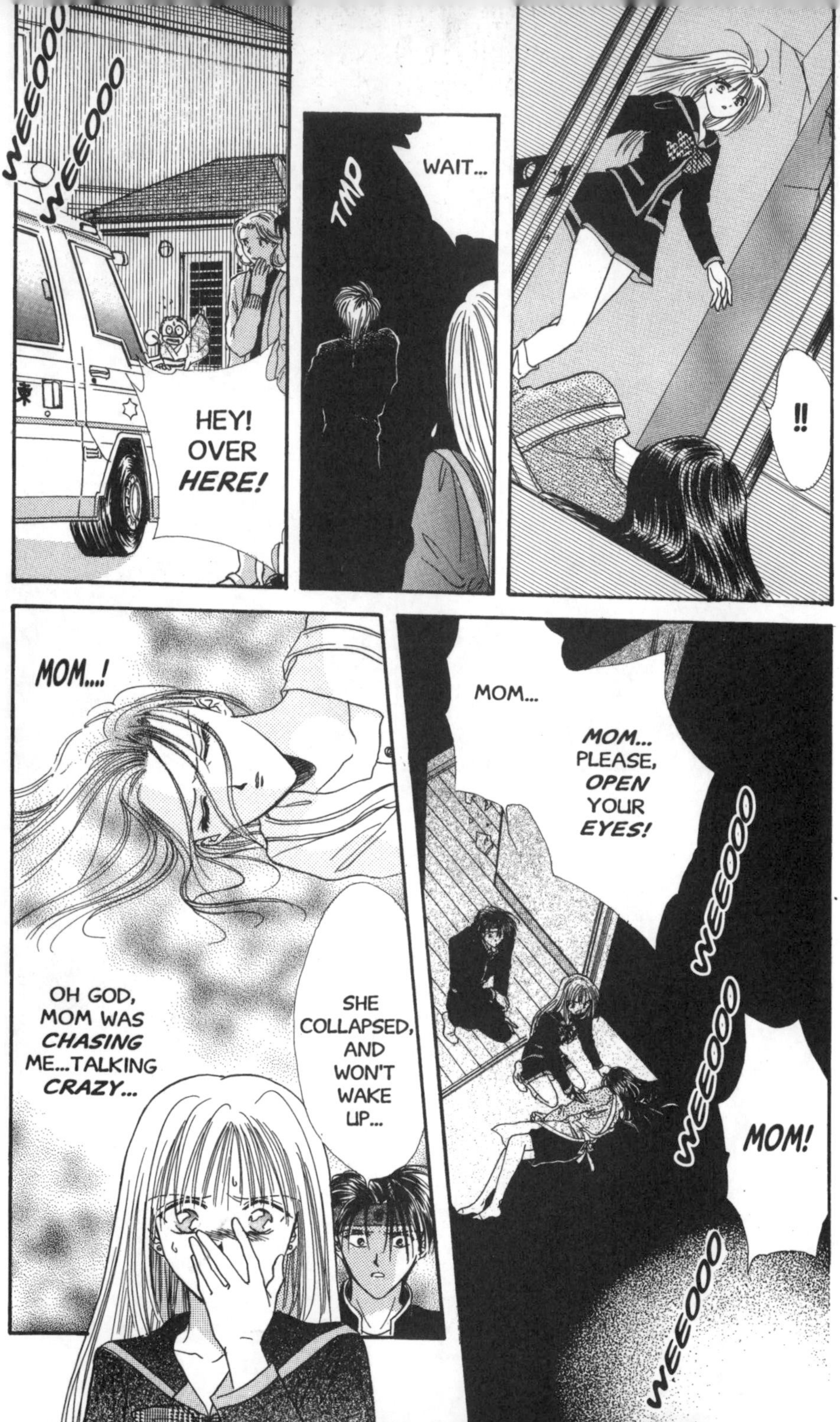
!!
TMP
WAIT...
WEEOOO
WEEOOO
HEY! OVER HERE!
MOM...
MOM... PLEASE, OPEN YOUR EYES!
WEEOOO
WEEOOO
MOM!
WEEOOO
MOM...!
SHE COLLAPSED, AND WON'T WAKE UP...
OH GOD, MOM WAS CHASING ME...TALKING CRAZY...

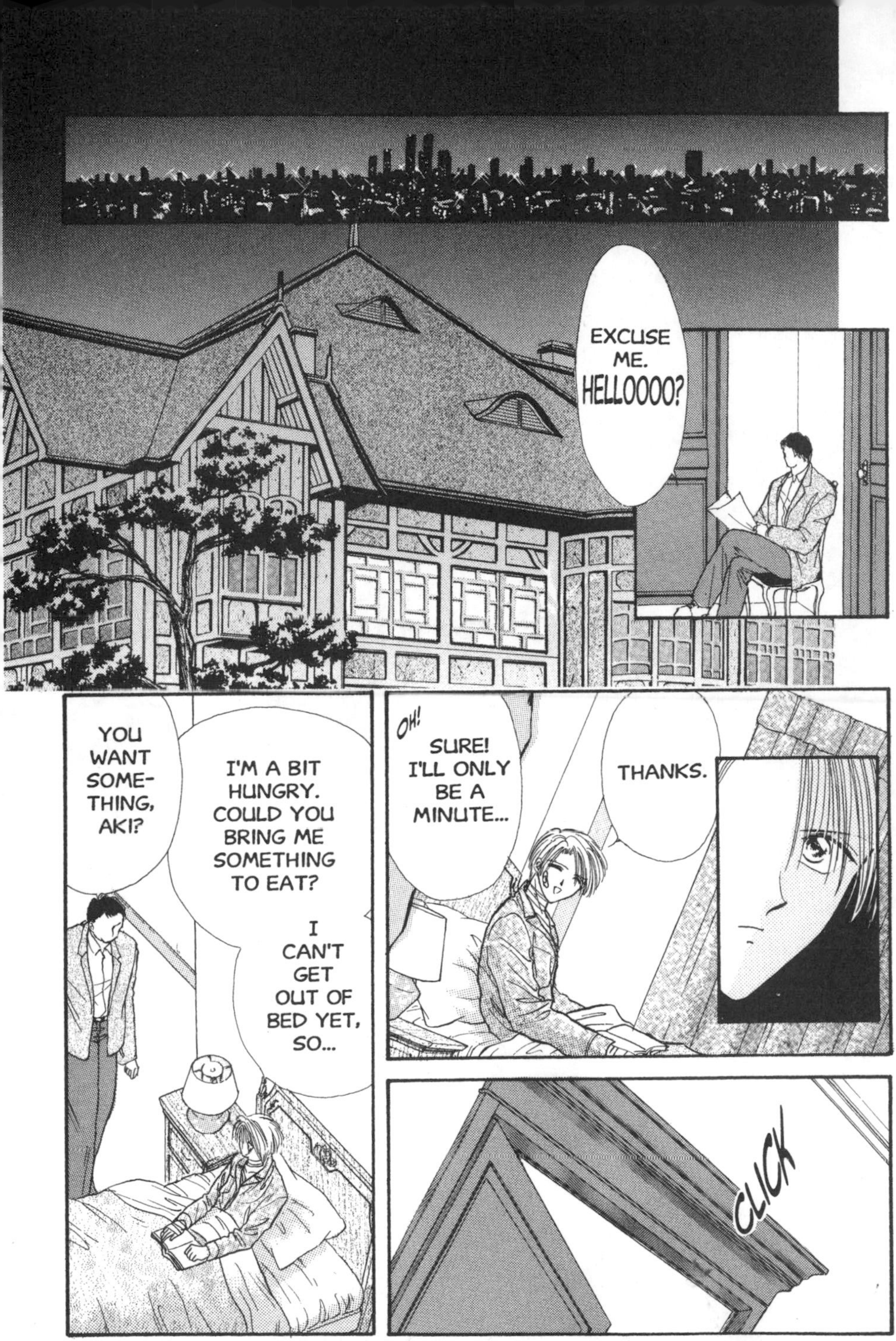
EXCUSE ME. HELLOOOO?
YOU WANT SOMETHING, AKI?
I'M A BIT HUNGRY. COULD YOU BRING ME SOMETHING TO EAT?
I CAN'T GET OUT OF BED YET, SO...
OH!
SURE! I'LL ONLY BE A MINUTE...
THANKS.
CLICK

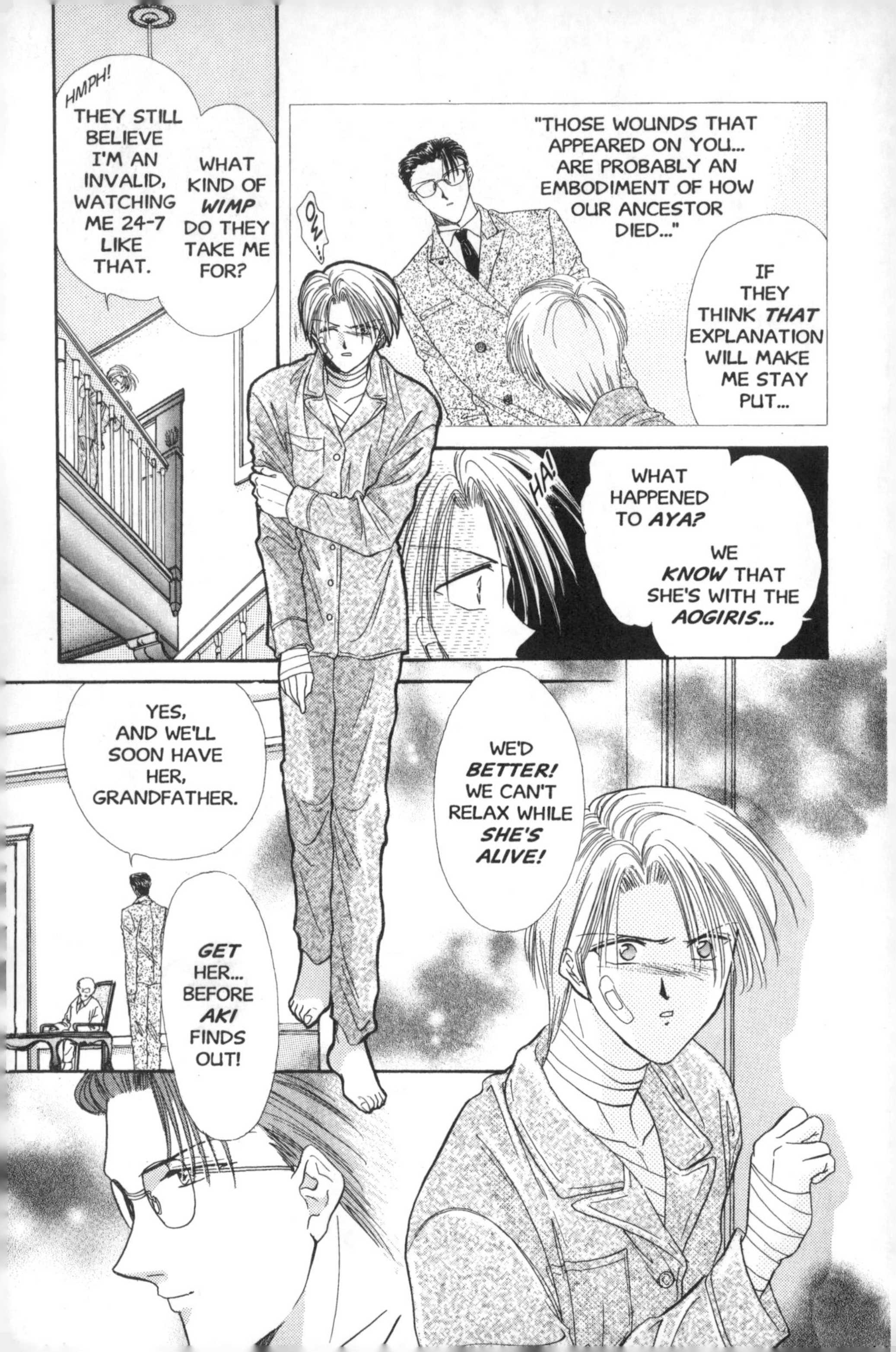
"THOSE WOUNDS THAT APPEARED ON YOU... ARE PROBABLY AN EMBODIMENT OF HOW OUR ANCESTOR DIED..."
OW...!
IF THEY THINK THAT EXPLANATION WILL MAKE ME STAY PUT...
HA!
WHAT HAPPENED TO AYA?
WE KNOW THAT SHE'S WITH THE AOGIRIS...
HMPH!
THEY STILL BELIEVE I'M AN INVALID, WATCHING ME 24-7 LIKE THAT.
WHAT KIND OF WIMP DO THEY TAKE ME FOR?
YES, AND WE'LL SOON HAVE HER, GRANDFATHER.
GET HER... BEFORE AKI FINDS OUT!
WE'D BETTER! WE CAN'T RELAX WHILE SHE'S ALIVE!

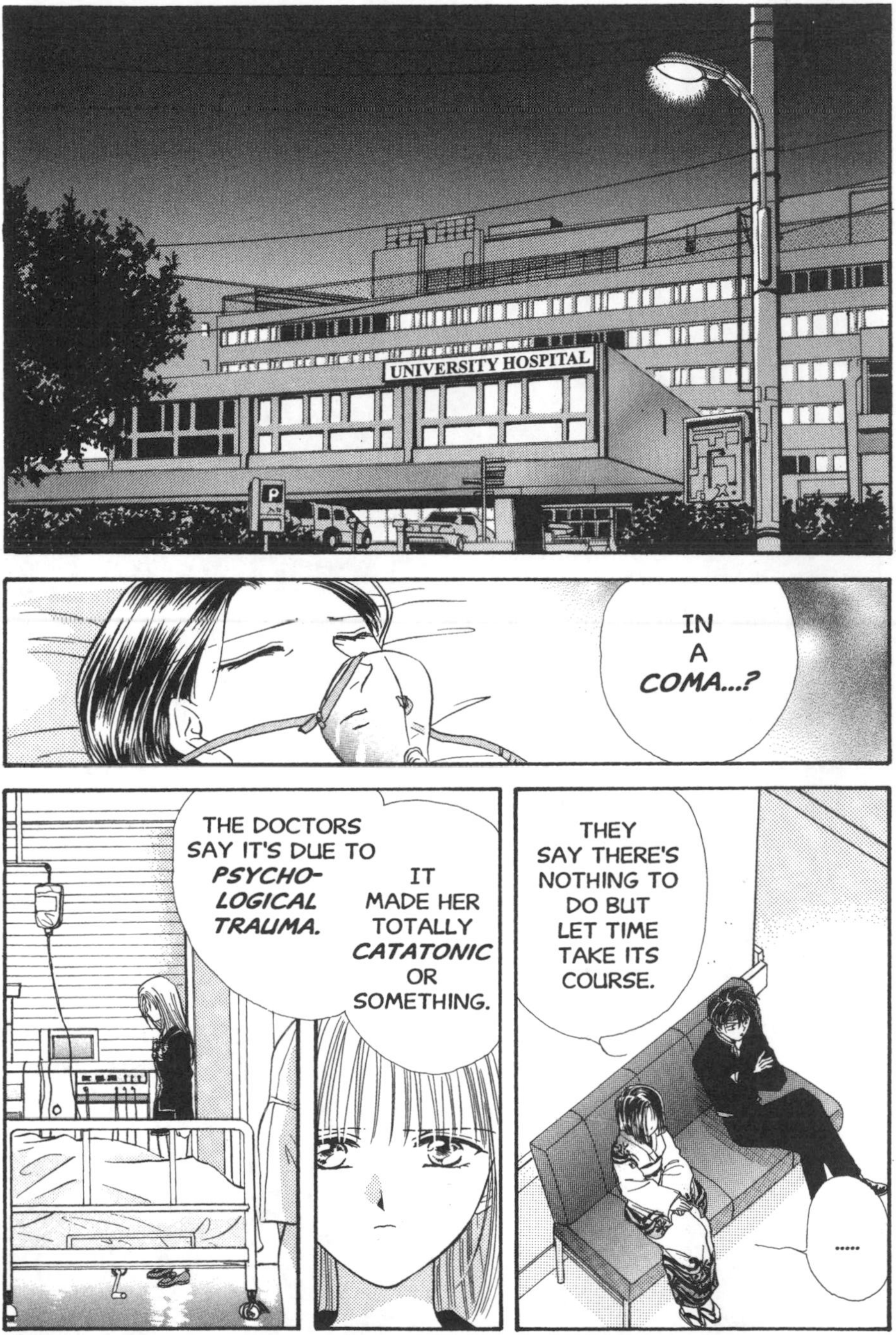
UNIVERSITY HOSPITAL
IN A COMA...?
THE DOCTORS SAY IT'S DUE TO PSYCHOLOGICAL TRAUMA.
IT MADE HER TOTALLY CATATONIC OR SOMETHING.
THEY SAY THERE'S NOTHING TO DO BUT LET TIME TAKE ITS COURSE.
.....

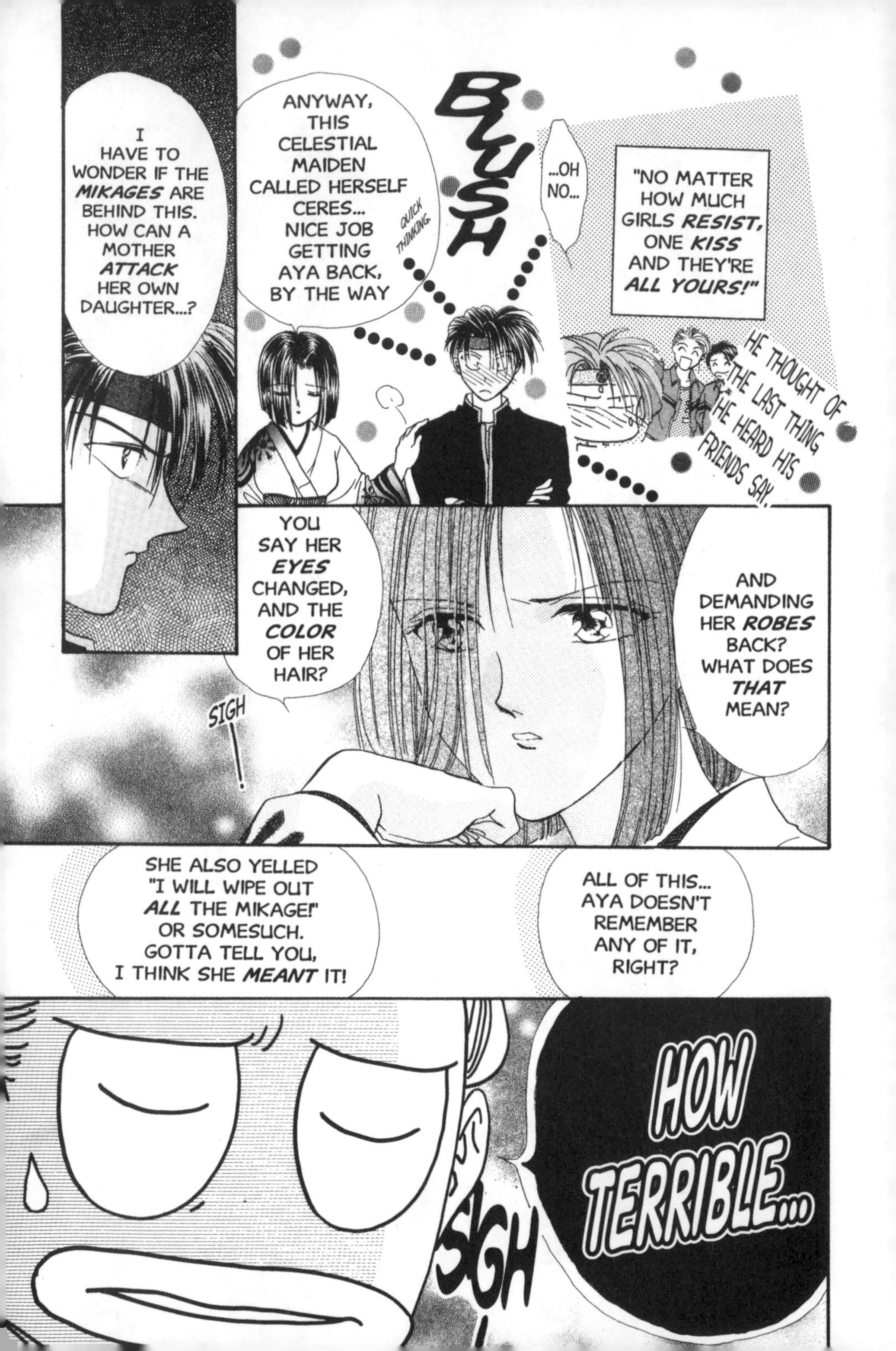

I HAVE TO WONDER IF THE MIKAGES ARE BEHIND THIS. HOW CAN A MOTHER ATTACK HER OWN DAUGHTER...?
ANYWAY, THIS CELESTIAL MAIDEN CALLED HERSELF CERES... NICE JOB GETTING AYA BACK, BY THE WAY
QUICK THINKING.
BLUSH
...OH NO...
"NO MATTER HOW MUCH GIRLS RESIST, ONE KISS AND THEY'RE ALL YOURS!"
HE THOUGHT OF THE LAST THING HE HEARD HIS FRIENDS SAY.
YOU SAY HER EYES CHANGED, AND THE COLOR OF HER HAIR?
SIGH
AND DEMANDING HER ROBES BACK? WHAT DOES THAT MEAN?
SHE ALSO YELLED "I WILL WIPE OUT ALL THE MIKAGE!" OR SOMESUCH. GOTTA TELL YOU, I THINK SHE MEANT IT!
ALL OF THIS... AYA DOESN'T REMEMBER ANY OF IT, RIGHT?
SIGH
HOW TERRIBLE...

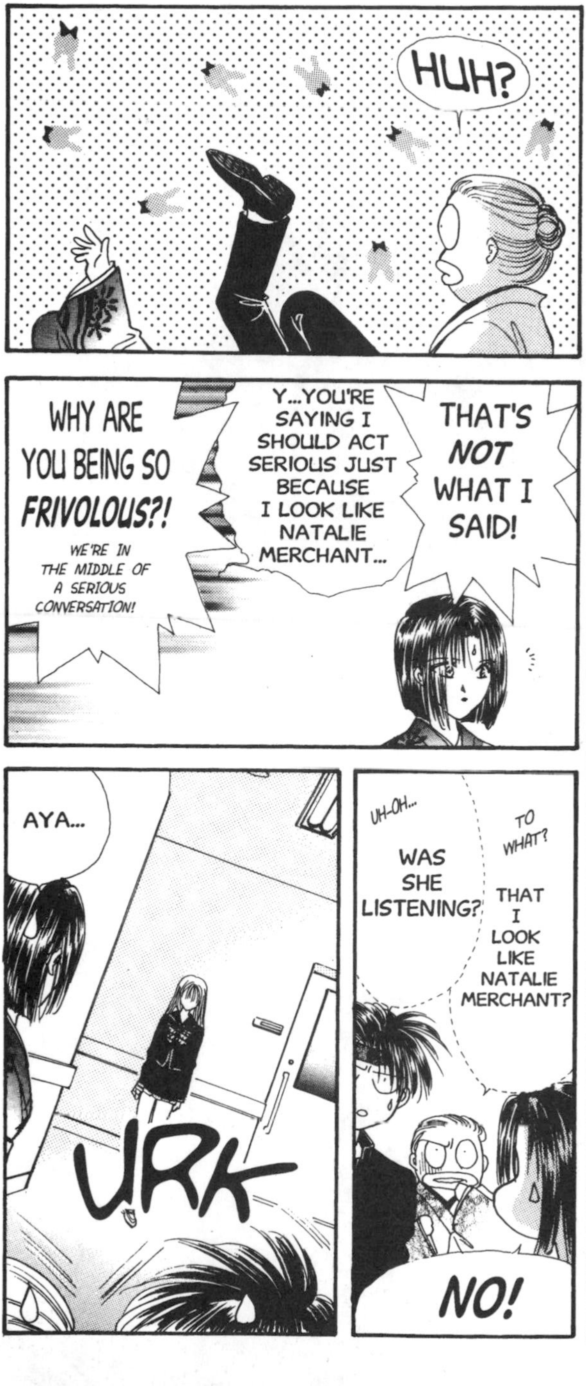
HUH?
WHY ARE YOU BEING SO *FRIVOLOUS?!*
WE'RE IN THE MIDDLE OF A SERIOUS CONVERSATION!
Y...YOU'RE SAYING I SHOULD ACT SERIOUS JUST BECAUSE I LOOK LIKE NATALIE MERCHANT...
THAT'S *NOT* WHAT I SAID!
AYA...
URK
UH-OH...
WAS SHE LISTENING?
TO WHAT?
THAT I LOOK LIKE NATALIE MERCHANT?
NO!

♦ Yūhi ♦

Here's volume number 2

Watase here. Ceres is safely into its second volume.
This story has a lot of mysteries, so I'm enjoying everyone's "guessing game." I'm sure some of them will become clear in this volume, but it's about to get more and more epic, so my head is spinning already. What am I supposed to do as the number of characters grow?
The one that's popular is actually "Kyū-chan" (Mrs. Q). ☺
Whenever she shows her face, She destroys any serious atmosphere up to that point, so I plan to make her show up often. She's more mysterious in some ways than Tōya. And according to my assistant, "her voice *has* to be Shigeru Chiba!" ...So since then, I hear Mr. Chiba in my head whenever I write her lines... ☺
I imagine that Aya sounds like Megumi Hayashibara...
The way she's so down to business.
Well in any case, Ceres is based on the "celestial maiden" story, but actually I had another idea as I was about to start a new series. And that was "something that's been overused and needed a fresh twist" according to my editor--"angels and devils." ☺
This concept has become cliché, but I felt challenged to depict it from a different angle... (My editor tells me that another overused concept that we don't need anymore is "the god of death." I think it depends on the way it's depicted.) So my editor was telling me, "something like vampires, except not so common" and I brought up the "celestial maidens" idea that I'd been thinking of. I was secretly plotting that if I draw that "angel story" after having done FY and Ceres, I could call it my **Celestial Trilogy!**
We'll see... Maybe it'll be totally different. The heavenly world might not appear in Ceres at all.

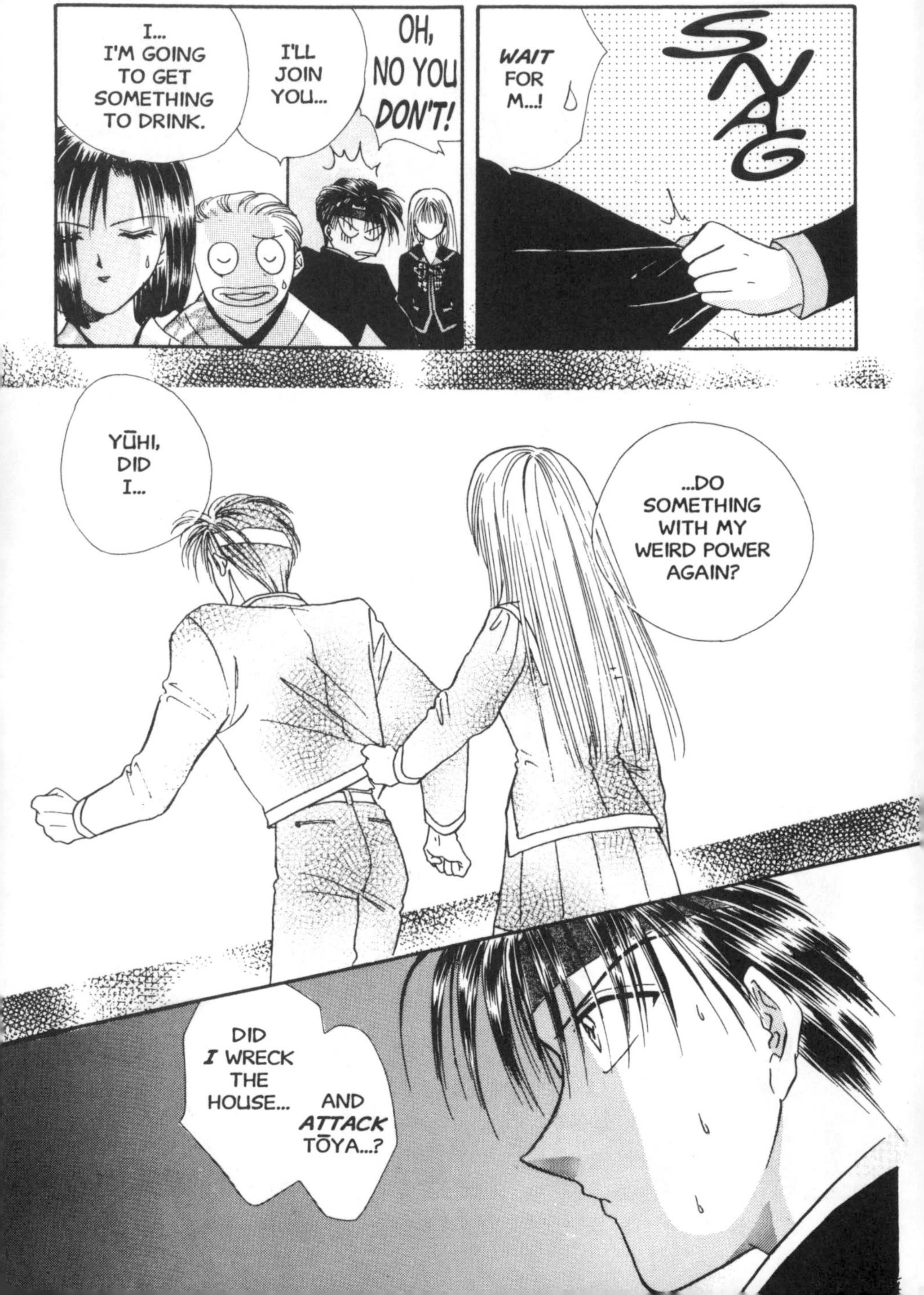
I... I'M GOING TO GET SOMETHING TO DRINK.
I'LL JOIN YOU...
OH, NO YOU DON'T!
WAIT FOR M...!
SNAG
YŪHI, DID I...
...DO SOMETHING WITH MY WEIRD POWER AGAIN?
DID I WRECK THE HOUSE...
AND ATTACK TŌYA...?

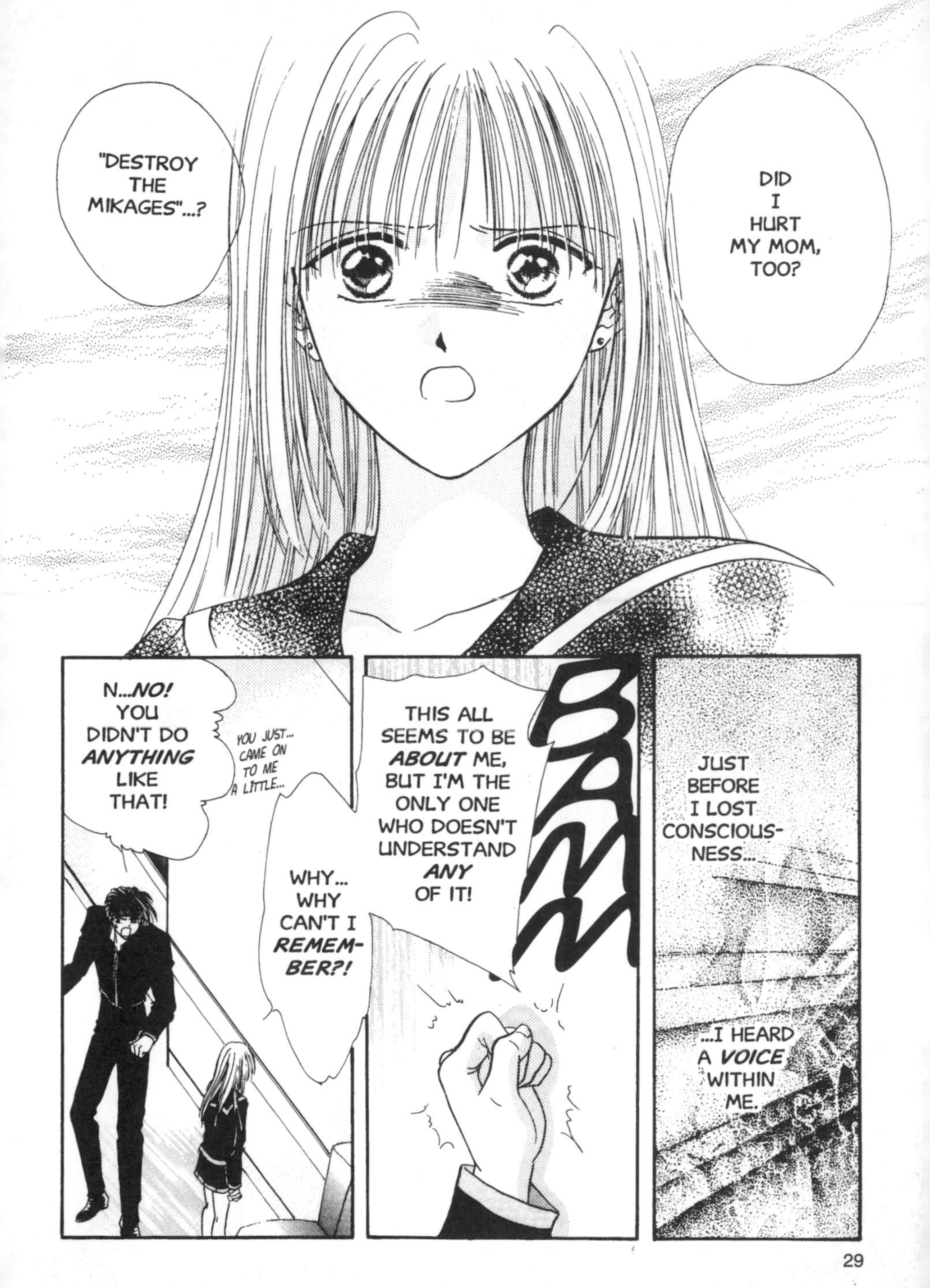
"DESTROY THE MIKAGES"...?
DID I HURT MY MOM, TOO?
N...*NO!* YOU DIDN'T DO *ANYTHING* LIKE THAT!
YOU JUST... CAME ON TO ME A LITTLE...
WHY... WHY CAN'T I *REMEMBER?!*
BAM
THIS ALL SEEMS TO BE *ABOUT* ME, BUT I'M THE ONLY ONE WHO DOESN'T UNDERSTAND *ANY* OF IT!
JUST BEFORE I LOST CONSCIOUSNESS...
...I HEARD A *VOICE* WITHIN ME.

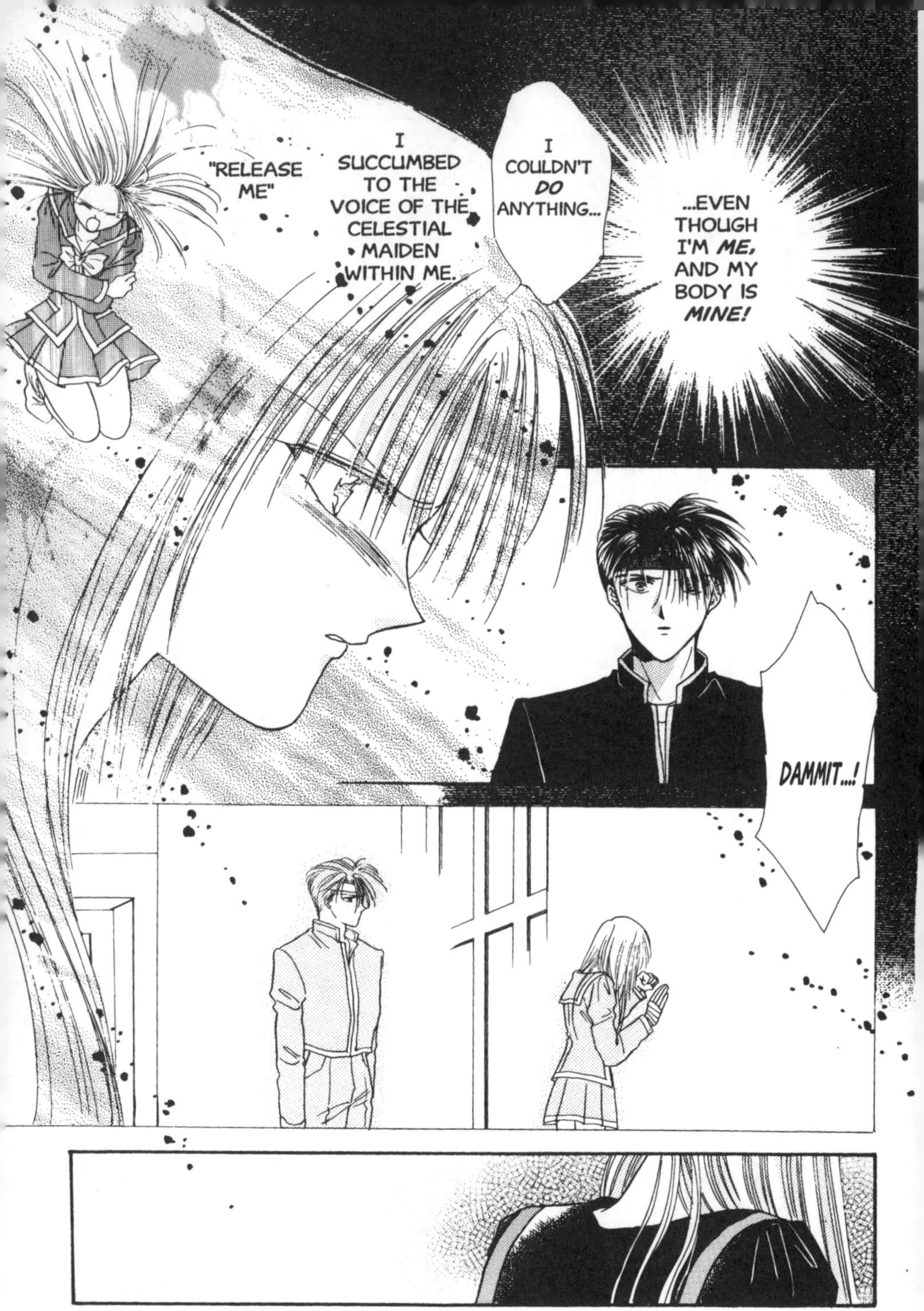
...EVEN THOUGH I'M *ME,* AND MY BODY IS *MINE!*
I COULDN'T *DO* ANYTHING...
I SUCCUMBED TO THE VOICE OF THE CELESTIAL MAIDEN WITHIN ME.
"RELEASE ME"
DAMMIT...!

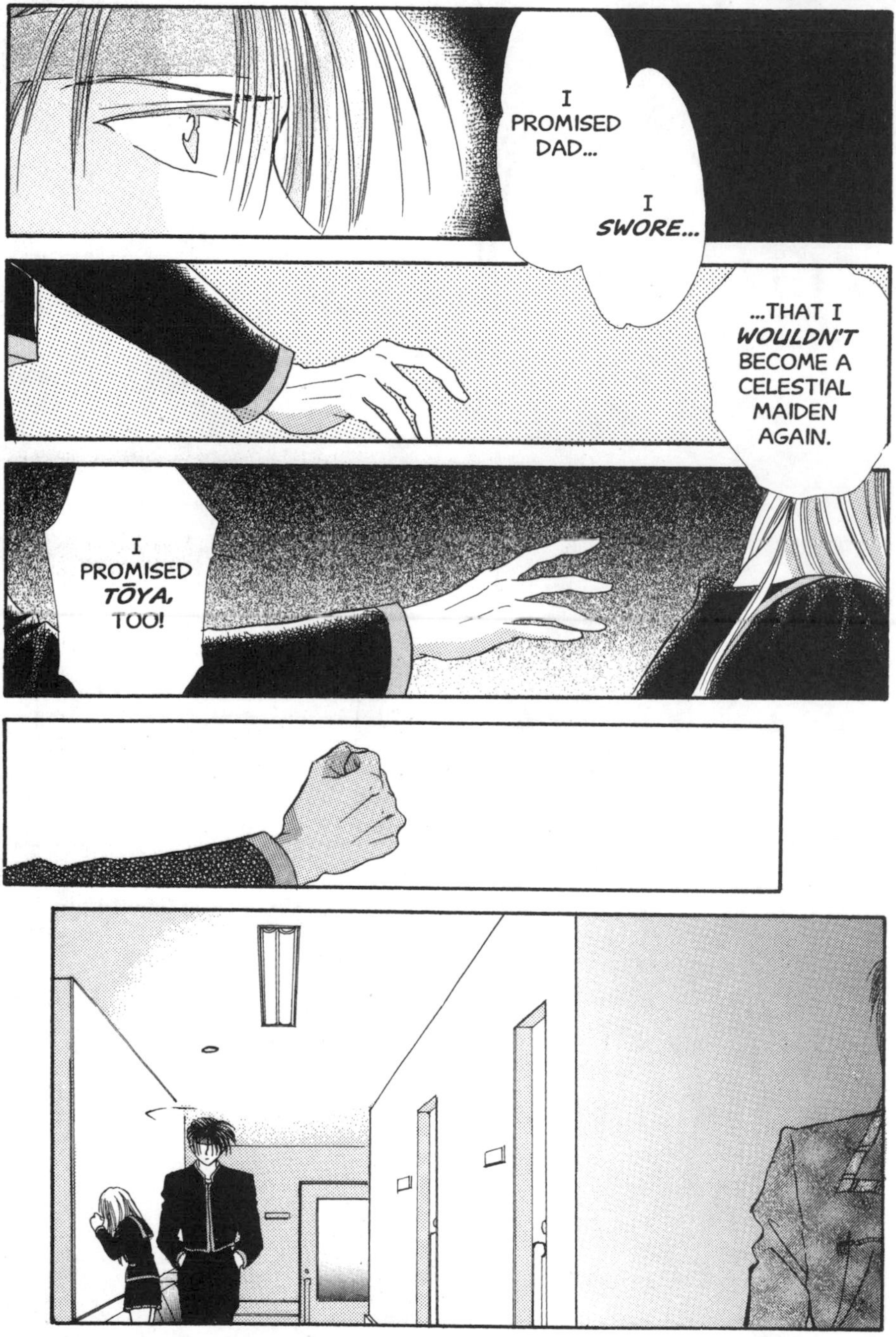
I PROMISED DAD...
I SWORE...
...THAT I WOULDN'T BECOME A CELESTIAL MAIDEN AGAIN.
I PROMISED TŌYA, TOO!

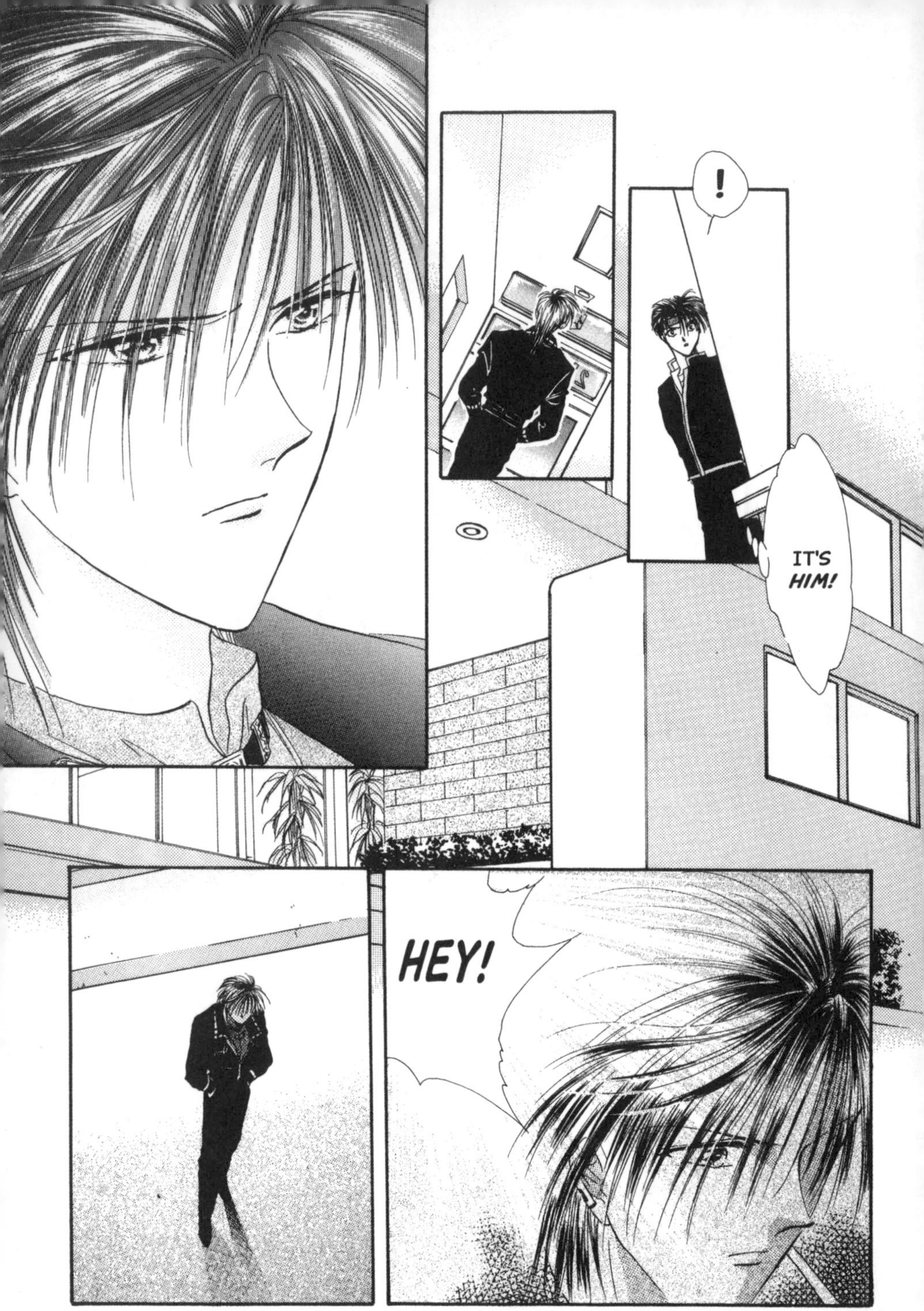
!
IT'S HIM!
HEY!

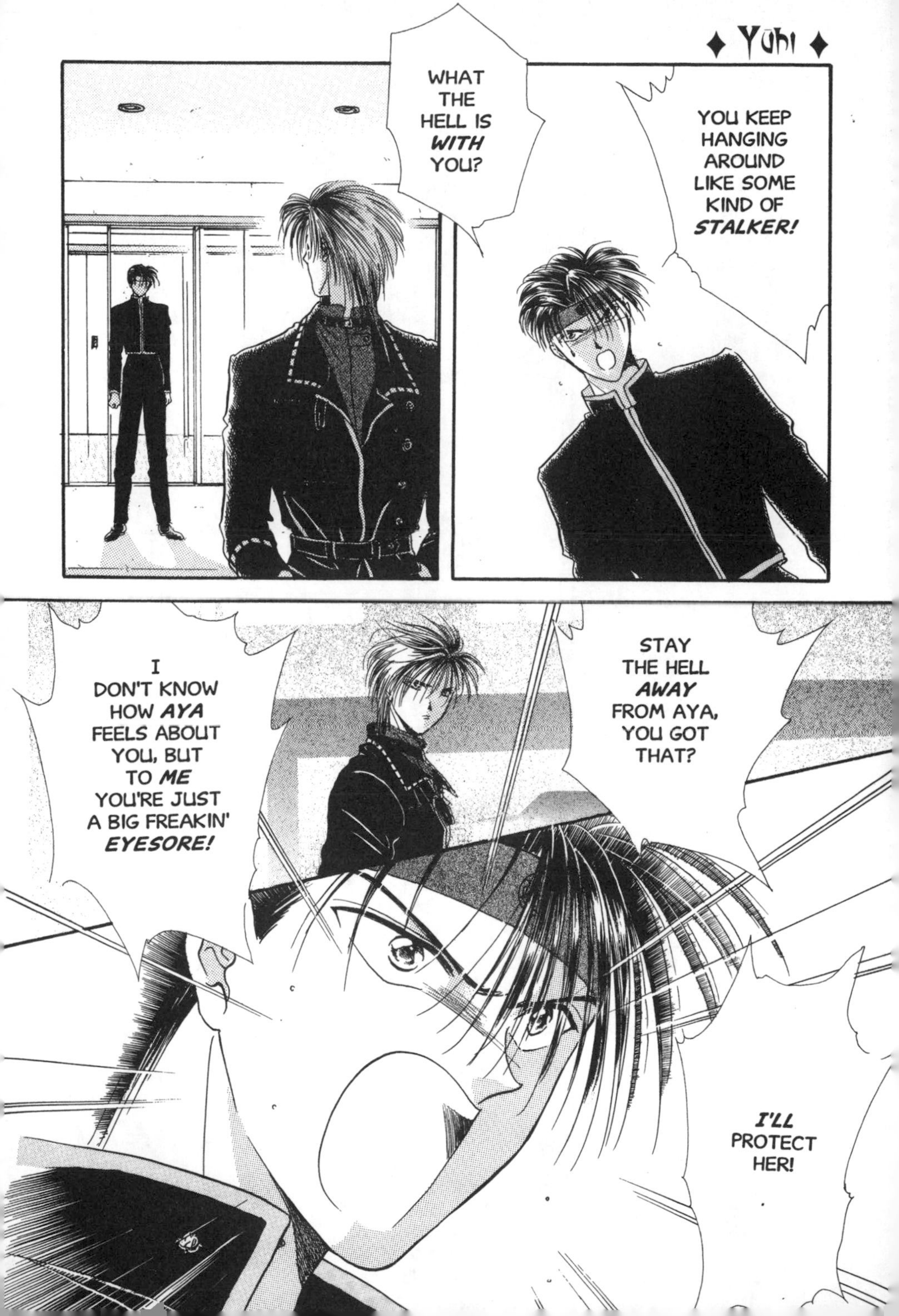
YOU KEEP HANGING AROUND LIKE SOME KIND OF STALKER!
WHAT THE HELL IS WITH YOU?
STAY THE HELL AWAY FROM AYA, YOU GOT THAT?
I DON'T KNOW HOW AYA FEELS ABOUT YOU, BUT TO ME YOU'RE JUST A BIG FREAKIN' EYESORE!
I'LL PROTECT HER!

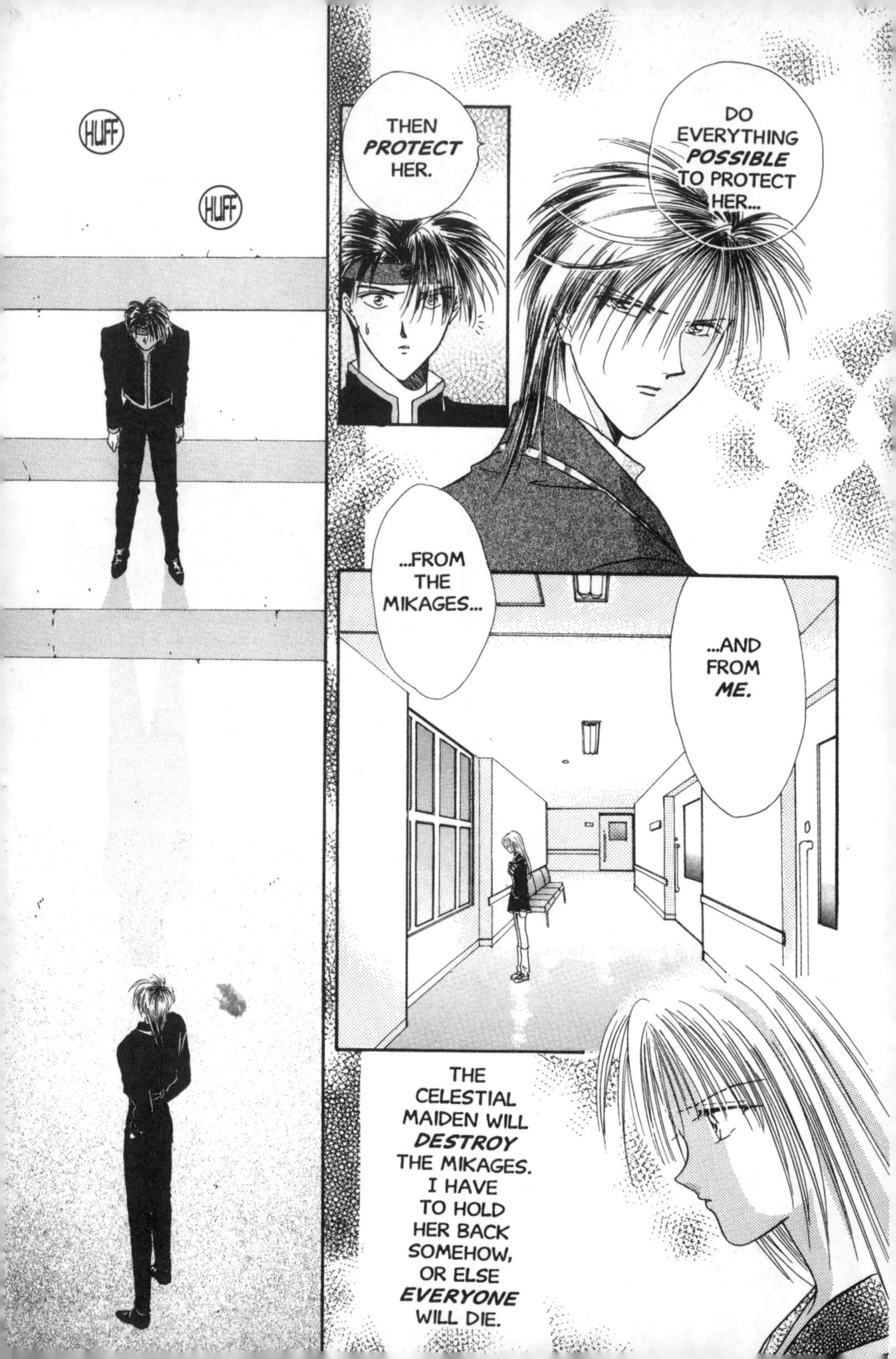
THEN PROTECT HER.
DO EVERYTHING POSSIBLE TO PROTECT HER...
...FROM THE MIKAGES...
...AND FROM ME.
THE CELESTIAL MAIDEN WILL DESTROY THE MIKAGES. I HAVE TO HOLD HER BACK SOMEHOW, OR ELSE EVERYONE WILL DIE.
HUFF
HUFF

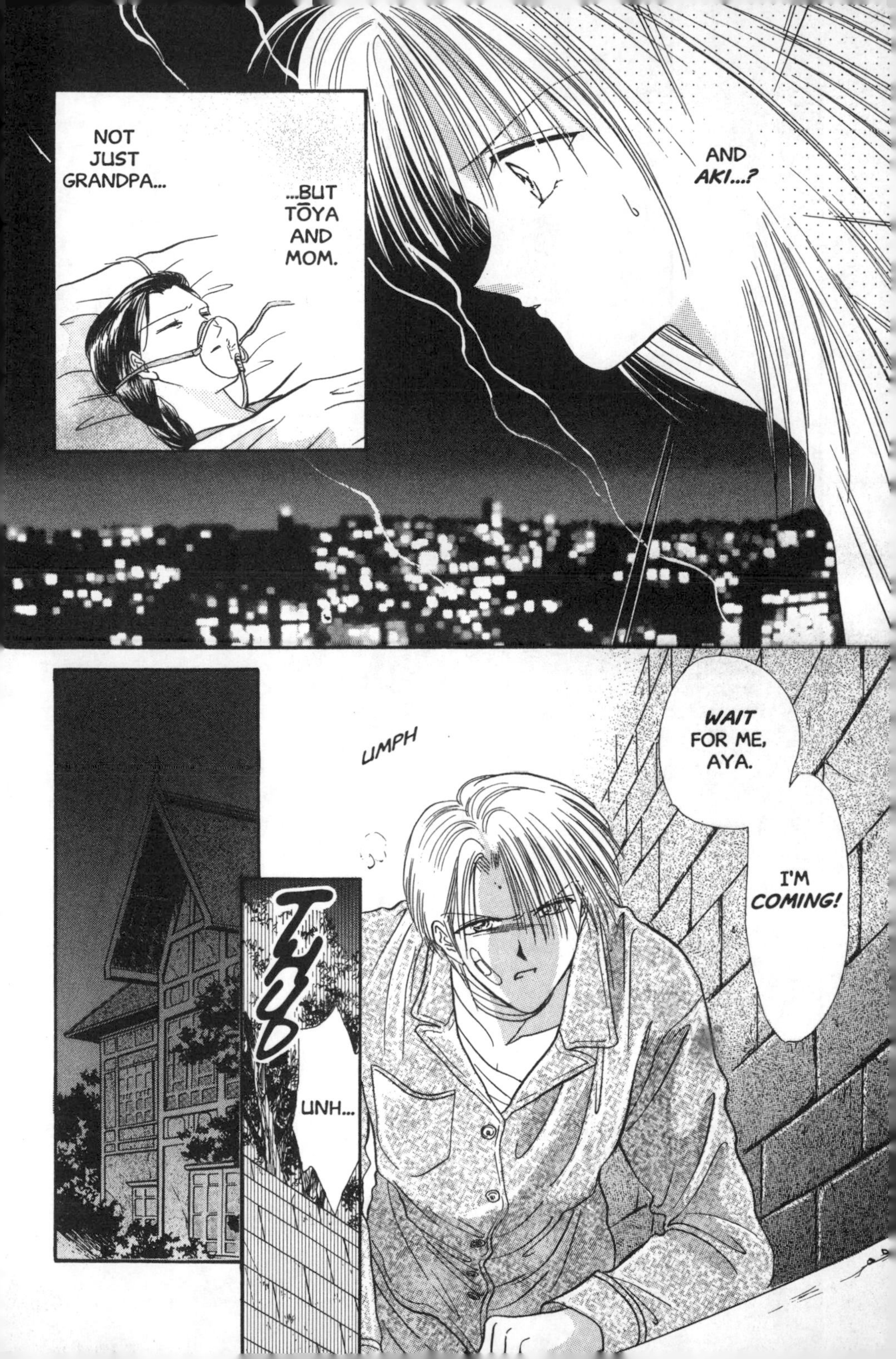
NOT JUST GRANDPA...
...BUT TŌYA AND MOM.
AND *AKI*...?
WAIT FOR ME, AYA.
I'M *COMING!*
UMPH
THUD
UNH...

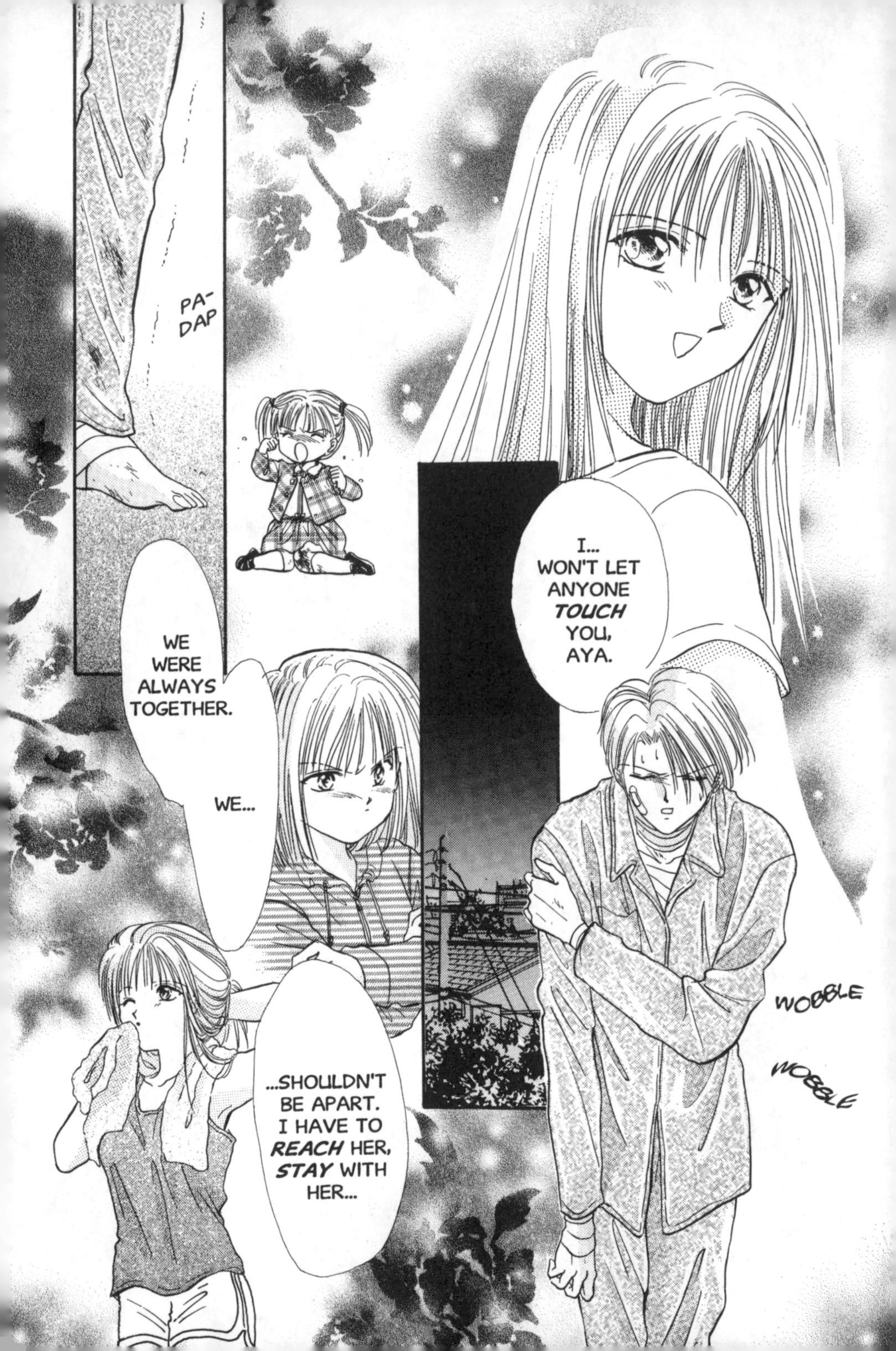
I... WON'T LET ANYONE TOUCH YOU, AYA.
PA-DAP
WE WERE ALWAYS TOGETHER.
WE...
WOBBLE
WOBBLE
...SHOULDN'T BE APART. I HAVE TO REACH HER, STAY WITH HER...

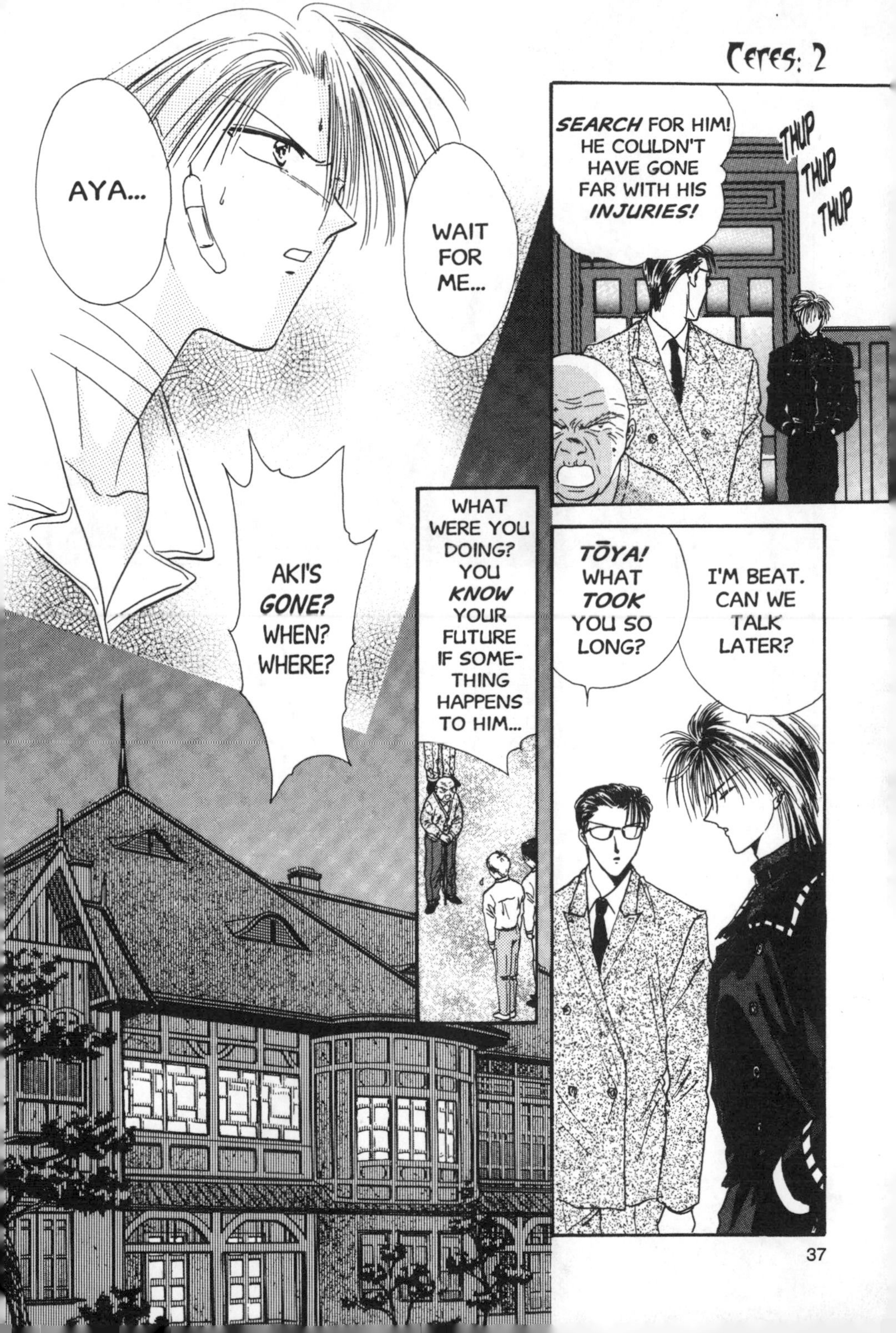
AKI'S GONE? WHEN? WHERE?
WHAT WERE YOU DOING? YOU KNOW YOUR FUTURE IF SOMETHING HAPPENS TO HIM...
SEARCH FOR HIM! HE COULDN'T HAVE GONE FAR WITH HIS INJURIES!
THUP THUP THUP
TŌYA! WHAT TOOK YOU SO LONG?
I'M BEAT. CAN WE TALK LATER?
AYA...
WAIT FOR ME...

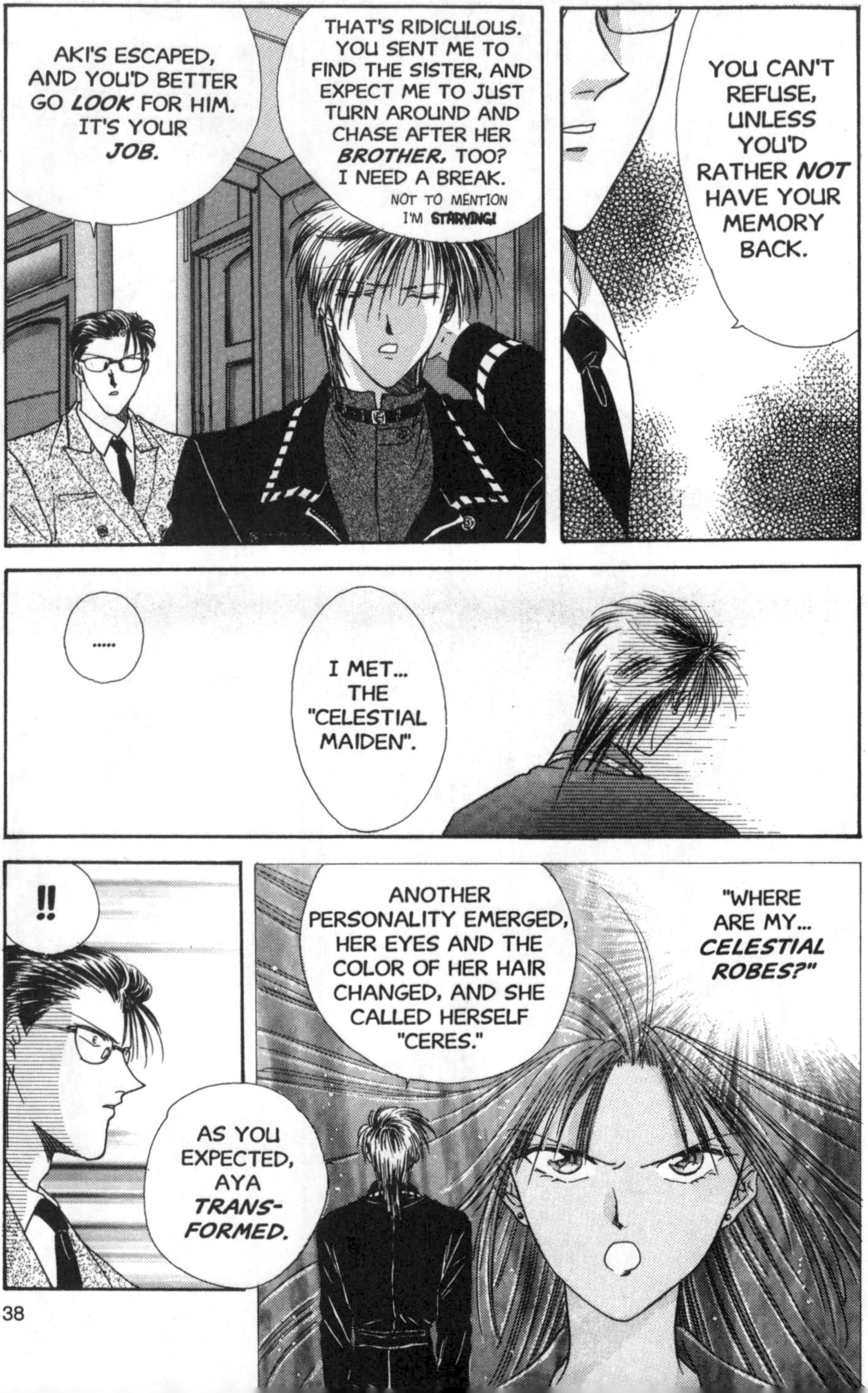
AKI'S ESCAPED, AND YOU'D BETTER GO *LOOK* FOR HIM. IT'S YOUR *JOB.*
THAT'S RIDICULOUS. YOU SENT ME TO FIND THE SISTER, AND EXPECT ME TO JUST TURN AROUND AND CHASE AFTER HER *BROTHER,* TOO? I NEED A BREAK.
NOT TO MENTION I'M STARVING!
YOU CAN'T REFUSE, UNLESS YOU'D RATHER *NOT* HAVE YOUR MEMORY BACK.
.....
I MET... THE "CELESTIAL MAIDEN".
!!
ANOTHER PERSONALITY EMERGED, HER EYES AND THE COLOR OF HER HAIR CHANGED, AND SHE CALLED HERSELF "CERES."
"WHERE ARE MY... *CELESTIAL ROBES?"*
AS YOU EXPECTED, AYA *TRANS-FORMED.*

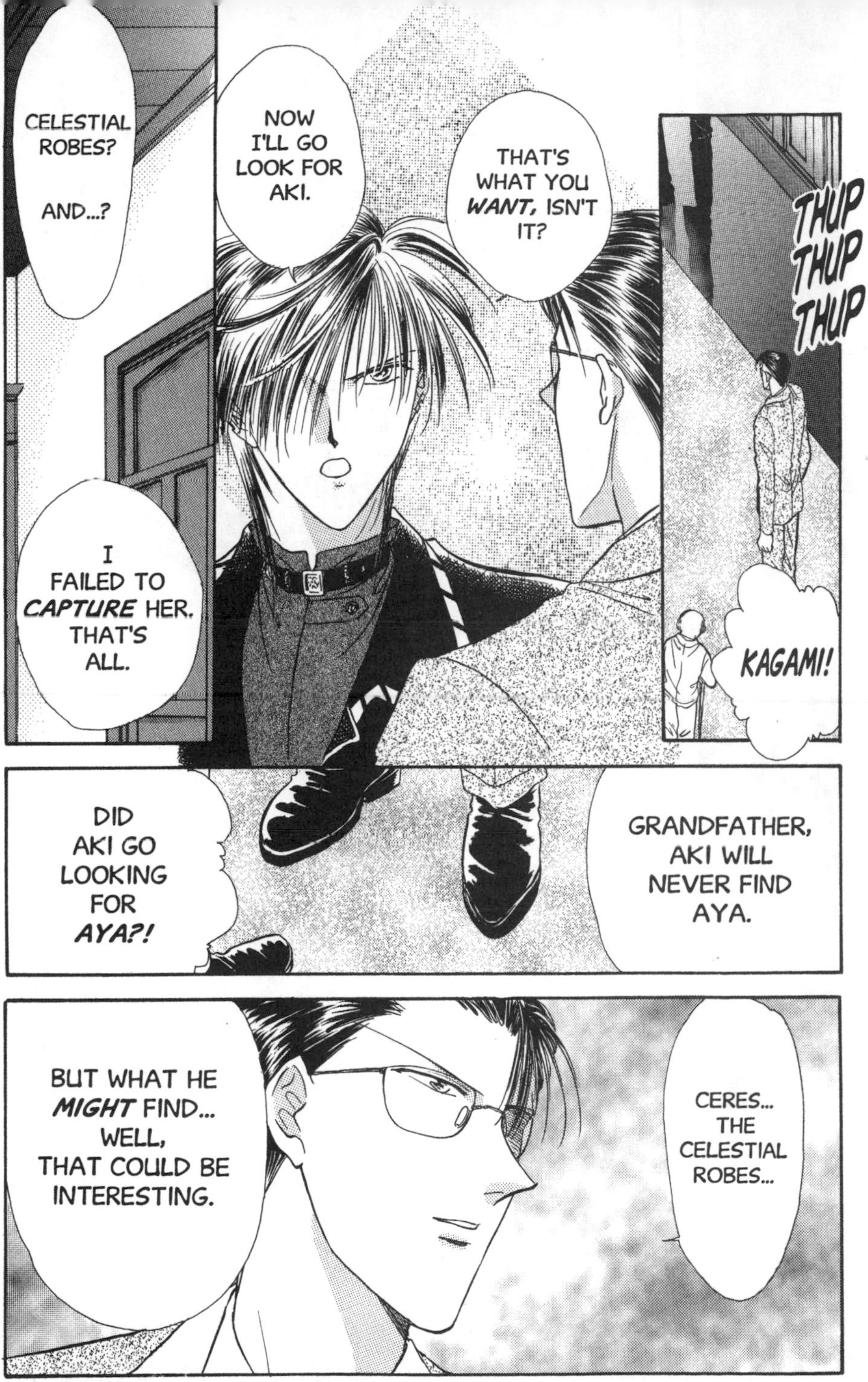
CELESTIAL ROBES?
AND...?
I FAILED TO CAPTURE HER. THAT'S ALL.
NOW I'LL GO LOOK FOR AKI.
THAT'S WHAT YOU WANT, ISN'T IT?
THUP THUP THUP
KAGAMI!
DID AKI GO LOOKING FOR AYA?!
GRANDFATHER, AKI WILL NEVER FIND AYA.
BUT WHAT HE MIGHT FIND... WELL, THAT COULD BE INTERESTING.
CERES... THE CELESTIAL ROBES...

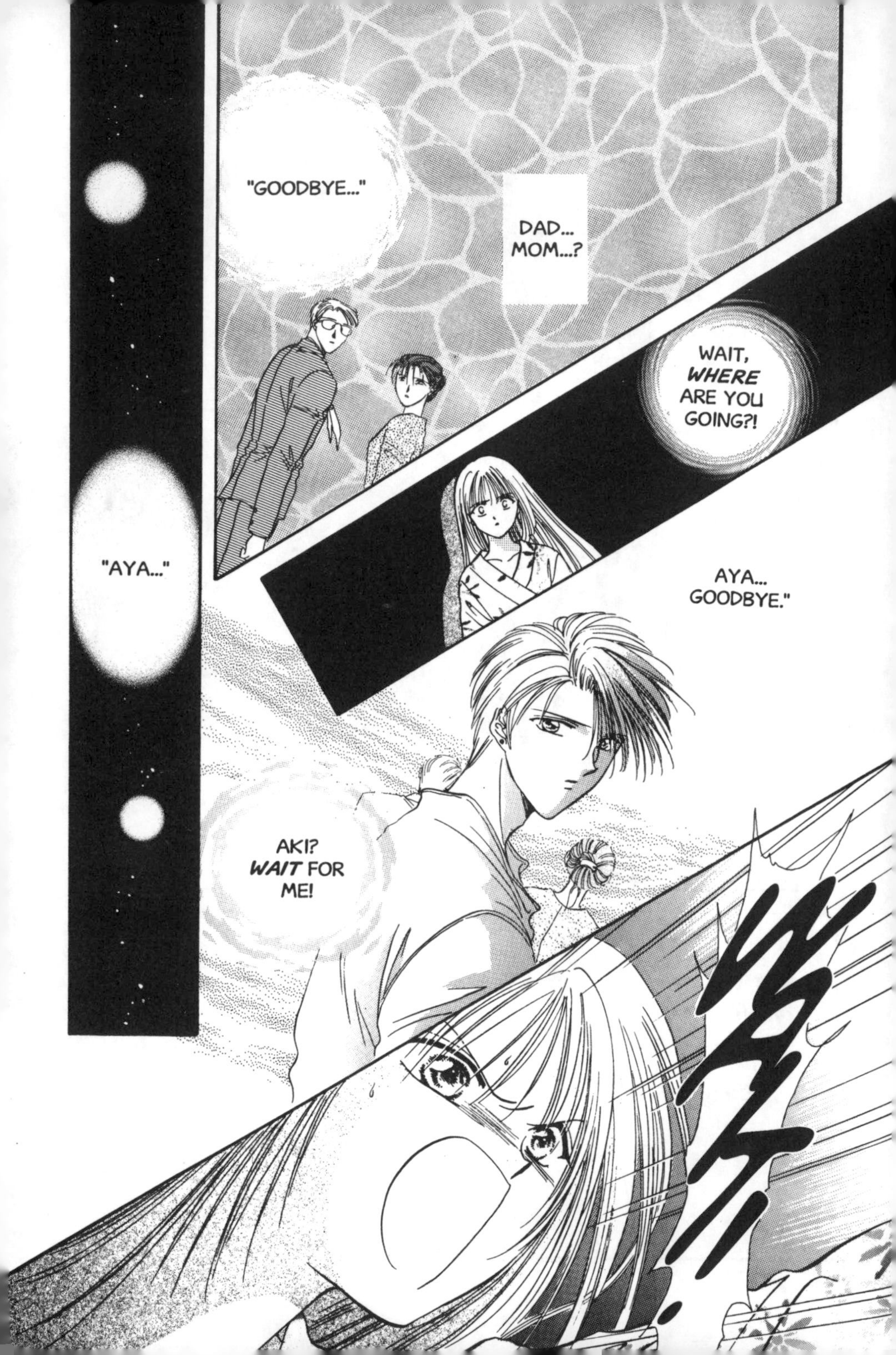
DAD... MOM...?
"GOODBYE..."
WAIT, **WHERE** ARE YOU GOING?!
"AYA..."
AYA... GOODBYE."
AKI? **WAIT** FOR ME!

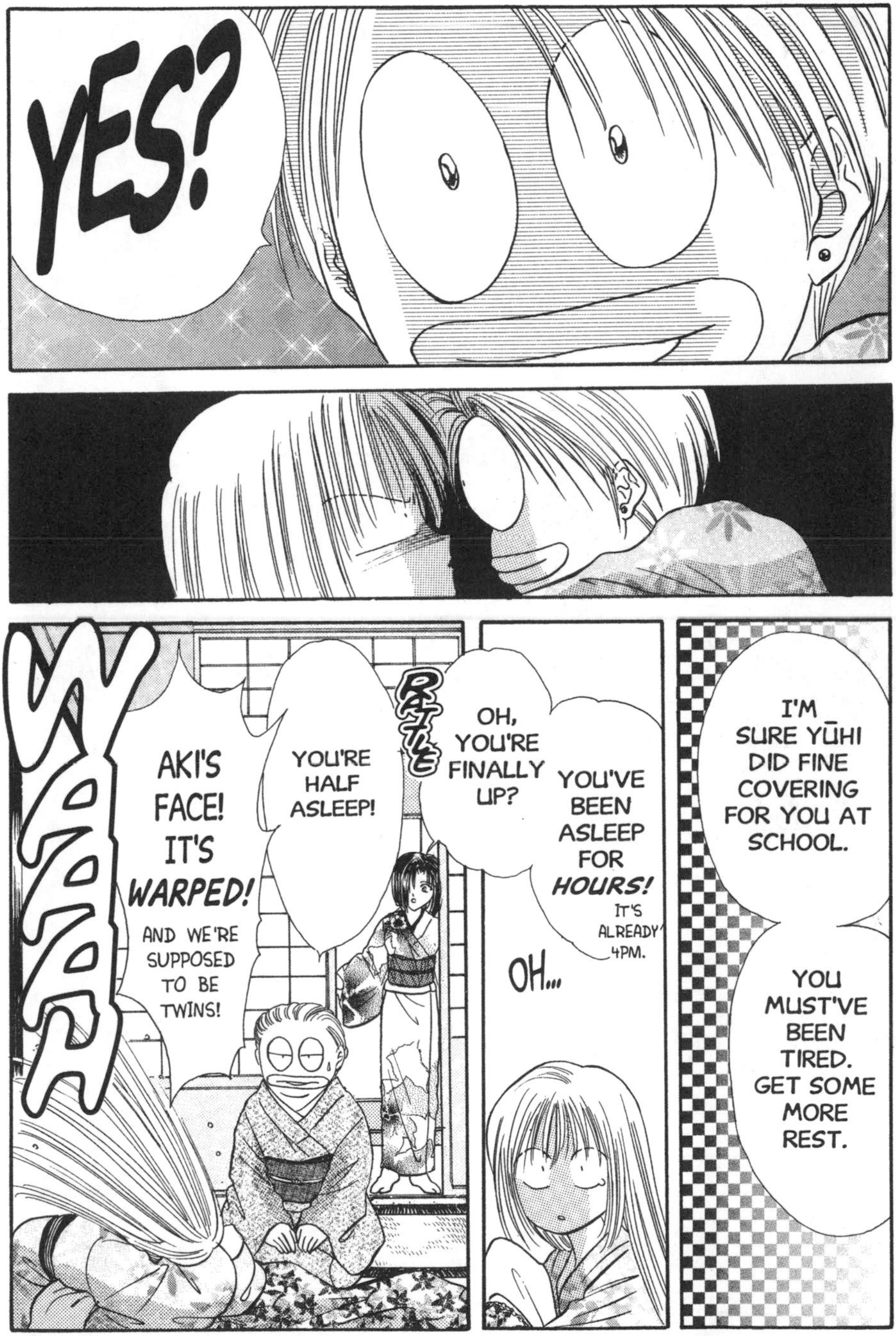
YES?
I'M SURE YŪHI DID FINE COVERING FOR YOU AT SCHOOL.
YOU MUST'VE BEEN TIRED. GET SOME MORE REST.
OH...
OH, YOU'RE FINALLY UP?
YOU'VE BEEN ASLEEP FOR HOURS!
IT'S ALREADY 4PM.
RATTLE
YOU'RE HALF ASLEEP!
AKI'S FACE! IT'S WARPED!
AND WE'RE SUPPOSED TO BE TWINS!

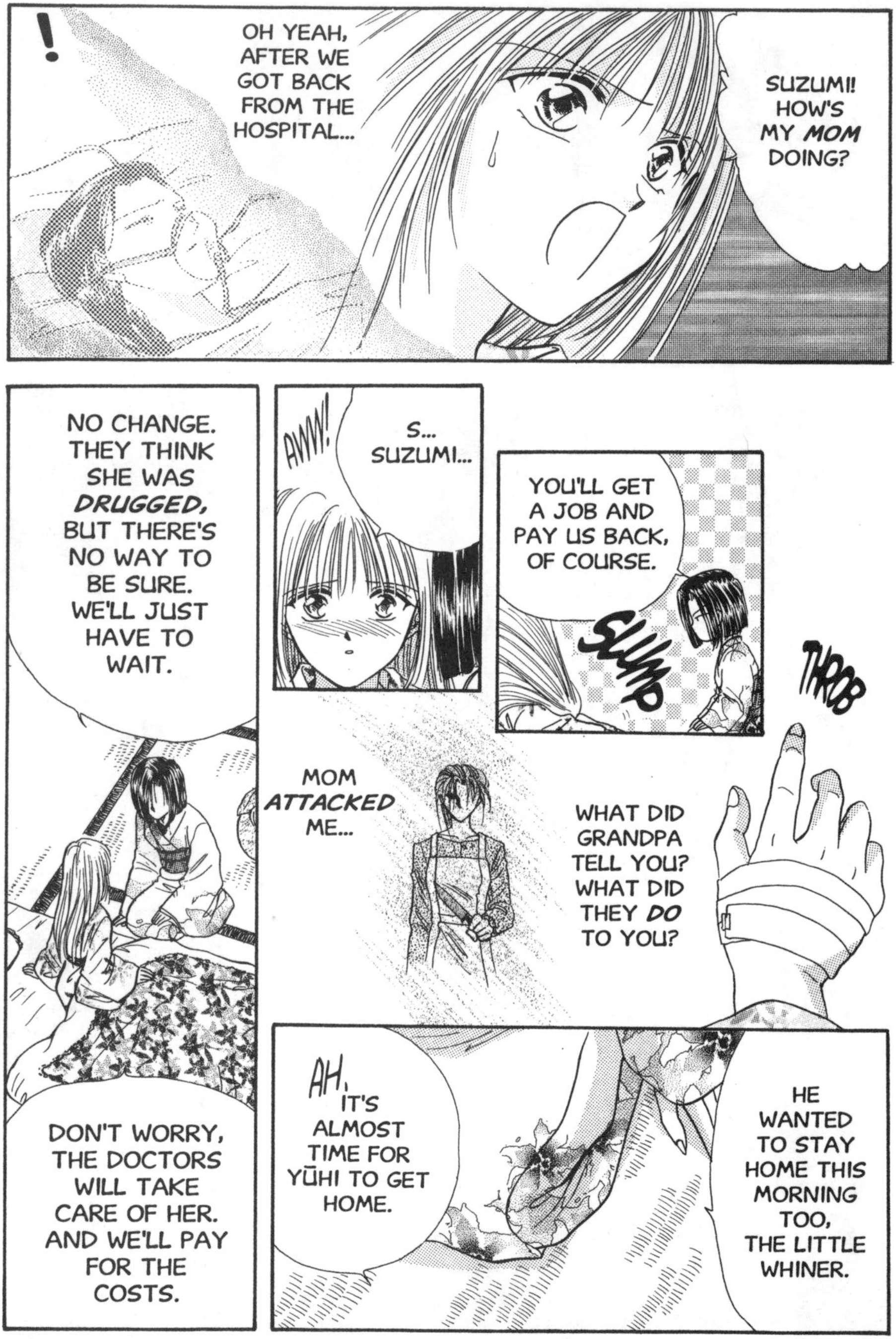
!
OH YEAH, AFTER WE GOT BACK FROM THE HOSPITAL...
SUZUMI!! HOW'S MY *MOM* DOING?
NO CHANGE. THEY THINK SHE WAS *DRUGGED,* BUT THERE'S NO WAY TO BE SURE. WE'LL JUST HAVE TO WAIT.
DON'T WORRY, THE DOCTORS WILL TAKE CARE OF HER. AND WE'LL PAY FOR THE COSTS.
AWWW!
S... SUZUMI...
YOU'LL GET A JOB AND PAY US BACK, OF COURSE.
SLUMP
THROB
MOM *ATTACKED* ME...
WHAT DID GRANDPA TELL YOU? WHAT DID THEY *DO* TO YOU?
AH, IT'S ALMOST TIME FOR YŪHI TO GET HOME.
HE WANTED TO STAY HOME THIS MORNING TOO, THE LITTLE WHINER.

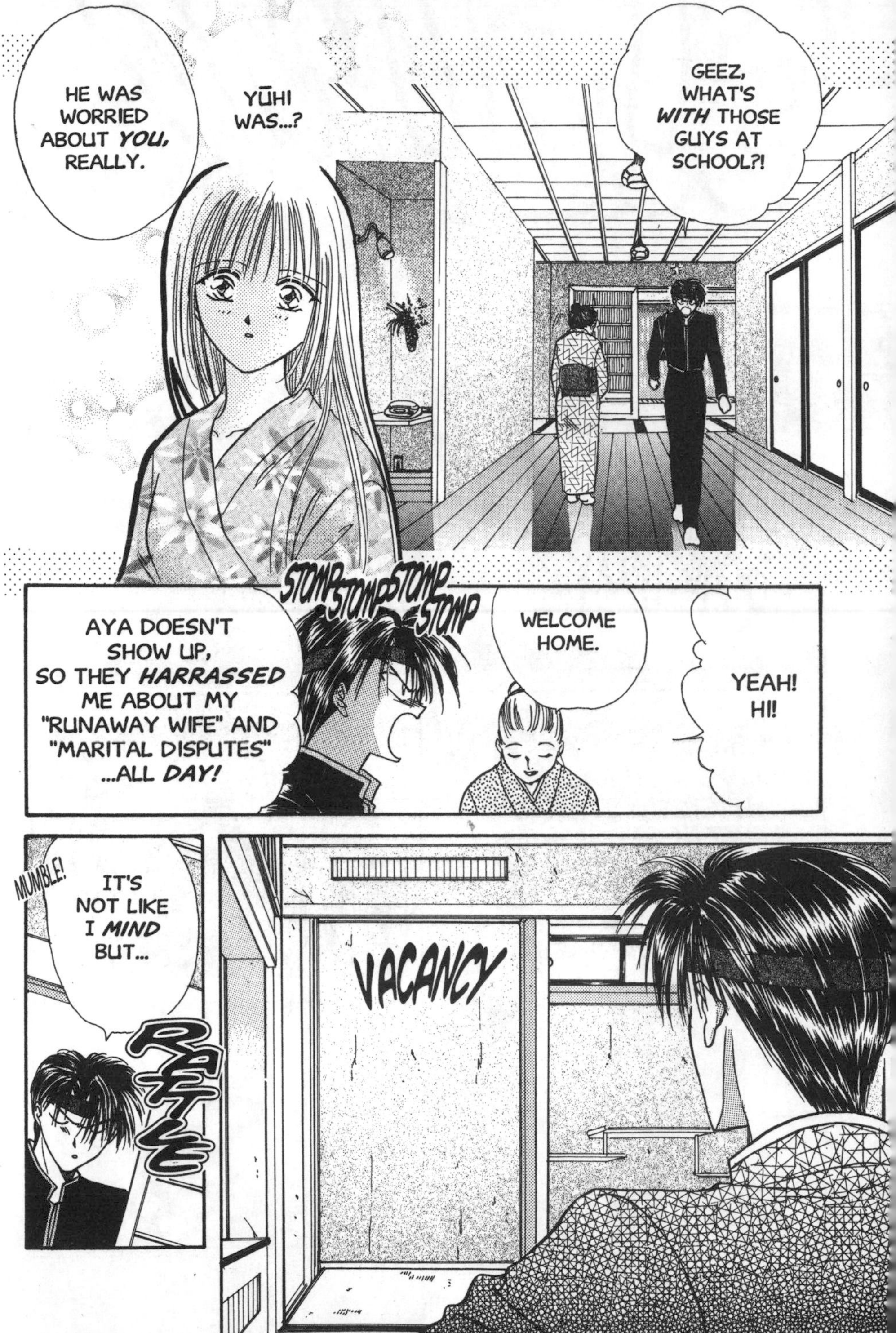
GEEZ, WHAT'S *WITH* THOSE GUYS AT SCHOOL?!
YŪHI WAS...?
HE WAS WORRIED ABOUT *YOU,* REALLY.
YEAH! HI!
WELCOME HOME.
STOMP STOMP STOMP STOMP
AYA DOESN'T SHOW UP, SO THEY *HARRASSED* ME ABOUT MY "RUNAWAY WIFE" AND "MARITAL DISPUTES" ...ALL *DAY!*
VACANCY
RATTLE
MUMBLE!
IT'S NOT LIKE I *MIND* BUT...

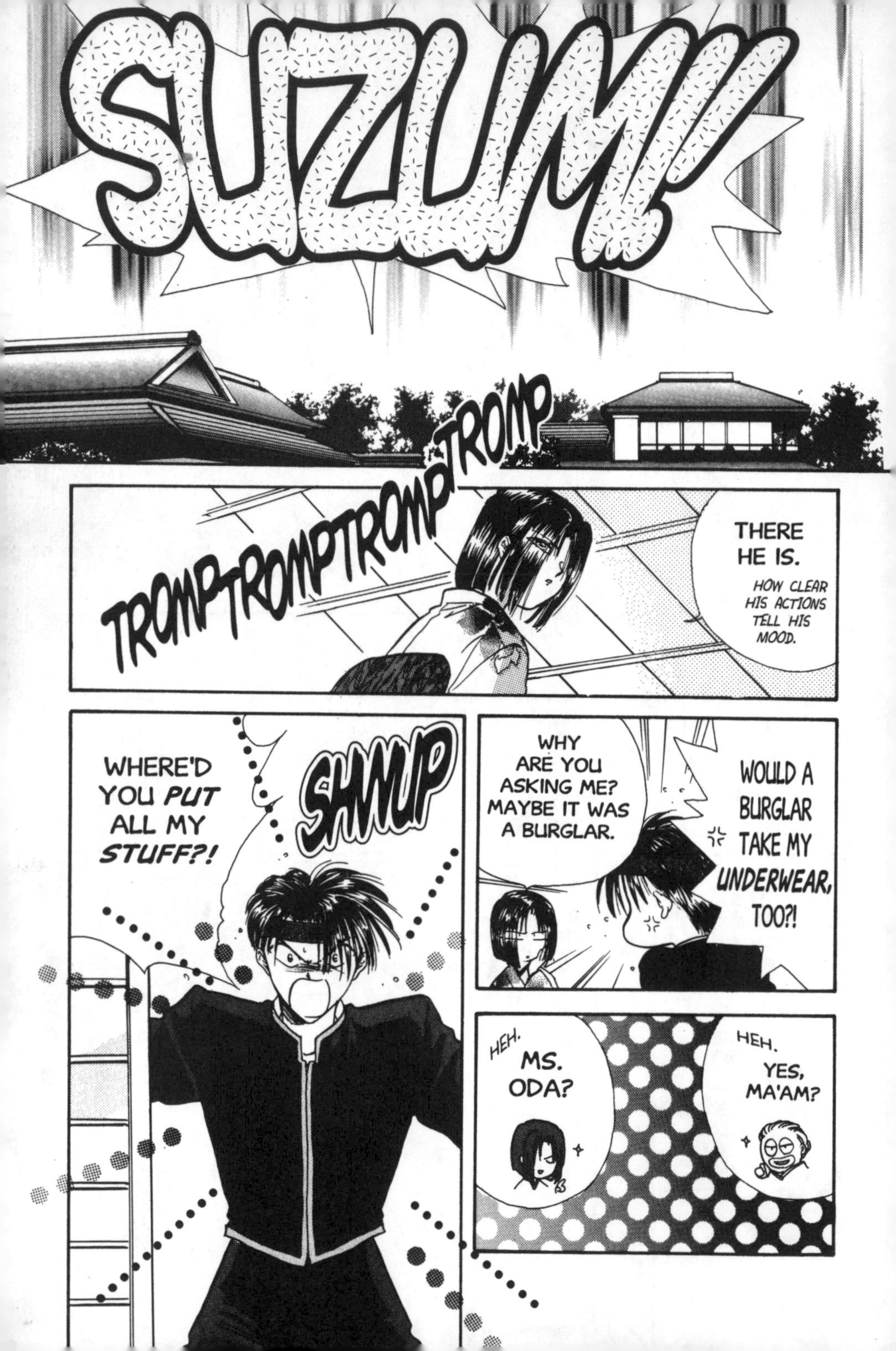
SUZUM!
TROMPTROMPTROMPTROMP
THERE HE IS.
HOW CLEAR HIS ACTIONS TELL HIS MOOD.
WHERE'D YOU PUT ALL MY STUFF?!
SHWUP
WHY ARE YOU ASKING ME? MAYBE IT WAS A BURGLAR.
WOULD A BURGLAR TAKE MY UNDERWEAR, TOO?!
HEH. MS. ODA?
HEH. YES, MA'AM?

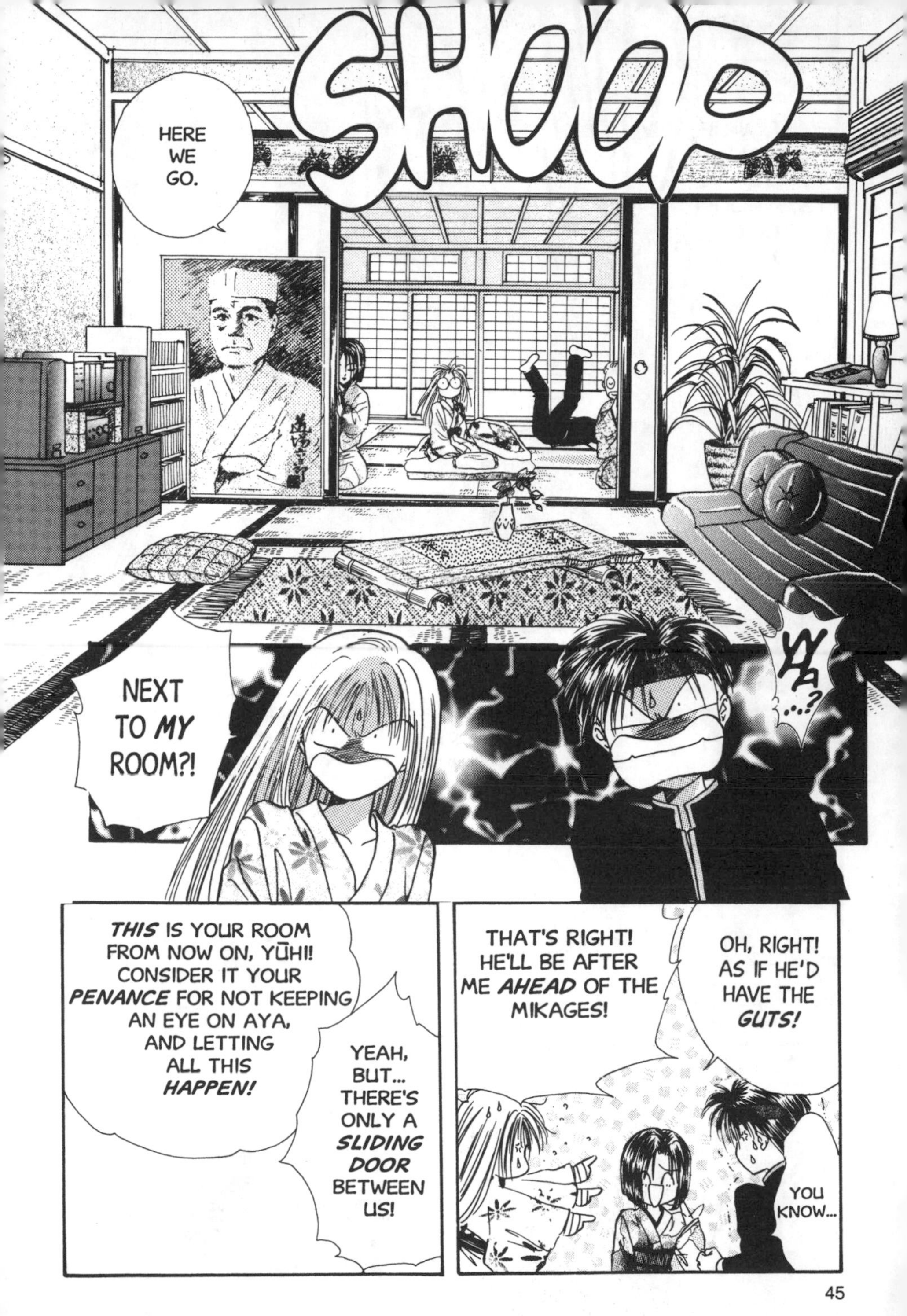
HERE WE GO.
SHOOP
NEXT TO *MY* ROOM?!
WHA...?
THIS IS YOUR ROOM FROM NOW ON, YŪHI! CONSIDER IT YOUR *PENANCE* FOR NOT KEEPING AN EYE ON AYA, AND LETTING ALL THIS *HAPPEN!*
YEAH, BUT... THERE'S ONLY A *SLIDING DOOR* BETWEEN US!
THAT'S RIGHT! HE'LL BE AFTER ME *AHEAD* OF THE MIKAGES!
OH, RIGHT! AS IF HE'D HAVE THE *GUTS!*
YOU KNOW...

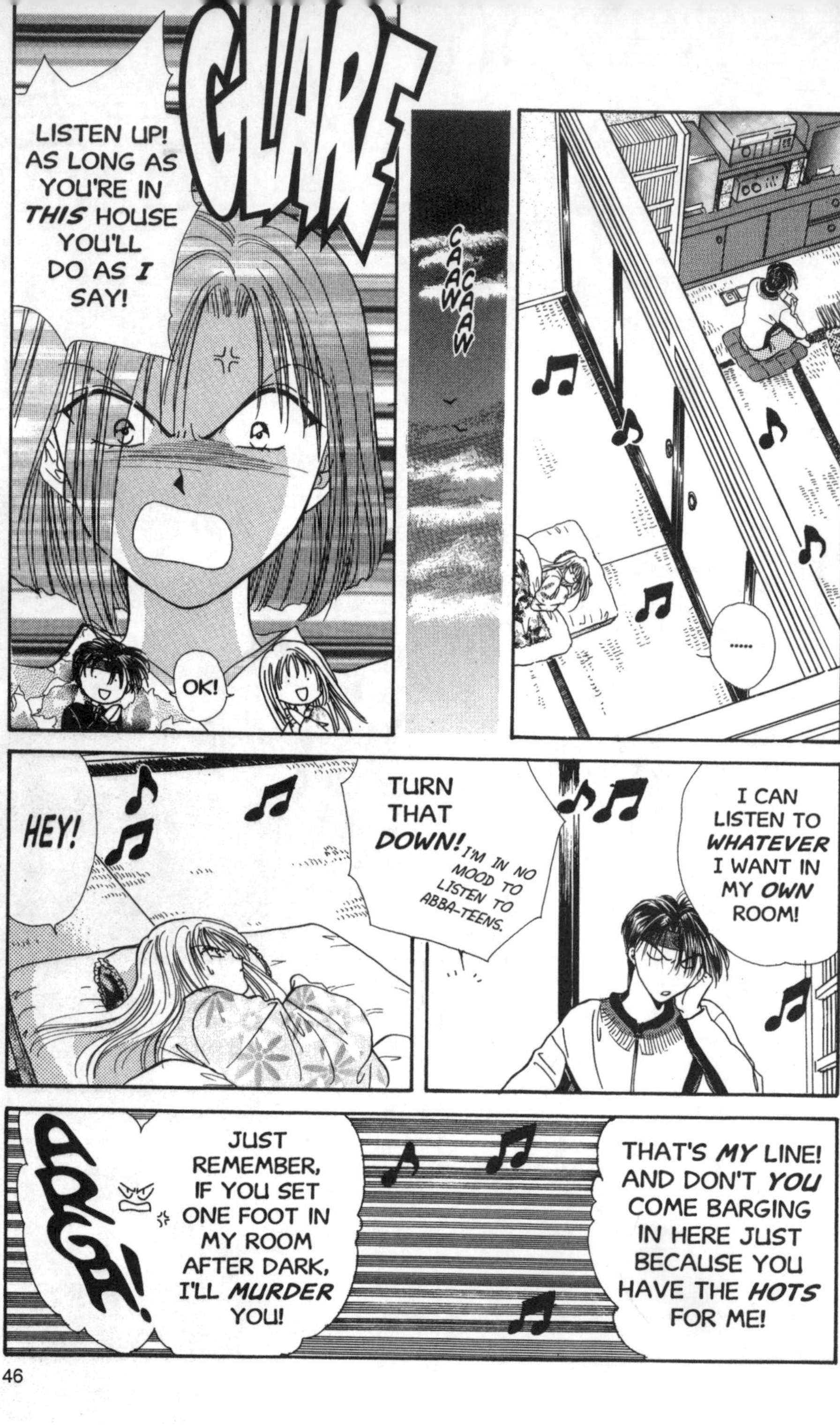
GLARE
LISTEN UP! AS LONG AS YOU'RE IN *THIS* HOUSE YOU'LL DO AS *I* SAY!
OK!
CAAAW CAAAW
......
HEY!
TURN THAT *DOWN!*
I'M IN NO MOOD TO LISTEN TO ABBA-TEENS.
I CAN LISTEN TO *WHATEVER* I WANT IN MY *OWN* ROOM!
JUST REMEMBER, IF YOU SET ONE FOOT IN MY ROOM AFTER DARK, I'LL *MURDER* YOU!
THAT'S *MY* LINE! AND DON'T *YOU* COME BARGING IN HERE JUST BECAUSE YOU HAVE THE *HOTS* FOR ME!

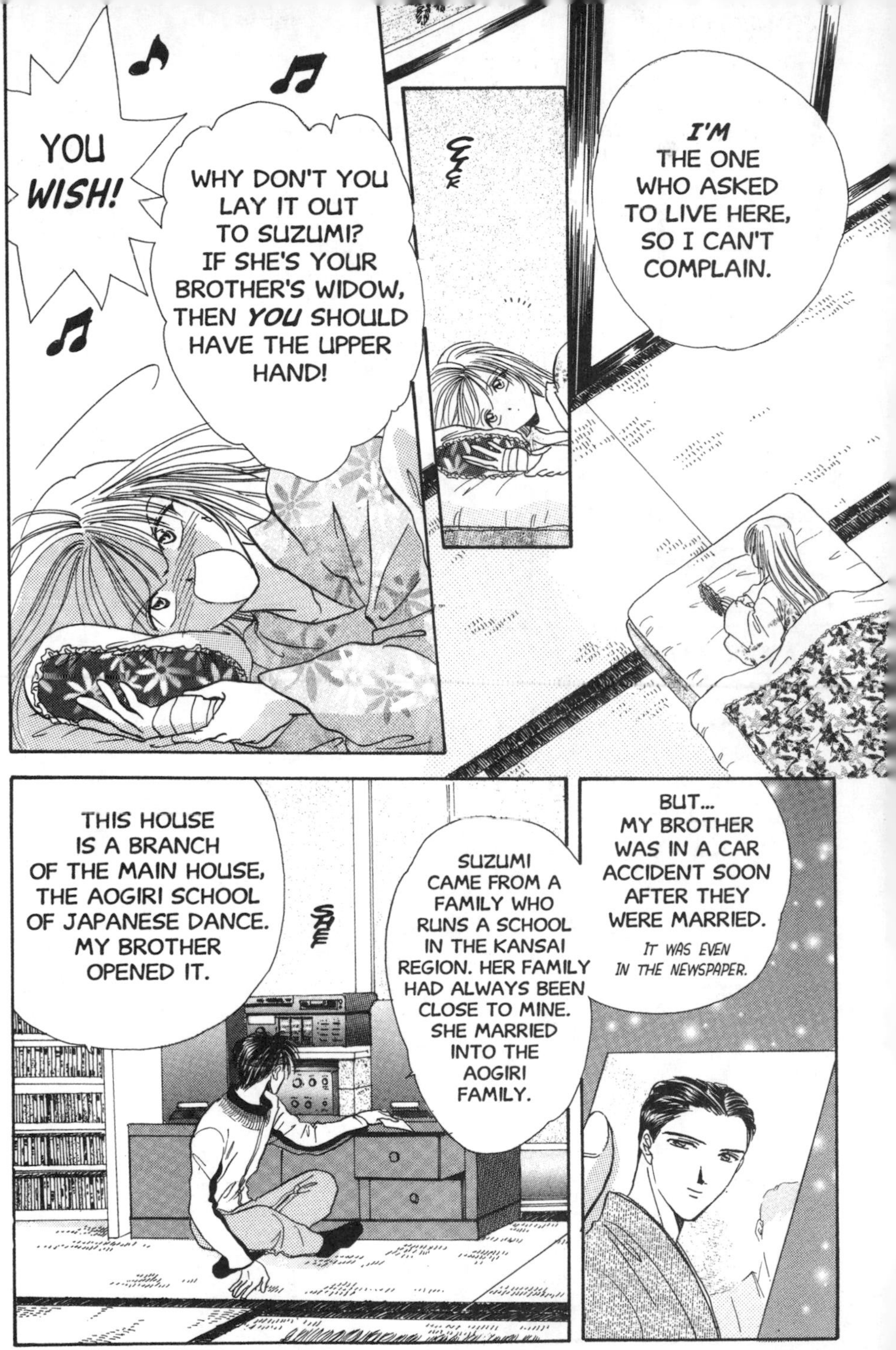
I'M THE ONE WHO ASKED TO LIVE HERE, SO I CAN'T COMPLAIN.
CLICK
WHY DON'T YOU LAY IT OUT TO SUZUMI? IF SHE'S YOUR BROTHER'S WIDOW, THEN *YOU* SHOULD HAVE THE UPPER HAND!
YOU *WISH!*
BUT... MY BROTHER WAS IN A CAR ACCIDENT SOON AFTER THEY WERE MARRIED.
IT WAS EVEN IN THE NEWSPAPER.
THIS HOUSE IS A BRANCH OF THE MAIN HOUSE, THE AOGIRI SCHOOL OF JAPANESE DANCE. MY BROTHER OPENED IT.
SHFF
SUZUMI CAME FROM A FAMILY WHO RUNS A SCHOOL IN THE KANSAI REGION. HER FAMILY HAD ALWAYS BEEN CLOSE TO MINE. SHE MARRIED INTO THE AOGIRI FAMILY.

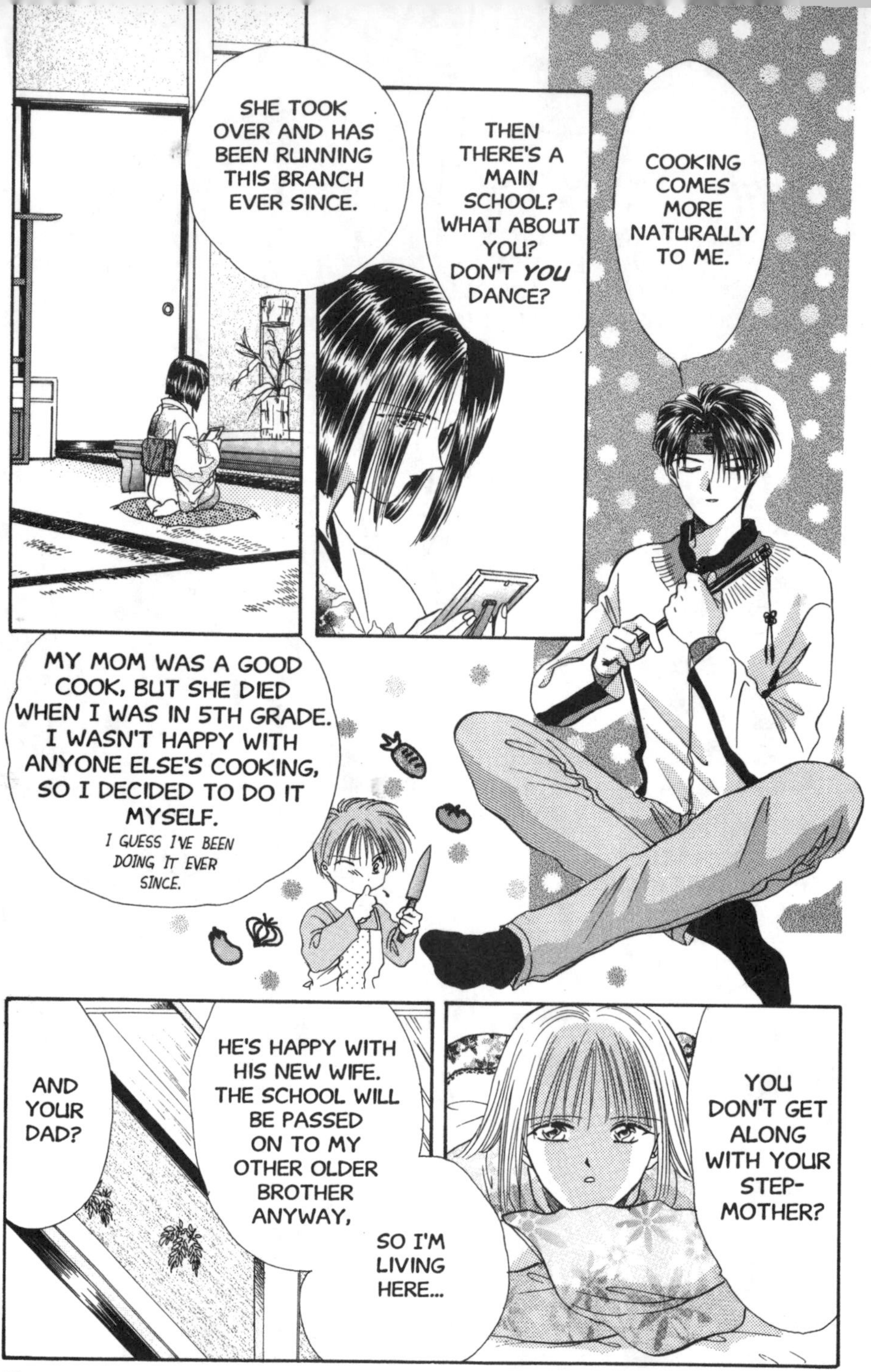
SHE TOOK OVER AND HAS BEEN RUNNING THIS BRANCH EVER SINCE.
THEN THERE'S A MAIN SCHOOL? WHAT ABOUT YOU? DON'T *YOU* DANCE?
COOKING COMES MORE NATURALLY TO ME.
MY MOM WAS A GOOD COOK, BUT SHE DIED WHEN I WAS IN 5TH GRADE. I WASN'T HAPPY WITH ANYONE ELSE'S COOKING, SO I DECIDED TO DO IT MYSELF.
I GUESS I'VE BEEN DOING IT EVER SINCE.
AND YOUR DAD?
HE'S HAPPY WITH HIS NEW WIFE. THE SCHOOL WILL BE PASSED ON TO MY OTHER OLDER BROTHER ANYWAY,
SO I'M LIVING HERE...
YOU DON'T GET ALONG WITH YOUR STEP-MOTHER?

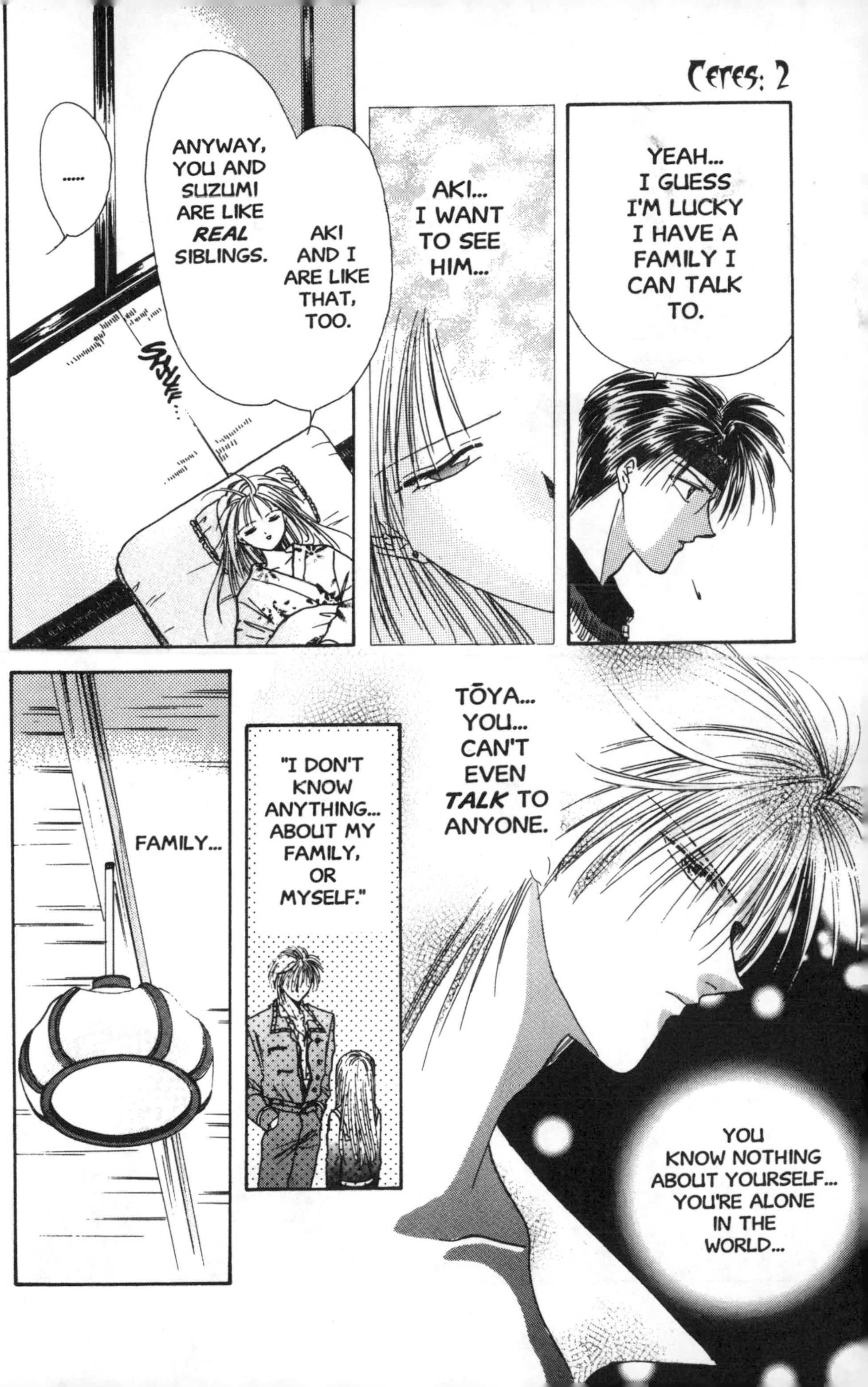
YEAH... I GUESS I'M LUCKY I HAVE A FAMILY I CAN TALK TO.
AKI... I WANT TO SEE HIM...
ANYWAY, YOU AND SUZUMI ARE LIKE *REAL* SIBLINGS.
AKI AND I ARE LIKE THAT, TOO.
.....
TŌYA... YOU... CAN'T EVEN *TALK* TO ANYONE.
YOU KNOW NOTHING ABOUT YOURSELF... YOU'RE ALONE IN THE WORLD...
"I DON'T KNOW ANYTHING... ABOUT MY FAMILY, OR MYSELF."
FAMILY...

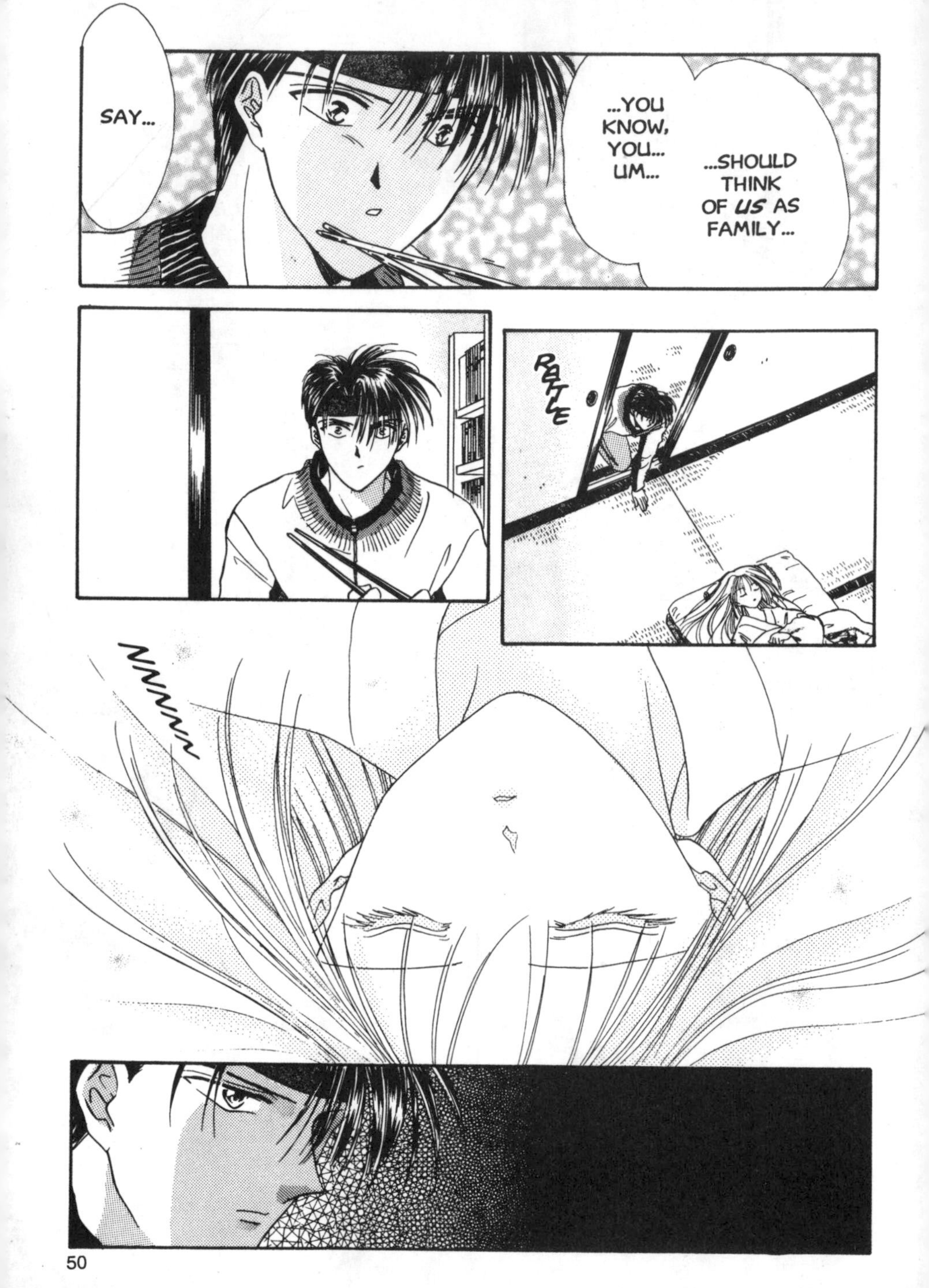

SAY...
...YOU KNOW, YOU... UM...
...SHOULD THINK OF *US* AS FAMILY...
RATTLE
NNNNNN

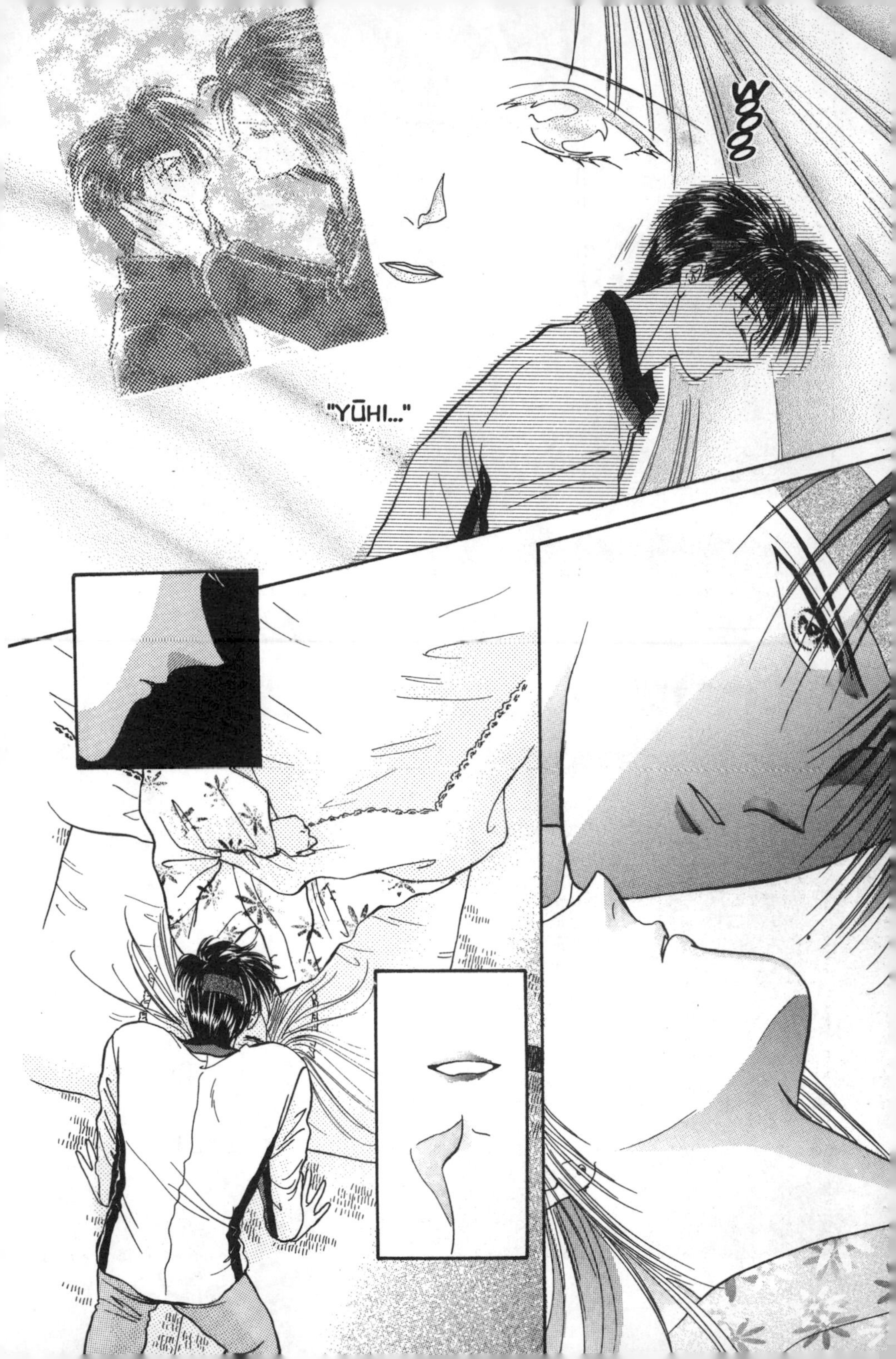
SOOOO
"YŪHI..."

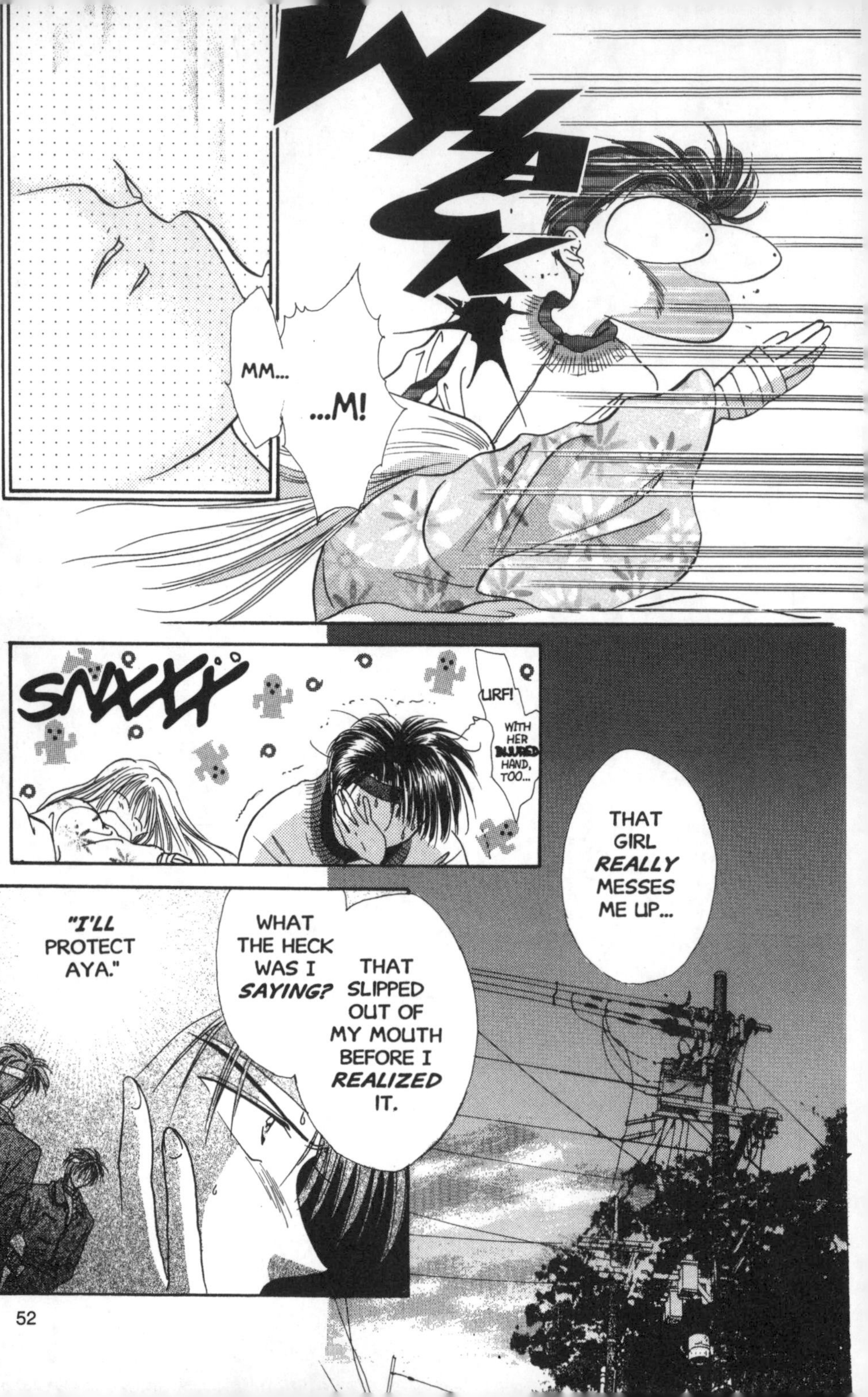
WHACK
MM...
...M!
URF!
WITH HER INJURED HAND, TOO...
THAT GIRL REALLY MESSES ME UP...
"I'LL PROTECT AYA."
WHAT THE HECK WAS I SAYING?
THAT SLIPPED OUT OF MY MOUTH BEFORE I REALIZED IT.

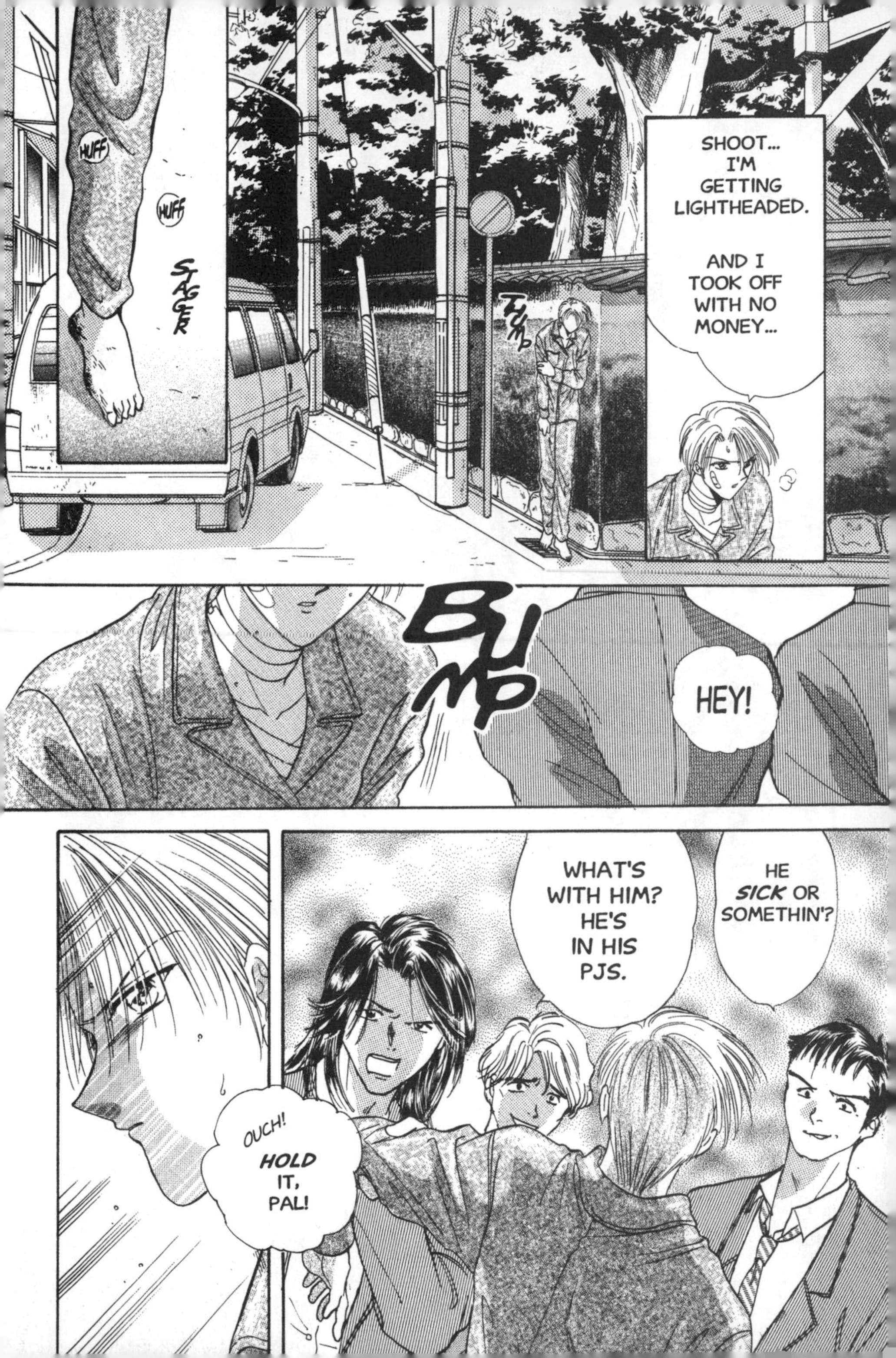
SHOOT... I'M GETTING LIGHTHEADED.
AND I TOOK OFF WITH NO MONEY...
THUMP
HUFF
HUFF
STAGGER
BUMP
HEY!
HE SICK OR SOMETHIN'?
WHAT'S WITH HIM? HE'S IN HIS PJS.
OUCH! HOLD IT, PAL!

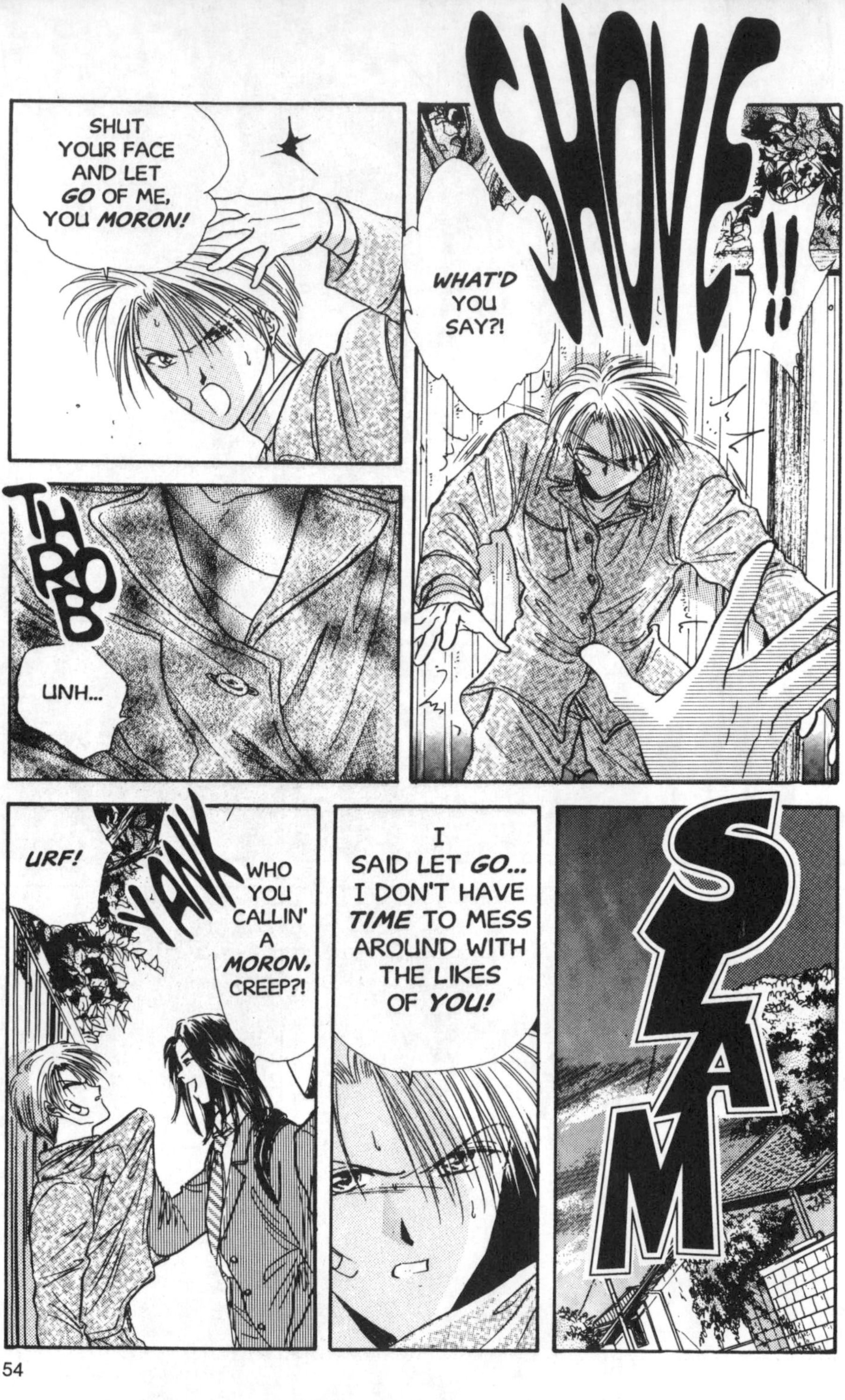

SHUT YOUR FACE AND LET GO OF ME, YOU MORON!
THROB
UNH...
WHAT'D YOU SAY?!
SHOVE!!
URF!
YANK
WHO YOU CALLIN' A MORON, CREEP?!
I SAID LET GO... I DON'T HAVE TIME TO MESS AROUND WITH THE LIKES OF YOU!
SLAM

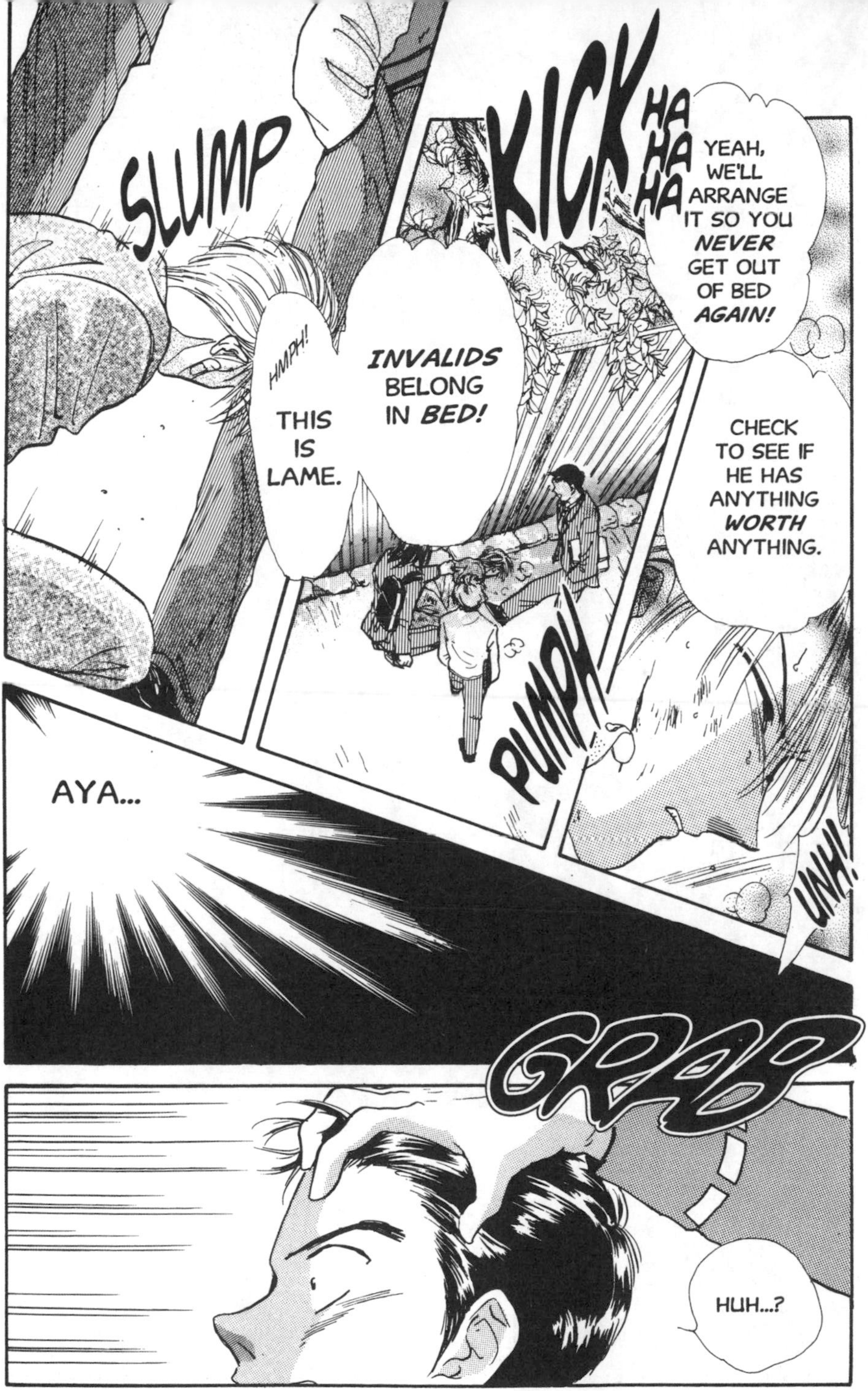
YEAH, WE'LL ARRANGE IT SO YOU NEVER GET OUT OF BED AGAIN!
CHECK TO SEE IF HE HAS ANYTHING WORTH ANYTHING.
PUMPH
UNH!
KICK
HA HA HA
INVALIDS BELONG IN BED!
HMPH!
THIS IS LAME.
SLUMP
AYA...
GRAB
HUH...?

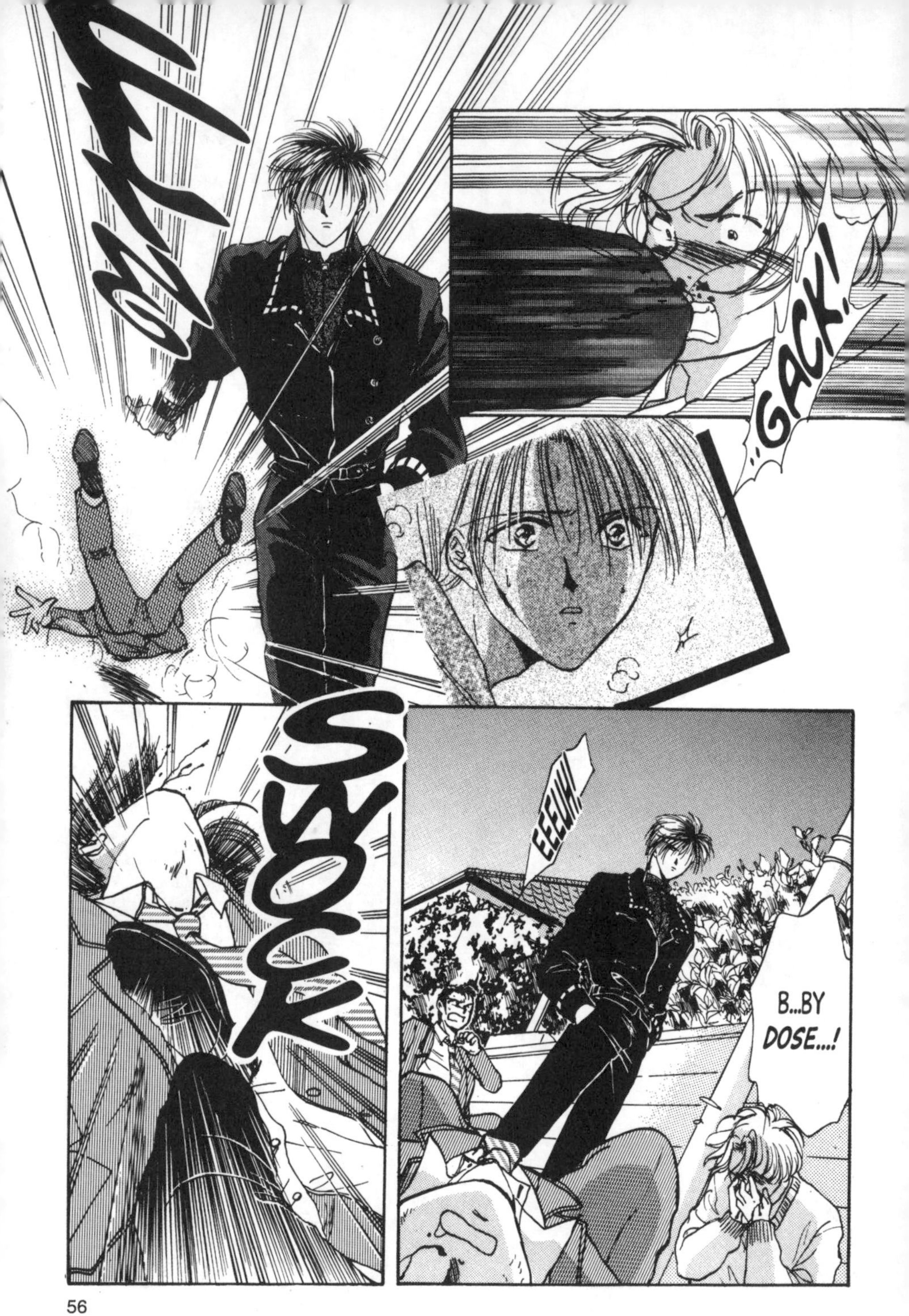
..GACK!
WHAM
EEEUH!
B...BY DOSE...!
SMACK

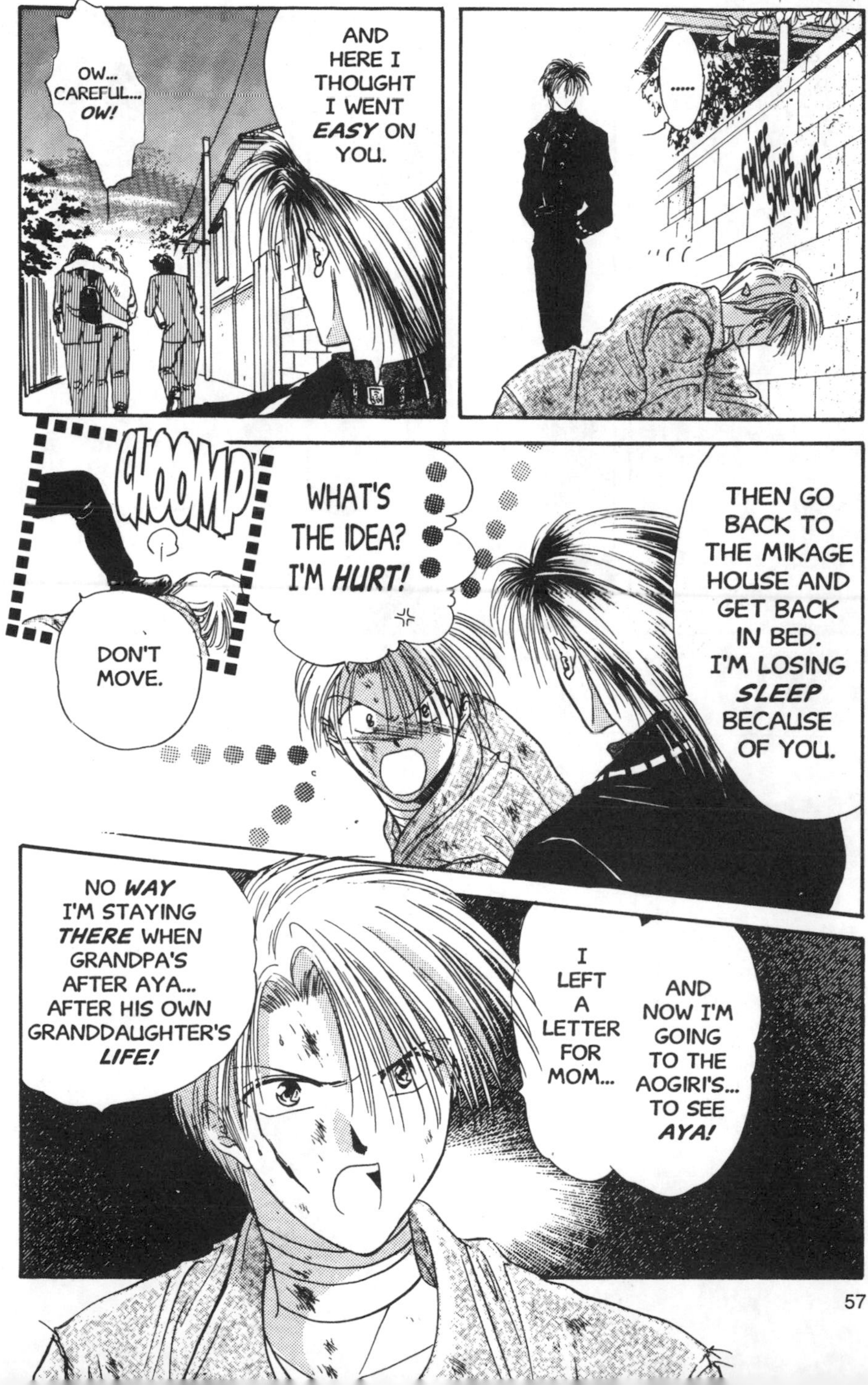
OW... CAREFUL... OW!
AND HERE I THOUGHT I WENT EASY ON YOU.
......
SNIFF SNIFF SNIFF
CHOOMP
DON'T MOVE.
WHAT'S THE IDEA? I'M HURT!
THEN GO BACK TO THE MIKAGE HOUSE AND GET BACK IN BED. I'M LOSING SLEEP BECAUSE OF YOU.
NO WAY I'M STAYING THERE WHEN GRANDPA'S AFTER AYA... AFTER HIS OWN GRANDDAUGHTER'S LIFE!
I LEFT A LETTER FOR MOM...
AND NOW I'M GOING TO THE AOGIRI'S... TO SEE AYA!

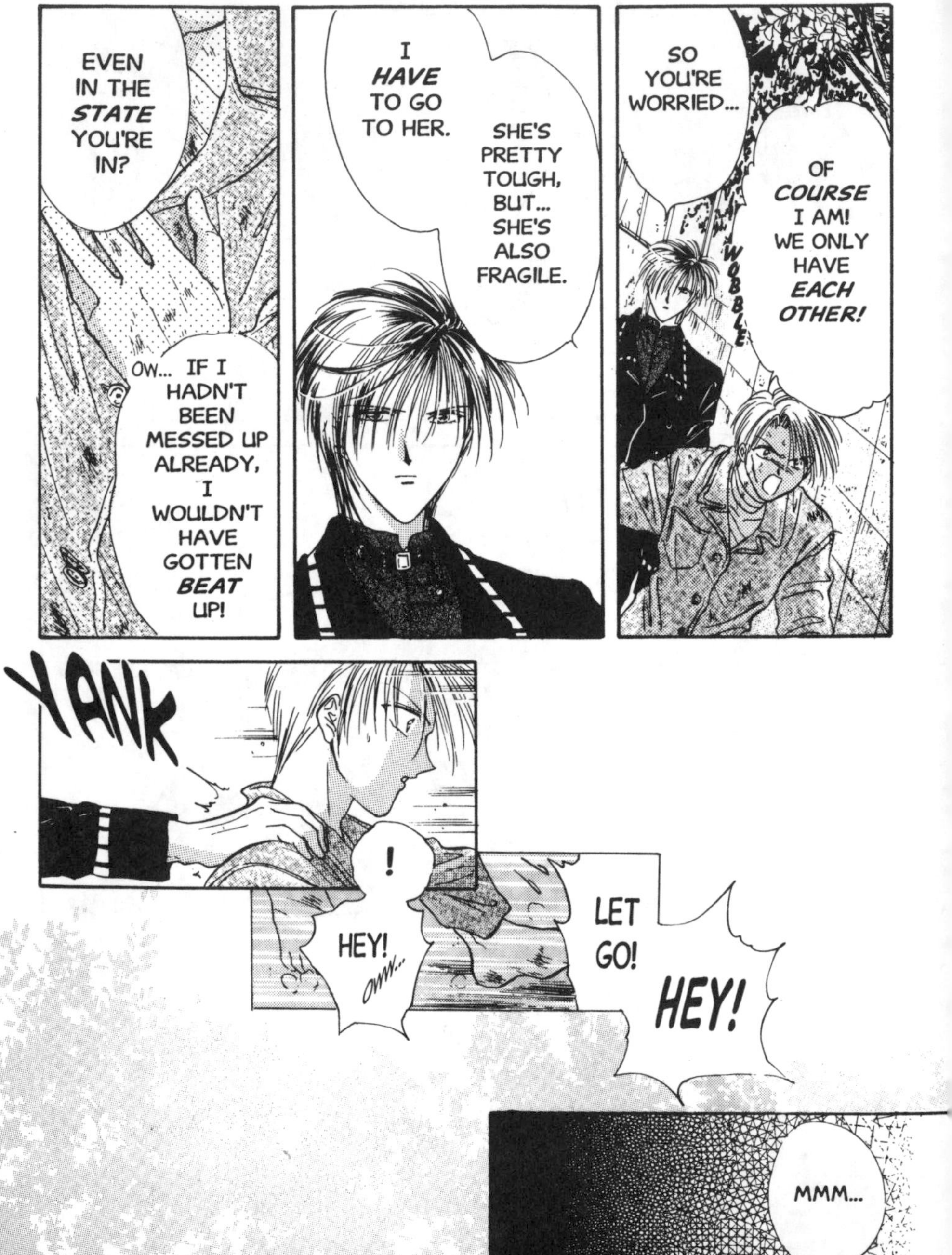
EVEN IN THE *STATE* YOU'RE IN?
OW... IF I HADN'T BEEN MESSED UP ALREADY, I WOULDN'T HAVE GOTTEN *BEAT* UP!
I *HAVE* TO GO TO HER.
SHE'S PRETTY TOUGH, BUT... SHE'S ALSO FRAGILE.
SO YOU'RE WORRIED...
WOBBLE
OF *COURSE* I AM! WE ONLY HAVE *EACH OTHER!*
YANK
!
HEY!
OWW...
LET GO!
HEY!
MMM...

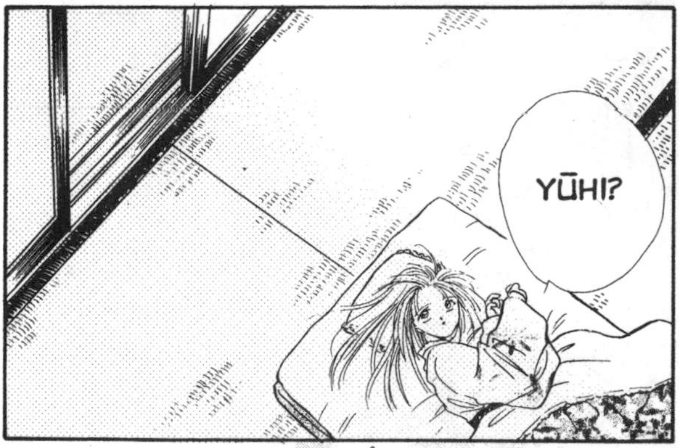
YŪHI?

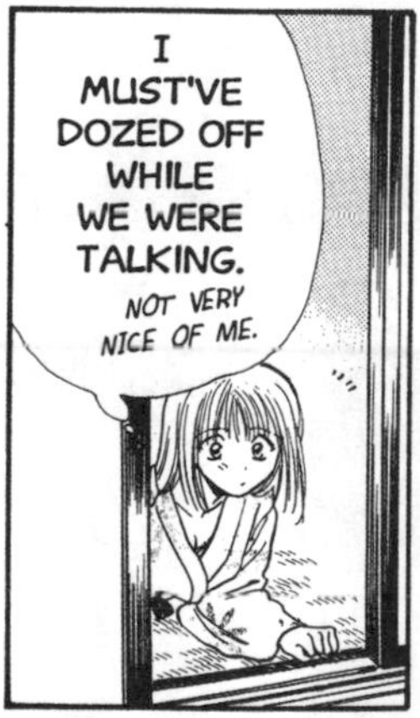
I MUST'VE DOZED OFF WHILE WE WERE TALKING.
NOT VERY NICE OF ME.

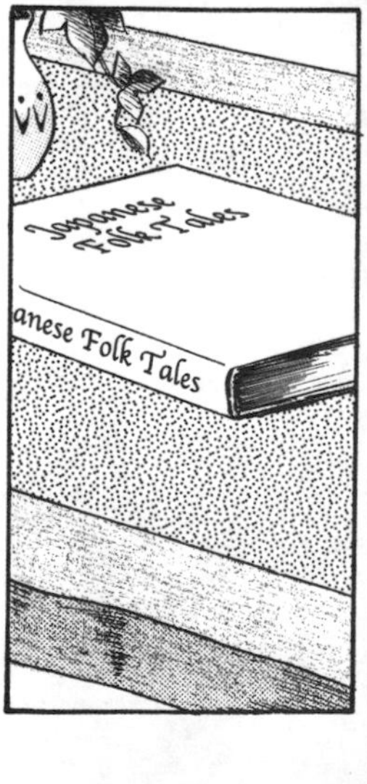
Japanese Folk Tales
anese Folk Tales

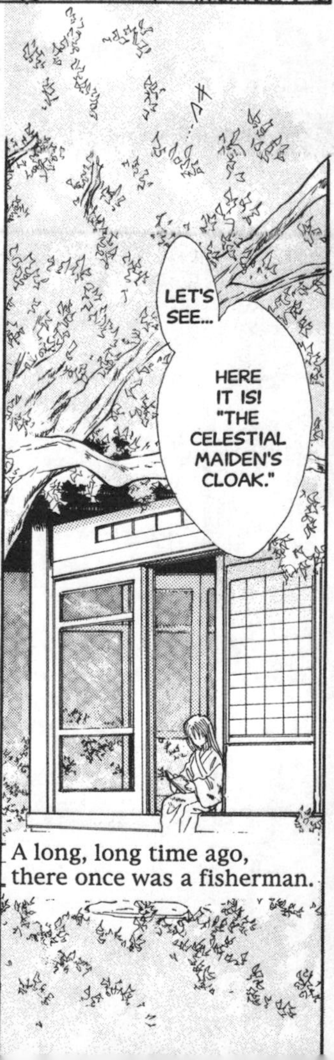
LET'S SEE...
HERE IT IS! "THE CELESTIAL MAIDEN'S CLOAK."
A long, long time ago, there once was a fisherman.

A little announcement here. **"FY part 2 is going to be an OVA! Six volumes will be released starting in May '97."** There might (?!) be some more events timed to the video releases, so people should keep checking Shōjo Comic comics anthology for info. And I don't know what'll happen just now (Jan. '97), but... **"there might be an FY CD-ROM?!"** --So please keep checking back on that too. Unfortunately, people without a computer are out of luck... They're planning on a digest of all 52 episodes of the TV series and a Q&A corner for the voice actors, among other things... The contents might change (well, if it even gets produced that is).

Oh yeah! For the video of part 2... **I'll be drawing new art for all six video covers!** I think the same art will be used for the LDs... So you'll be able to see Miaka and the seven celestial warriors again. It'll be worth the wait. I'm about to die though...

The novels? ...Huh? ...

Well, so be patient... :)

x x x

By the way, I've succeeded in dieting! I lost 8kg (17 1/2lbs) in 5 months starting in May '96... And I lost 2 more kg (4 more pounds) but everyone said, "You don't have to get any thinner." So 17 1/2lbs it is. Now I eat normally, but I haven't gained the weight back. I have to exercise and get some muscle tone... What I'm most happy about is the feeling of accomplishment, that "I can do it if I try." So I'm a lot thinner than the picture taken for the FY artbook (and I even cut and bleached my hair! to brown...) ...So I look like a totally different person. I'd lost weight since the FY event in '96 too...

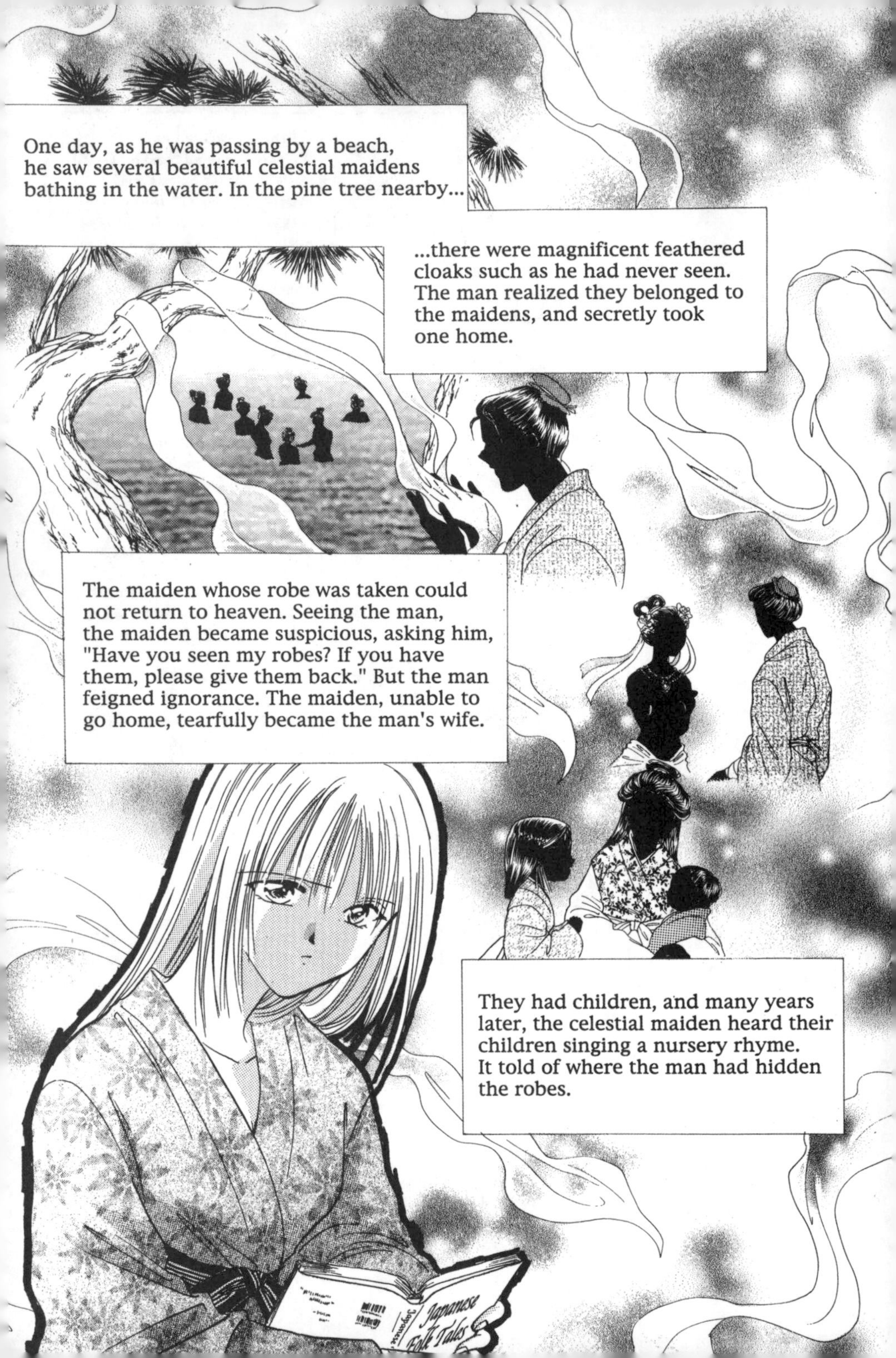
One day, as he was passing by a beach, he saw several beautiful celestial maidens bathing in the water. In the pine tree nearby...
...there were magnificent feathered cloaks such as he had never seen. The man realized they belonged to the maidens, and secretly took one home.
The maiden whose robe was taken could not return to heaven. Seeing the man, the maiden became suspicious, asking him, "Have you seen my robes? If you have them, please give them back." But the man feigned ignorance. The maiden, unable to go home, tearfully became the man's wife.
They had children, and many years later, the celestial maiden heard their children singing a nursery rhyme. It told of where the man had hidden the robes.
Japanese Folk Tales

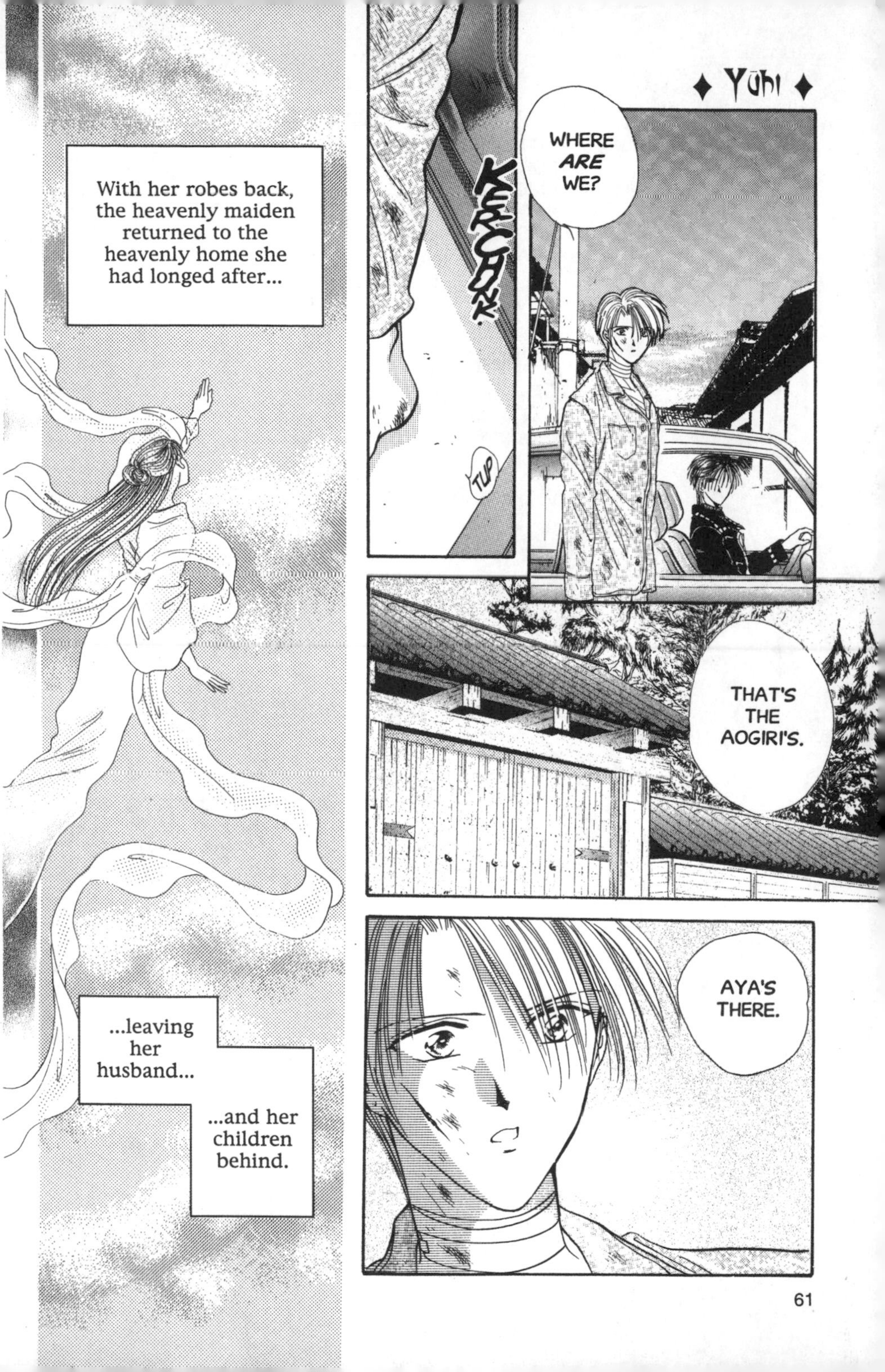
WHERE *ARE* WE?
KERCHUNK.
TUP
THAT'S THE AOGIRI'S.
AYA'S THERE.
With her robes back, the heavenly maiden returned to the heavenly home she had longed after...
...leaving her husband...
...and her children behind.

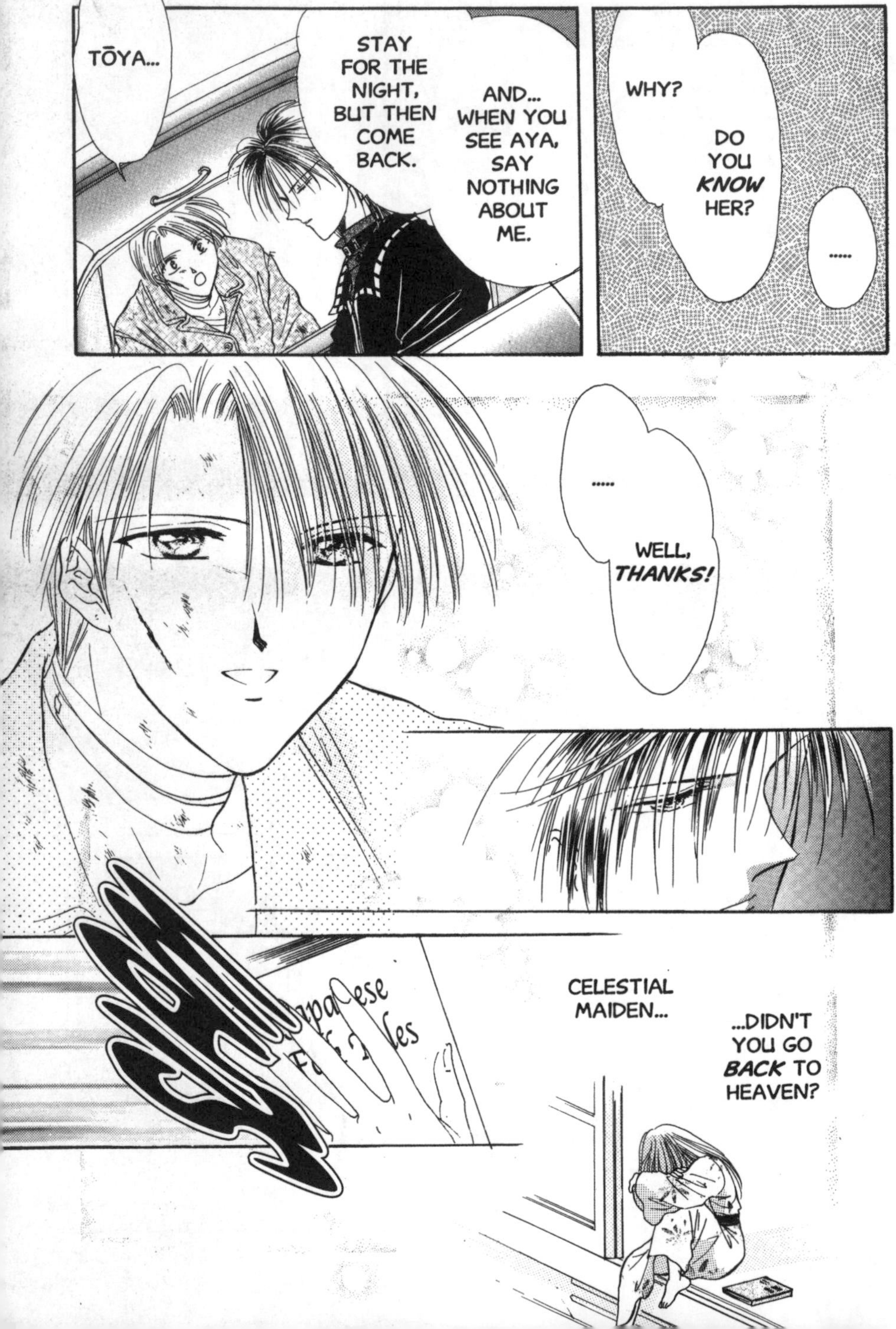
TŌYA...
STAY FOR THE NIGHT, BUT THEN COME BACK.
AND... WHEN YOU SEE AYA, SAY NOTHING ABOUT ME.
WHY?
DO YOU *KNOW* HER?
......
......
WELL, ***THANKS!***
CELESTIAL MAIDEN...
...DIDN'T YOU GO *BACK* TO HEAVEN?

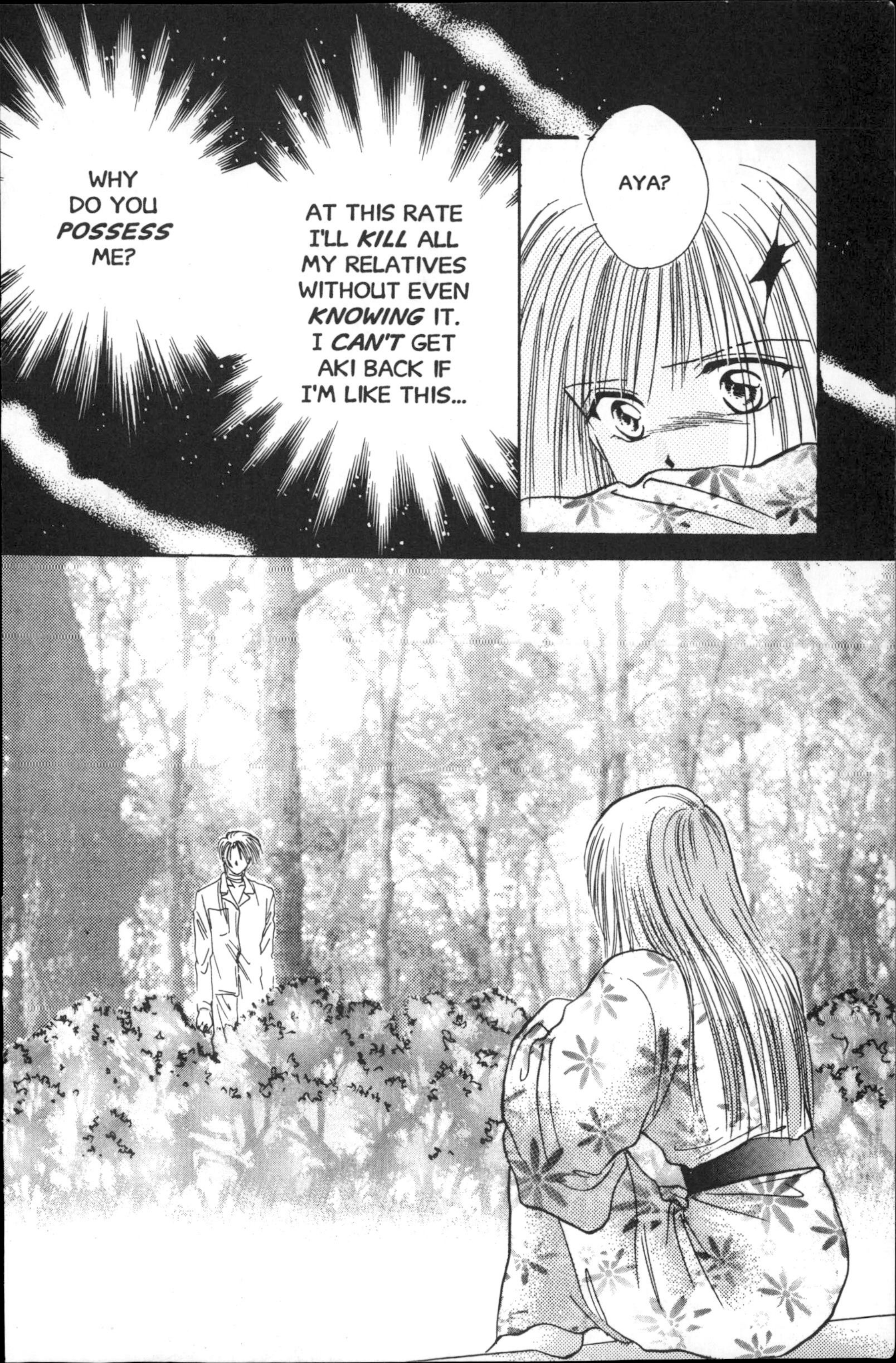
WHY DO YOU *POSSESS* ME?
AT THIS RATE I'LL *KILL* ALL MY RELATIVES WITHOUT EVEN *KNOWING* IT. I *CAN'T* GET AKI BACK IF I'M LIKE THIS...
AYA?

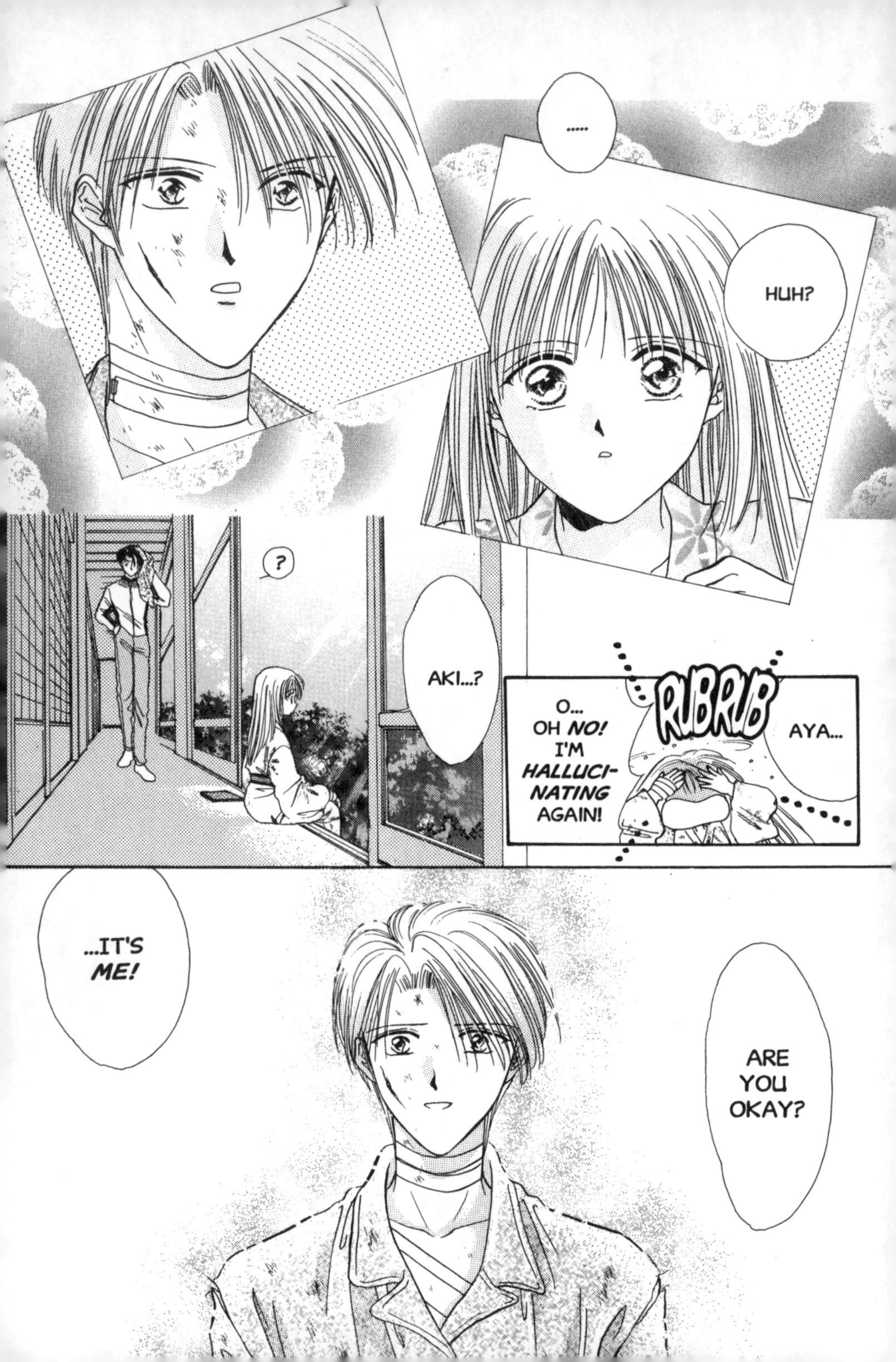

......
HUH?
?
AKI...?
O... OH NO! I'M HALLUCINATING AGAIN!
RUBRUB
AYA...
...IT'S ME!
ARE YOU OKAY?

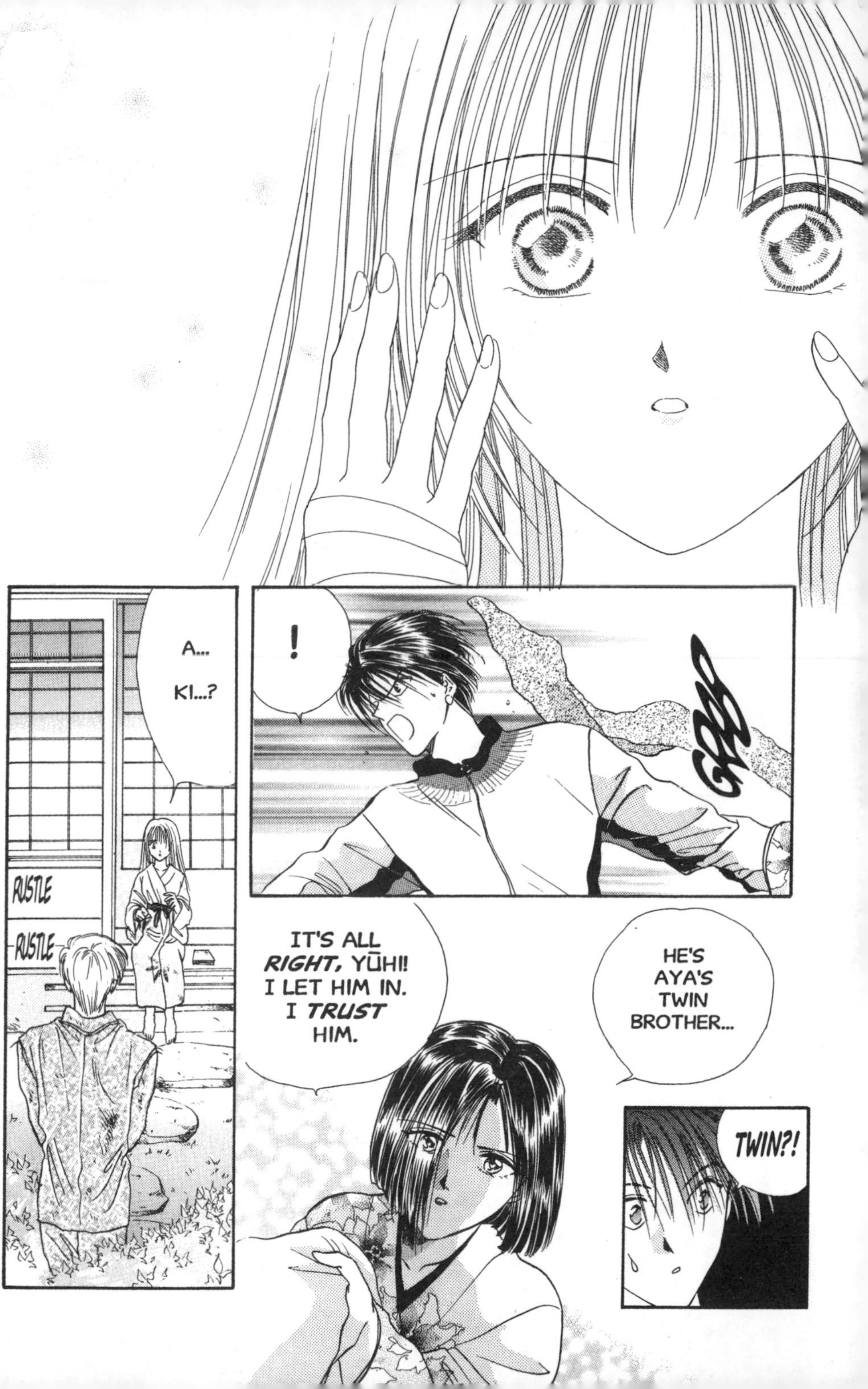
!
GRAB
IT'S ALL *RIGHT,* YŪHI! I LET HIM IN. I *TRUST* HIM.
HE'S AYA'S TWIN BROTHER...
TWIN?!
A... KI...?
RUSTLE
RUSTLE

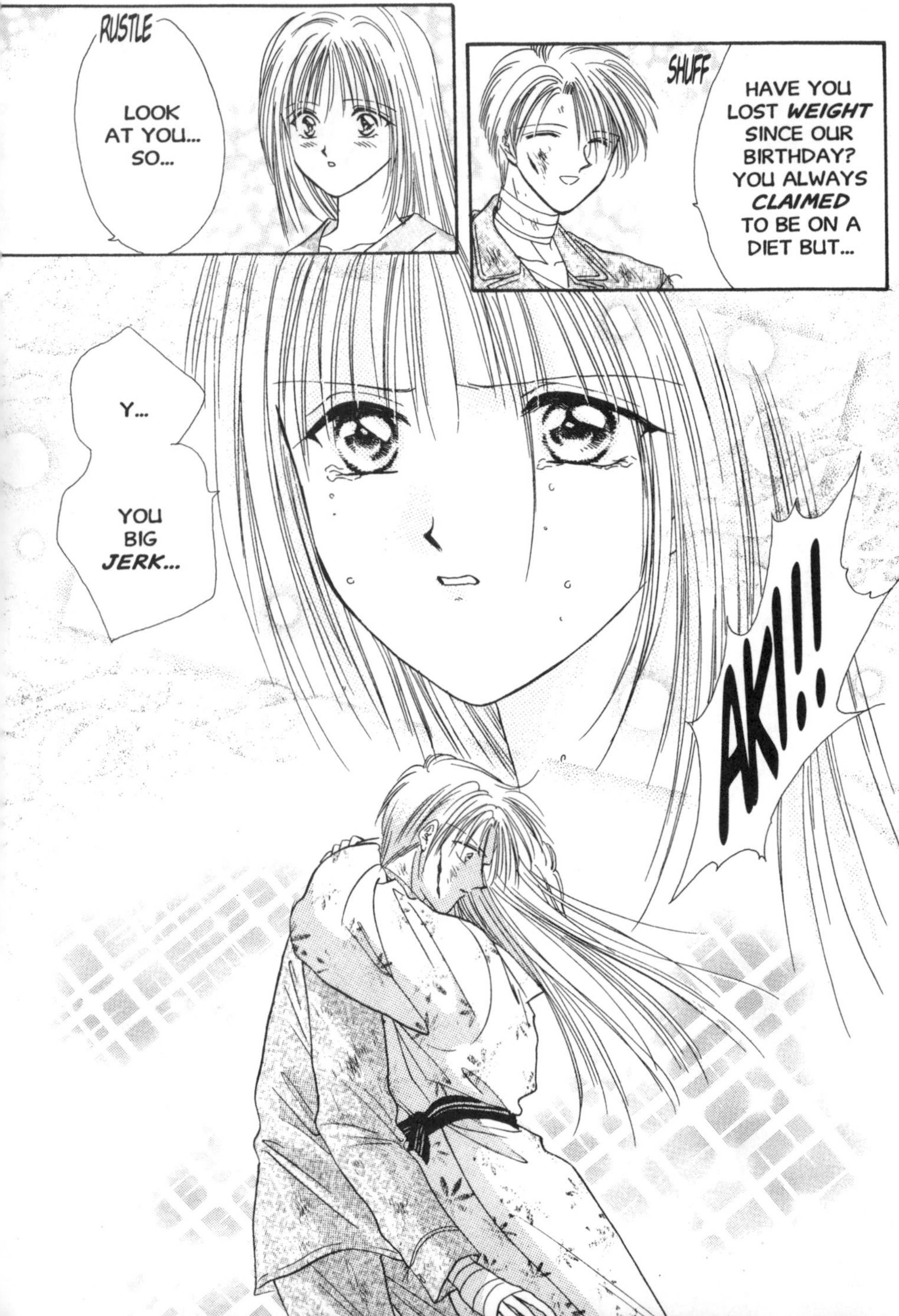
SHUFF
HAVE YOU LOST WEIGHT SINCE OUR BIRTHDAY? YOU ALWAYS CLAIMED TO BE ON A DIET BUT...
RUSTLE
LOOK AT YOU... SO...
Y...
YOU BIG JERK...
AKI!!!

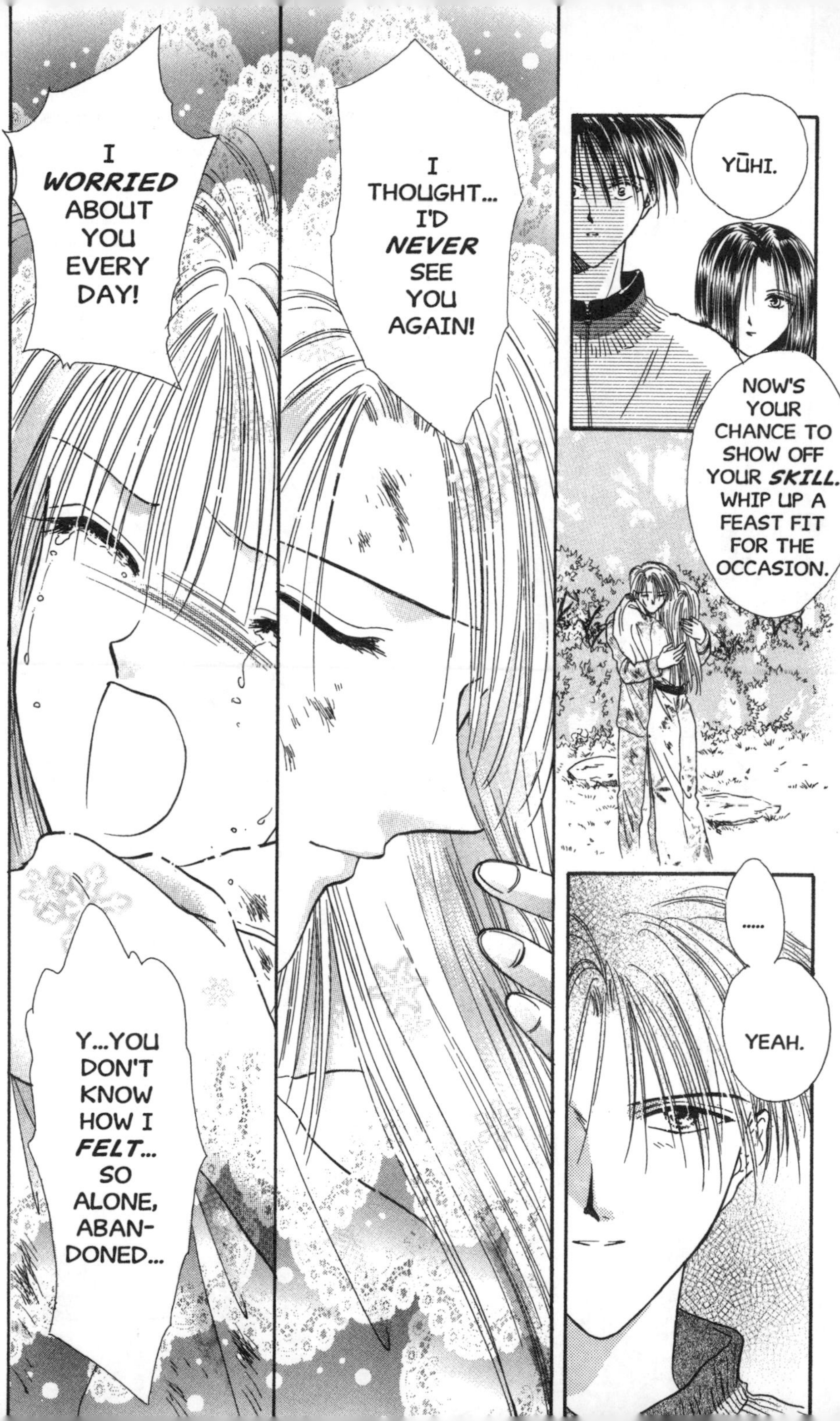
YŪHI.
NOW'S YOUR CHANCE TO SHOW OFF YOUR SKILL. WHIP UP A FEAST FIT FOR THE OCCASION.
......
YEAH.
I THOUGHT... I'D NEVER SEE YOU AGAIN!
I WORRIED ABOUT YOU EVERY DAY!
Y...YOU DON'T KNOW HOW I FELT... SO ALONE, ABAN-DONED...

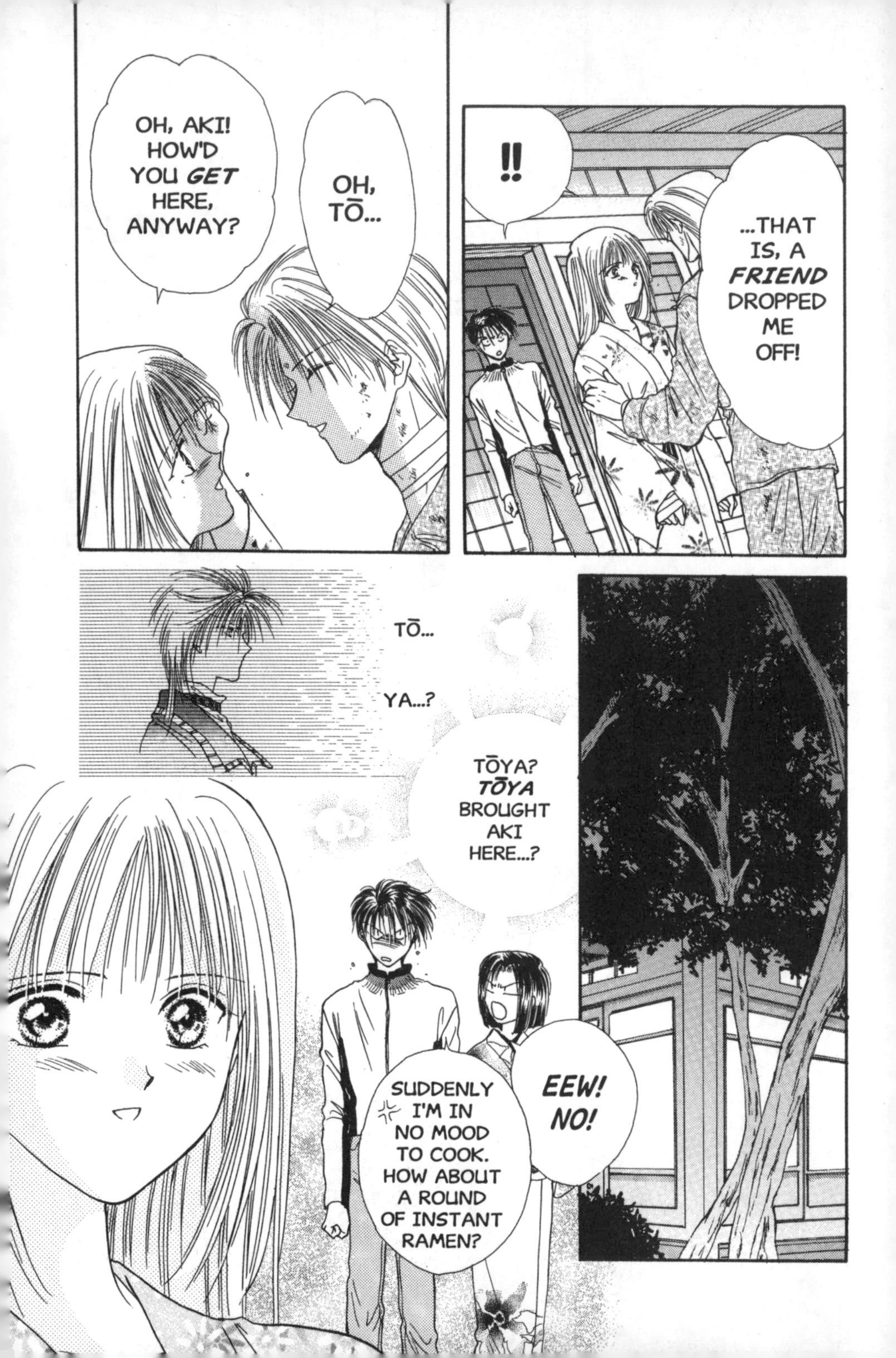
OH, AKI! HOW'D YOU *GET* HERE, ANYWAY?
OH, TŌ...
!!
...THAT IS, A *FRIEND* DROPPED ME OFF!
TŌ...
YA...?
TŌYA? *TŌYA* BROUGHT AKI HERE...?
SUDDENLY I'M IN NO MOOD TO COOK. HOW ABOUT A ROUND OF INSTANT RAMEN?
EEW! NO!

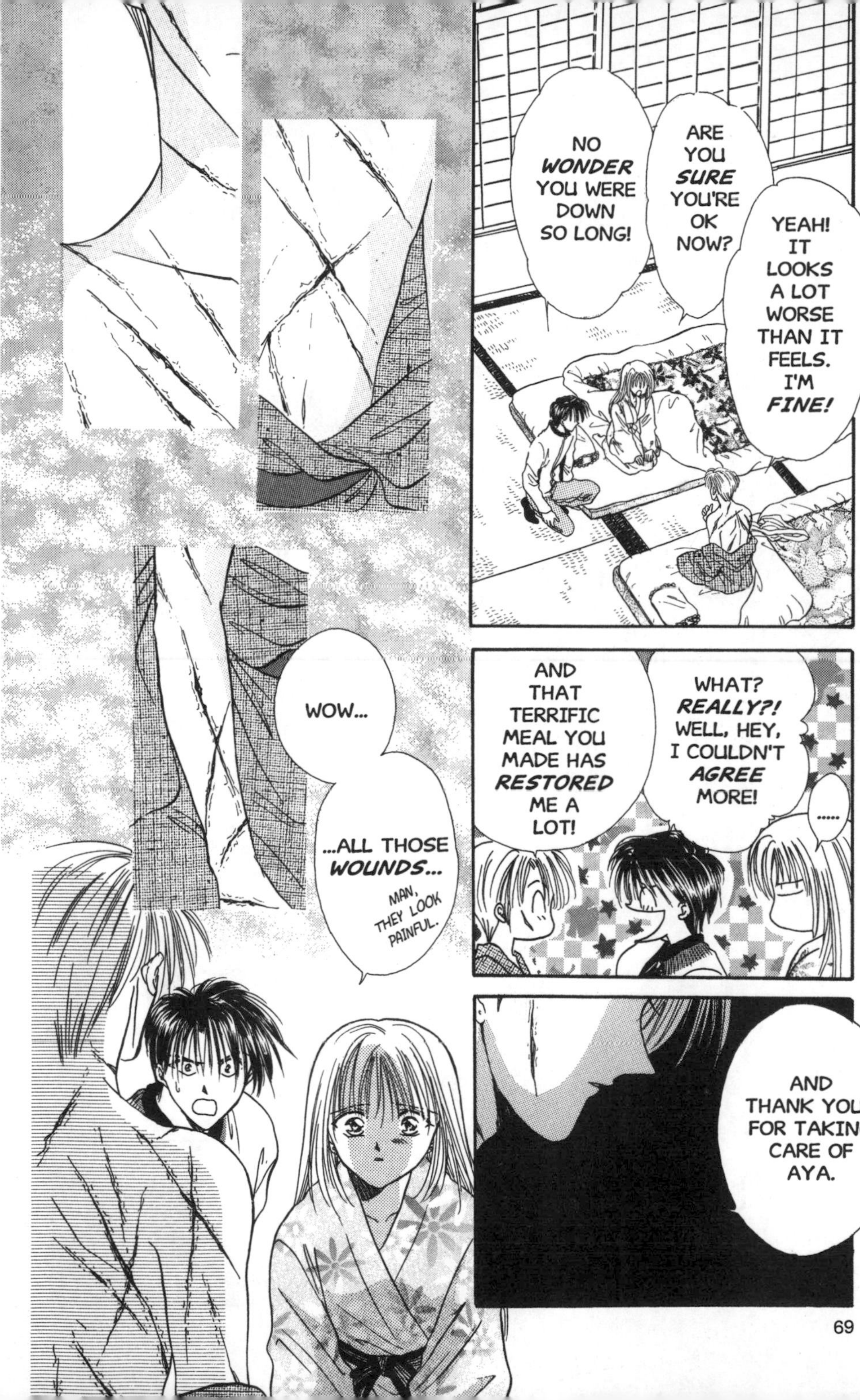
WOW...
...ALL THOSE WOUNDS...
MAN, THEY LOOK PAINFUL.
NO WONDER YOU WERE DOWN SO LONG!
ARE YOU SURE YOU'RE OK NOW?
YEAH! IT LOOKS A LOT WORSE THAN IT FEELS. I'M FINE!
AND THAT TERRIFIC MEAL YOU MADE HAS RESTORED ME A LOT!
WHAT? REALLY?! WELL, HEY, I COULDN'T AGREE MORE!
.....
AND THANK YOU... FOR TAKING CARE OF AYA.

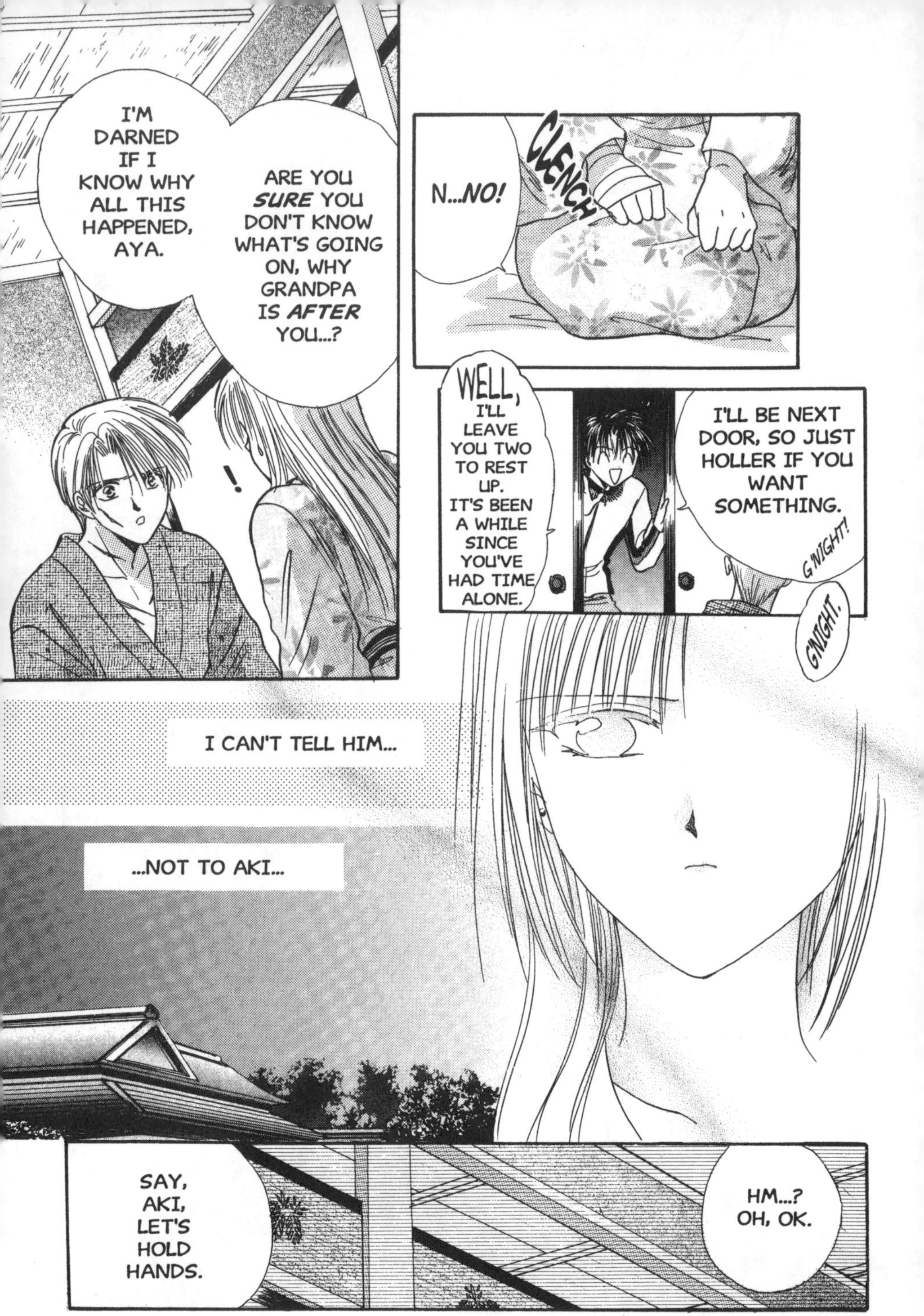
I'M DARNED IF I KNOW WHY ALL THIS HAPPENED, AYA.
ARE YOU *SURE* YOU DON'T KNOW WHAT'S GOING ON, WHY GRANDPA IS *AFTER* YOU...?
!
CLENCH
N...*NO!*
WELL, I'LL LEAVE YOU TWO TO REST UP. IT'S BEEN A WHILE SINCE YOU'VE HAD TIME ALONE.
I'LL BE NEXT DOOR, SO JUST HOLLER IF YOU WANT SOMETHING.
G'NIGHT!
G'NIGHT.
I CAN'T TELL HIM...
...NOT TO AKI...
SAY, AKI, LET'S HOLD HANDS.
HM...? OH, OK.

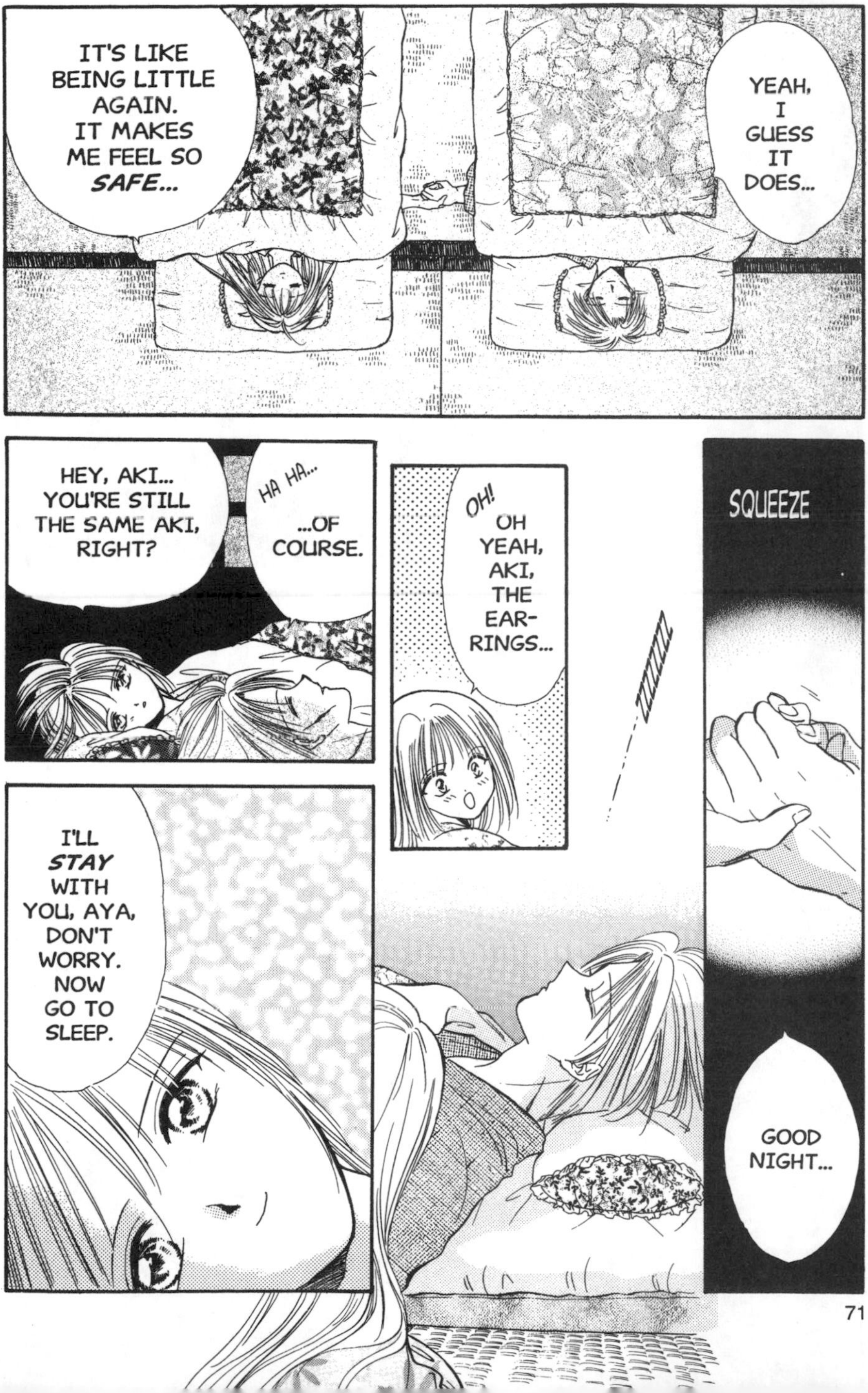
IT'S LIKE BEING LITTLE AGAIN. IT MAKES ME FEEL SO *SAFE...*
YEAH, I GUESS IT DOES...
HEY, AKI... YOU'RE STILL THE SAME AKI, RIGHT?
HA HA...
...OF COURSE.
OH!
OH YEAH, AKI, THE EAR-RINGS...
ZZZZZZZZ
I'LL *STAY* WITH YOU, AYA, DON'T WORRY. NOW GO TO SLEEP.
SQUEEZE
GOOD NIGHT...

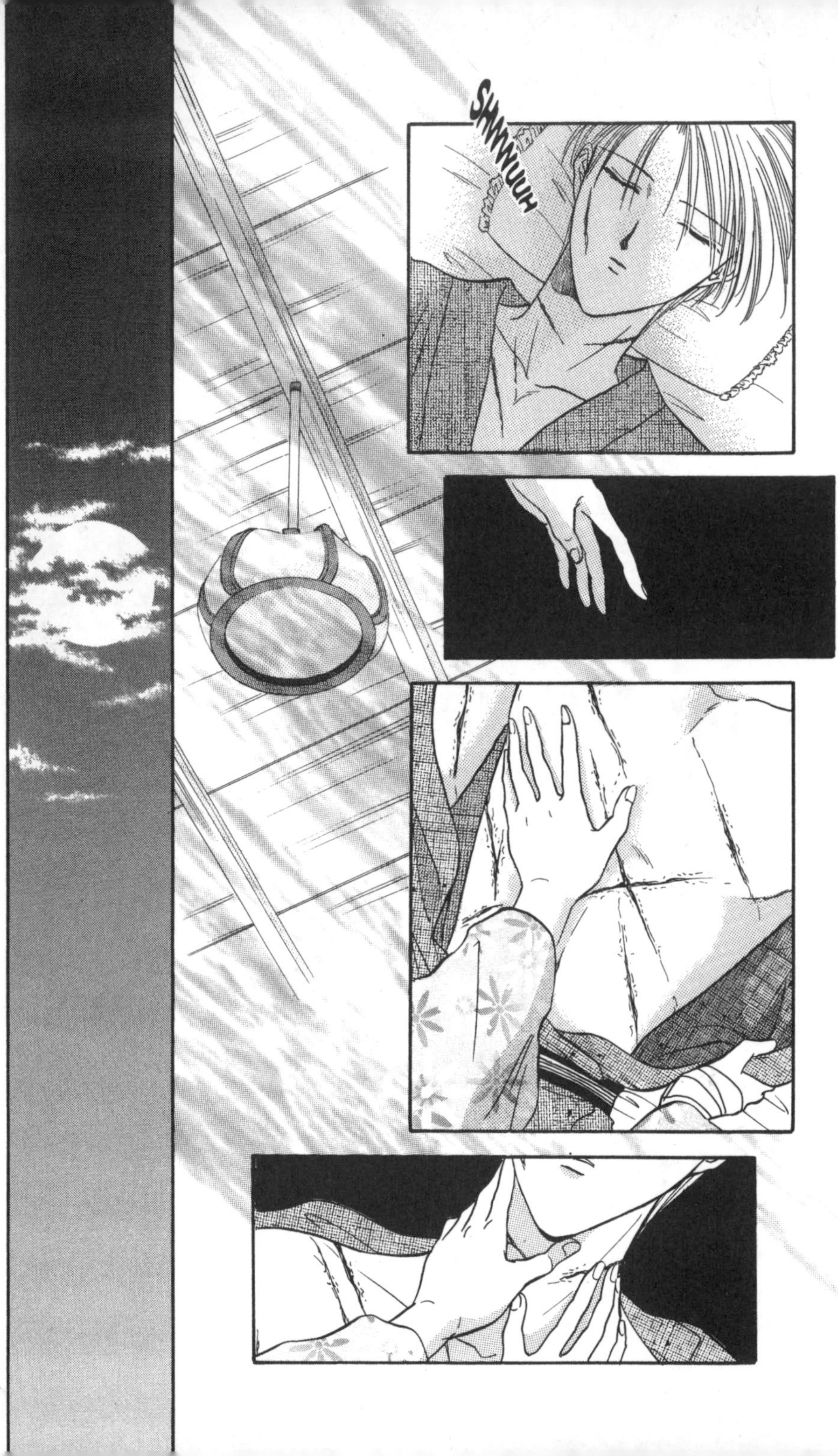
SHWWUUH

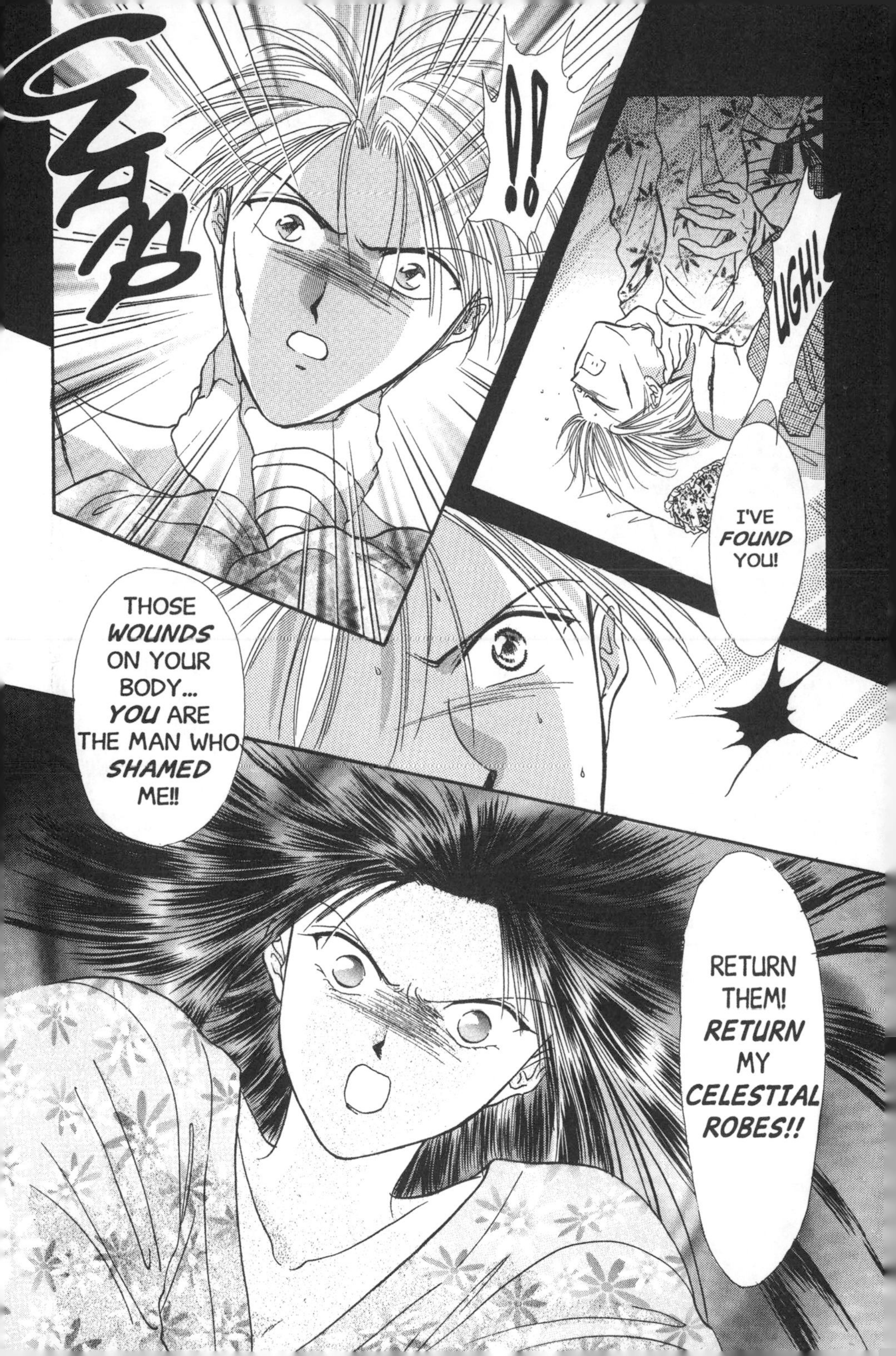
CLAMP
!!
UGH!
I'VE *FOUND* YOU!
THOSE *WOUNDS* ON YOUR BODY... *YOU* ARE THE MAN WHO *SHAMED* ME!!
RETURN THEM! *RETURN* MY *CELESTIAL ROBES!!*

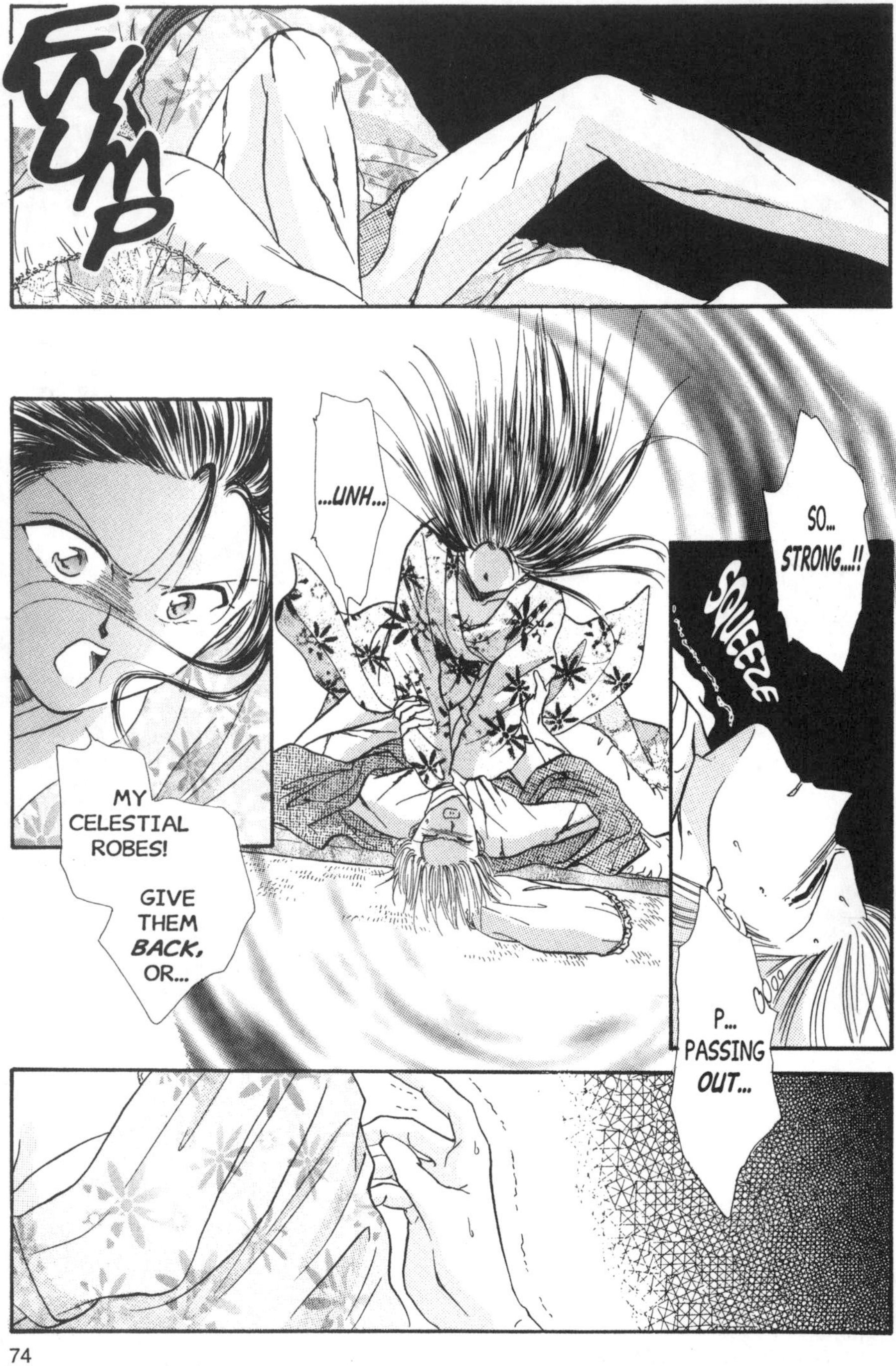
FWUMP
SO... STRONG...!!
SQUEEZE
P... PASSING OUT...
...UNH...
MY CELESTIAL ROBES!
GIVE THEM BACK, OR...

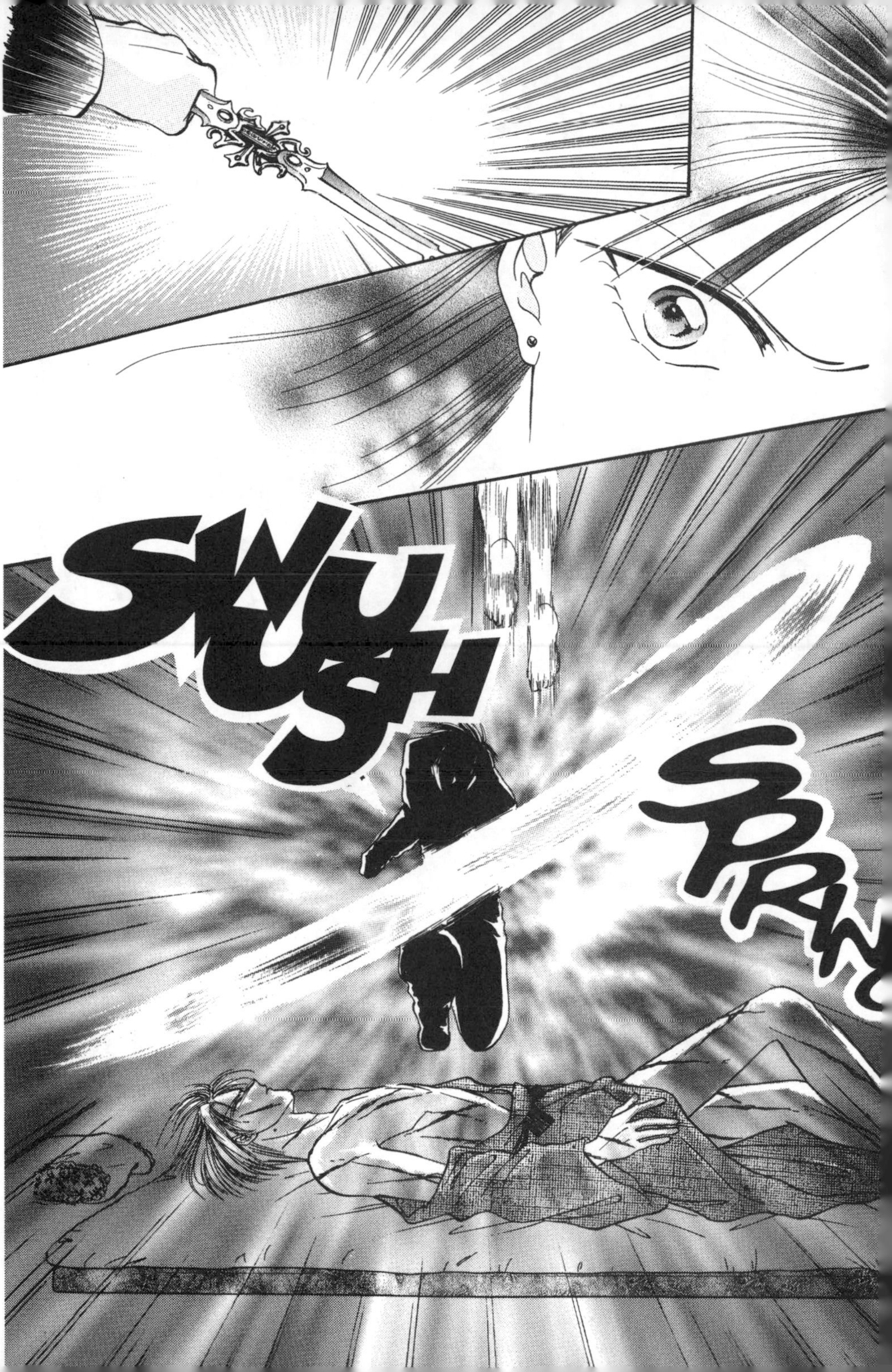
SWUSH!
SPRAN

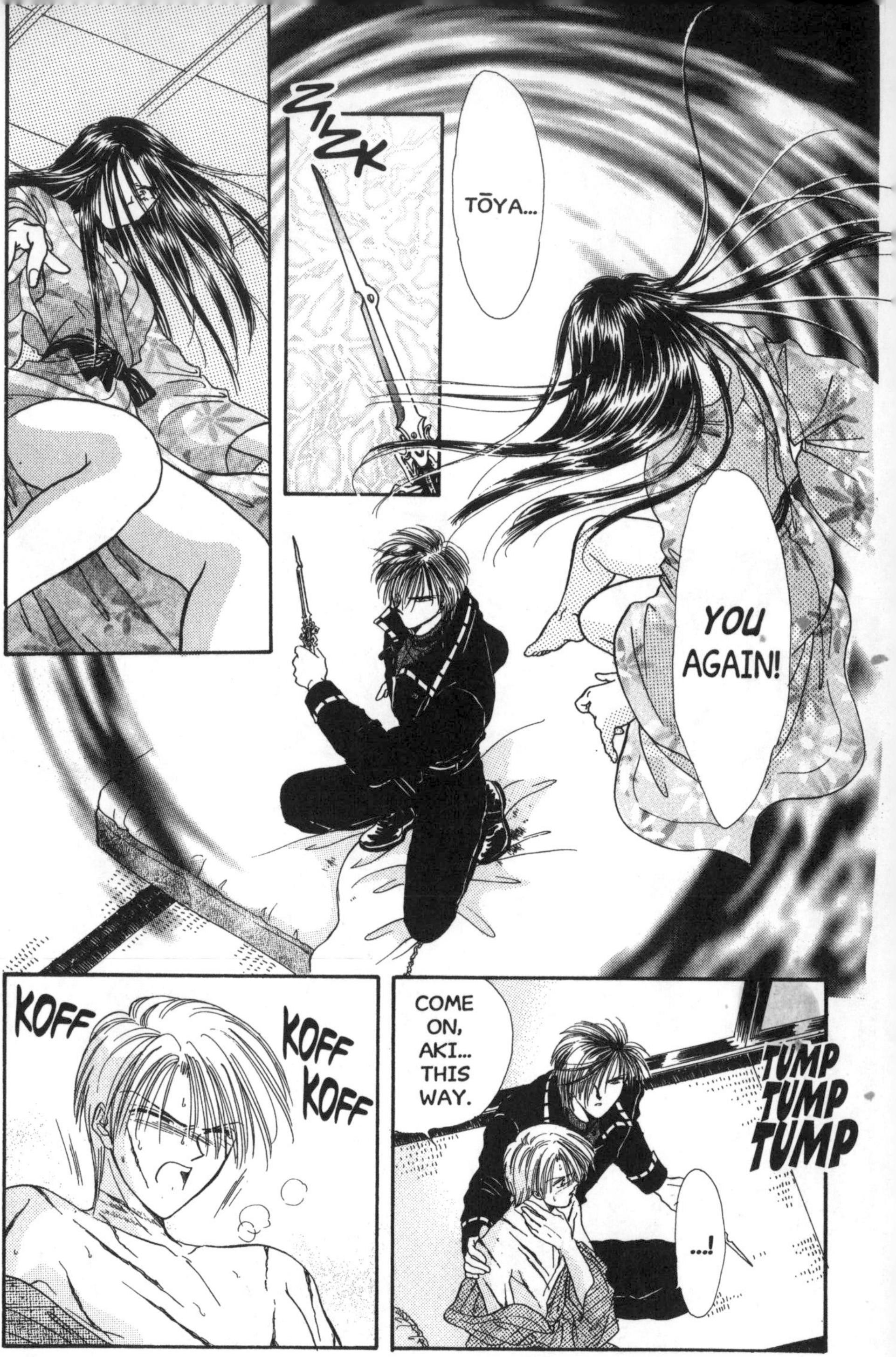
TŌYA...
ZZZK
YOU AGAIN!
TUMP TUMP TUMP
COME ON, AKI... THIS WAY.
...!
KOFF
KOFF KOFF

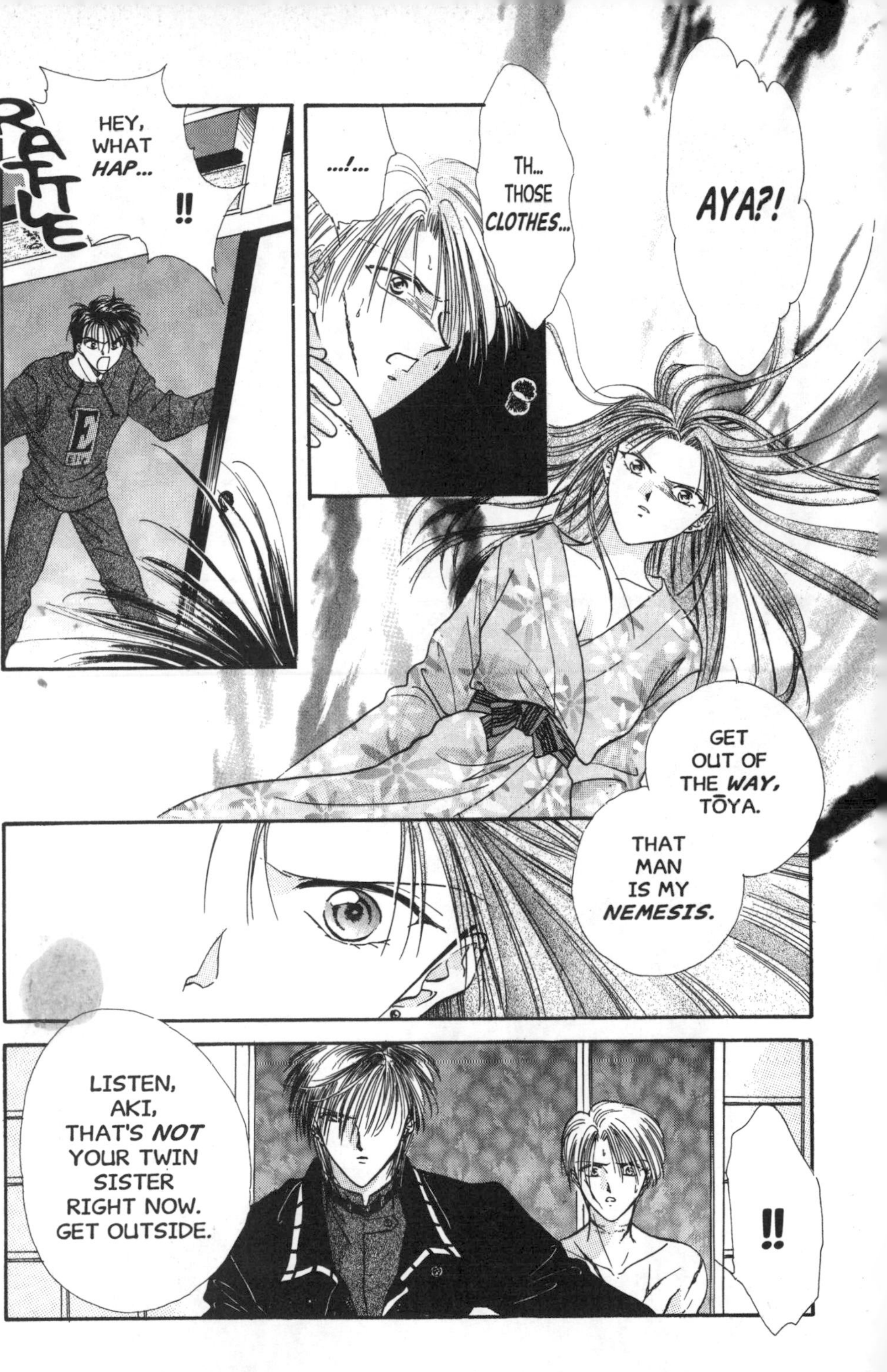
RATTLE
HEY, WHAT *HAP*...
!!
...!...
TH... THOSE *CLOTHES*...
AYA?!
GET OUT OF THE *WAY,* TŌYA.
THAT MAN IS MY *NEMESIS.*
LISTEN, AKI, THAT'S *NOT* YOUR TWIN SISTER RIGHT NOW. GET OUTSIDE.
!!

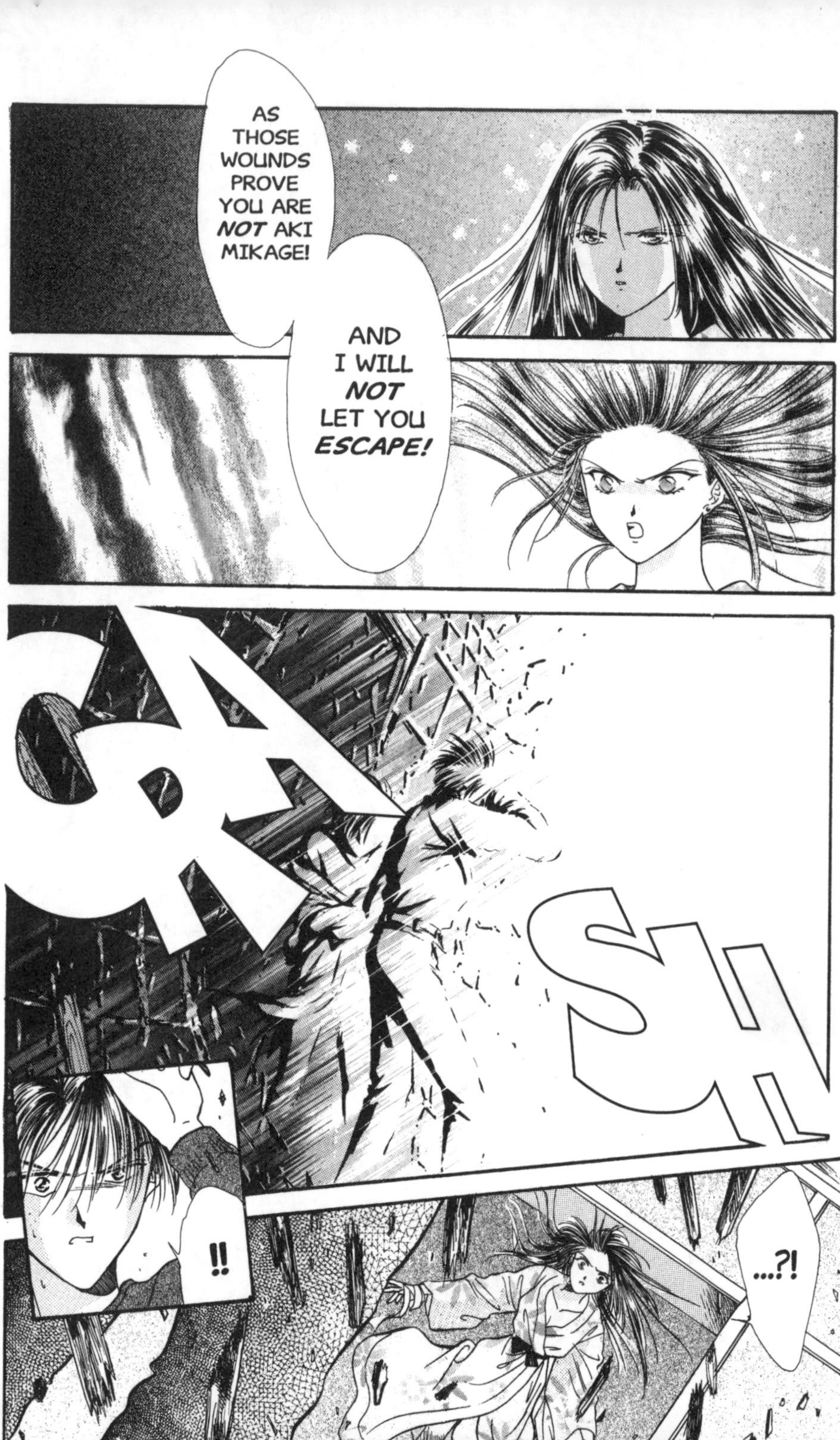
AS THOSE WOUNDS PROVE YOU ARE NOT AKI MIKAGE!
AND I WILL NOT LET YOU ESCAPE!
SH
SA
...?!
!!

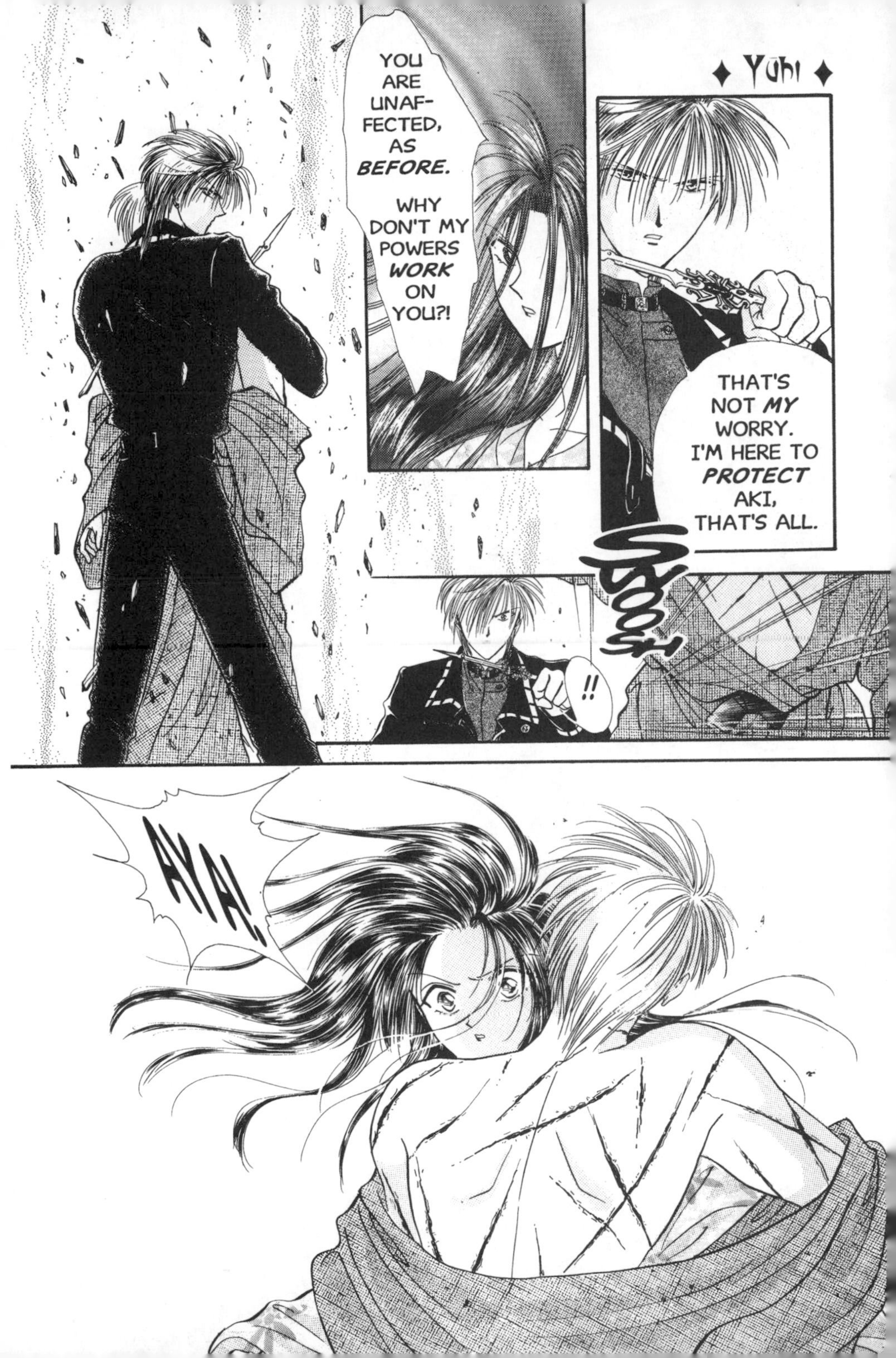
YOU ARE UNAFFECTED, AS *BEFORE.*
WHY DON'T MY POWERS *WORK* ON YOU?!
THAT'S NOT *MY* WORRY. I'M HERE TO *PROTECT* AKI, THAT'S ALL.
SWOOSH
!!
AYA!

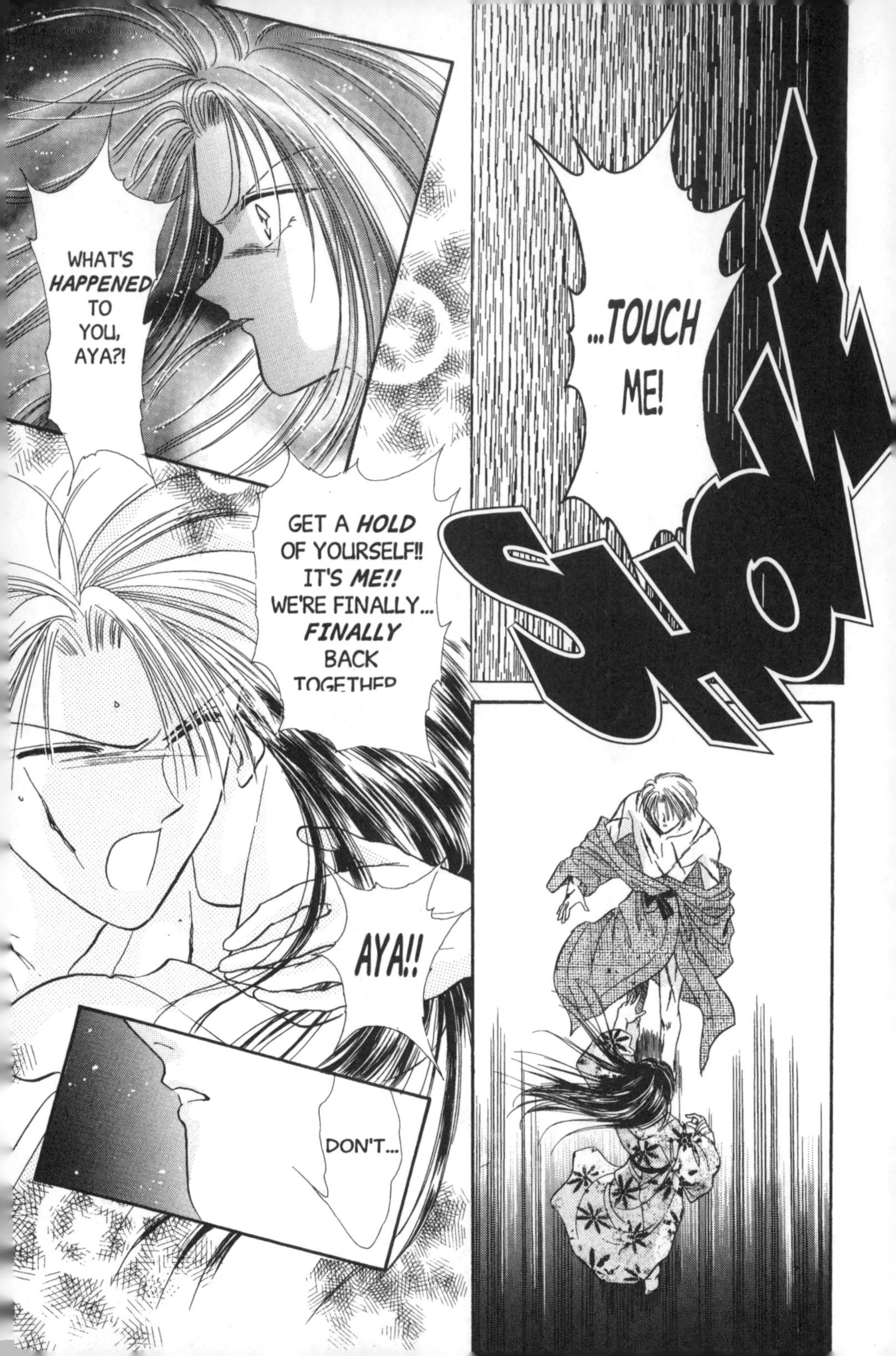
WHAT'S *HAPPENED* TO YOU, AYA?!
GET A *HOLD* OF YOURSELF!! IT'S *ME!!* WE'RE FINALLY... *FINALLY* BACK TOGETHER
AYA!!
DON'T...
...TOUCH ME!

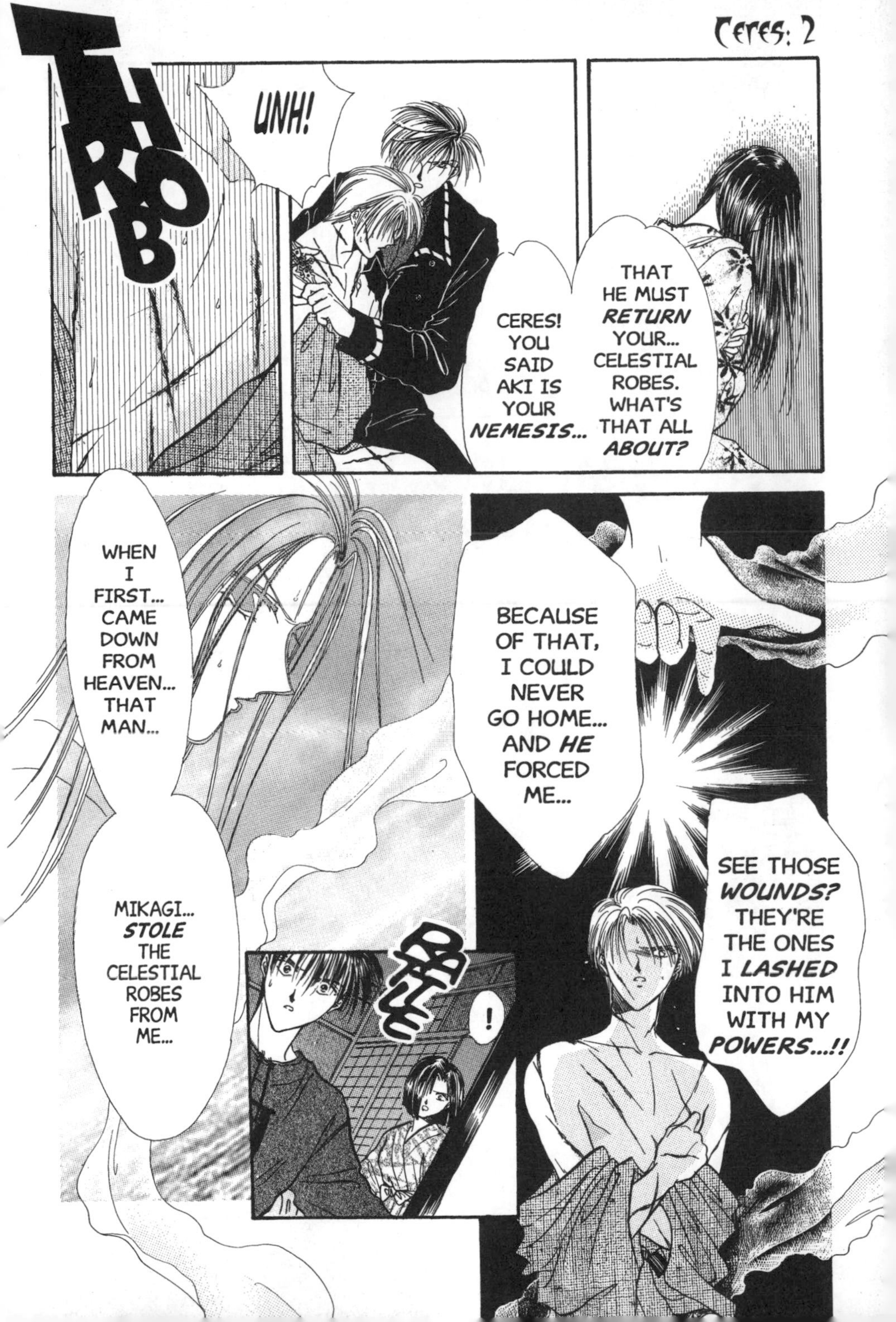
CERES! YOU SAID AKI IS YOUR *NEMESIS...*
THAT HE MUST *RETURN* YOUR... CELESTIAL ROBES. WHAT'S THAT ALL *ABOUT?*
UNH!
THROB
WHEN I FIRST... CAME DOWN FROM HEAVEN... THAT MAN...
MIKAGI... *STOLE* THE CELESTIAL ROBES FROM ME...
BECAUSE OF THAT, I COULD NEVER GO HOME... AND *HE* FORCED ME...
SEE THOSE *WOUNDS?* THEY'RE THE ONES I *LASHED* INTO HIM WITH MY *POWERS...!!*
!

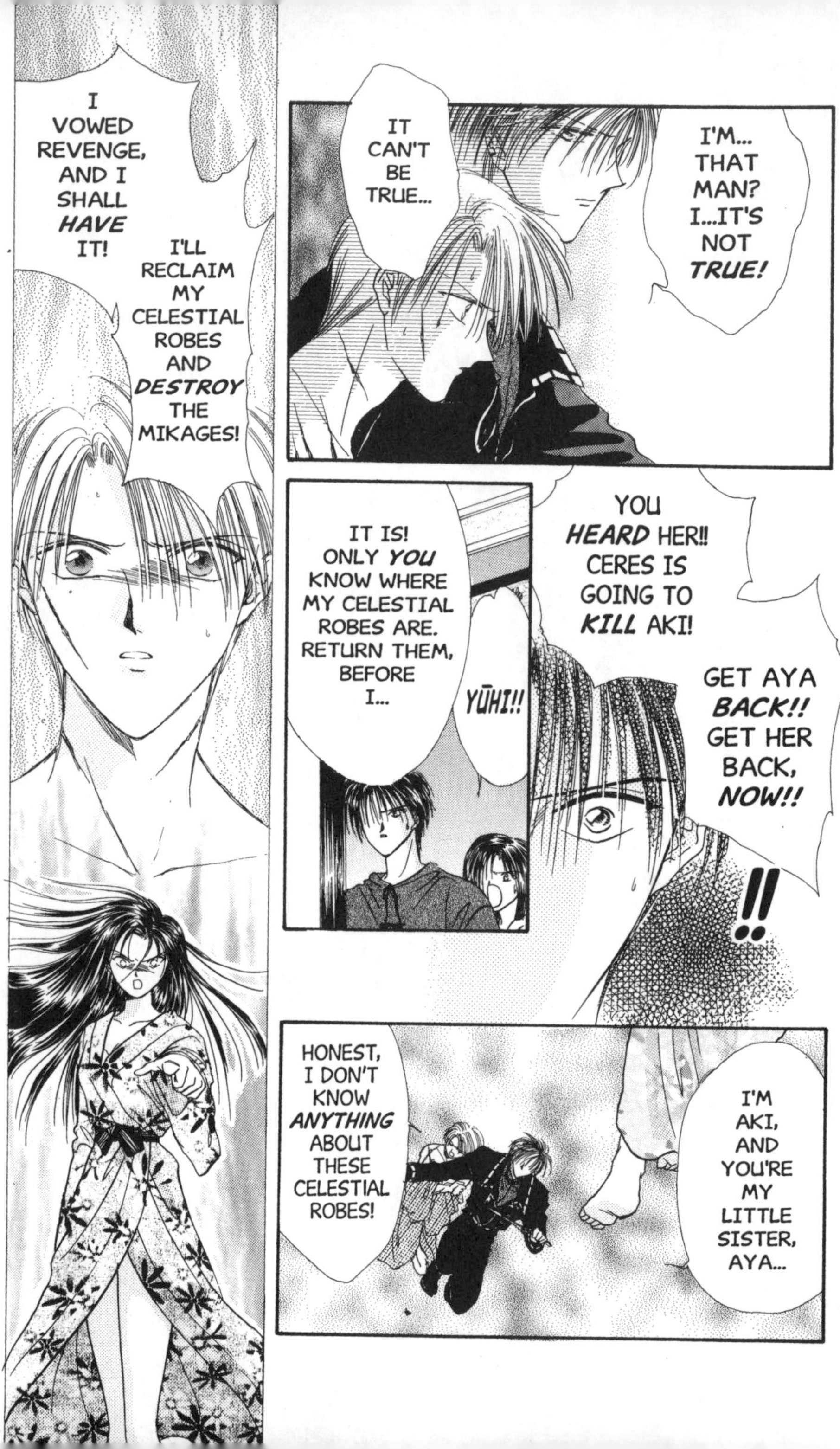
I'M... THAT MAN? I...IT'S NOT TRUE!
IT CAN'T BE TRUE...
YOU HEARD HER!! CERES IS GOING TO KILL AKI!
GET AYA BACK!! GET HER BACK, NOW!!
!!
IT IS! ONLY YOU KNOW WHERE MY CELESTIAL ROBES ARE. RETURN THEM, BEFORE I...
YŪHI!!
I'M AKI, AND YOU'RE MY LITTLE SISTER, AYA...
HONEST, I DON'T KNOW ANYTHING ABOUT THESE CELESTIAL ROBES!
I VOWED REVENGE, AND I SHALL HAVE IT!
I'LL RECLAIM MY CELESTIAL ROBES AND DESTROY THE MIKAGES!

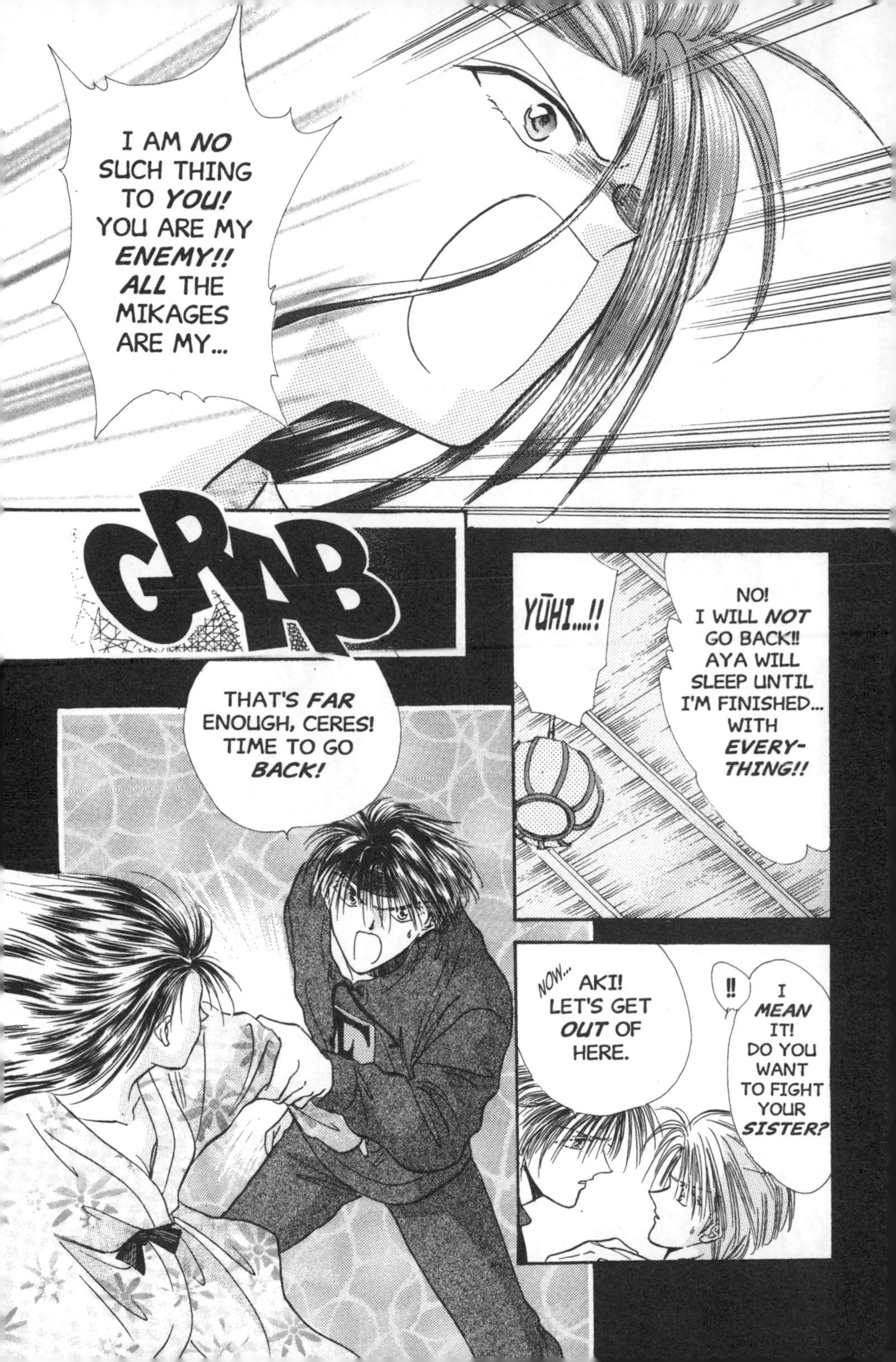
I AM *NO* SUCH THING TO *YOU!* YOU ARE MY *ENEMY!!* *ALL* THE MIKAGES ARE MY...
GRAB
THAT'S *FAR* ENOUGH, CERES! TIME TO GO *BACK!*
YŪHI...!!
NO! I WILL *NOT* GO BACK!! AYA WILL SLEEP UNTIL I'M FINISHED... WITH *EVERY-THING!!*
NOW... AKI! LET'S GET *OUT* OF HERE.
!!
I *MEAN* IT! DO YOU WANT TO FIGHT YOUR *SISTER?*

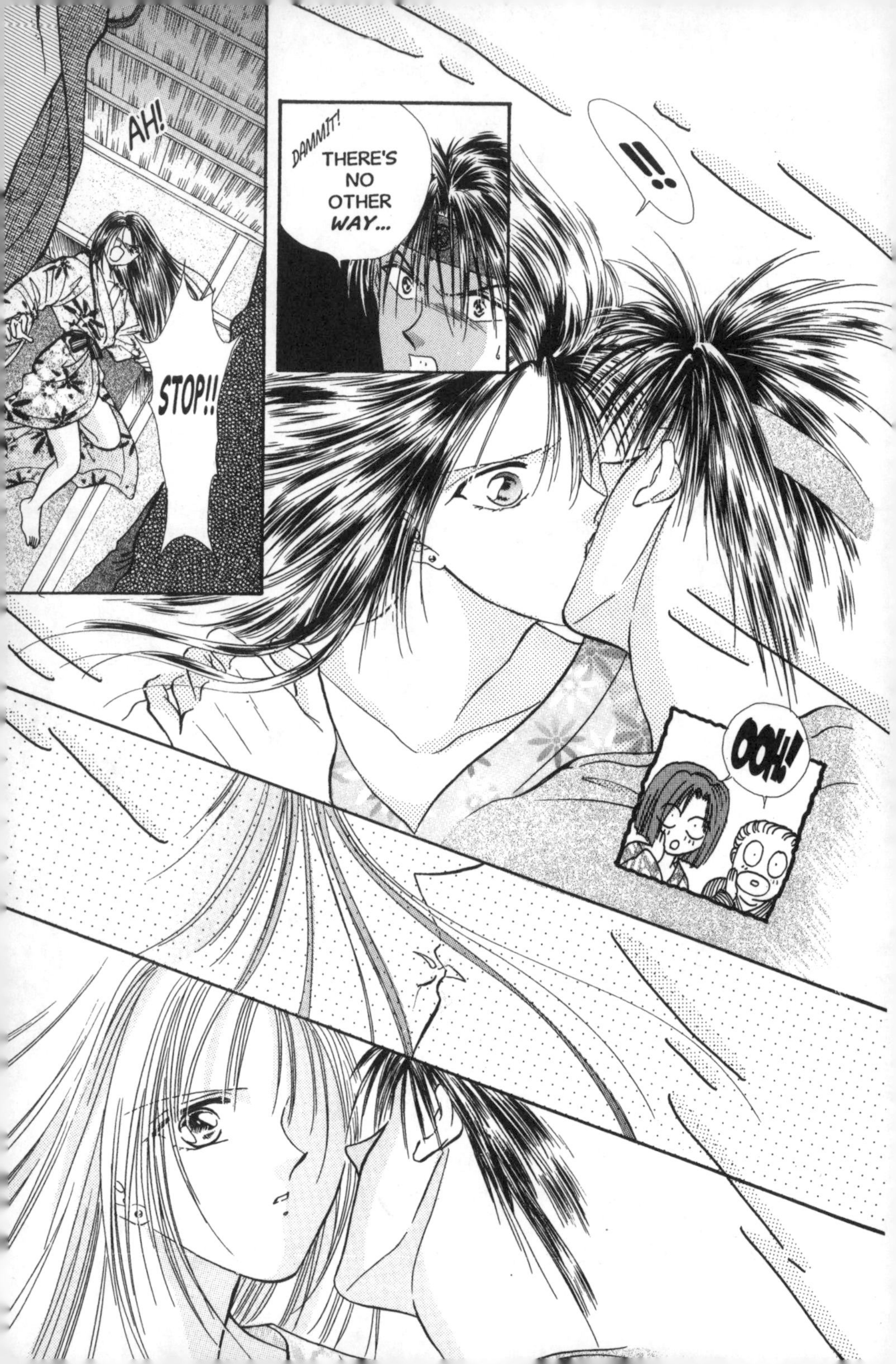
!!
DAMMIT!
THERE'S NO OTHER WAY...
AH!
STOP!!
OOH!

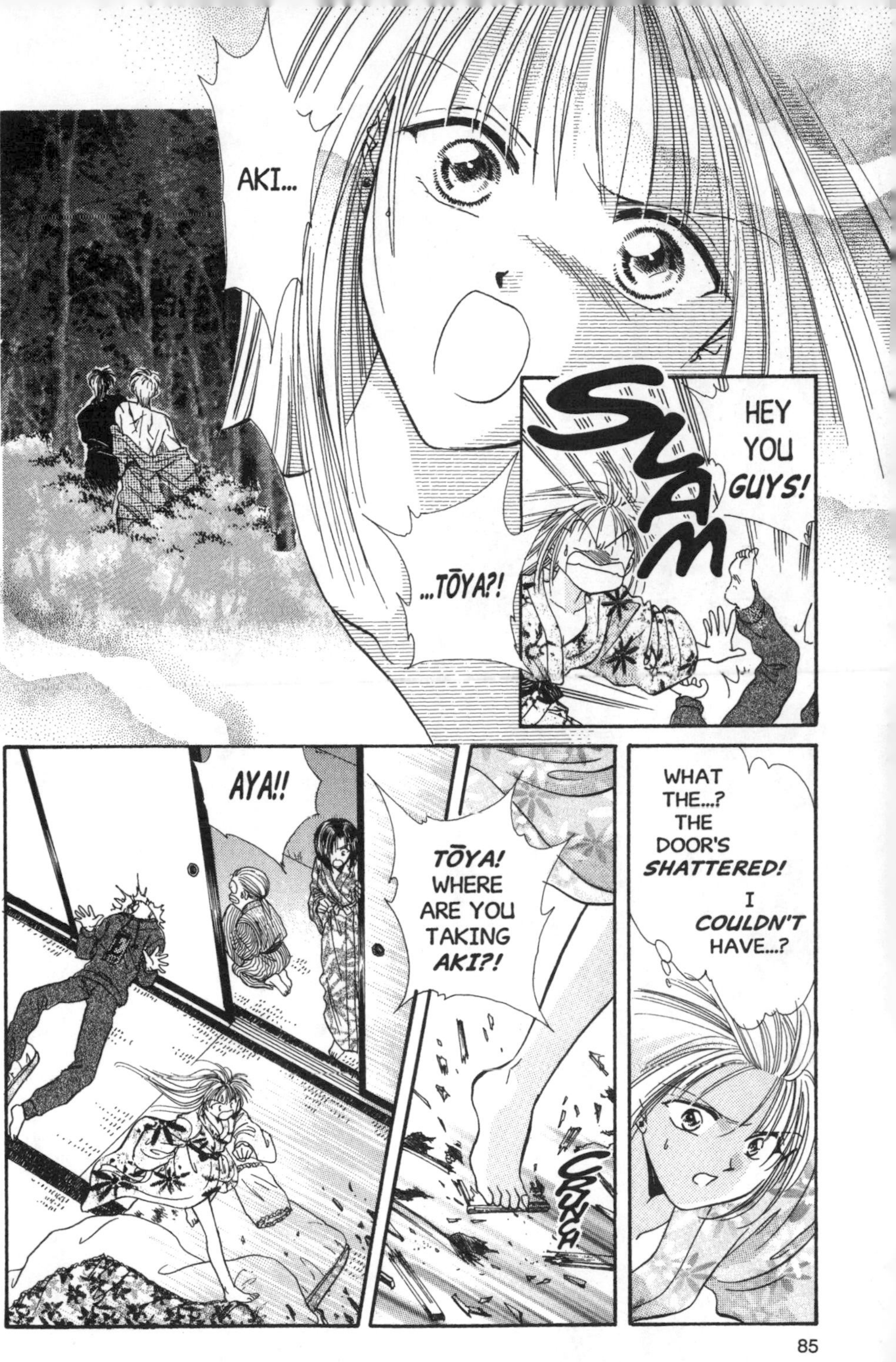
AKI...
...TŌYA?!
SLAM
HEY YOU GUYS!
WHAT THE...? THE DOOR'S SHATTERED!
I COULDN'T HAVE...?
TŌYA! WHERE ARE YOU TAKING AKI?!
CRUNCH
AYA!!

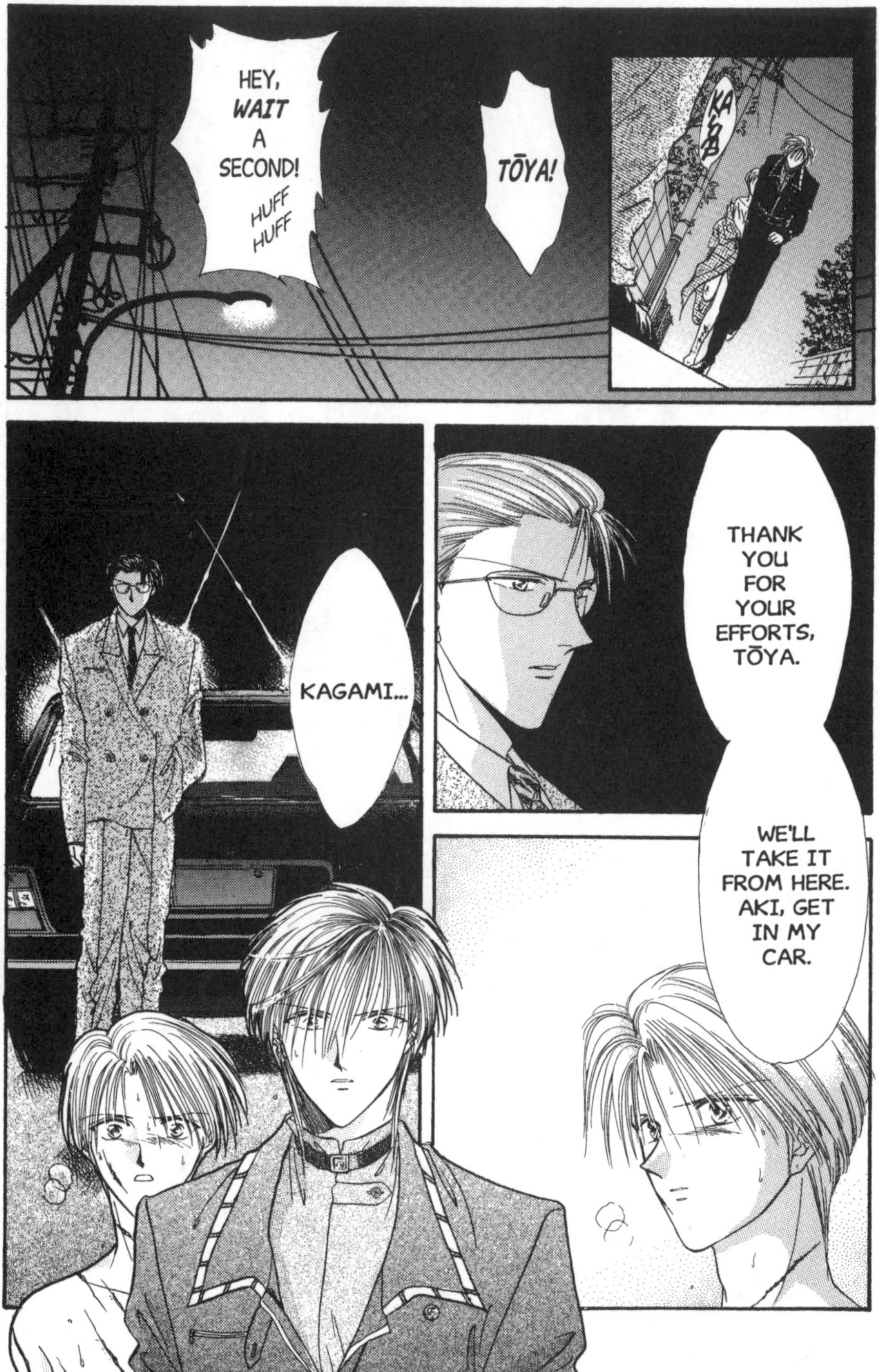
TŌYA!
HEY, WAIT A SECOND!
HUFF HUFF
THANK YOU FOR YOUR EFFORTS, TŌYA.
WE'LL TAKE IT FROM HERE. AKI, GET IN MY CAR.
KAGAMI...

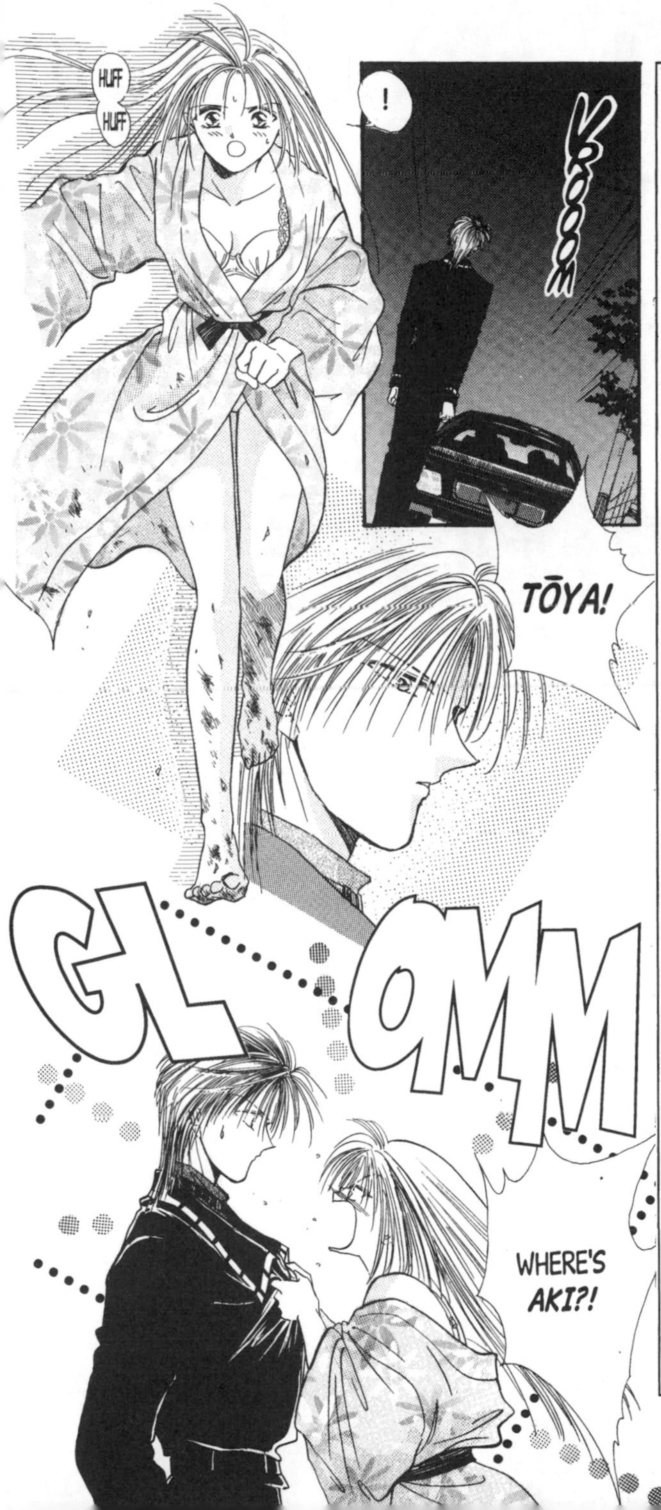
!
VROOOOM
HUFF
HUFF
TŌYA!
GLOMM
WHERE'S AKI?!

Oh, recently I got hooked to a certain food! ...And that's **"natto"** (a fermented soybean treat)!! My family disapproved of it on the general theory that "Kansai people (western Japan) don't eat much natto." I was the only one among them who winced at the smell, but that's now a distant memory...
I'm pretty fussy about my food, but I was listening to the people on TV extol natto's virtues--it's nutritious; it's good for the brain; and it fights bad bacteria--one good thing after another! I thought, "I gotta try this!" So I made it more palatable by using the mustard that comes with it, and adding perilla leaf (Japanese basil) dressing (adding vinegar is good too. Oh! and red pepper! and scallions!)
It's sooo good!
I got so hooked that I get depressed if I don't eat it every morning. I could eat it three times a day! Nowadays I can eat it without the mustard or anything! I never thought such a delicacy existed... (Okay, I'm exaggerating.)
I guess as you get older, your tastes, including the foods you like, change. I don't like fried and greasy foods anymore, for example.
Aside from food, other things like the way I think are changing a lot these days. I get irritable recently, and there's all this defiance welling up inside me. Then one of my acquaintances said, "That means you're trying to break out of your previous shell," "Your ego is growing," and so forth. "It's like that when teenagers become delinquent." ...What?! Does that mean that I'm going to be a delinquent at **my** age?! ...But I hear that it happens even to people in their 30's.

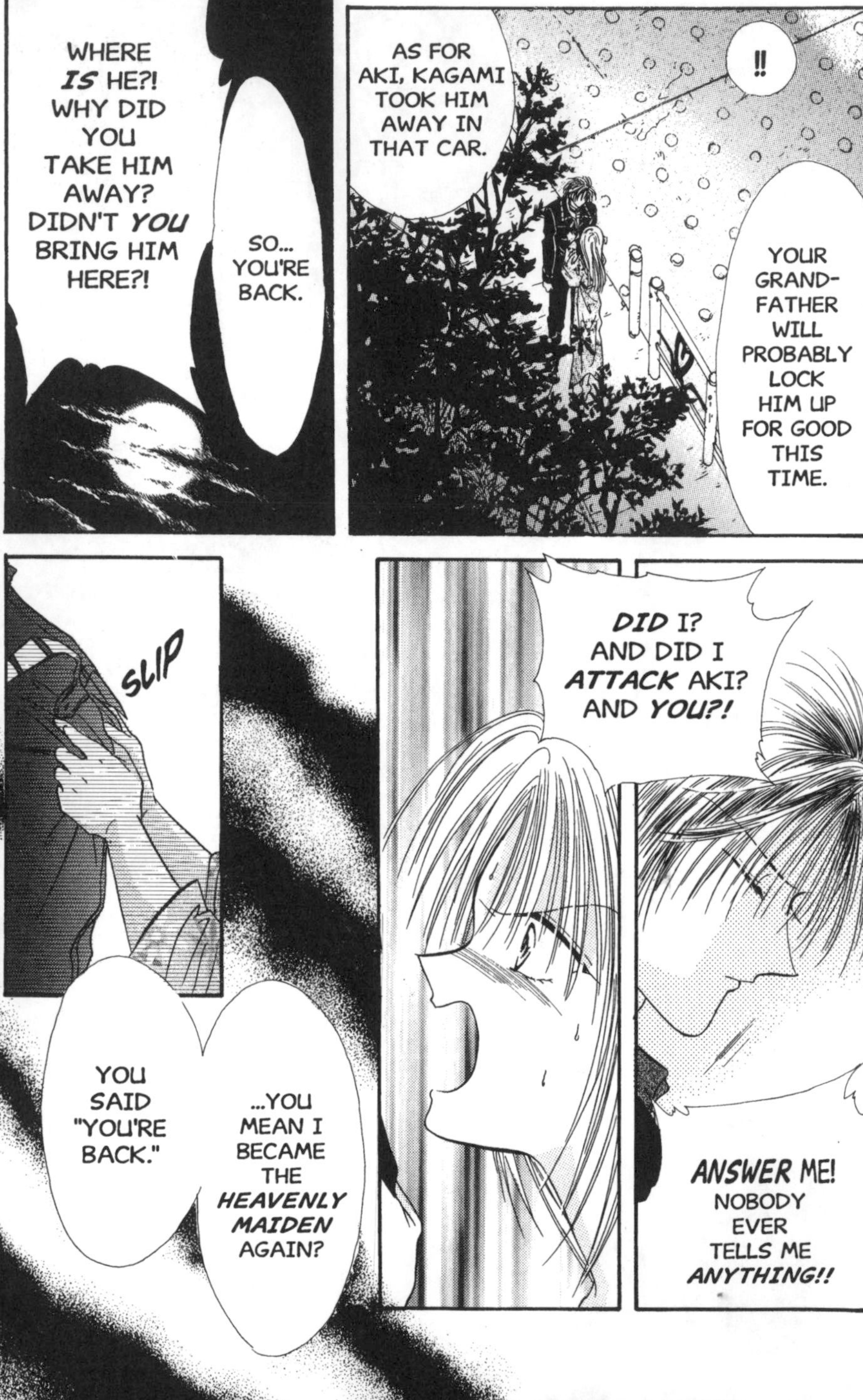
!!
AS FOR AKI, KAGAMI TOOK HIM AWAY IN THAT CAR.
YOUR GRANDFATHER WILL PROBABLY LOCK HIM UP FOR GOOD THIS TIME.
WHERE *IS* HE?! WHY DID YOU TAKE HIM AWAY? DIDN'T *YOU* BRING HIM HERE?!
SO... YOU'RE BACK.
DID I? AND DID I *ATTACK* AKI? AND *YOU?!*
ANSWER ME! NOBODY EVER TELLS ME *ANYTHING!!*
SLIP
YOU SAID "YOU'RE BACK."
...YOU MEAN I BECAME THE *HEAVENLY MAIDEN* AGAIN?

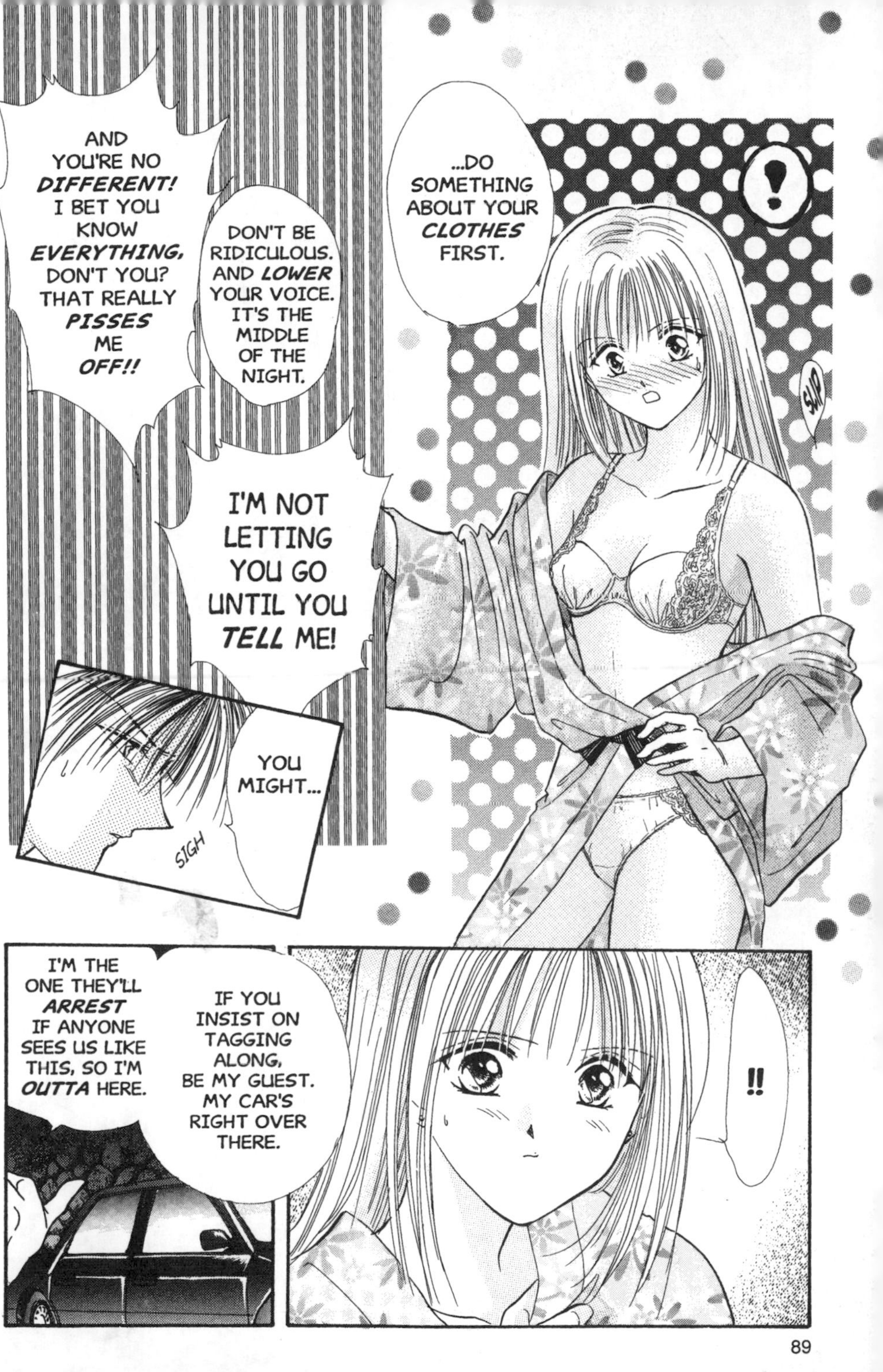
AND YOU'RE NO *DIFFERENT!* I BET YOU KNOW *EVERYTHING,* DON'T YOU? THAT REALLY *PISSES* ME *OFF!!*
DON'T BE RIDICULOUS. AND *LOWER* YOUR VOICE. IT'S THE MIDDLE OF THE NIGHT.
I'M NOT LETTING YOU GO UNTIL YOU *TELL* ME!
YOU MIGHT...
SIGH
...DO SOMETHING ABOUT YOUR *CLOTHES* FIRST.
!
SLIP
I'M THE ONE THEY'LL *ARREST* IF ANYONE SEES US LIKE THIS, SO I'M *OUTTA* HERE.
IF YOU INSIST ON TAGGING ALONG, BE MY GUEST. MY CAR'S RIGHT OVER THERE.
!!

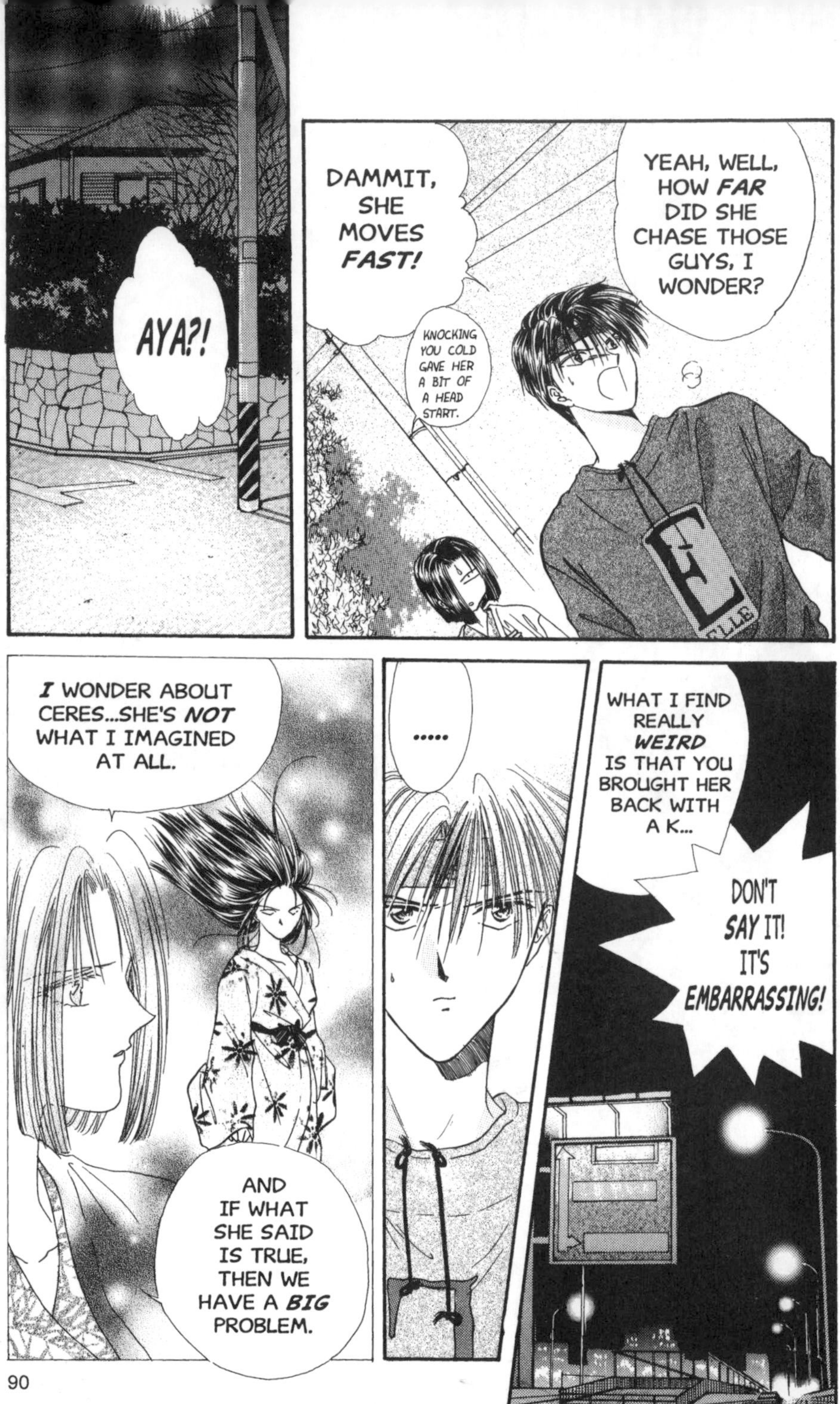
YEAH, WELL, HOW FAR DID SHE CHASE THOSE GUYS, I WONDER?
DAMMIT, SHE MOVES FAST!
KNOCKING YOU COLD GAVE HER A BIT OF A HEAD START.
AYA?!
WHAT I FIND REALLY WEIRD IS THAT YOU BROUGHT HER BACK WITH A K...
DON'T SAY IT! IT'S EMBARRASSING!
......
I WONDER ABOUT CERES...SHE'S NOT WHAT I IMAGINED AT ALL.
AND IF WHAT SHE SAID IS TRUE, THEN WE HAVE A BIG PROBLEM.

HEY! *WHERE* ARE WE GOING? BET YOU DON'T EVEN HAVE A DRIVER'S LICENSE.

MY CONDO.

OH.

SAY WHAT?!

I'M GOING HOME. THE WORKDAY IS LONG OVER.

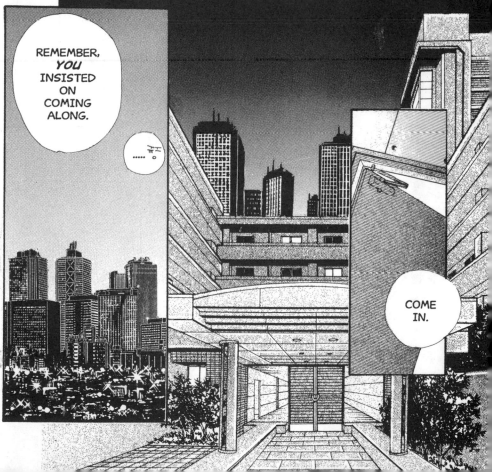

REMEMBER, *YOU* INSISTED ON COMING ALONG.

.....

COME IN.

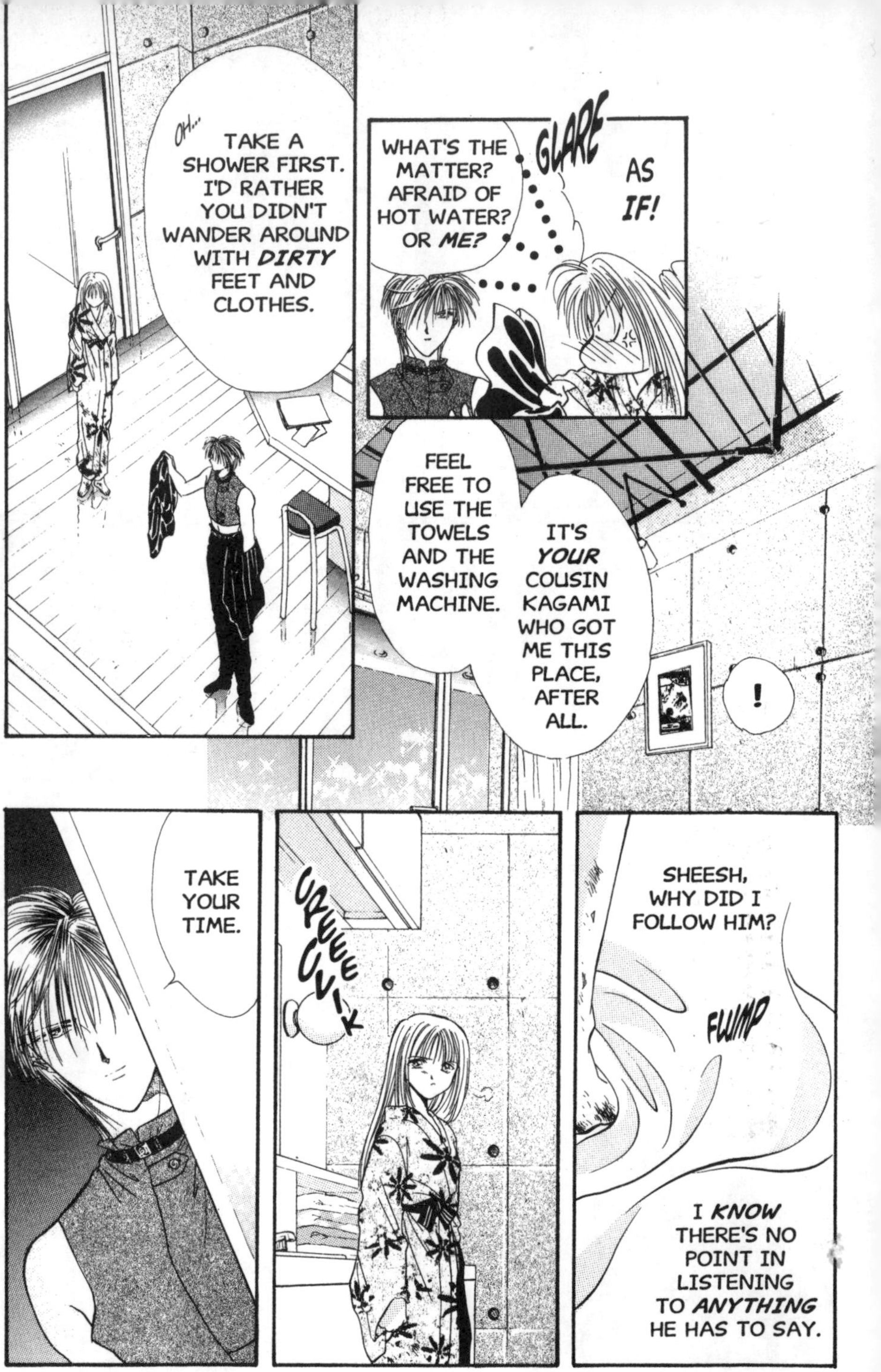
OH...
TAKE A SHOWER FIRST. I'D RATHER YOU DIDN'T WANDER AROUND WITH *DIRTY* FEET AND CLOTHES.
WHAT'S THE MATTER? AFRAID OF HOT WATER? OR *ME?*
GLARE
AS *IF!*
FEEL FREE TO USE THE TOWELS AND THE WASHING MACHINE.
IT'S *YOUR* COUSIN KAGAMI WHO GOT ME THIS PLACE, AFTER ALL.
!
TAKE YOUR TIME.
CREEEE CVIK
SHEESH, WHY DID I FOLLOW HIM?
FLUMP
I *KNOW* THERE'S NO POINT IN LISTENING TO *ANYTHING* HE HAS TO SAY.

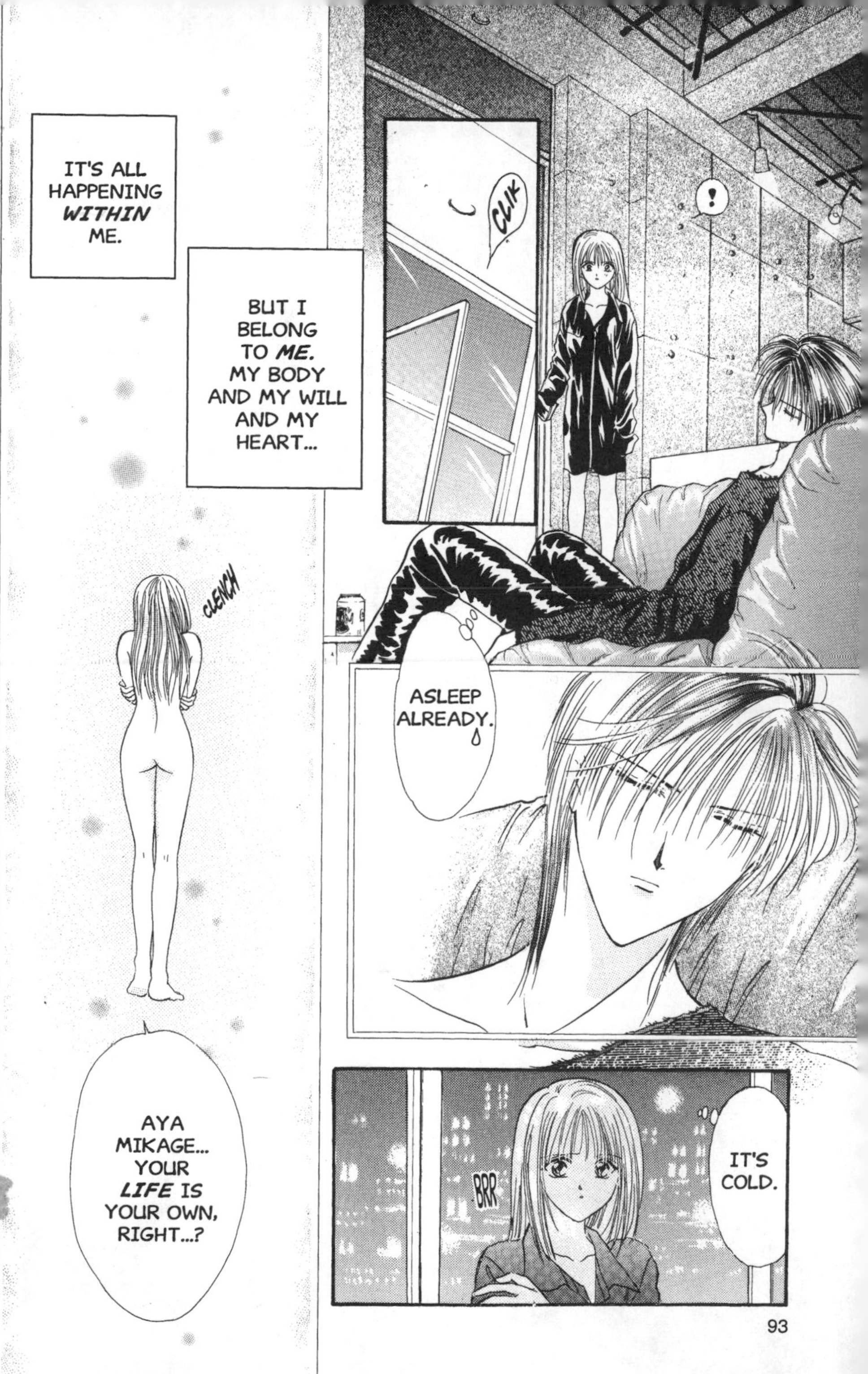
CLIK
!
ASLEEP ALREADY.
IT'S COLD.
BRR
IT'S ALL HAPPENING WITHIN ME.
BUT I BELONG TO ME. MY BODY AND MY WILL AND MY HEART...
CLENCH
AYA MIKAGE... YOUR LIFE IS YOUR OWN, RIGHT...?

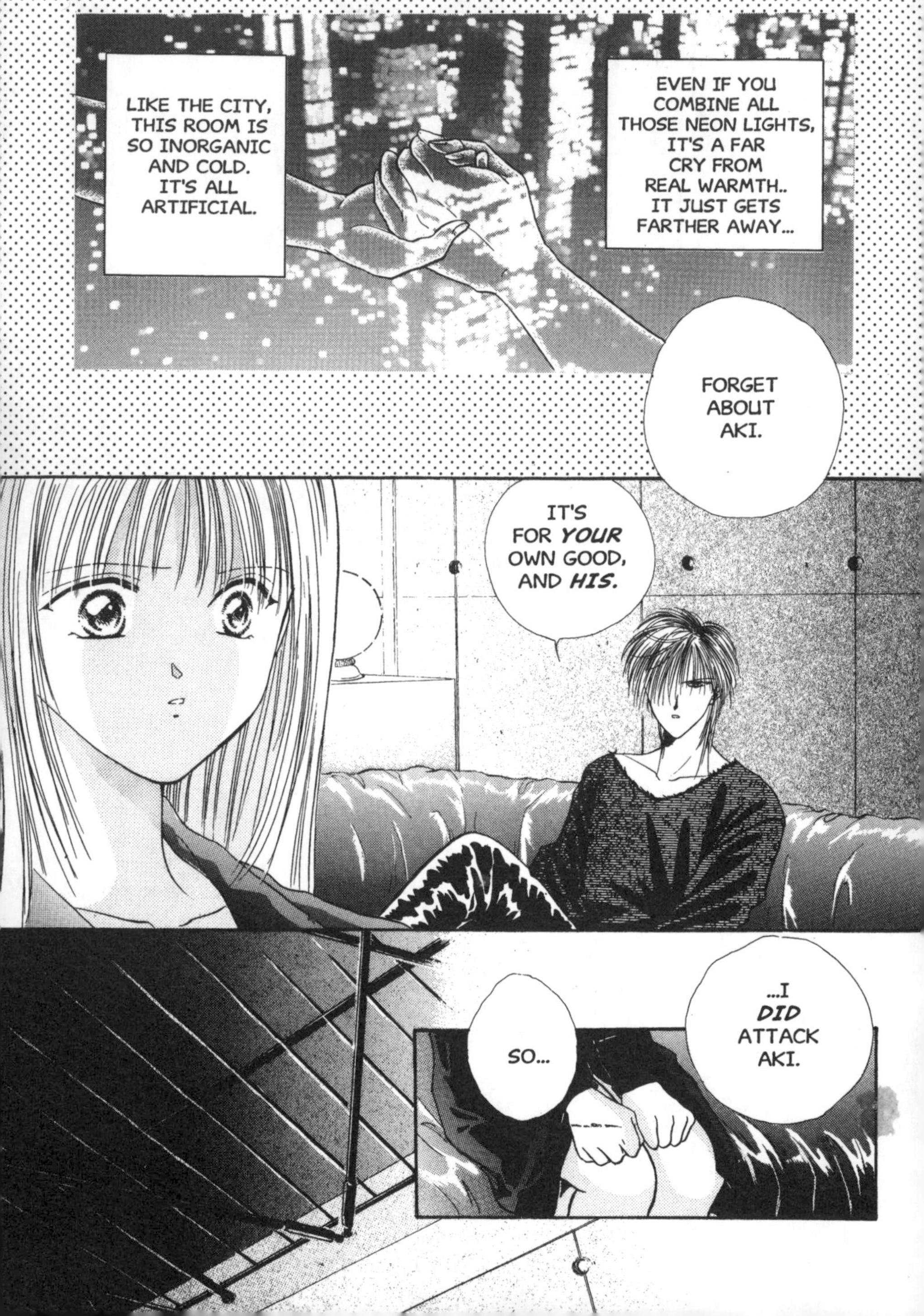
LIKE THE CITY, THIS ROOM IS SO INORGANIC AND COLD. IT'S ALL ARTIFICIAL.
EVEN IF YOU COMBINE ALL THOSE NEON LIGHTS, IT'S A FAR CRY FROM REAL WARMTH.. IT JUST GETS FARTHER AWAY...
FORGET ABOUT AKI.
IT'S FOR *YOUR* OWN GOOD, AND *HIS.*
SO...
...I *DID* ATTACK AKI.

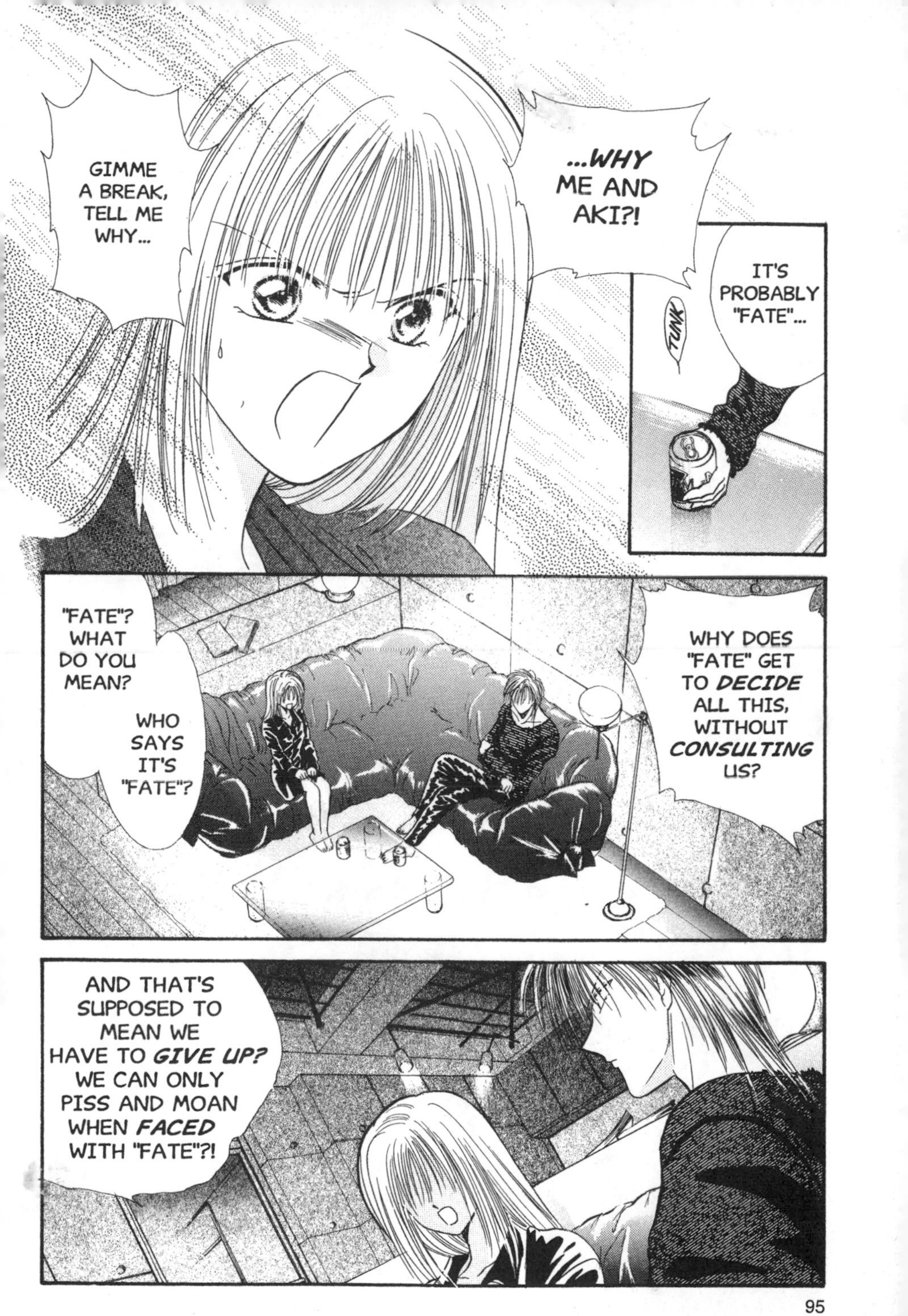
GIMME A BREAK, TELL ME WHY...
...WHY ME AND AKI?!
TUNK
IT'S PROBABLY "FATE"...
"FATE"? WHAT DO YOU MEAN?
WHO SAYS IT'S "FATE"?
WHY DOES "FATE" GET TO DECIDE ALL THIS, WITHOUT CONSULTING US?
AND THAT'S SUPPOSED TO MEAN WE HAVE TO GIVE UP? WE CAN ONLY PISS AND MOAN WHEN FACED WITH "FATE"?!

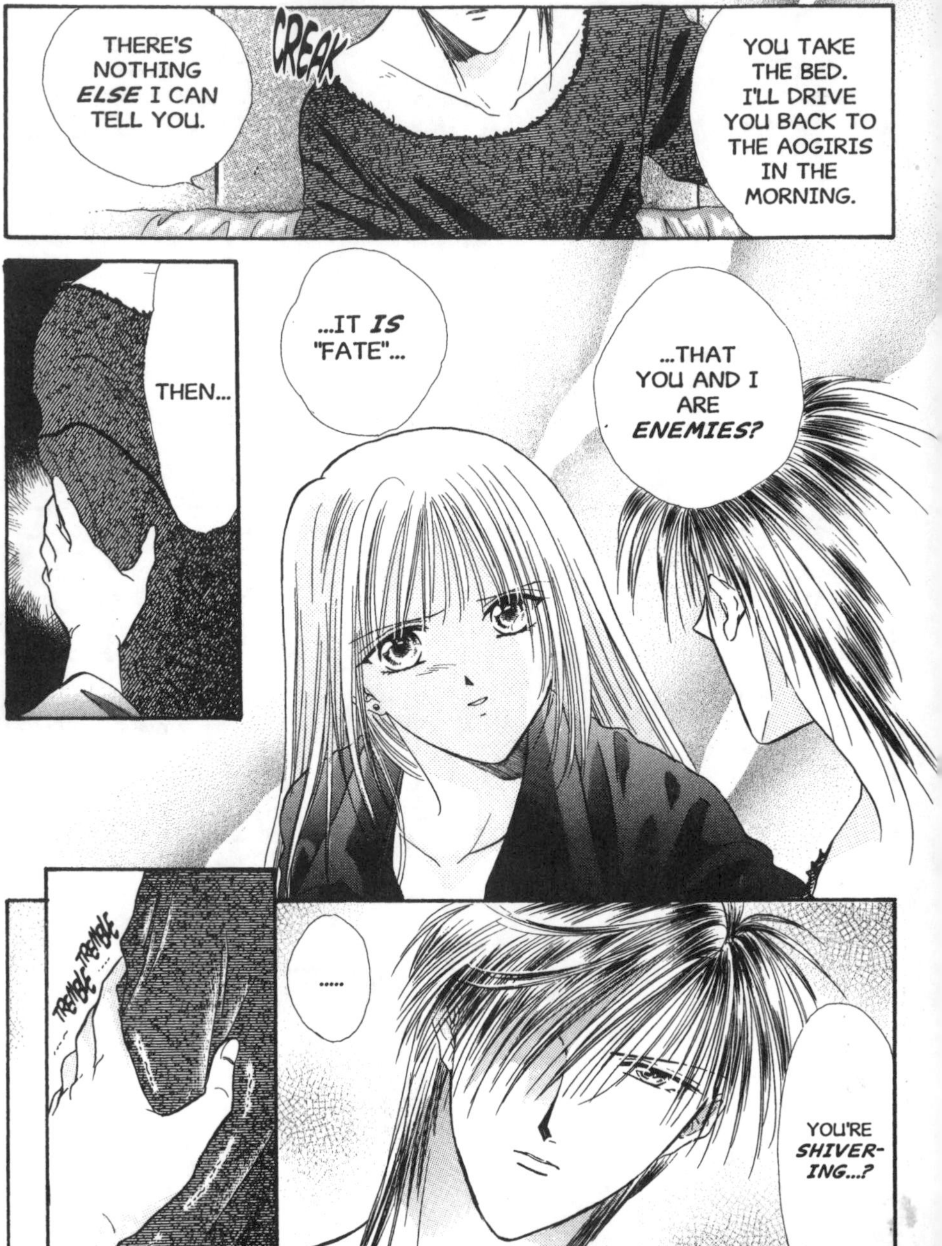
THERE'S NOTHING *ELSE* I CAN TELL YOU.
CREAK
YOU TAKE THE BED. I'LL DRIVE YOU BACK TO THE AOGIRIS IN THE MORNING.
THEN...
...IT *IS* "FATE"...
...THAT YOU AND I ARE *ENEMIES?*
TREMBLE TREMBLE
.....
YOU'RE *SHIVER-ING...?*

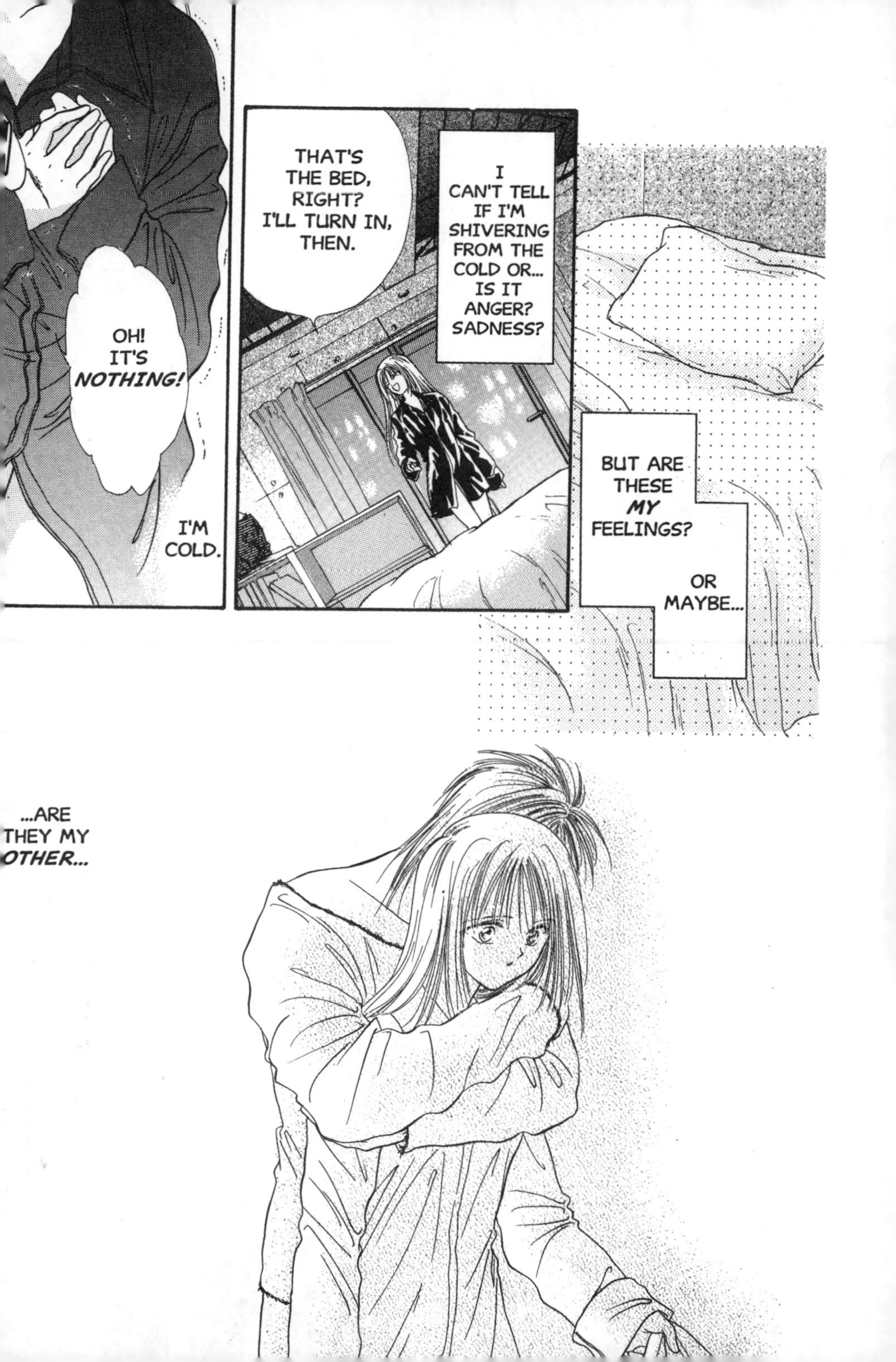
BUT ARE THESE *MY* FEELINGS?
OR MAYBE...
I CAN'T TELL IF I'M SHIVERING FROM THE COLD OR... IS IT ANGER? SADNESS?
THAT'S THE BED, RIGHT? I'LL TURN IN, THEN.
OH! IT'S *NOTHING!*
I'M COLD.
...ARE THEY MY *OTHER...*

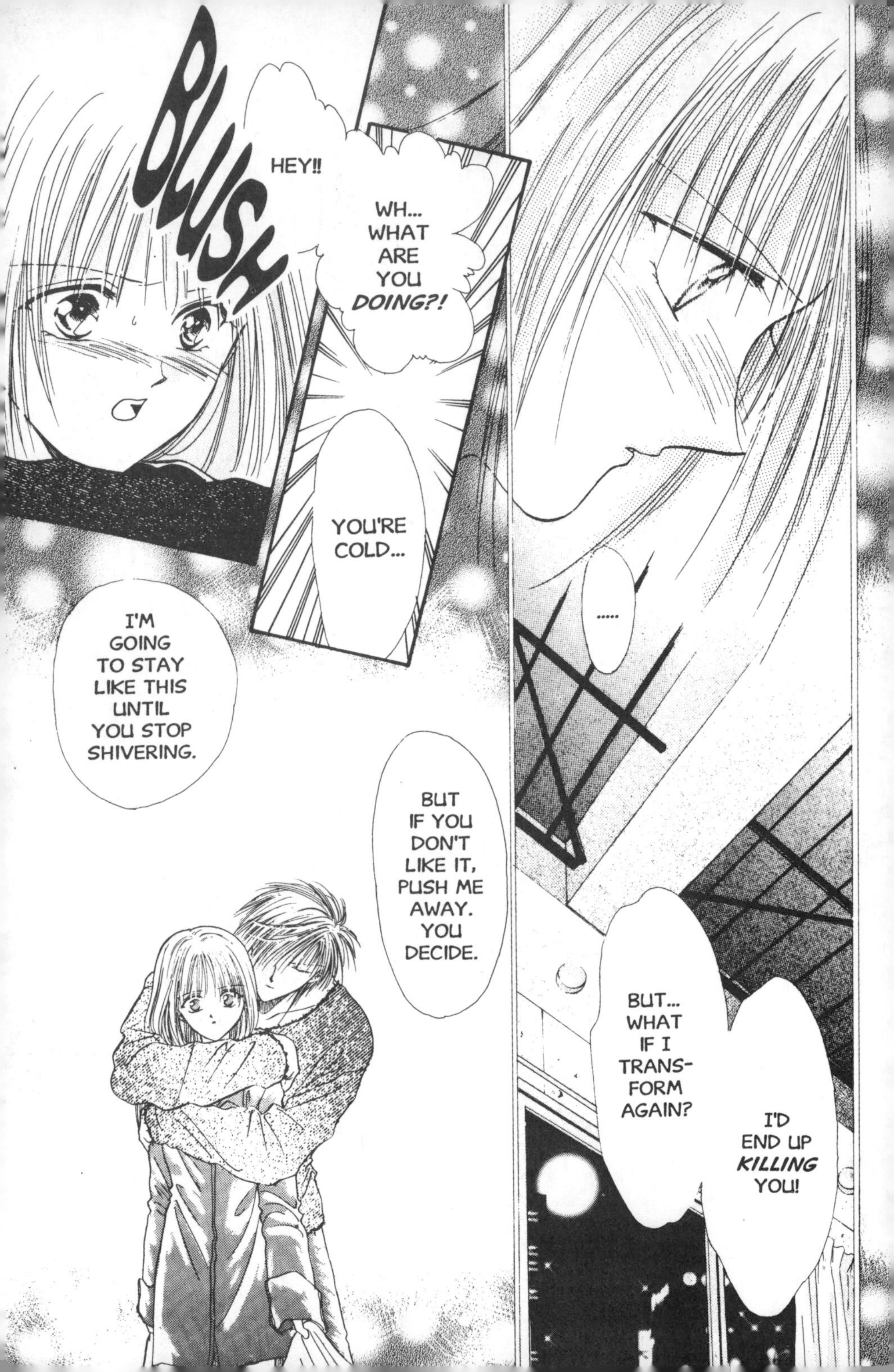
BLUSH
HEY!!
WH... WHAT ARE YOU DOING?!
YOU'RE COLD...
I'M GOING TO STAY LIKE THIS UNTIL YOU STOP SHIVERING.
BUT IF YOU DON'T LIKE IT, PUSH ME AWAY. YOU DECIDE.
.....
BUT... WHAT IF I TRANSFORM AGAIN?
I'D END UP KILLING YOU!

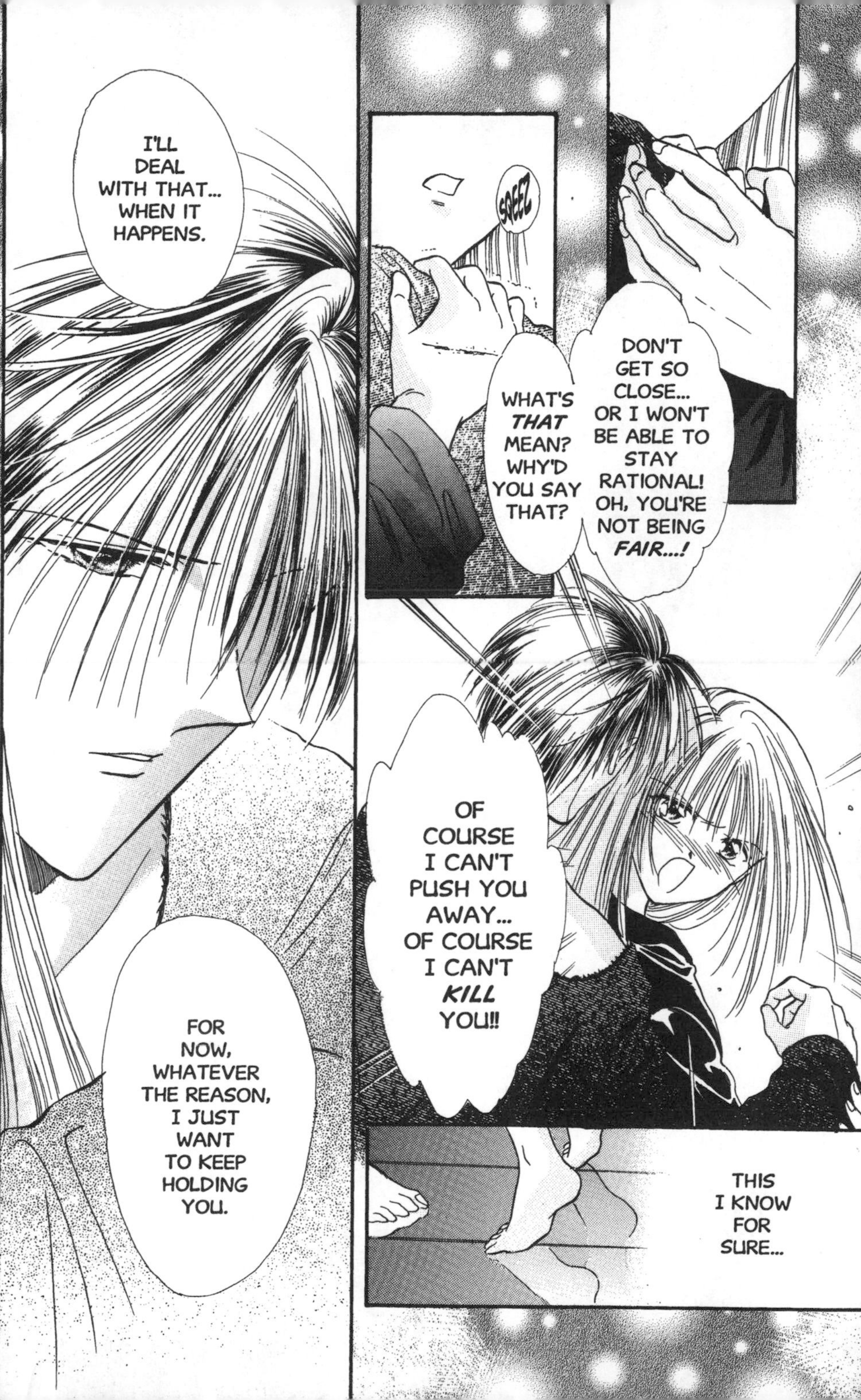
DON'T GET SO CLOSE... OR I WON'T BE ABLE TO STAY RATIONAL! OH, YOU'RE NOT BEING *FAIR...!*
SQEEZ
WHAT'S *THAT* MEAN? WHY'D YOU SAY THAT?
OF COURSE I CAN'T PUSH YOU AWAY... OF COURSE I CAN'T ***KILL*** YOU!!
THIS I KNOW FOR SURE...
I'LL DEAL WITH THAT... WHEN IT HAPPENS.
FOR NOW, WHATEVER THE REASON, I JUST WANT TO KEEP HOLDING YOU.

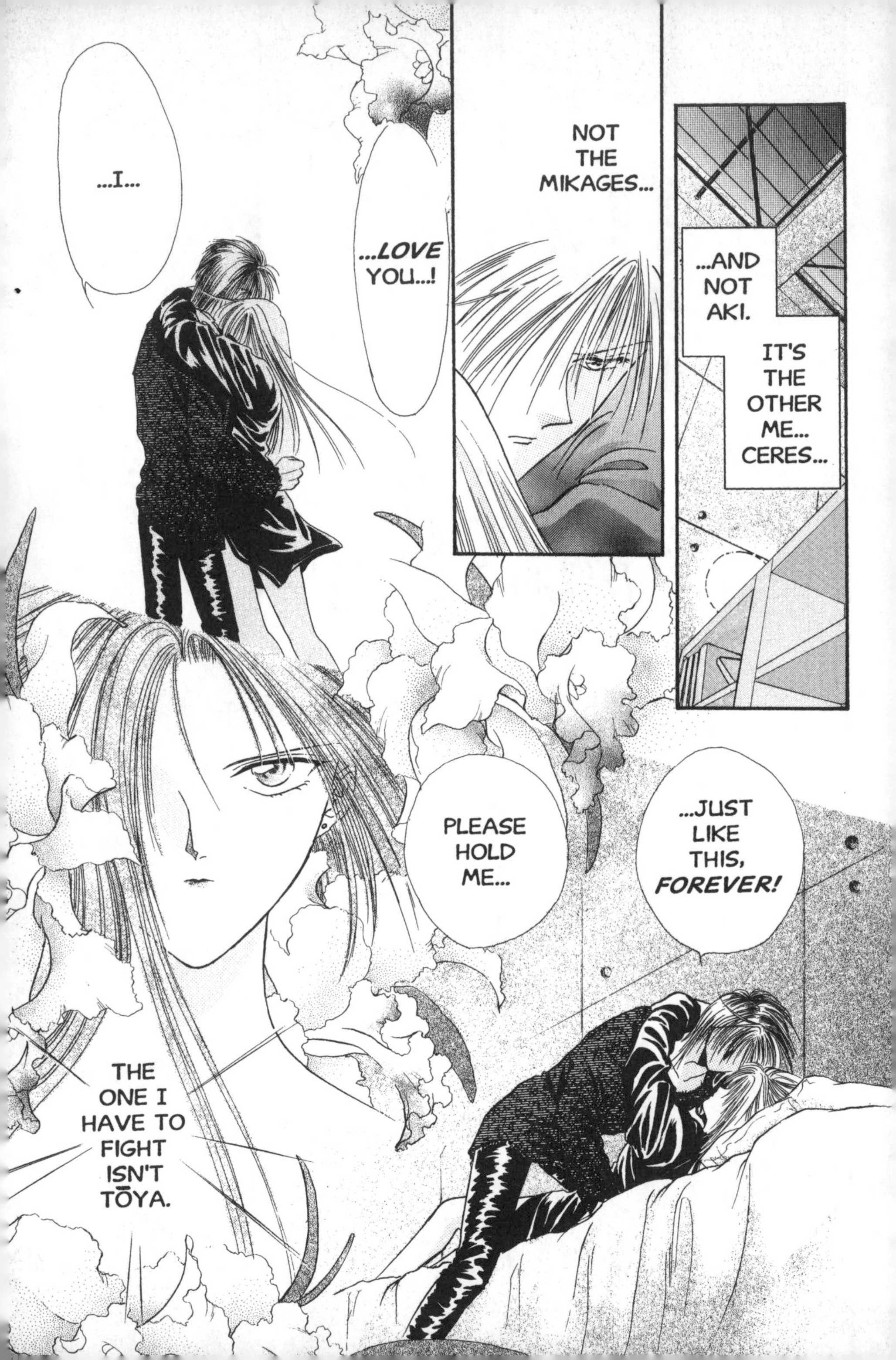
...I...
...LOVE YOU...!
PLEASE HOLD ME...
...JUST LIKE THIS, FOREVER!
THE ONE I HAVE TO FIGHT ISN'T TŌYA.
NOT THE MIKAGES...
...AND NOT AKI.
IT'S THE OTHER ME... CERES...

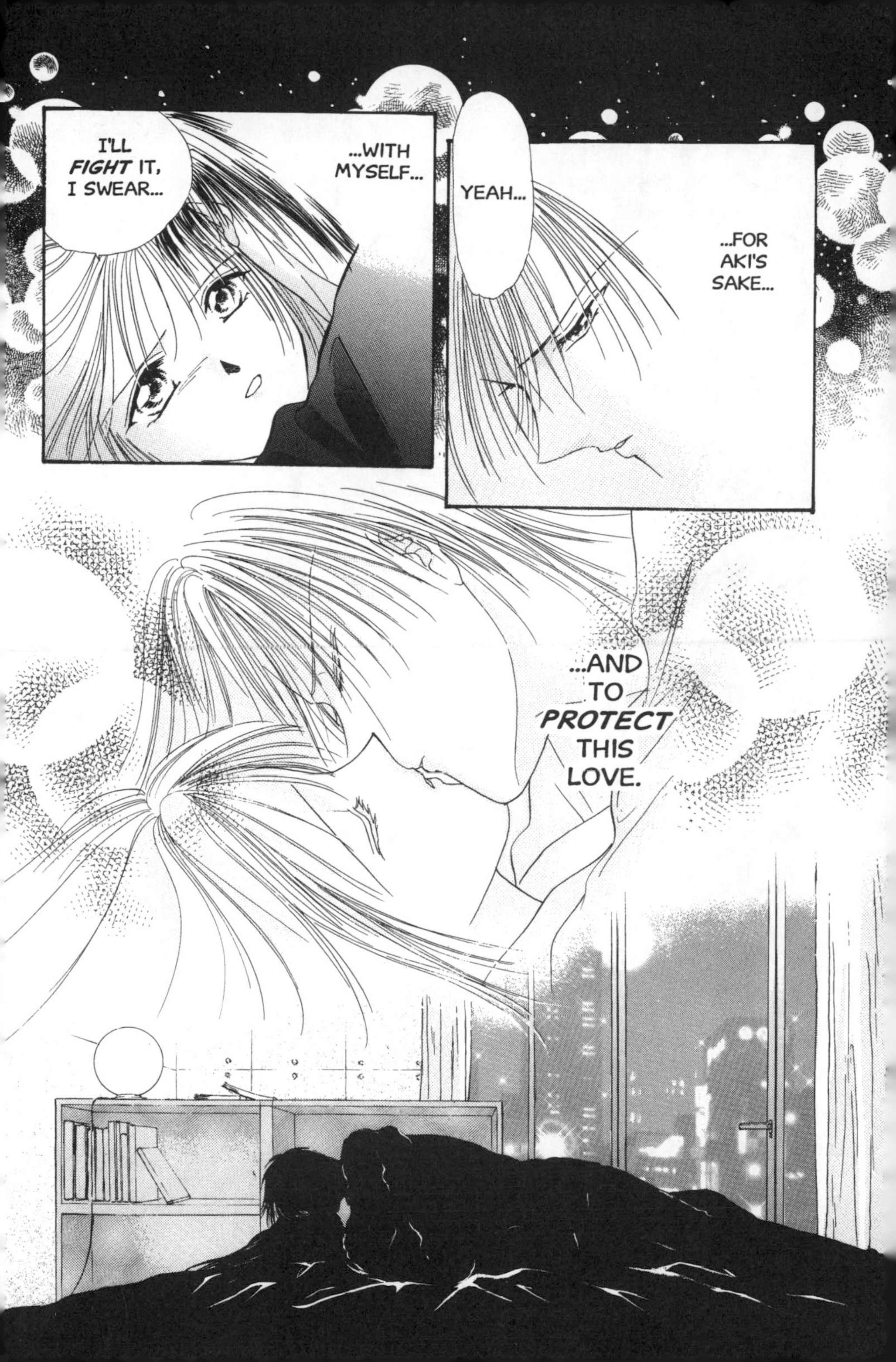
I'LL *FIGHT* IT, I SWEAR...
...WITH MYSELF...
YEAH...
...FOR AKI'S SAKE...
...AND TO *PROTECT* THIS LOVE.

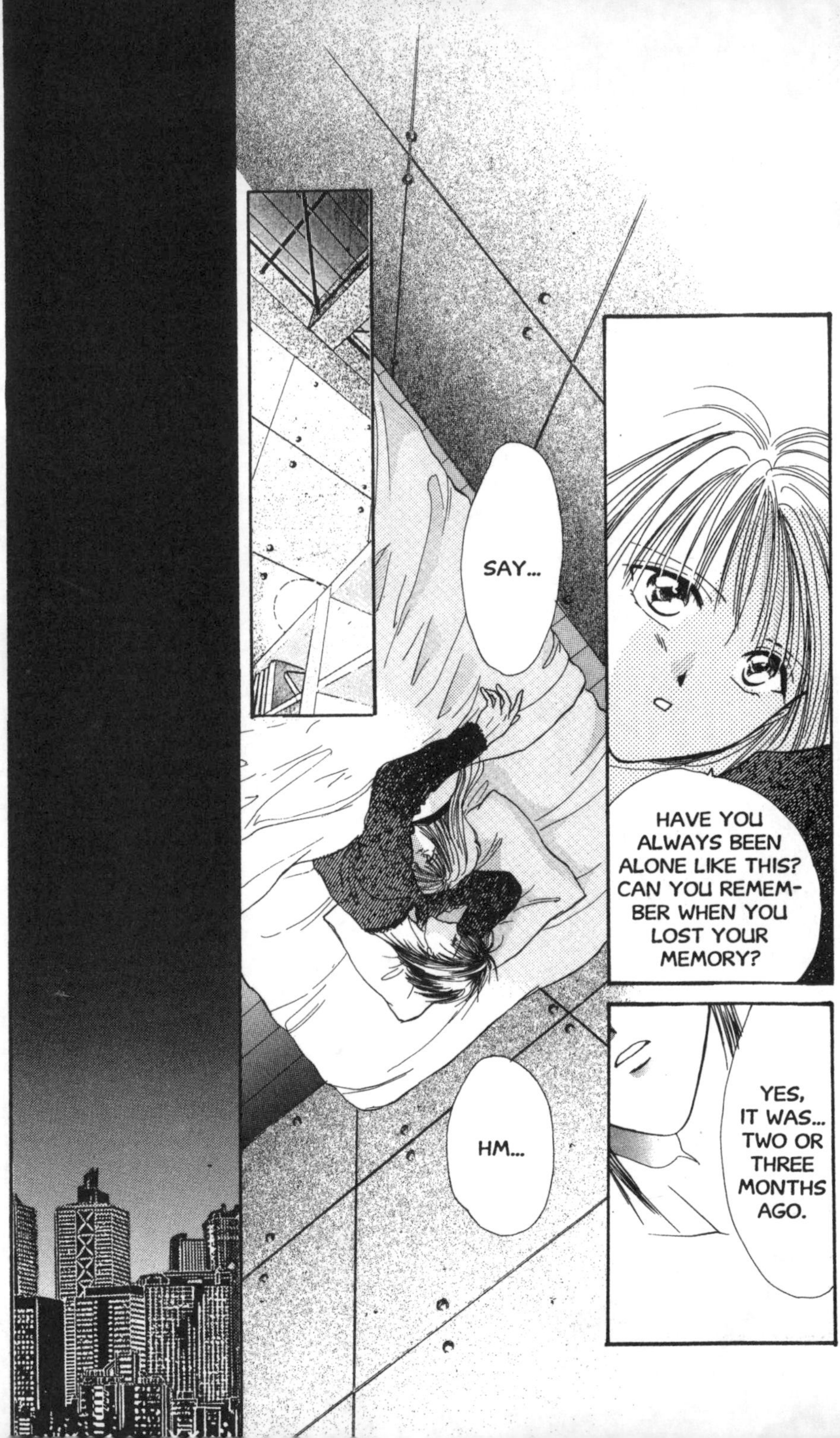
SAY...
HAVE YOU ALWAYS BEEN ALONE LIKE THIS? CAN YOU REMEMBER WHEN YOU LOST YOUR MEMORY?
HM...
YES, IT WAS... TWO OR THREE MONTHS AGO.

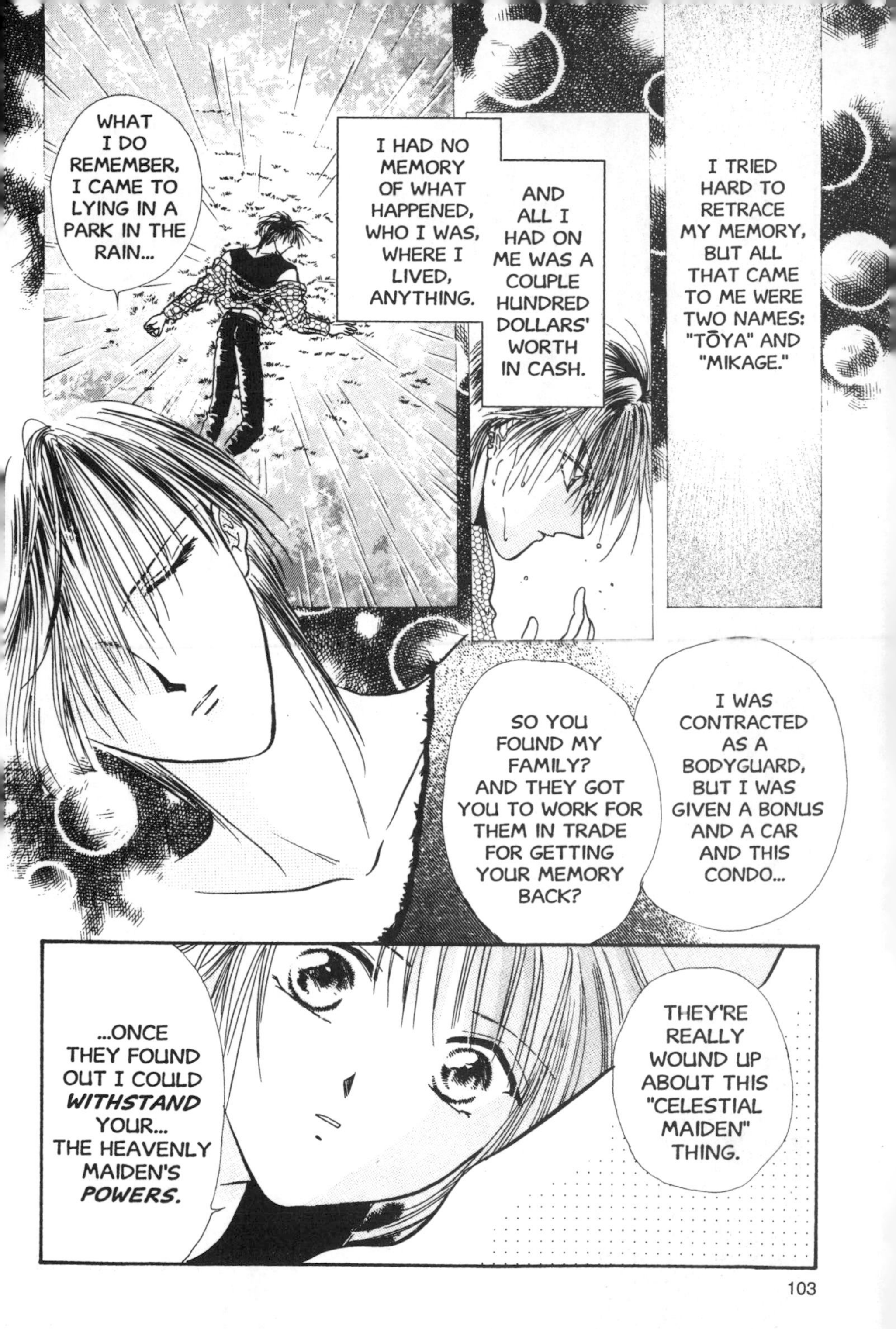
WHAT I DO REMEMBER, I CAME TO LYING IN A PARK IN THE RAIN...
I HAD NO MEMORY OF WHAT HAPPENED, WHO I WAS, WHERE I LIVED, ANYTHING.
AND ALL I HAD ON ME WAS A COUPLE HUNDRED DOLLARS' WORTH IN CASH.
I TRIED HARD TO RETRACE MY MEMORY, BUT ALL THAT CAME TO ME WERE TWO NAMES: "TŌYA" AND "MIKAGE."
SO YOU FOUND MY FAMILY? AND THEY GOT YOU TO WORK FOR THEM IN TRADE FOR GETTING YOUR MEMORY BACK?
I WAS CONTRACTED AS A BODYGUARD, BUT I WAS GIVEN A BONUS AND A CAR AND THIS CONDO...
...ONCE THEY FOUND OUT I COULD ***WITHSTAND*** YOUR... THE HEAVENLY MAIDEN'S ***POWERS.***
THEY'RE REALLY WOUND UP ABOUT THIS "CELESTIAL MAIDEN" THING.

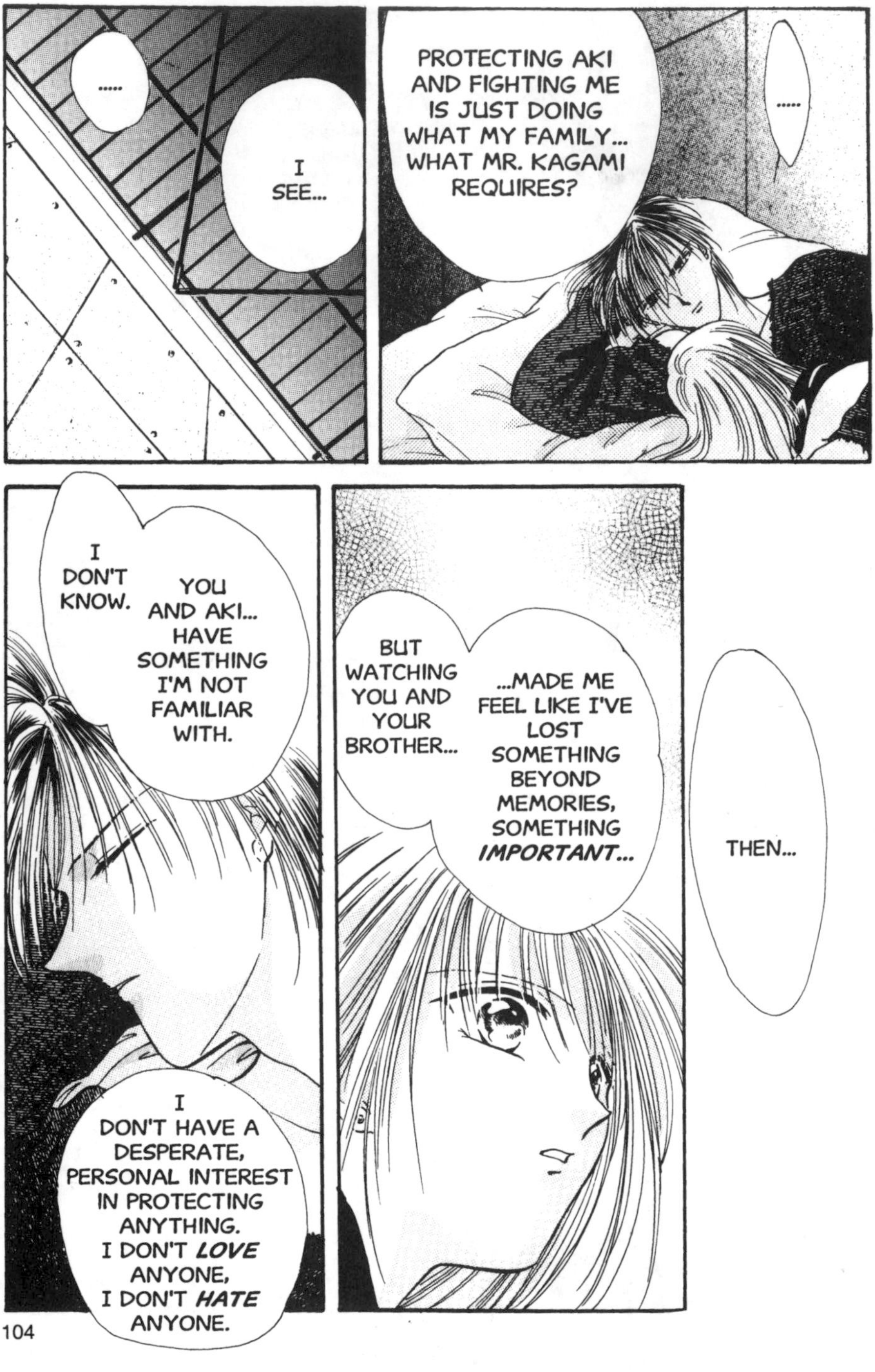
PROTECTING AKI AND FIGHTING ME IS JUST DOING WHAT MY FAMILY... WHAT MR. KAGAMI REQUIRES?
.....
.....
I SEE...
THEN...
BUT WATCHING YOU AND YOUR BROTHER...
...MADE ME FEEL LIKE I'VE LOST SOMETHING BEYOND MEMORIES, SOMETHING *IMPORTANT*...
I DON'T KNOW.
YOU AND AKI... HAVE SOMETHING I'M NOT FAMILIAR WITH.
I DON'T HAVE A DESPERATE, PERSONAL INTEREST IN PROTECTING ANYTHING. I DON'T *LOVE* ANYONE, I DON'T *HATE* ANYONE.

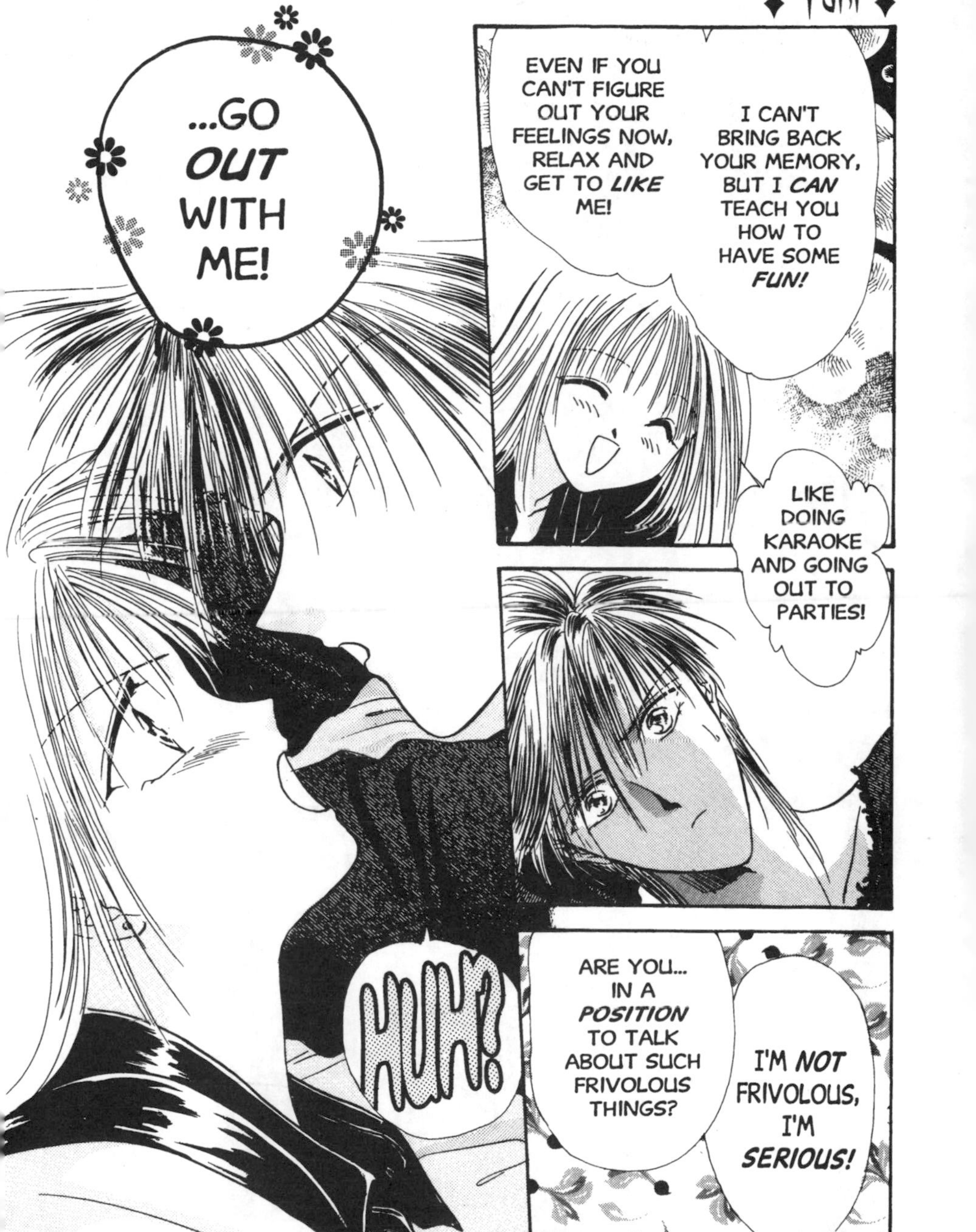
I CAN'T BRING BACK YOUR MEMORY, BUT I *CAN* TEACH YOU HOW TO HAVE SOME *FUN!*
EVEN IF YOU CAN'T FIGURE OUT YOUR FEELINGS NOW, RELAX AND GET TO *LIKE* ME!
LIKE DOING KARAOKE AND GOING OUT TO PARTIES!
...GO *OUT* WITH ME!
HUH?
ARE YOU... IN A *POSITION* TO TALK ABOUT SUCH FRIVOLOUS THINGS?
I'M *NOT* FRIVOLOUS, I'M *SERIOUS!*

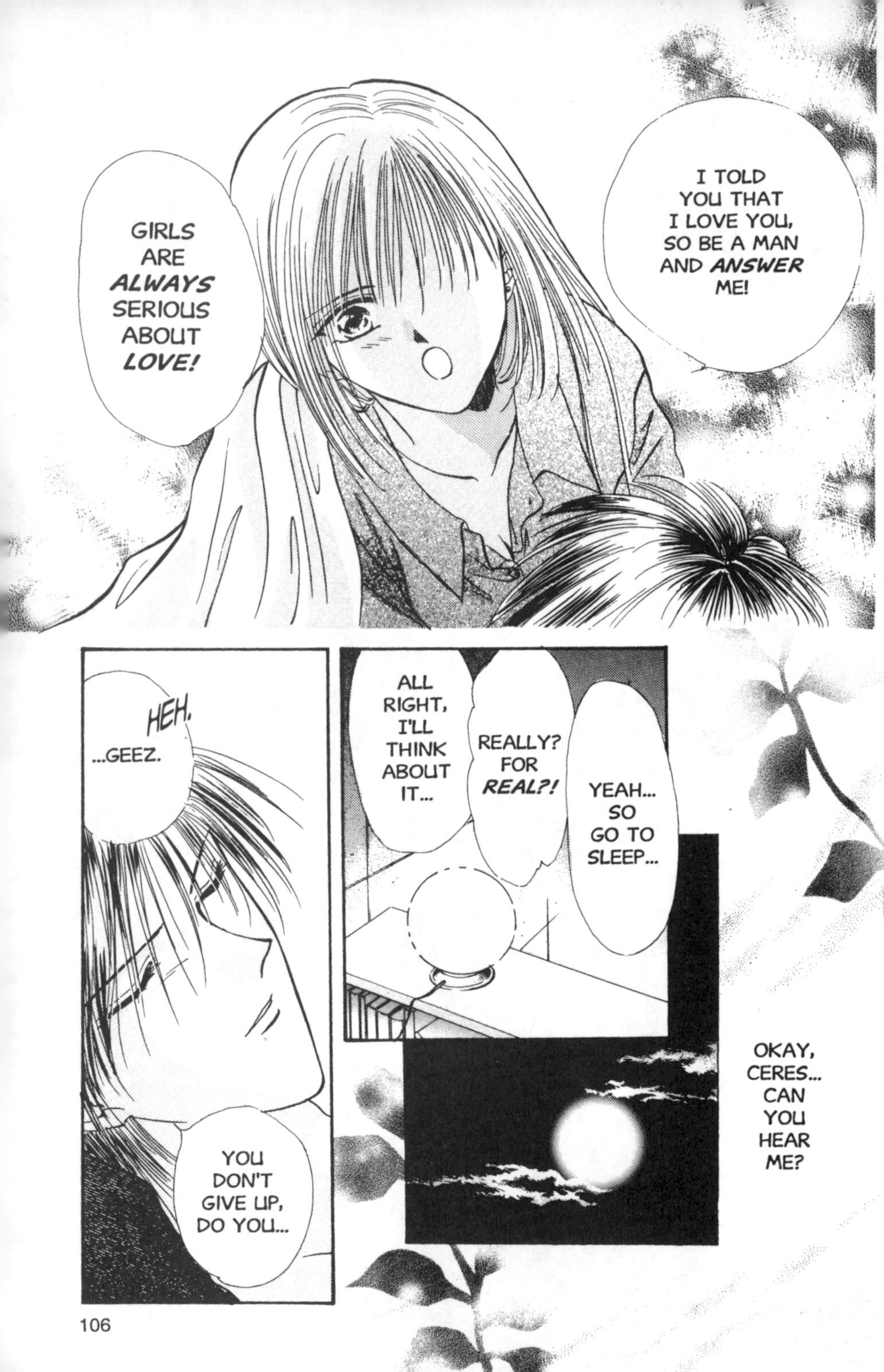
GIRLS ARE *ALWAYS* SERIOUS ABOUT *LOVE!*
I TOLD YOU THAT I LOVE YOU, SO BE A MAN AND *ANSWER* ME!
HEH.
...GEEZ.
YOU DON'T GIVE UP, DO YOU...
ALL RIGHT, I'LL THINK ABOUT IT...
REALLY? FOR *REAL?!*
YEAH... SO GO TO SLEEP...
OKAY, CERES... CAN YOU HEAR ME?

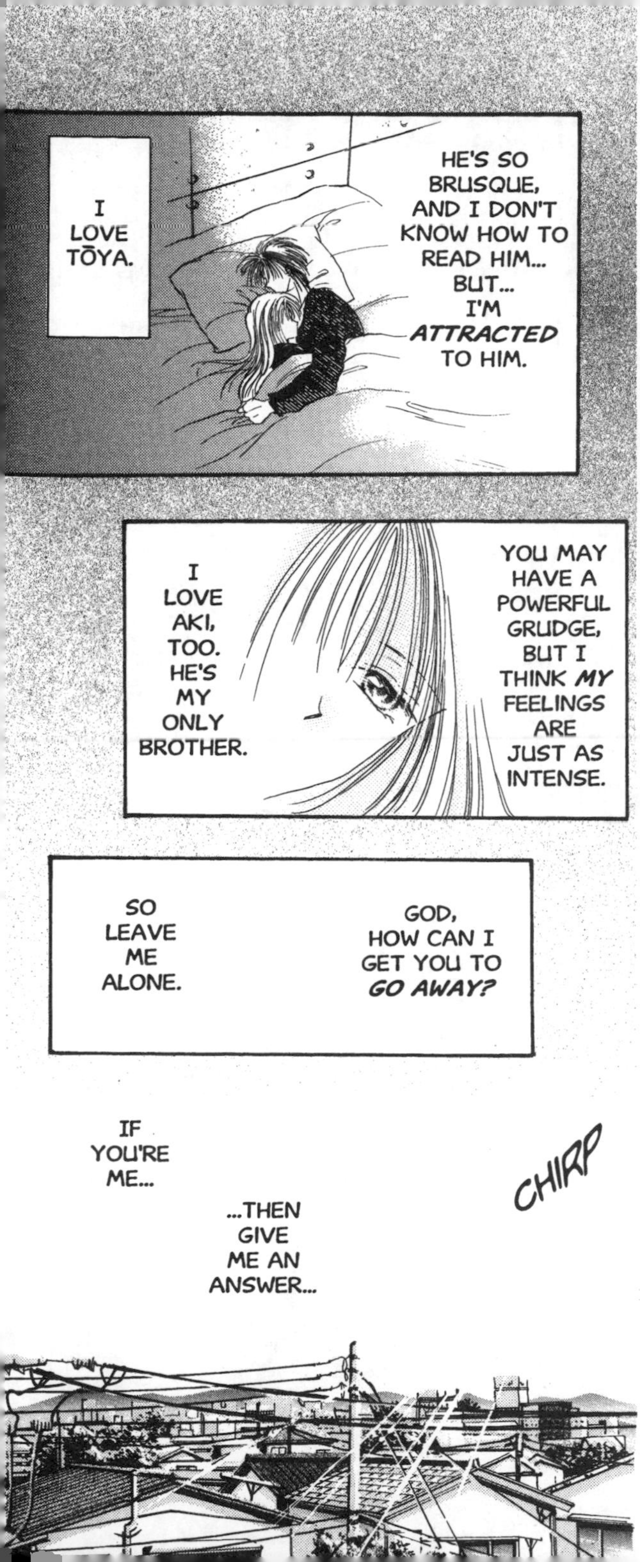
HE'S SO BRUSQUE, AND I DON'T KNOW HOW TO READ HIM... BUT... I'M *ATTRACTED* TO HIM.
I LOVE TŌYA.
YOU MAY HAVE A POWERFUL GRUDGE, BUT I THINK *MY* FEELINGS ARE JUST AS INTENSE.
I LOVE AKI, TOO. HE'S MY ONLY BROTHER.
GOD, HOW CAN I GET YOU TO *GO AWAY?*
SO LEAVE ME ALONE.
CHIRP
IF YOU'RE ME...
...THEN GIVE ME AN ANSWER...

...Yeah, these days I'm feeling kinda rebellious. I guess it happens even in your 20's. I feel it towards my work, too -- I feel like I just want to destroy everything I've made up to now. Before, it was all about love and hope. All candy-coated and sugary sweet, and looking at it now, it feels kinda, "Blech," or something. Well, my personality's pretty much the same as it's always been, but I honestly feel that way. Putting it in Ceres-related terms, it's probably because Ceres, a facet of the main character Aya, is someone from the dark side. She feels within her that, "Love and dreams and wimpy crap like that are only a fantasy" (though I'm sure she's not that vulgar). I think Aya's gotten the worst treatment I've ever doled out in any of my works. Her relatives are her enemies, and even the other self within her is an enemy of sorts! Once you step into the dark side of the world, you get really get caught up in it. The Aogiri family isn't so dark though... Tōya also has a bit of a rule-breaker side. I won't let Tōya have any lovey-dovey, cutesy, sugary-sweet love! He's more suited to straight-black coffee love... After all, he projects an image that suggests a guy who would look good covered in blood. I think I'll let him do that some time. SCARED? On the other hand, the straightforward, transparent type is Yūhi, so I'll be happy if he goes at it with a half-chipper, half-serious attitude. But I'm sure Tōya will be amazing when he actually does it.

...DOES WHAT?

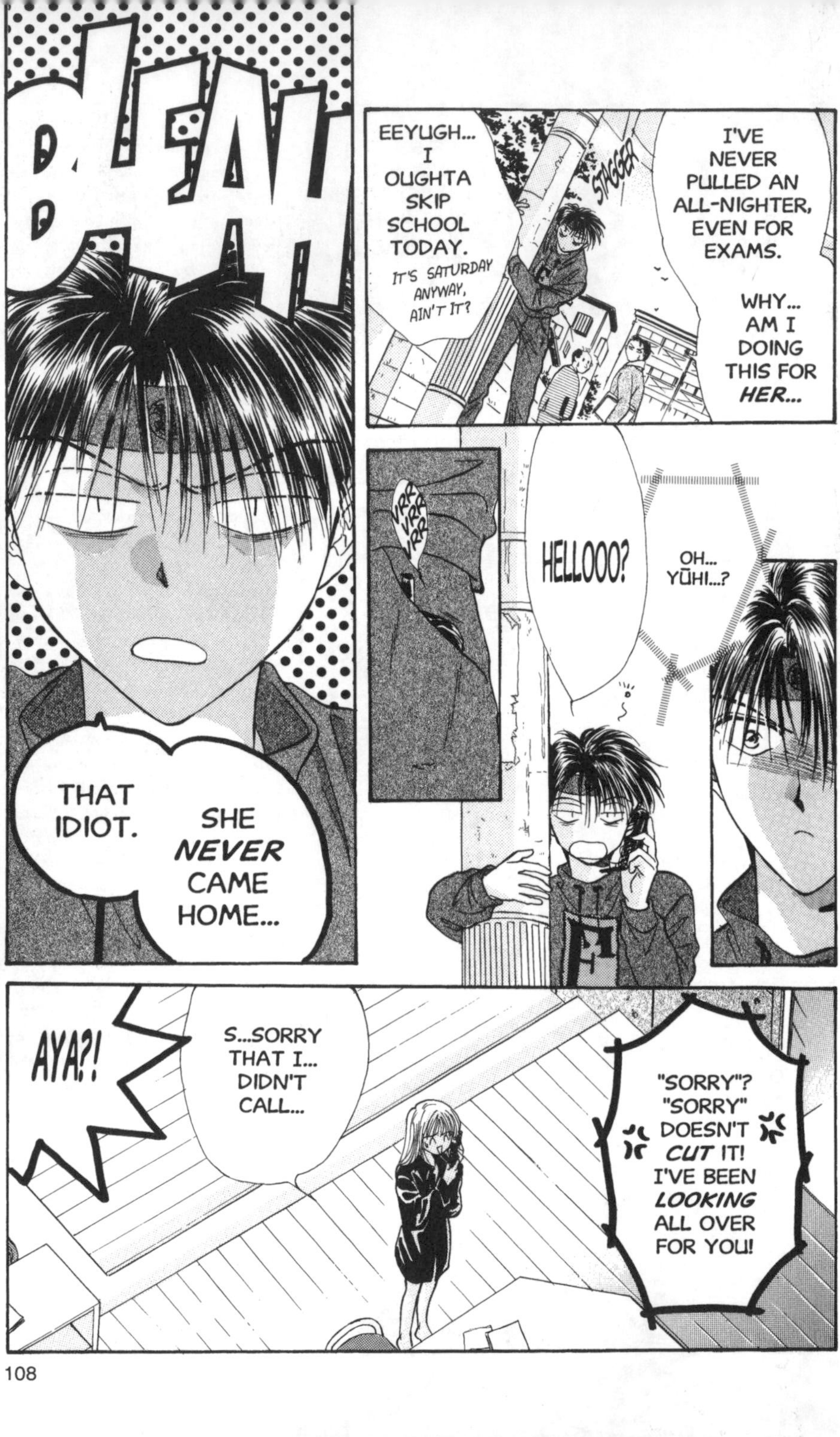
I'VE NEVER PULLED AN ALL-NIGHTER, EVEN FOR EXAMS.
WHY... AM I DOING THIS FOR HER...
STAGGER
EEYUGH... I OUGHTA SKIP SCHOOL TODAY.
IT'S SATURDAY ANYWAY, AIN'T IT?
VRR VRR VRR
HELLOOO?
OH... YŪHI...?
BLAH
THAT IDIOT.
SHE NEVER CAME HOME...
AYA?!
S...SORRY THAT I... DIDN'T CALL...
"SORRY"? "SORRY" DOESN'T CUT IT! I'VE BEEN LOOKING ALL OVER FOR YOU!

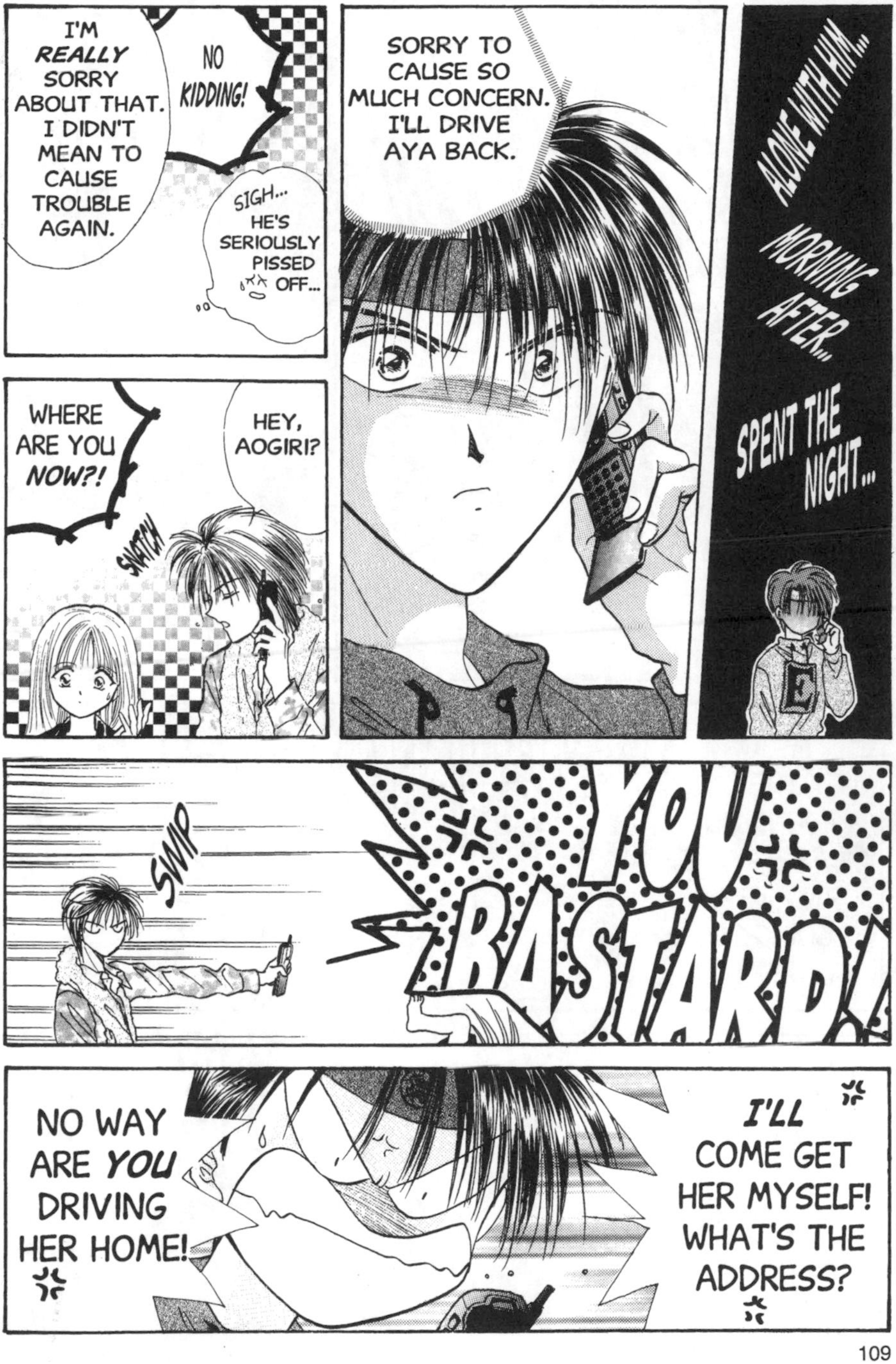
I'M REALLY SORRY ABOUT THAT. I DIDN'T MEAN TO CAUSE TROUBLE AGAIN.
NO KIDDING!
SIGH... HE'S SERIOUSLY PISSED OFF...
SNATCH
HEY, AOGIRI?
WHERE ARE YOU NOW?!
SORRY TO CAUSE SO MUCH CONCERN. I'LL DRIVE AYA BACK.
ALONE WITH HIM...
MORNING AFTER...
SPENT THE NIGHT...
SWIP
YOU BASTARD!!
NO WAY ARE YOU DRIVING HER HOME!
I'LL COME GET HER MYSELF! WHAT'S THE ADDRESS?

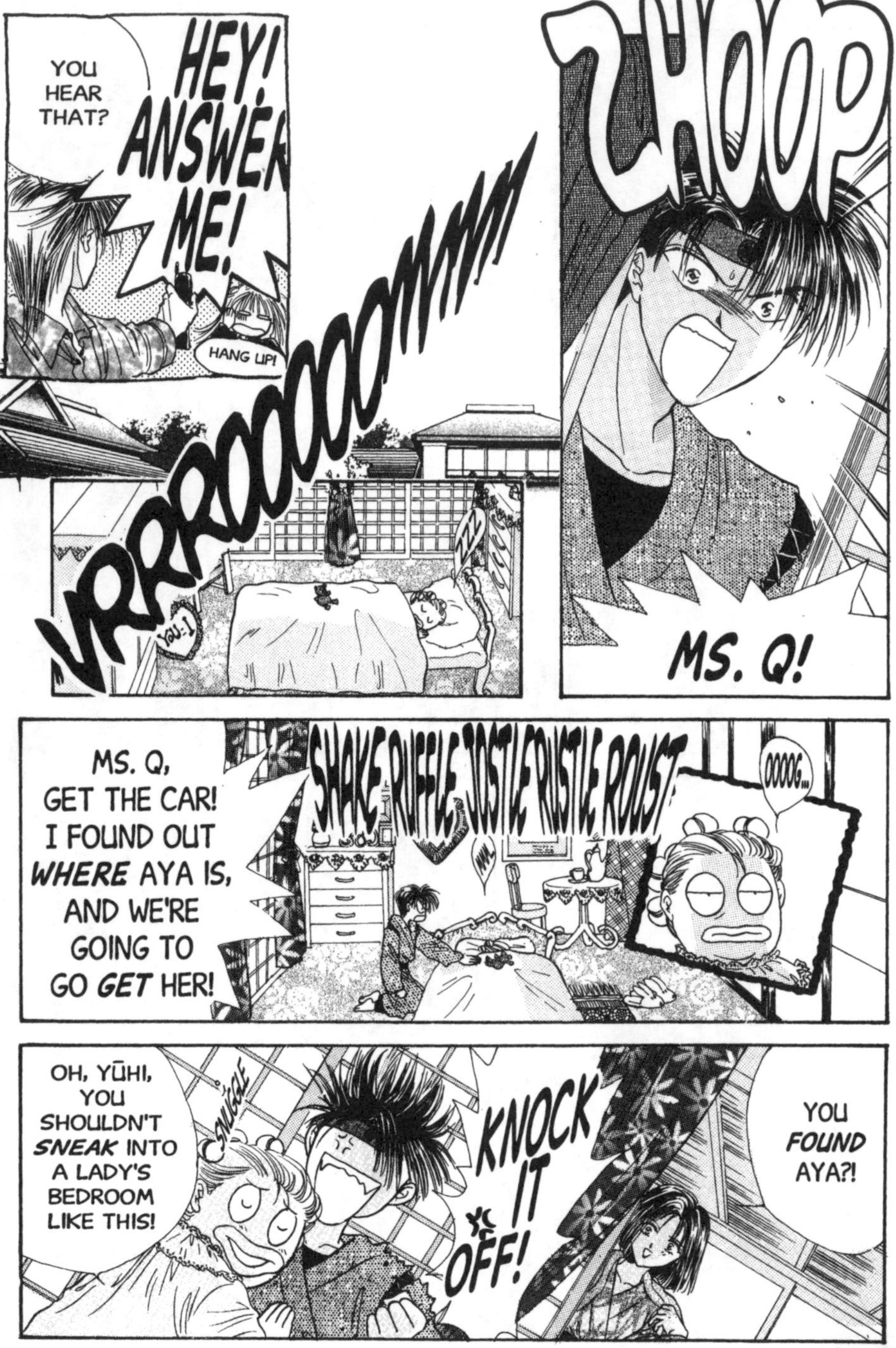
YOU HEAR THAT?
HEY! ANSWER ME!
HANG UP!
VRRROOOOOMMMM
ZHOOP
MS. Q!
MS. Q, GET THE CAR! I FOUND OUT *WHERE* AYA IS, AND WE'RE GOING TO GO *GET* HER!
SHAKE RUFFLE JOSTLE RUSTLE ROUST
OOOOG...
OH, YŪHI, YOU SHOULDN'T *SNEAK* INTO A LADY'S BEDROOM LIKE THIS!
SNUGGLE
KNOCK IT OFF!
YOU *FOUND* AYA?!

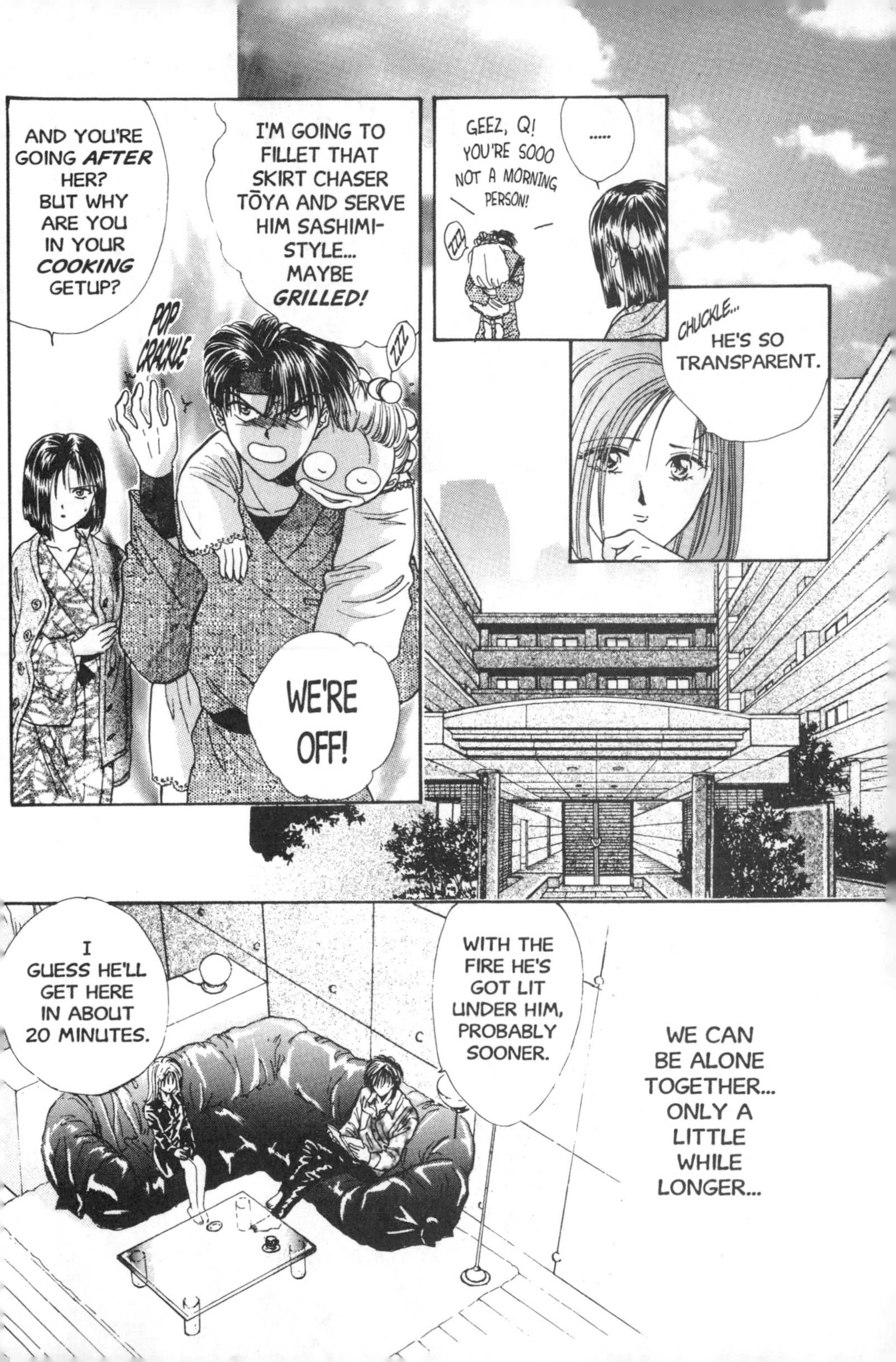
AND YOU'RE GOING *AFTER* HER? BUT WHY ARE YOU IN YOUR *COOKING* GETUP?
I'M GOING TO FILLET THAT SKIRT CHASER TŌYA AND SERVE HIM SASHIMI-STYLE... MAYBE *GRILLED!*
POP CRACKLE
ZZZ
WE'RE OFF!
GEEZ, Q! YOU'RE SOOO NOT A MORNING PERSON!
.....
ZZZ
CHUCKLE...
HE'S SO TRANSPARENT.
I GUESS HE'LL GET HERE IN ABOUT 20 MINUTES.
WITH THE FIRE HE'S GOT LIT UNDER HIM, PROBABLY SOONER.
WE CAN BE ALONE TOGETHER... ONLY A LITTLE WHILE LONGER...

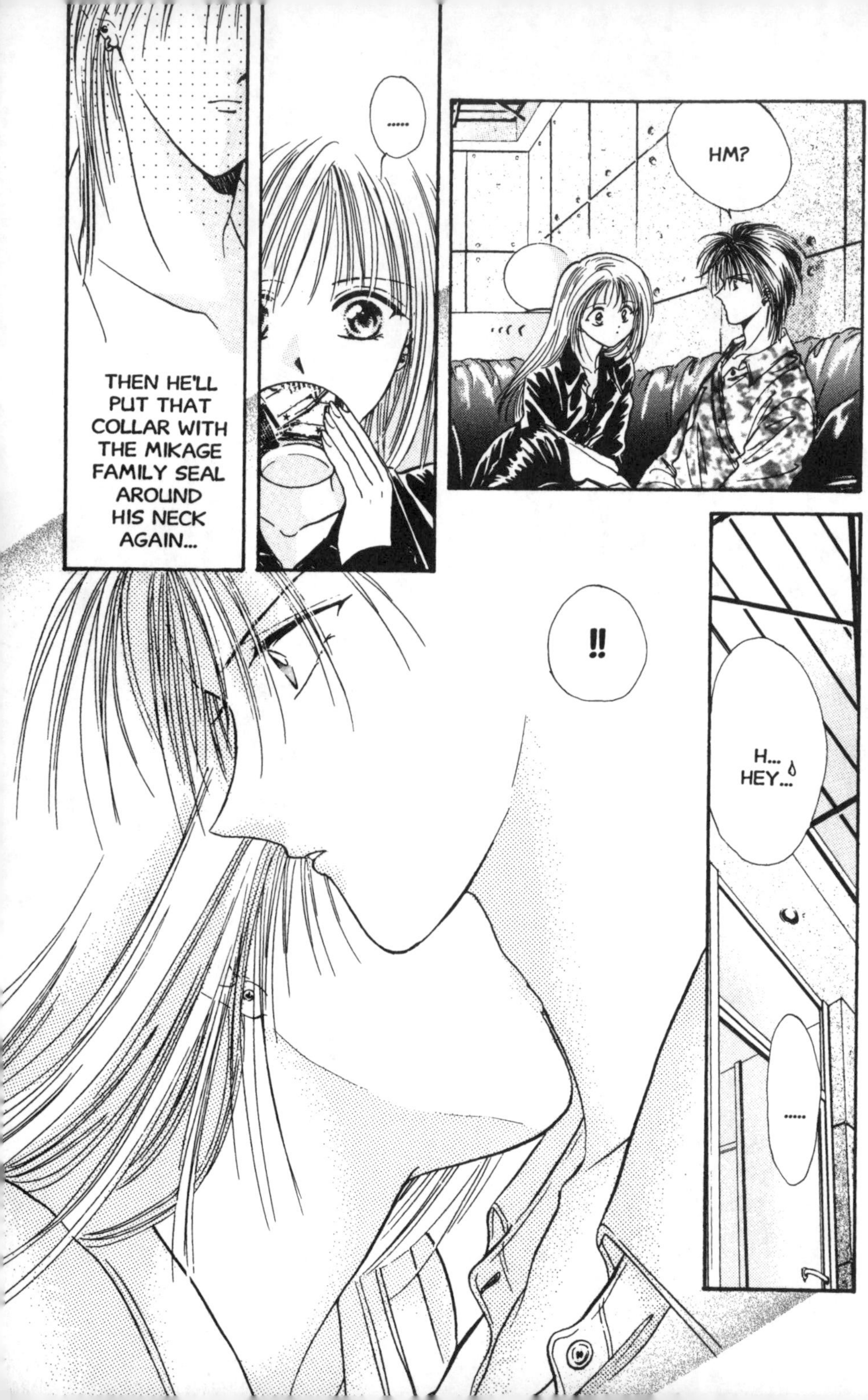
HM?
......
THEN HE'LL PUT THAT COLLAR WITH THE MIKAGE FAMILY SEAL AROUND HIS NECK AGAIN...
!!
H... HEY...
......

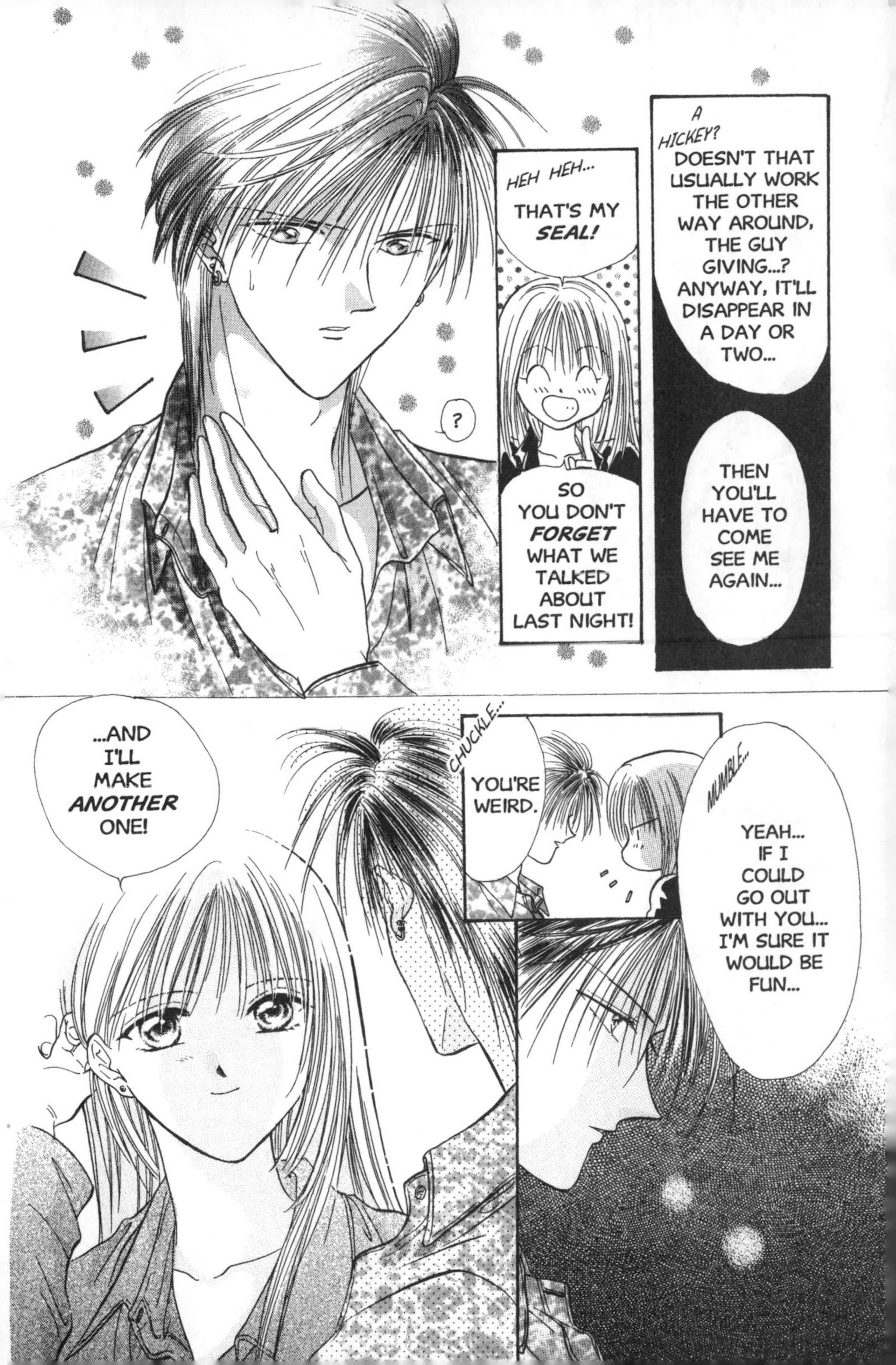
?
HEH HEH...
THAT'S MY SEAL!
SO YOU DON'T FORGET WHAT WE TALKED ABOUT LAST NIGHT!
A HICKEY?
DOESN'T THAT USUALLY WORK THE OTHER WAY AROUND, THE GUY GIVING...? ANYWAY, IT'LL DISAPPEAR IN A DAY OR TWO...
THEN YOU'LL HAVE TO COME SEE ME AGAIN...
...AND I'LL MAKE ANOTHER ONE!
CHUCKLE...
YOU'RE WEIRD.
MUMBLE...
YEAH... IF I COULD GO OUT WITH YOU... I'M SURE IT WOULD BE FUN...

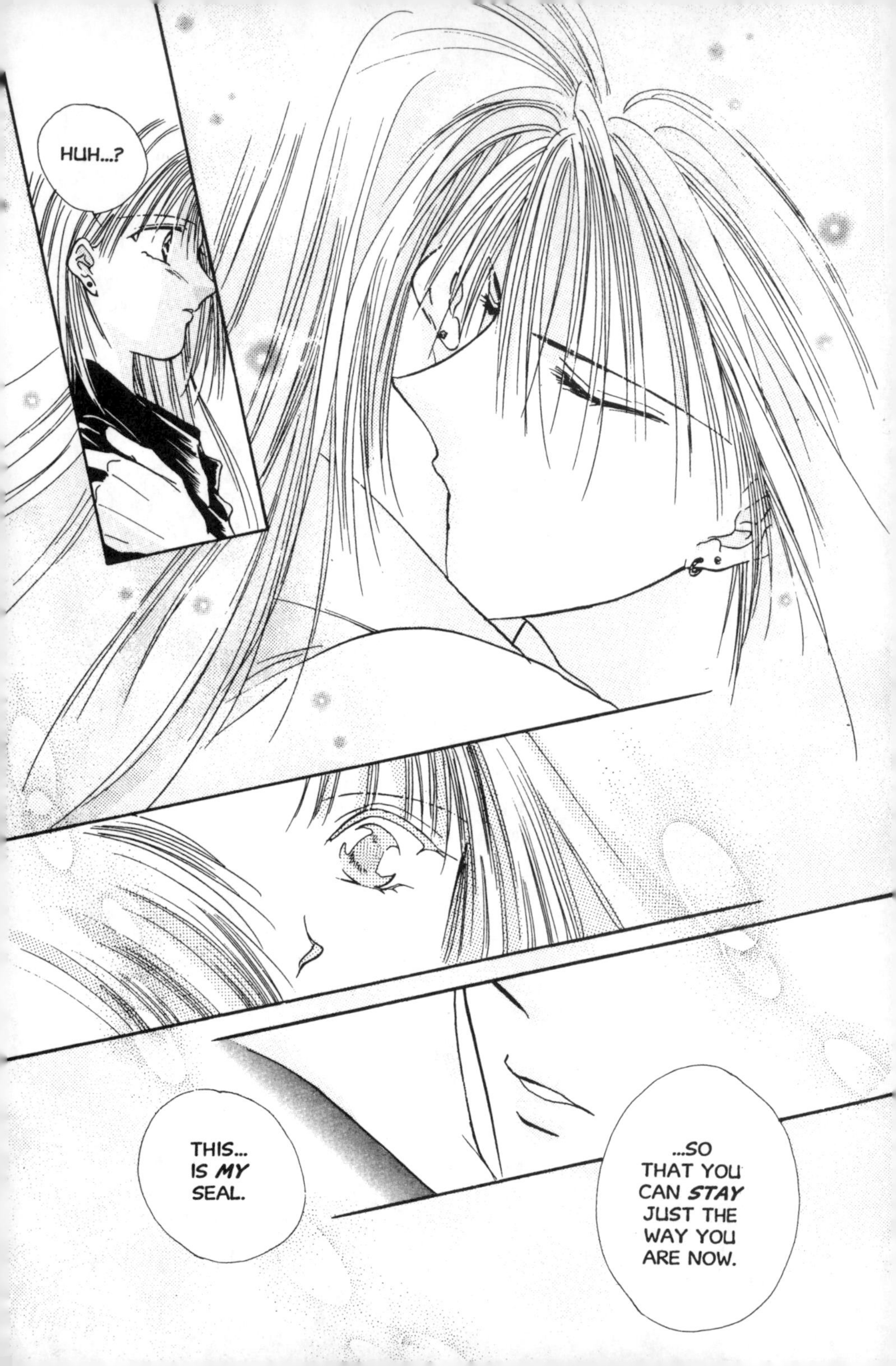
HUH...?
THIS... IS *MY* SEAL.
...SO THAT YOU CAN *STAY* JUST THE WAY YOU ARE NOW.

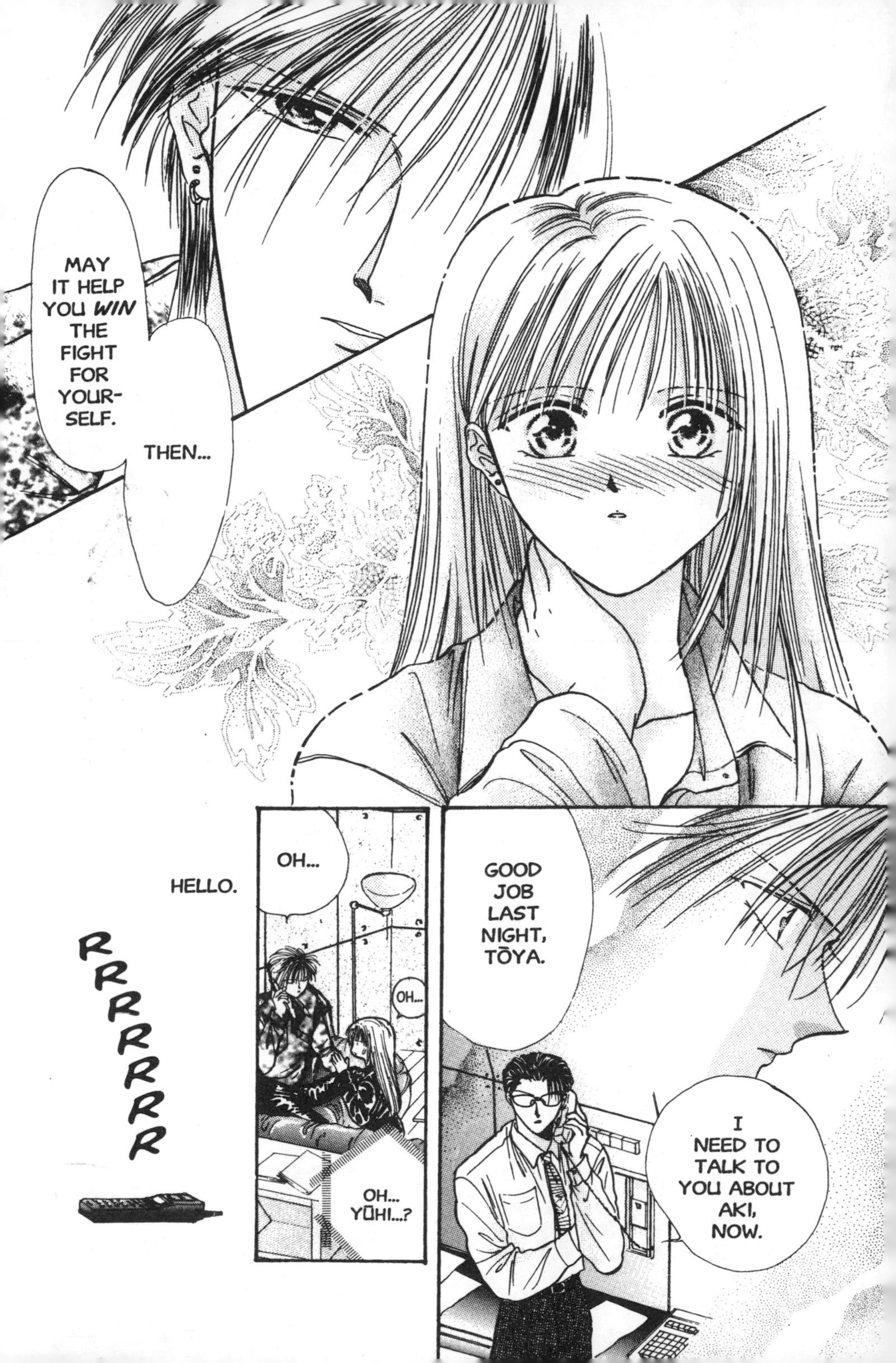
MAY IT HELP YOU *WIN* THE FIGHT FOR YOURSELF.
THEN...
GOOD JOB LAST NIGHT, TŌYA.
I NEED TO TALK TO YOU ABOUT AKI, NOW.
OH...
OH...
OH... YŪHI...?
HELLO.
RRRRRRR

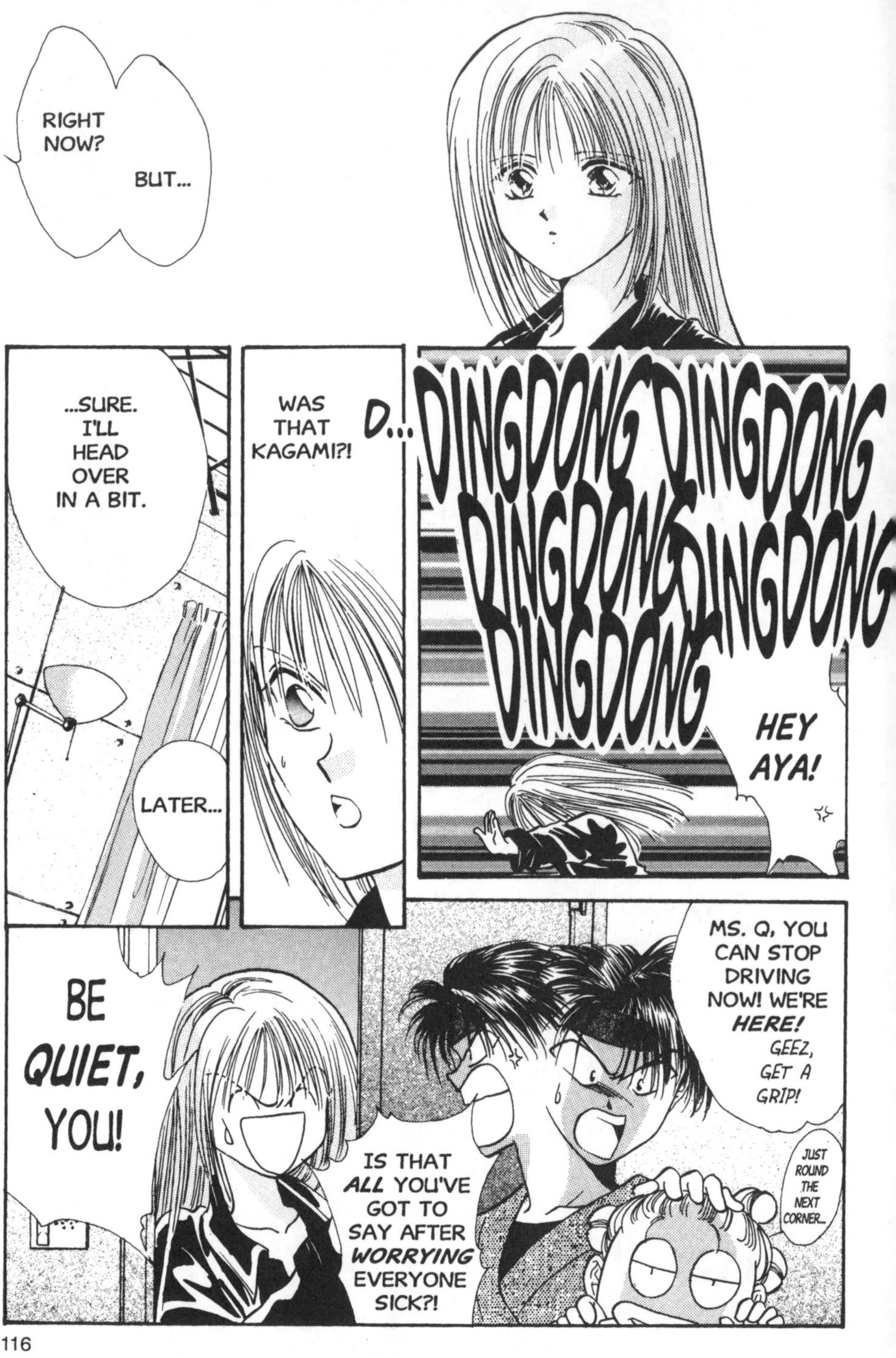
RIGHT NOW? BUT...
...SURE. I'LL HEAD OVER IN A BIT.
LATER...
D...
WAS THAT KAGAMI?!
DINGDONG DINGDONG DINGDONG DINGDONG DINGDONG
HEY AYA!
BE QUIET, YOU!
IS THAT ALL YOU'VE GOT TO SAY AFTER WORRYING EVERYONE SICK?!
MS. Q, YOU CAN STOP DRIVING NOW! WE'RE HERE!
GEEZ, GET A GRIP!
JUST ROUND THE NEXT CORNER...

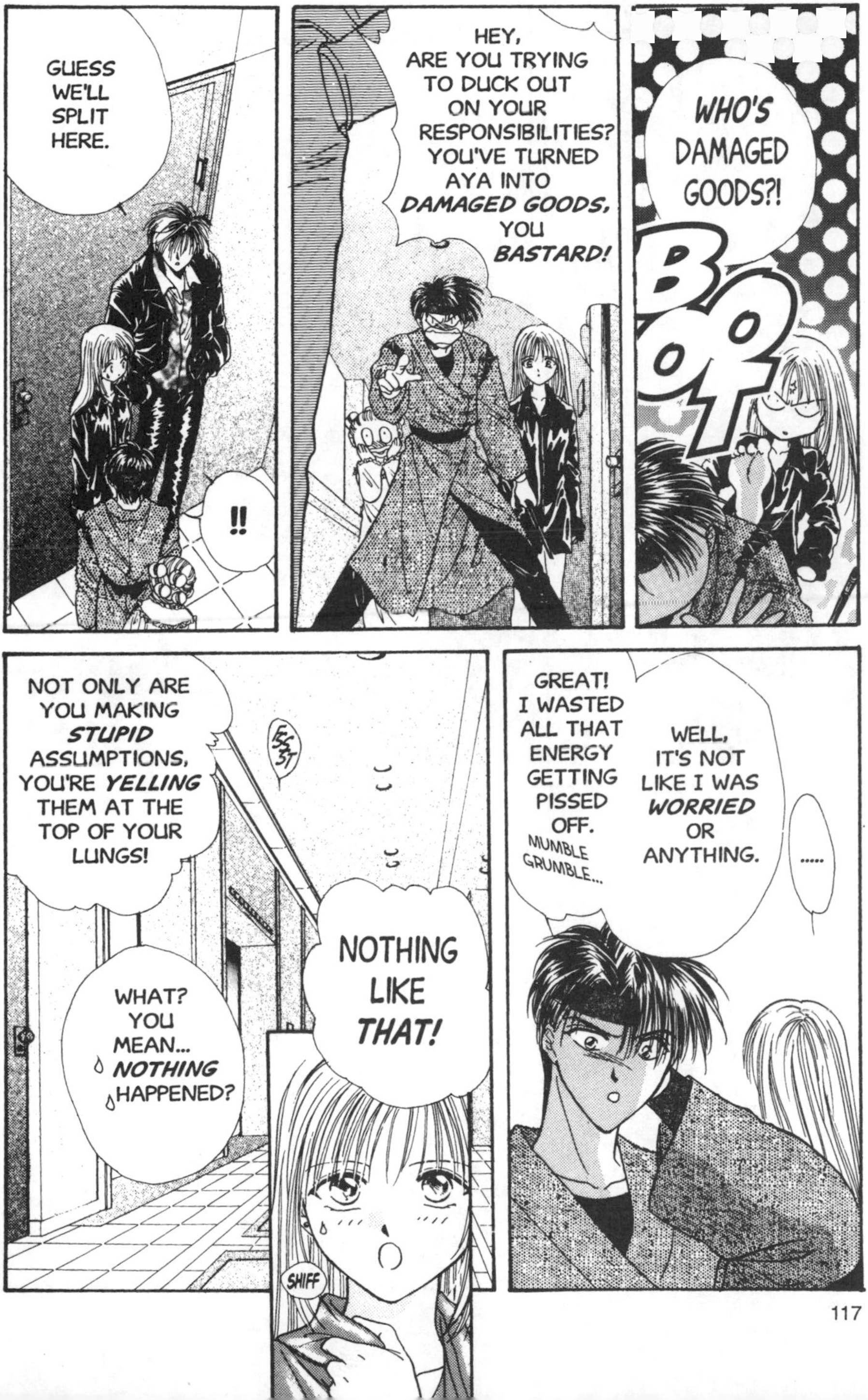
GUESS WE'LL SPLIT HERE.
!!
HEY, ARE YOU TRYING TO DUCK OUT ON YOUR RESPONSIBILITIES? YOU'VE TURNED AYA INTO DAMAGED GOODS, YOU BASTARD!
WHO'S DAMAGED GOODS?!
BOOF
NOT ONLY ARE YOU MAKING STUPID ASSUMPTIONS, YOU'RE YELLING THEM AT THE TOP OF YOUR LUNGS!
WHAT? YOU MEAN... NOTHING HAPPENED?
NOTHING LIKE THAT!
SNIFF
GREAT! I WASTED ALL THAT ENERGY GETTING PISSED OFF. MUMBLE GRUMBLE...
WELL, IT'S NOT LIKE I WAS WORRIED OR ANYTHING.
.....

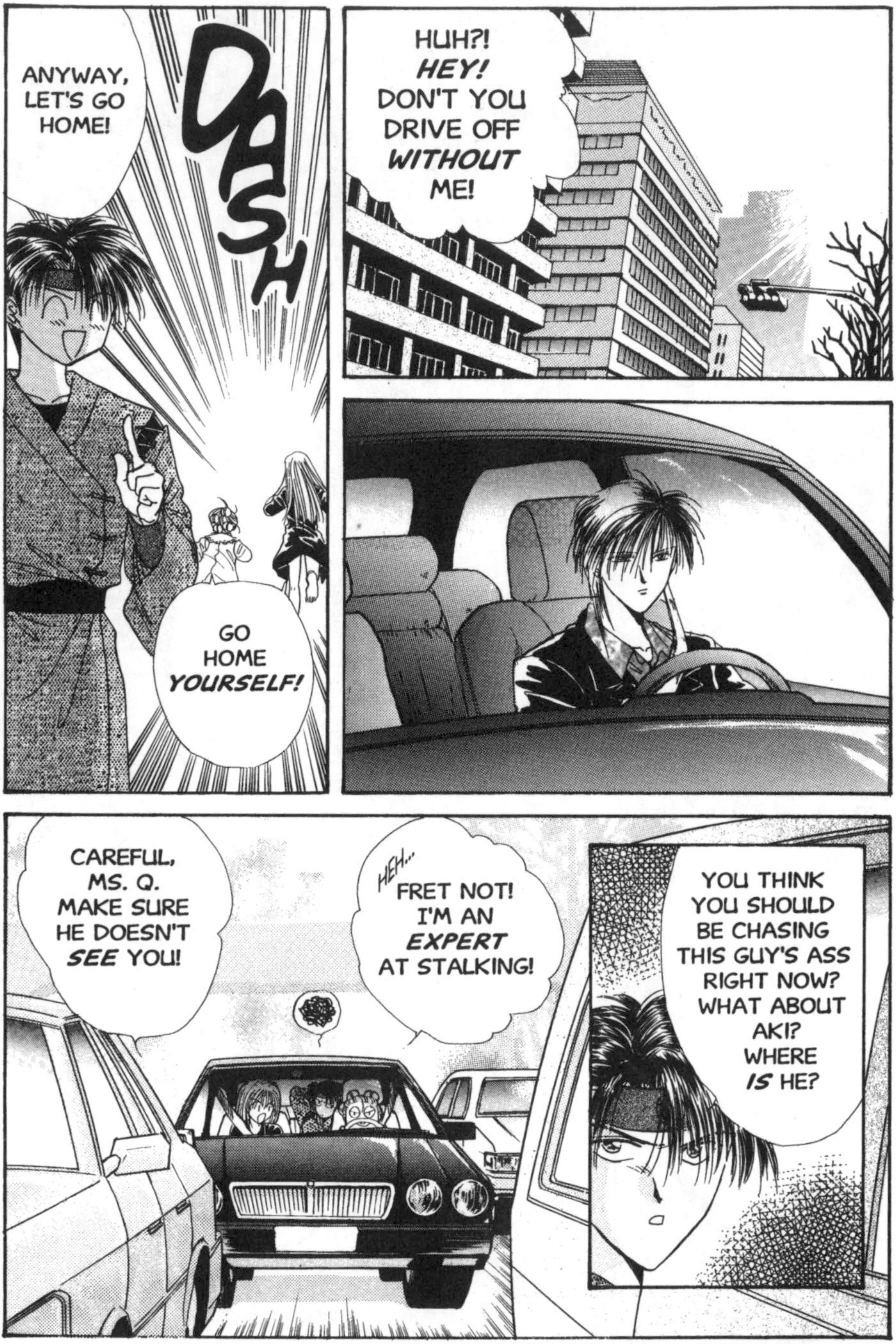
ANYWAY, LET'S GO HOME!
DASH
GO HOME *YOURSELF!*
HUH?! *HEY!* DON'T YOU DRIVE OFF *WITHOUT* ME!
CAREFUL, MS. Q. MAKE SURE HE DOESN'T *SEE* YOU!
HEH...
FRET NOT! I'M AN *EXPERT* AT STALKING!
YOU THINK YOU SHOULD BE CHASING THIS GUY'S ASS RIGHT NOW? WHAT ABOUT AKI? WHERE *IS* HE?

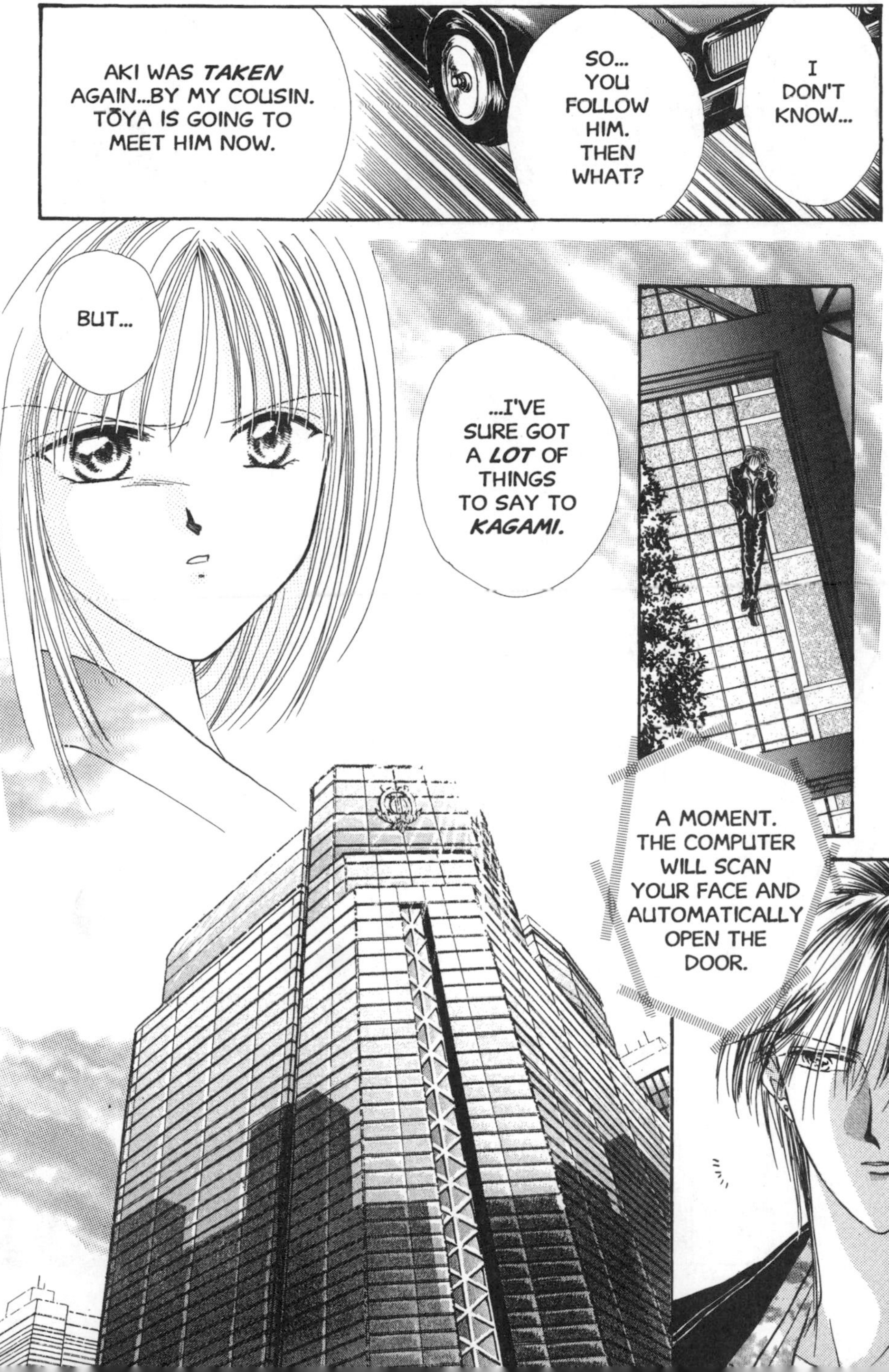
AKI WAS TAKEN AGAIN...BY MY COUSIN. TŌYA IS GOING TO MEET HIM NOW.
SO... YOU FOLLOW HIM. THEN WHAT?
I DON'T KNOW...
BUT...
...I'VE SURE GOT A LOT OF THINGS TO SAY TO KAGAMI.
A MOMENT. THE COMPUTER WILL SCAN YOUR FACE AND AUTOMATICALLY OPEN THE DOOR.

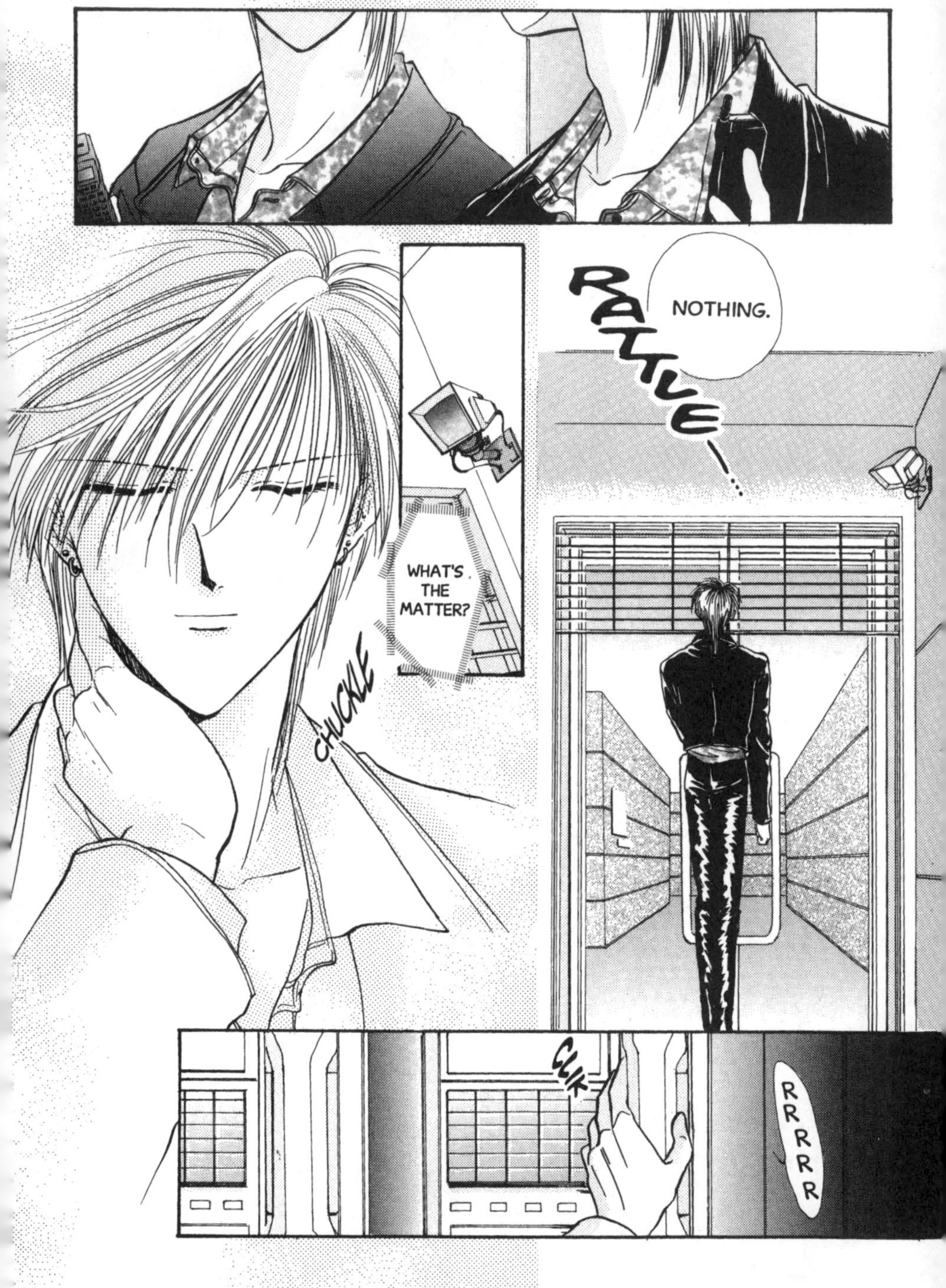
NOTHING.
RATTLE...
WHAT'S THE MATTER?
CHUCKLE
RRRRR
CLIK

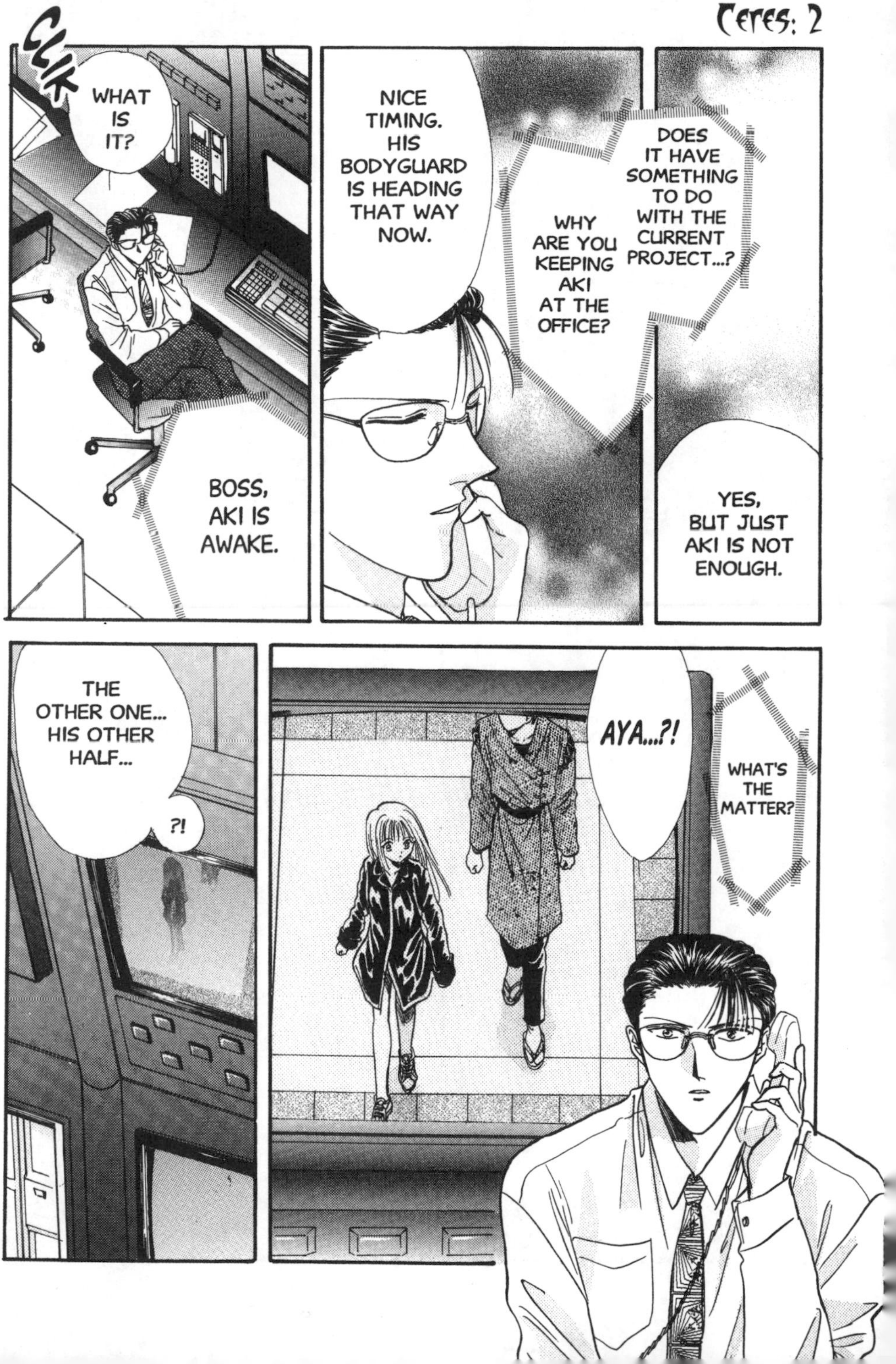
CLIK
WHAT IS IT?
BOSS, AKI IS AWAKE.
NICE TIMING. HIS BODYGUARD IS HEADING THAT WAY NOW.
WHY ARE YOU KEEPING AKI AT THE OFFICE?
DOES IT HAVE SOMETHING TO DO WITH THE CURRENT PROJECT...?
YES, BUT JUST AKI IS NOT ENOUGH.
THE OTHER ONE... HIS OTHER HALF...
?!
AYA...?!
WHAT'S THE MATTER?

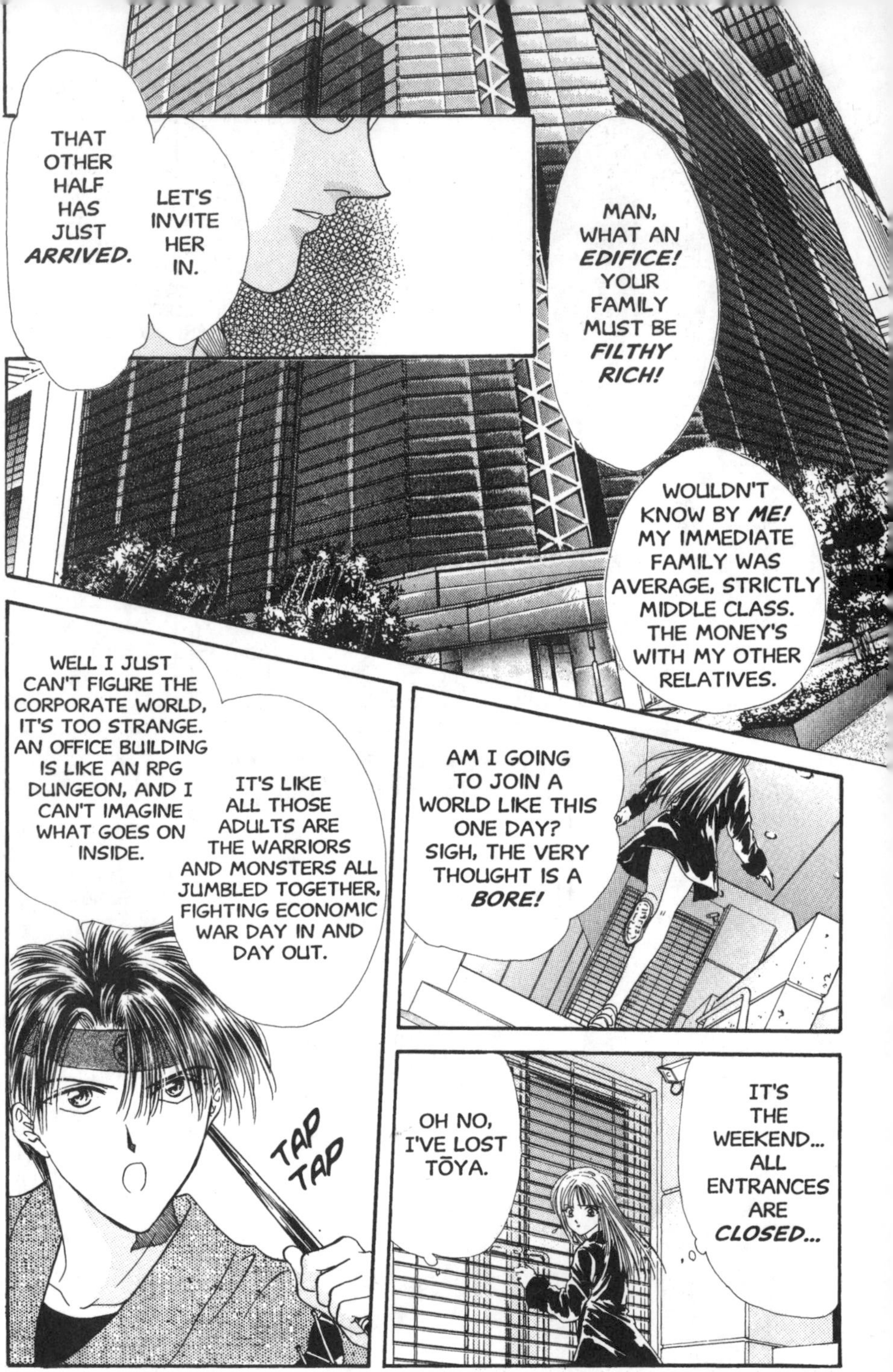
MAN, WHAT AN EDIFICE! YOUR FAMILY MUST BE FILTHY RICH!
WOULDN'T KNOW BY ME! MY IMMEDIATE FAMILY WAS AVERAGE, STRICTLY MIDDLE CLASS. THE MONEY'S WITH MY OTHER RELATIVES.
THAT OTHER HALF HAS JUST ARRIVED.
LET'S INVITE HER IN.
AM I GOING TO JOIN A WORLD LIKE THIS ONE DAY? SIGH, THE VERY THOUGHT IS A BORE!
IT'S THE WEEKEND... ALL ENTRANCES ARE CLOSED...
OH NO, I'VE LOST TŌYA.
WELL I JUST CAN'T FIGURE THE CORPORATE WORLD, IT'S TOO STRANGE. AN OFFICE BUILDING IS LIKE AN RPG DUNGEON, AND I CAN'T IMAGINE WHAT GOES ON INSIDE.
IT'S LIKE ALL THOSE ADULTS ARE THE WARRIORS AND MONSTERS ALL JUMBLED TOGETHER, FIGHTING ECONOMIC WAR DAY IN AND DAY OUT.
TAP TAP

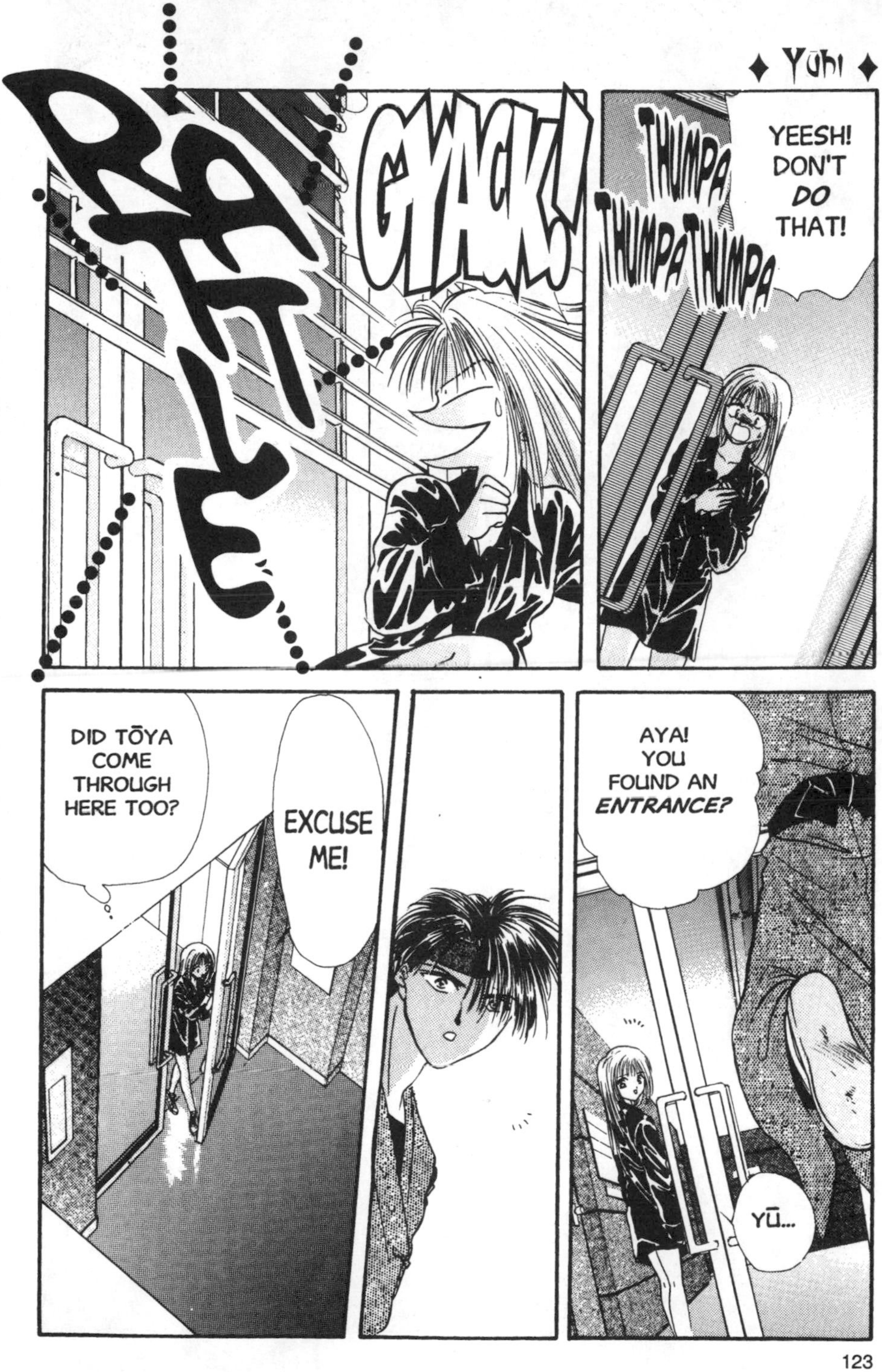
YEESH! DON'T *DO* THAT!
THUMPA THUMPA THUMPA
GYACK!
RATTLE
AYA! YOU FOUND AN *ENTRANCE?*
YŪ...
EXCUSE ME!
DID TŌYA COME THROUGH HERE TOO?

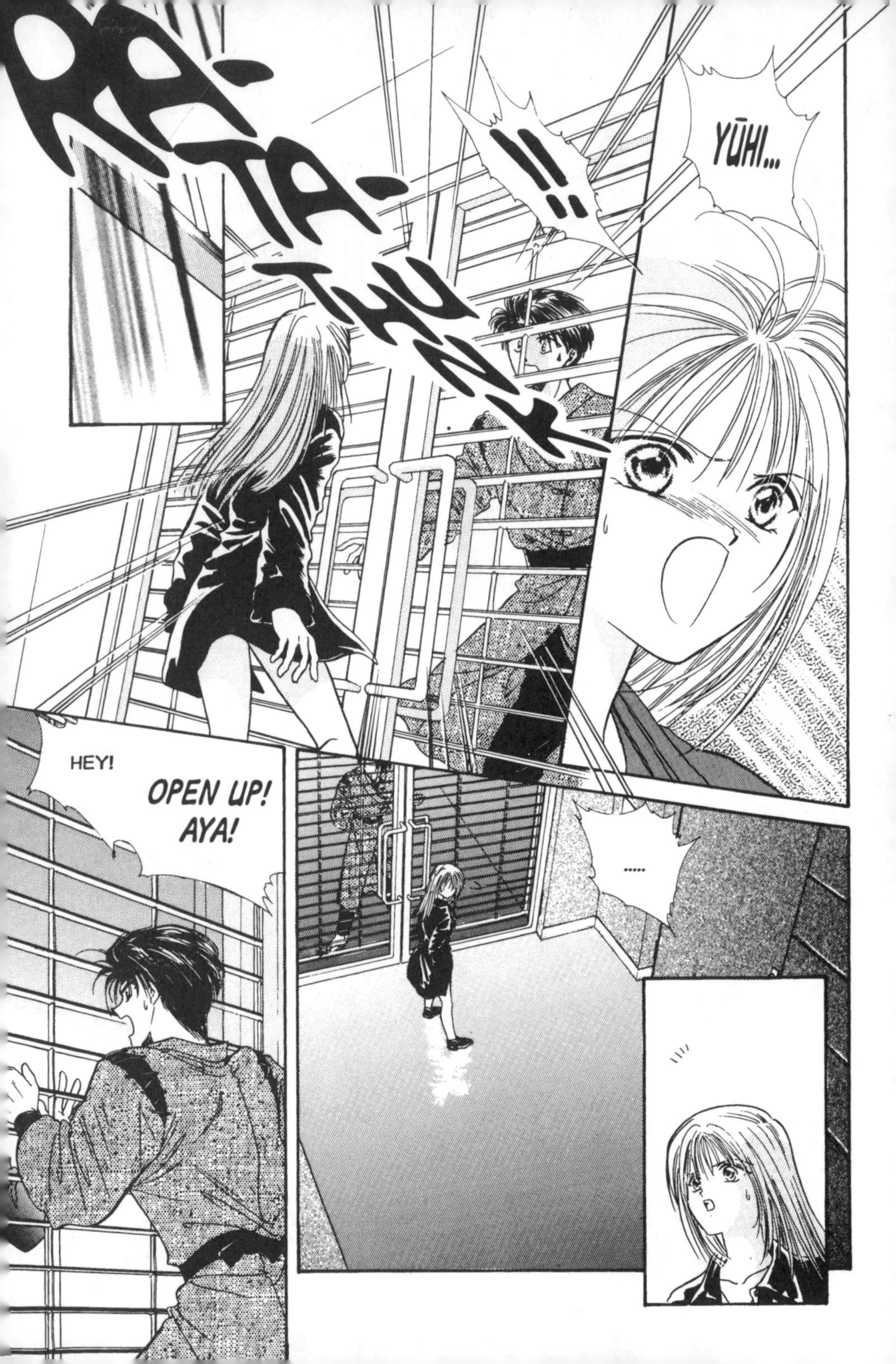
YŪHI...
RA-TA-THUNK!!
......
HEY!
OPEN UP! AYA!

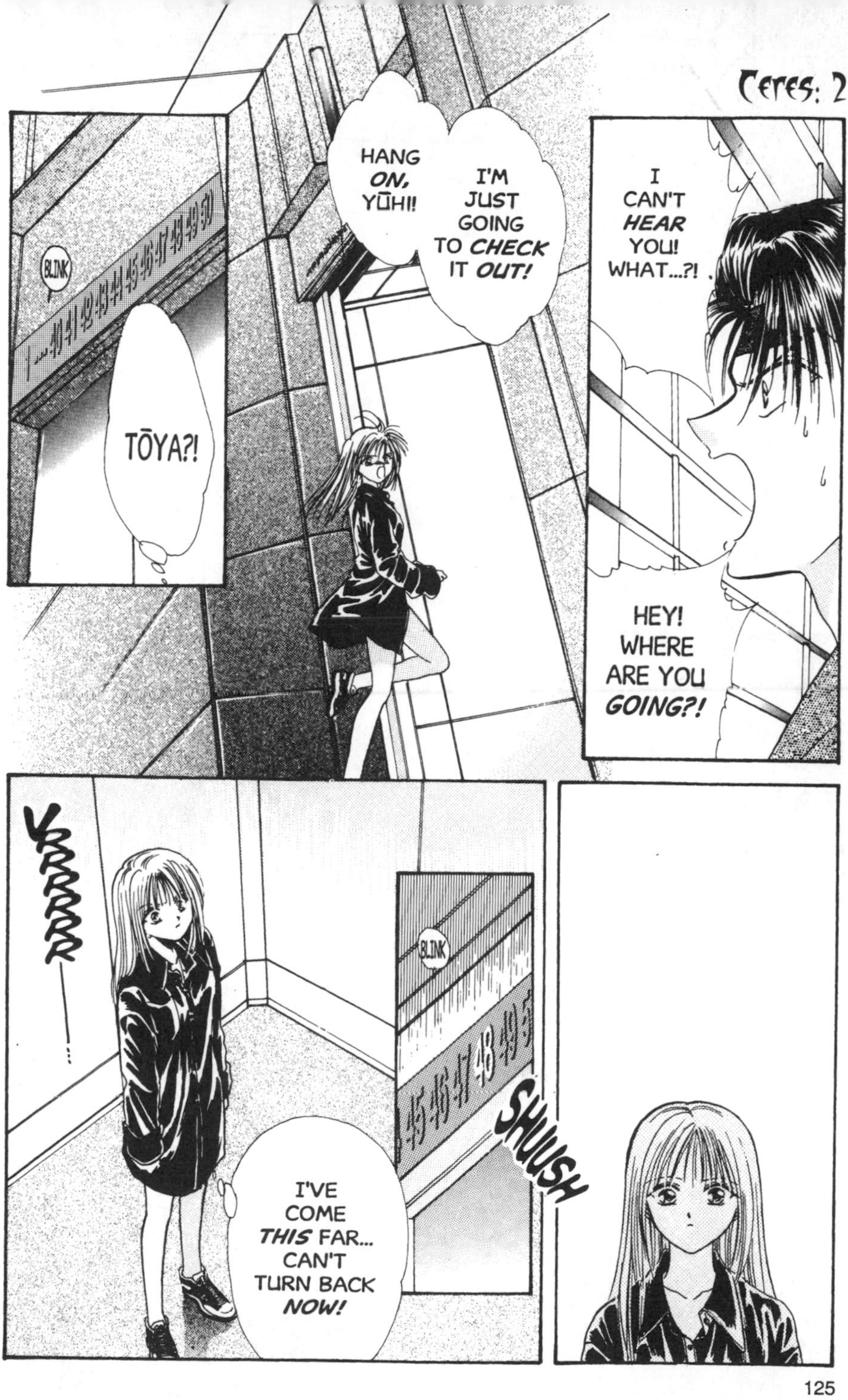
I CAN'T HEAR YOU! WHAT...?!
HEY! WHERE ARE YOU GOING?!
HANG ON, YŪHI!
I'M JUST GOING TO CHECK IT OUT!
BLINK
TŌYA?!
SHUUSH
BLINK
VRRRRRR
I'VE COME THIS FAR... CAN'T TURN BACK NOW!

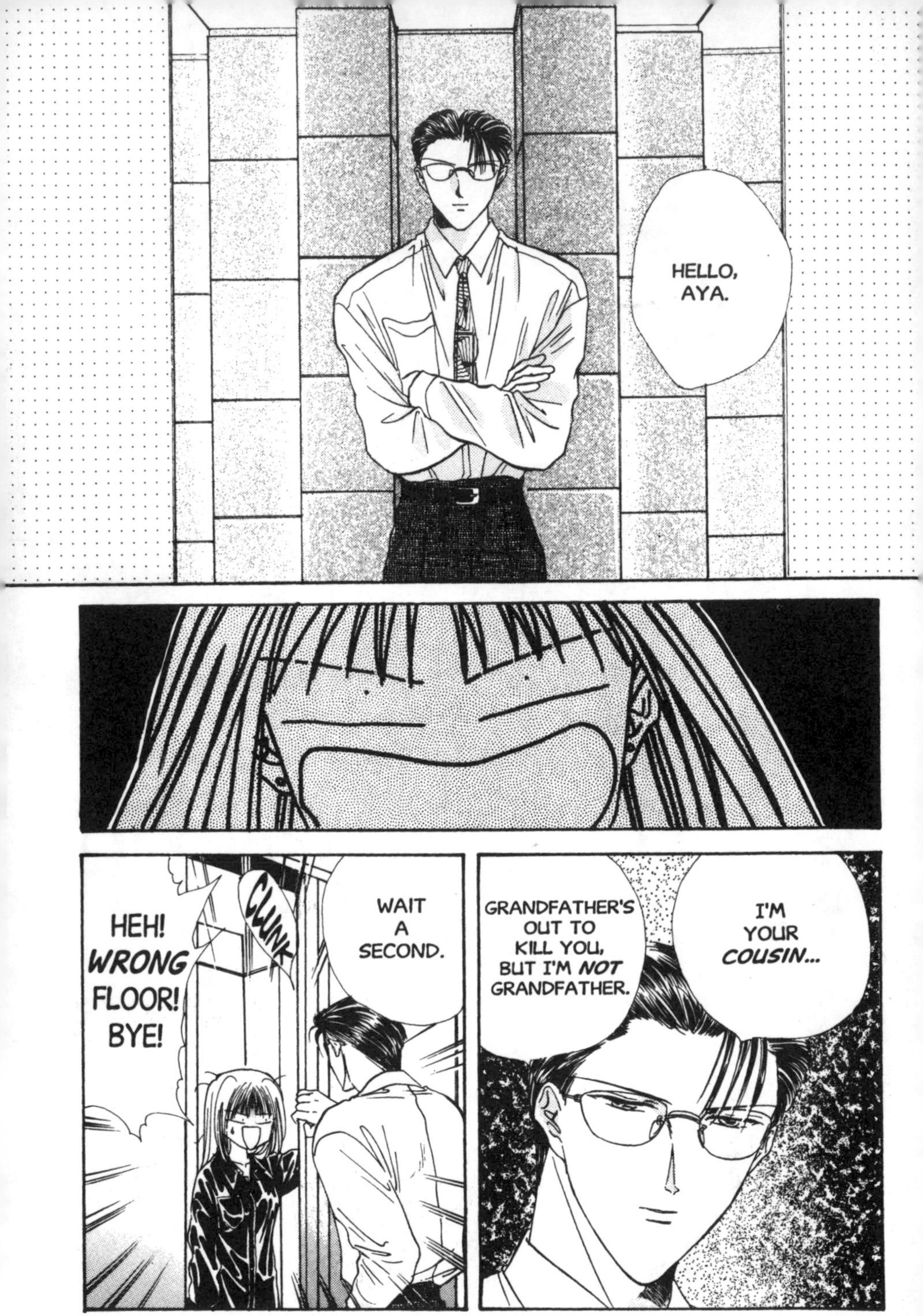
HELLO, AYA.
HEH! *WRONG* FLOOR! BYE!
CLUNK
WAIT A SECOND.
GRANDFATHER'S OUT TO KILL YOU, BUT I'M *NOT* GRANDFATHER.
I'M YOUR *COUSIN...*

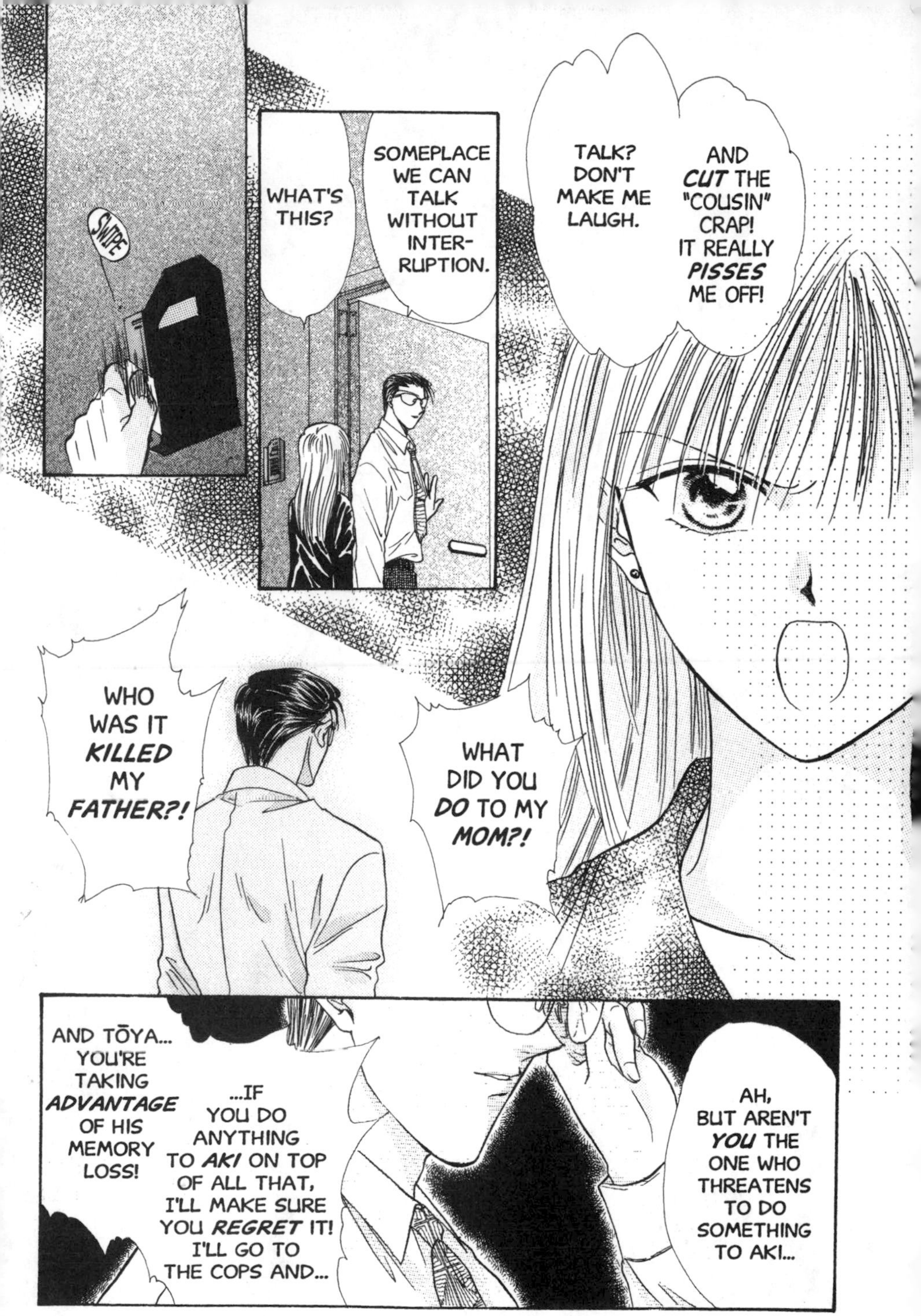
SWIPE
WHAT'S THIS?
SOMEPLACE WE CAN TALK WITHOUT INTER-RUPTION.
TALK? DON'T MAKE ME LAUGH.
AND *CUT* THE "COUSIN" CRAP! IT REALLY *PISSES* ME OFF!
WHO WAS IT *KILLED* MY *FATHER?!*
WHAT DID YOU *DO* TO MY *MOM?!*
AND TŌYA... YOU'RE TAKING *ADVANTAGE* OF HIS MEMORY LOSS!
...IF YOU DO ANYTHING TO *AKI* ON TOP OF ALL THAT, I'LL MAKE SURE YOU *REGRET* IT! I'LL GO TO THE COPS AND...
AH, BUT AREN'T *YOU* THE ONE WHO THREATENS TO DO SOMETHING TO AKI...

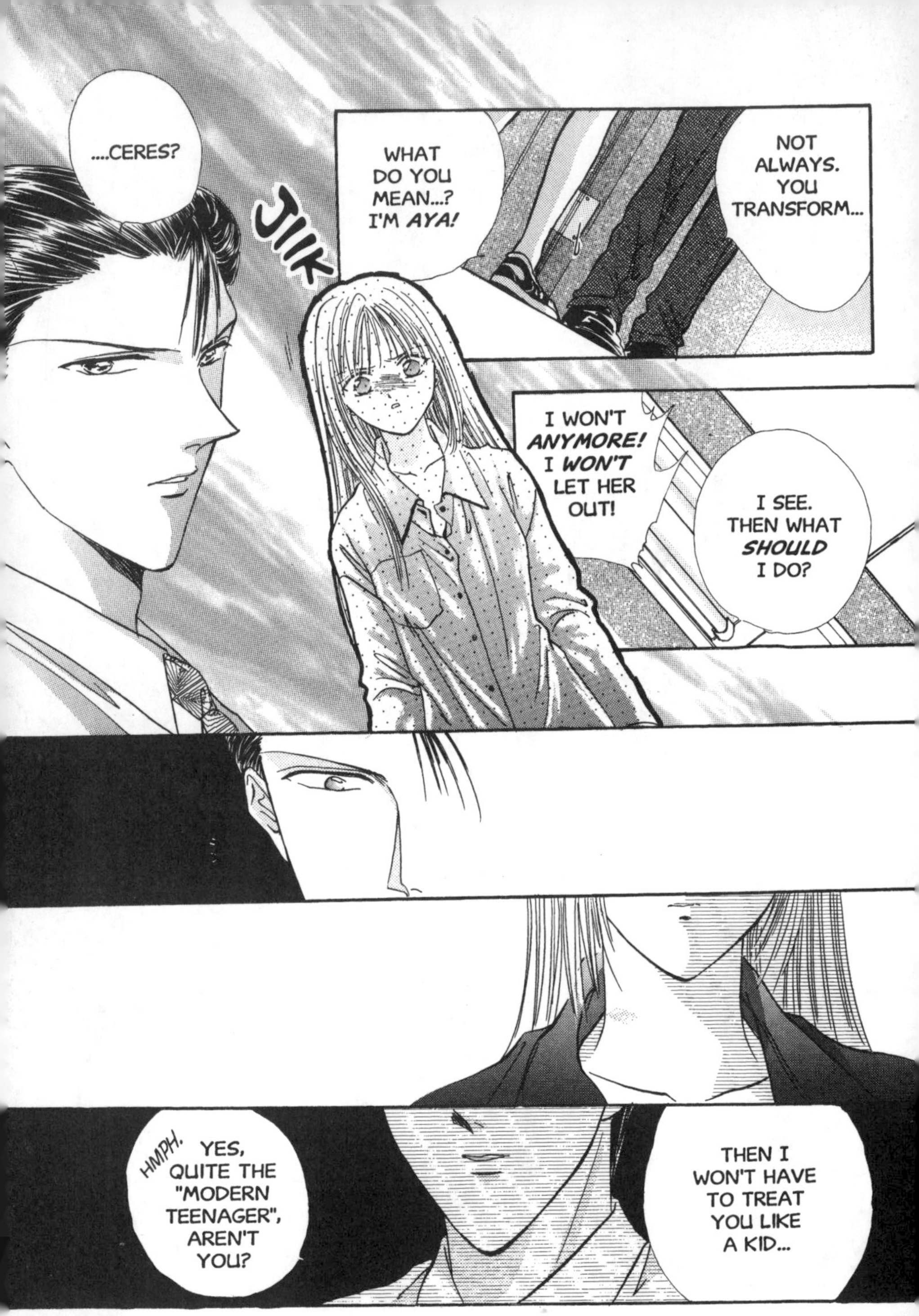
....CERES?
JIIK
WHAT DO YOU MEAN...? I'M *AYA!*
NOT ALWAYS. YOU TRANSFORM...
I WON'T ***ANYMORE!*** I ***WON'T*** LET HER OUT!
I SEE. THEN WHAT ***SHOULD*** I DO?
HMPH.
YES, QUITE THE "MODERN TEENAGER", AREN'T YOU?
THEN I WON'T HAVE TO TREAT YOU LIKE A KID...

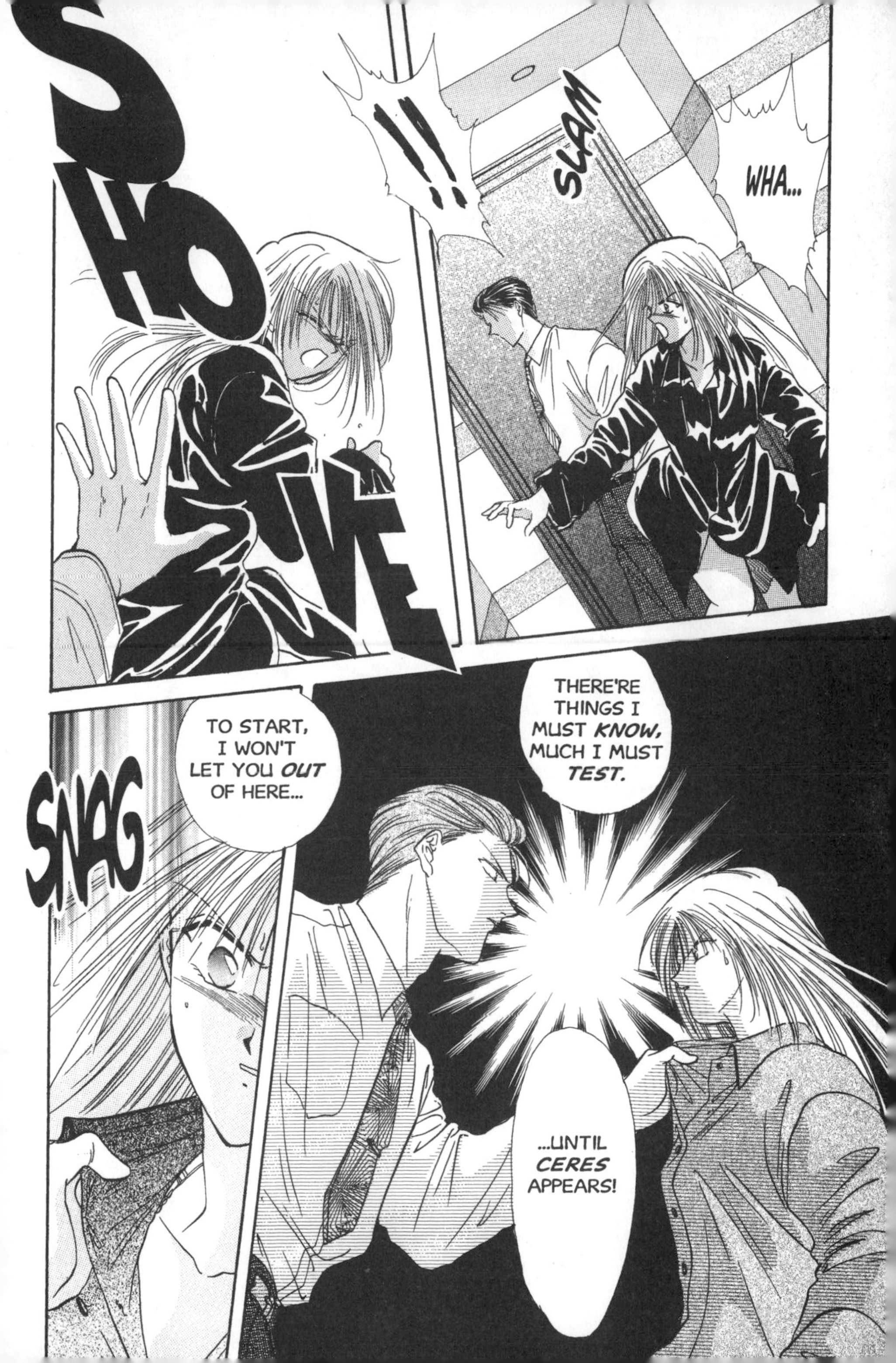
!!
SLAM
WHA...
SHOVE
THERE'RE THINGS I MUST *KNOW,* MUCH I MUST *TEST.*
TO START, I WON'T LET YOU *OUT* OF HERE...
SNAG
...UNTIL *CERES* APPEARS!

BIRTHDAY: Unknown (estimated age 20-24)

BLOODTYPE: AB (confirmed by lab results)

HEIGHT: 184cm (6') all other statistics unknown

Above average intelligence, athletics, and

muscular strength, but lacking in emotional expression.

TŌYA

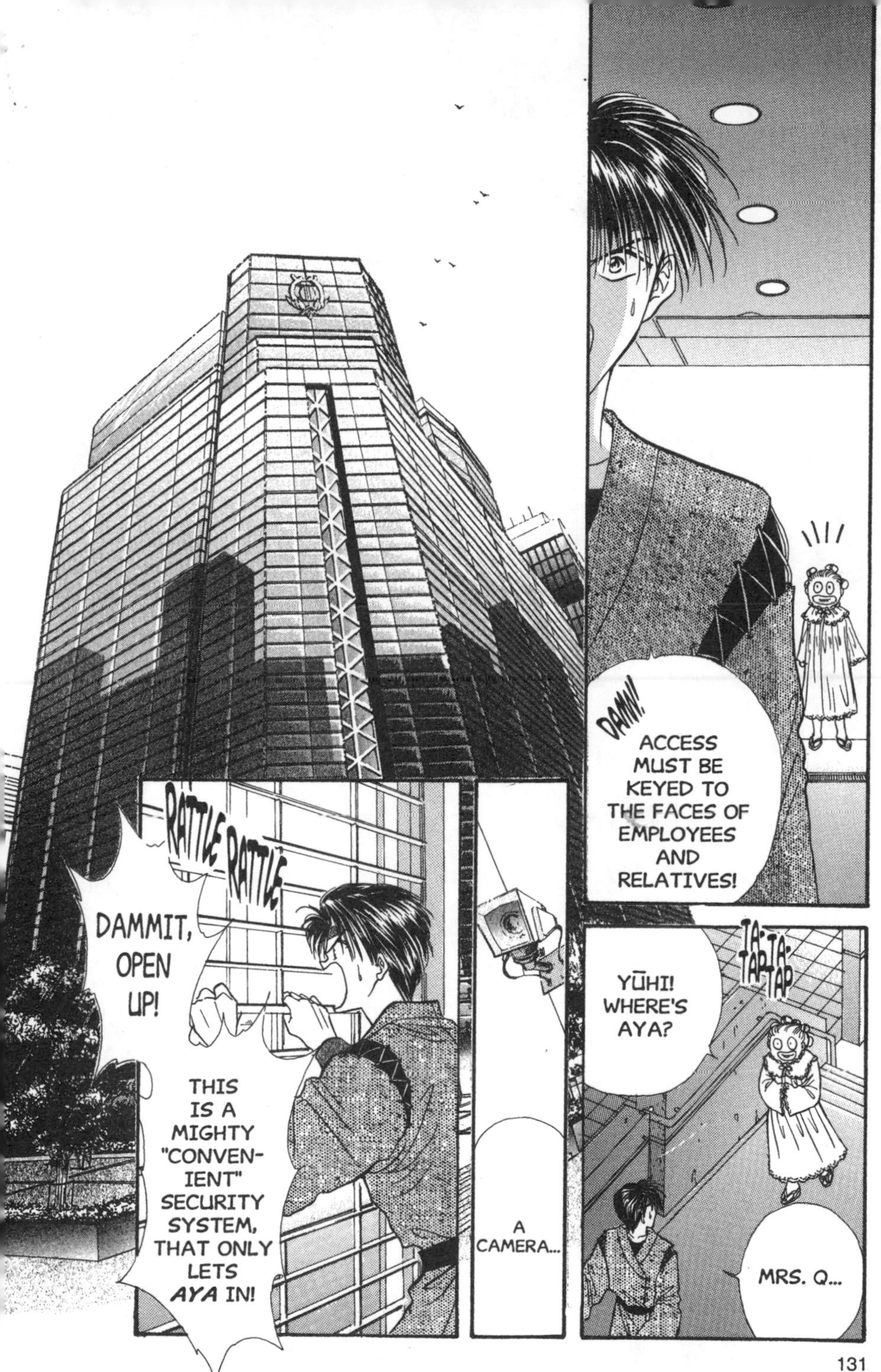
RATTLE RATTLE
DAMMIT, OPEN UP!
THIS IS A MIGHTY "CONVEN-IENT" SECURITY SYSTEM, THAT ONLY LETS AYA IN!
A CAMERA...
DAMN!
ACCESS MUST BE KEYED TO THE FACES OF EMPLOYEES AND RELATIVES!
TA-TA-TAPTAP
YŪHI! WHERE'S AYA?
MRS. Q...

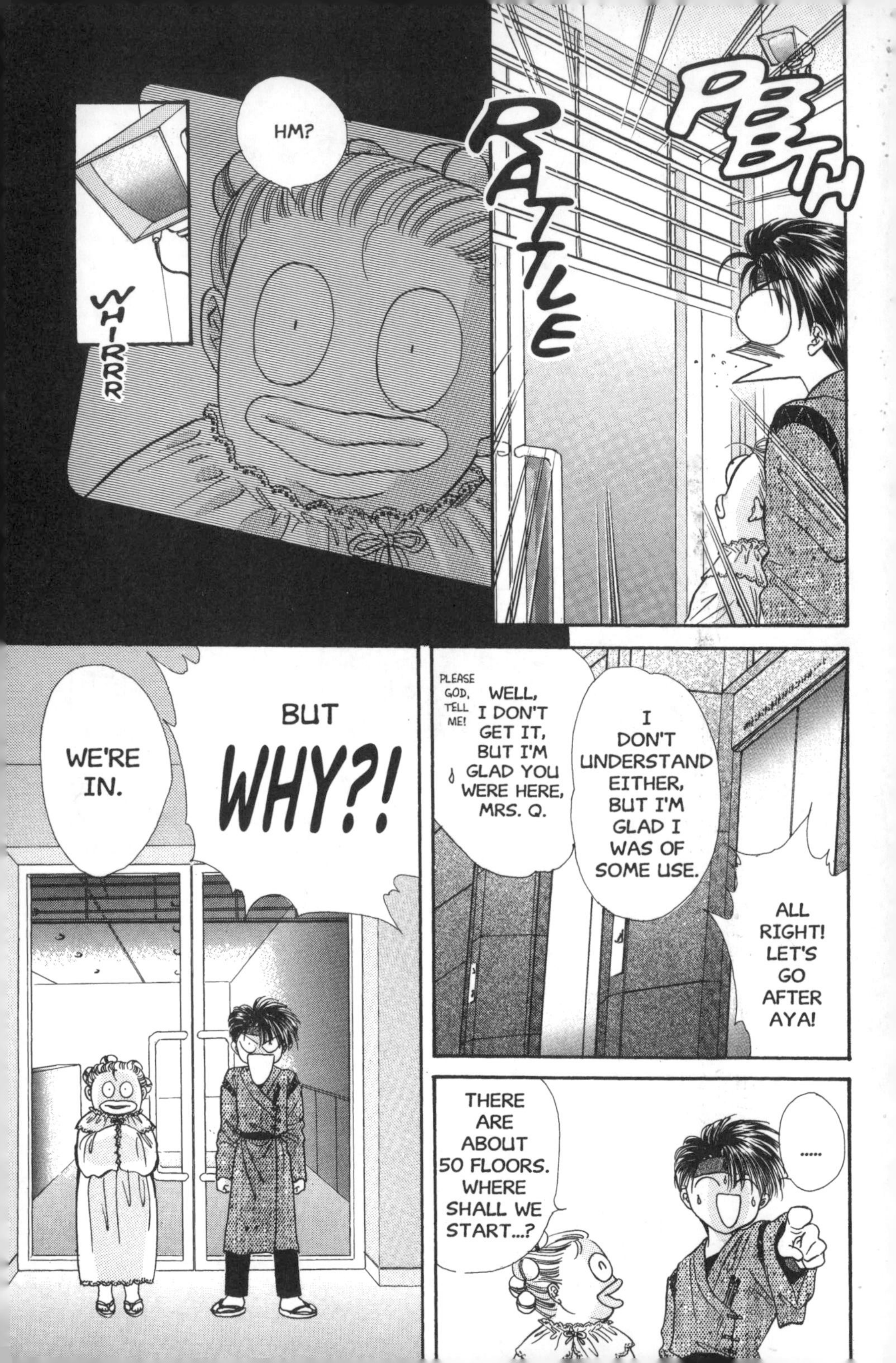
PBBTH
RATTLE
HM?
WHIRRR
WELL, I DON'T GET IT, BUT I'M GLAD YOU WERE HERE, MRS. Q.
PLEASE GOD, TELL ME!
I DON'T UNDERSTAND EITHER, BUT I'M GLAD I WAS OF SOME USE.
ALL RIGHT! LET'S GO AFTER AYA!
.....
THERE ARE ABOUT 50 FLOORS. WHERE SHALL WE START...?
WE'RE IN.
BUT WHY?!

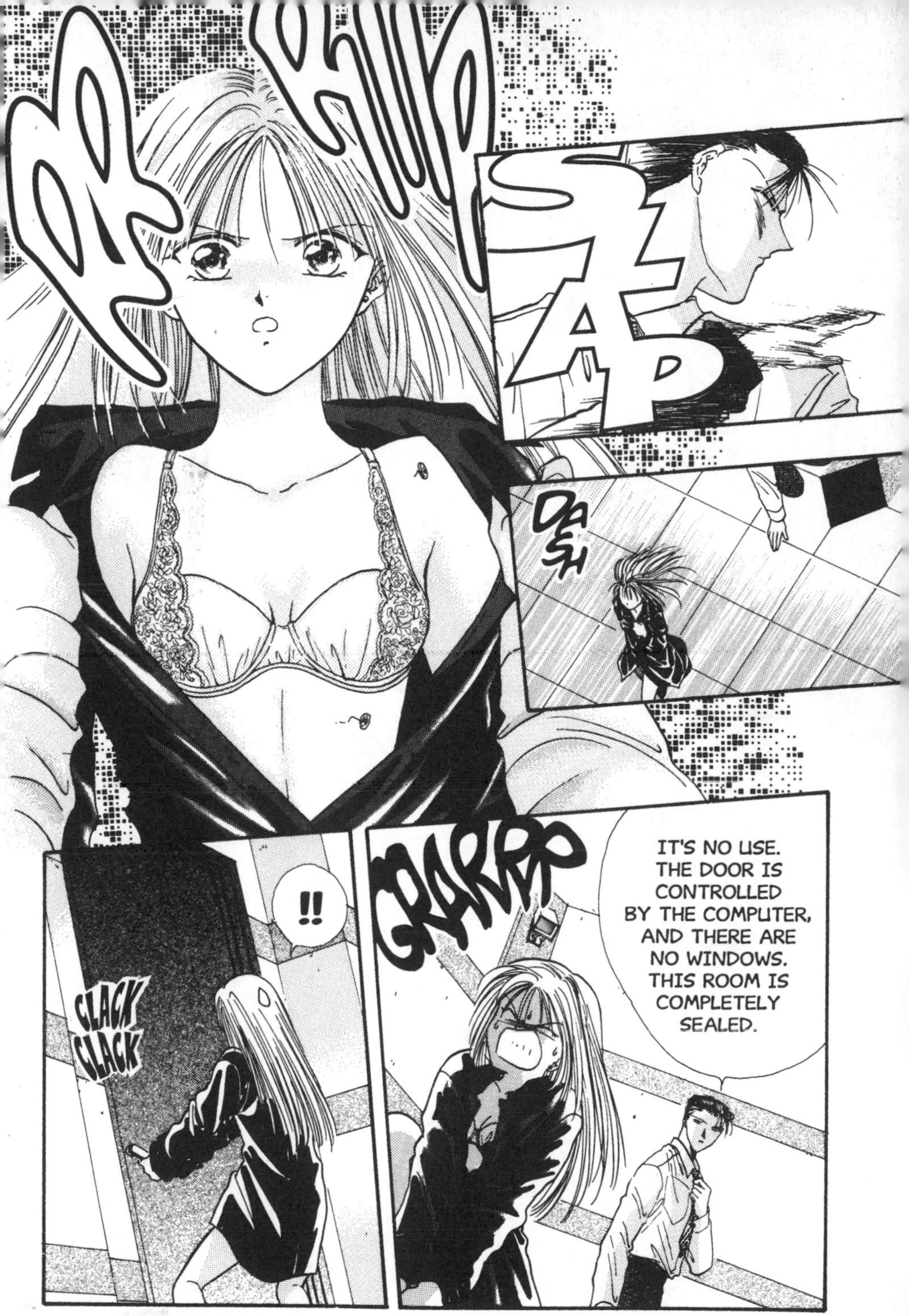
SLAP
DASH
IT'S NO USE. THE DOOR IS CONTROLLED BY THE COMPUTER, AND THERE ARE NO WINDOWS. THIS ROOM IS COMPLETELY SEALED.
!!
CLACK CLACK

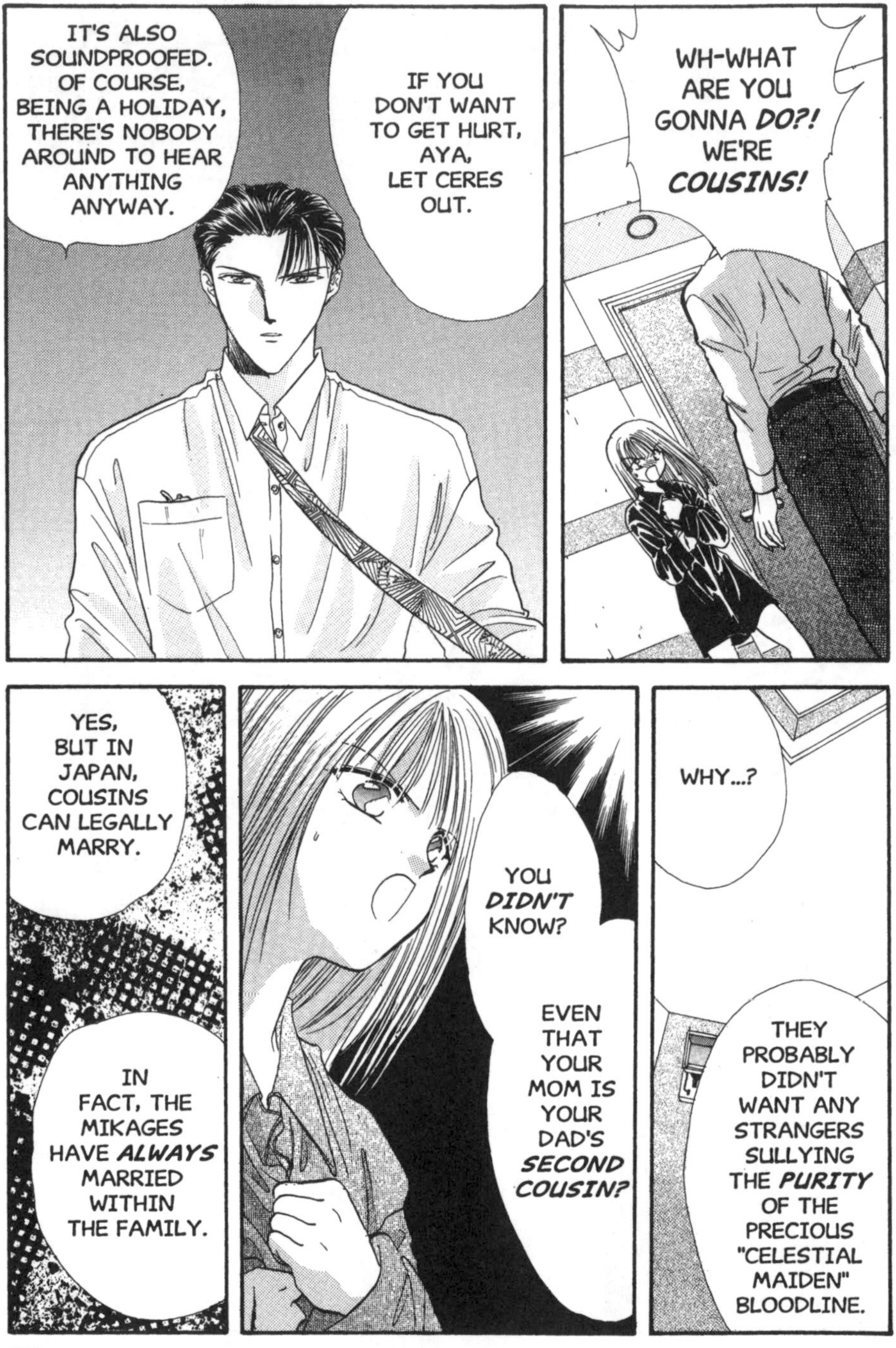
IT'S ALSO SOUNDPROOFED. OF COURSE, BEING A HOLIDAY, THERE'S NOBODY AROUND TO HEAR ANYTHING ANYWAY.
IF YOU DON'T WANT TO GET HURT, AYA, LET CERES OUT.
WH-WHAT ARE YOU GONNA *DO?!* WE'RE *COUSINS!*
YES, BUT IN JAPAN, COUSINS CAN LEGALLY MARRY.
IN FACT, THE MIKAGES HAVE *ALWAYS* MARRIED WITHIN THE FAMILY.
YOU *DIDN'T* KNOW?
EVEN THAT YOUR MOM IS YOUR DAD'S *SECOND COUSIN?*
WHY...?
THEY PROBABLY DIDN'T WANT ANY STRANGERS SULLYING THE *PURITY* OF THE PRECIOUS "CELESTIAL MAIDEN" BLOODLINE.

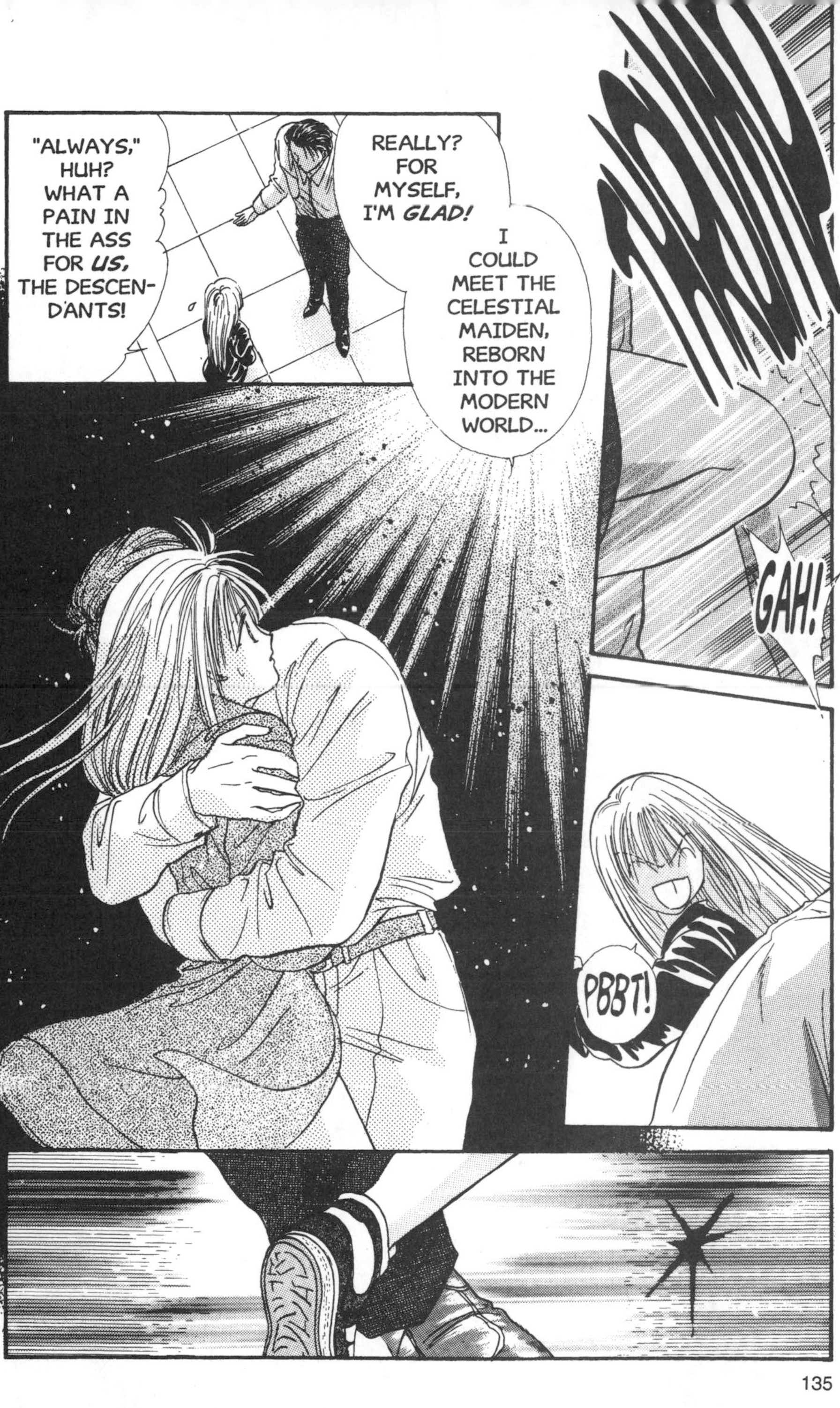
"ALWAYS," HUH? WHAT A PAIN IN THE ASS FOR *US,* THE DESCENDANTS!
REALLY? FOR MYSELF, I'M *GLAD!*
I COULD MEET THE CELESTIAL MAIDEN, REBORN INTO THE MODERN WORLD...
GAH!
PBBT!

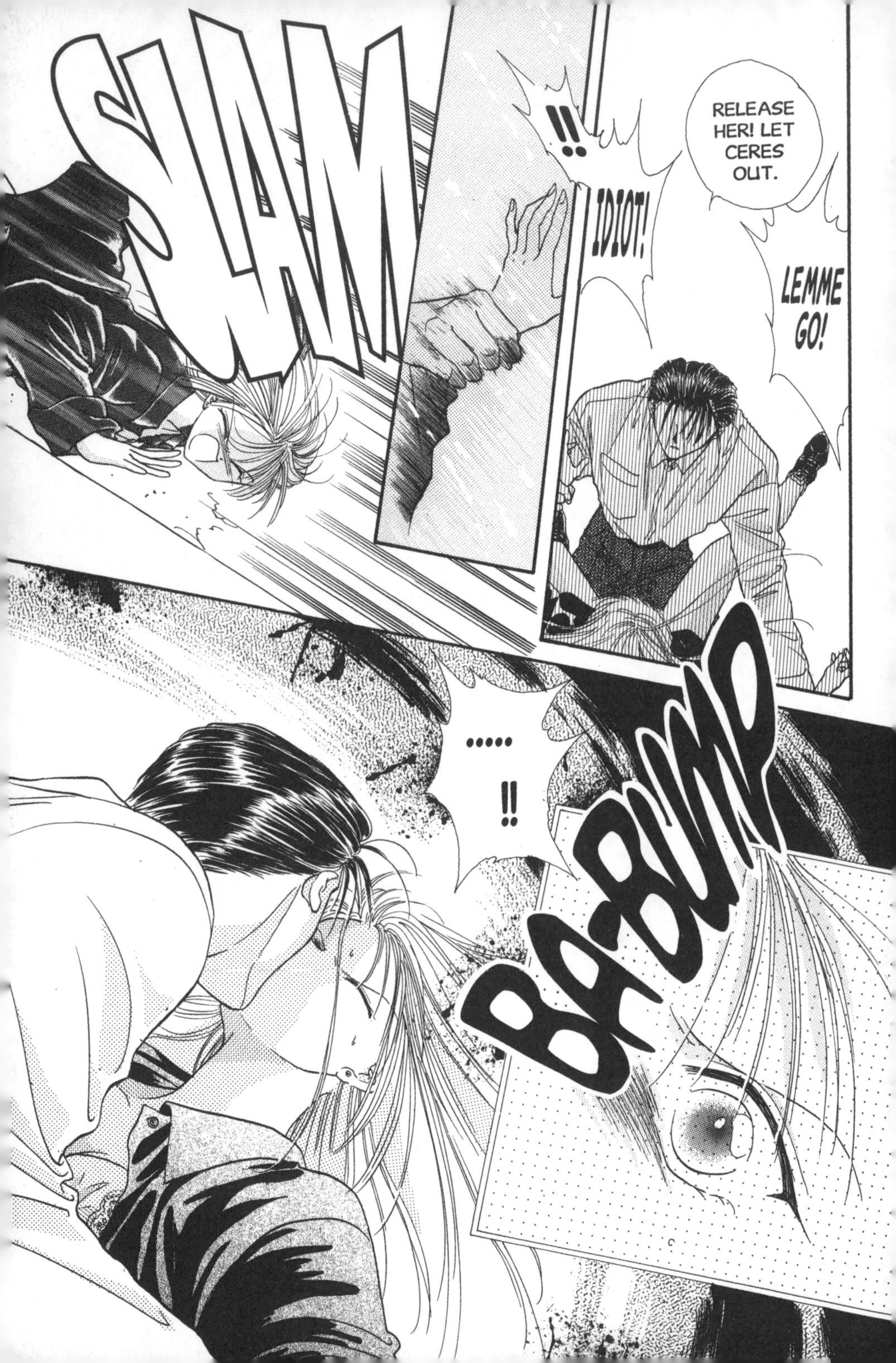
RELEASE HER! LET CERES OUT.
IDIOT!
LEMME GO!
!!
SLAM
BA-BUMP
.....
!!

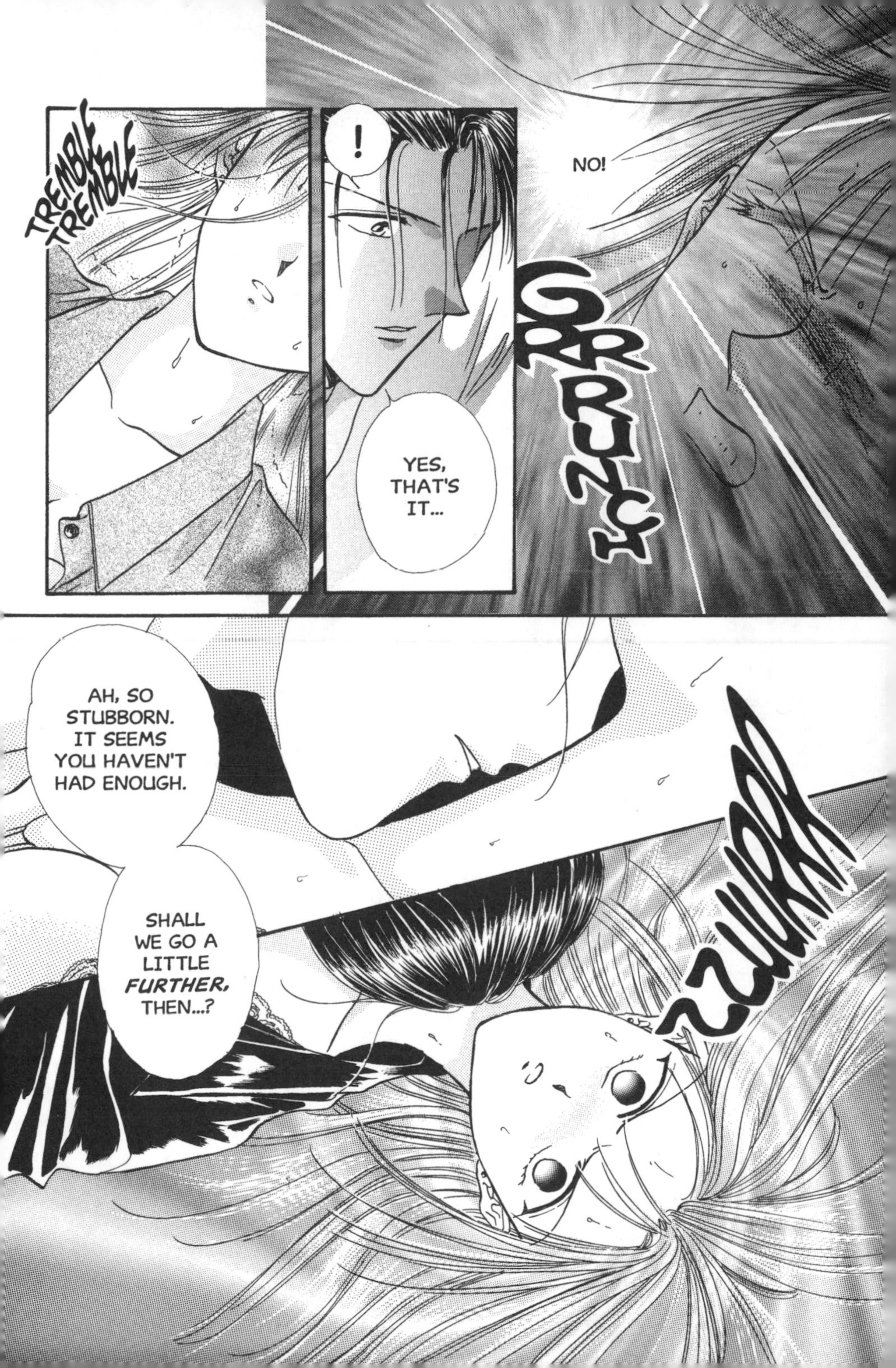
NO!
GRRUNCH!
!
YES, THAT'S IT...
TREMBLE TREMBLE
AH, SO STUBBORN. IT SEEMS YOU HAVEN'T HAD ENOUGH.
SHALL WE GO A LITTLE *FURTHER,* THEN...?
ZWRRR

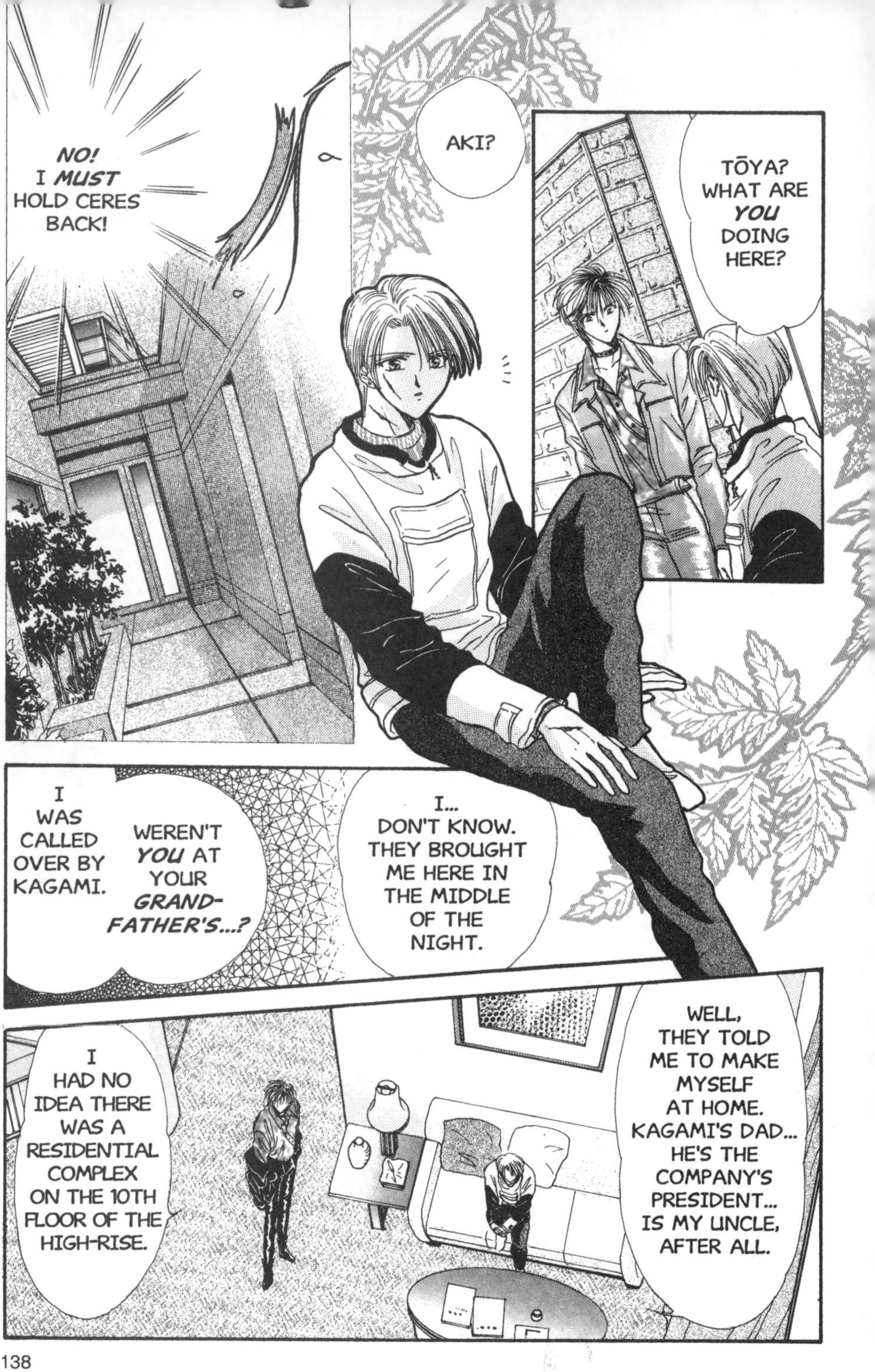
NO! I MUST HOLD CERES BACK!
AKI?
TŌYA? WHAT ARE YOU DOING HERE?
I WAS CALLED OVER BY KAGAMI.
WEREN'T YOU AT YOUR GRAND-FATHER'S...?
I... DON'T KNOW. THEY BROUGHT ME HERE IN THE MIDDLE OF THE NIGHT.
I HAD NO IDEA THERE WAS A RESIDENTIAL COMPLEX ON THE 10TH FLOOR OF THE HIGH-RISE.
WELL, THEY TOLD ME TO MAKE MYSELF AT HOME. KAGAMI'S DAD... HE'S THE COMPANY'S PRESIDENT... IS MY UNCLE, AFTER ALL.

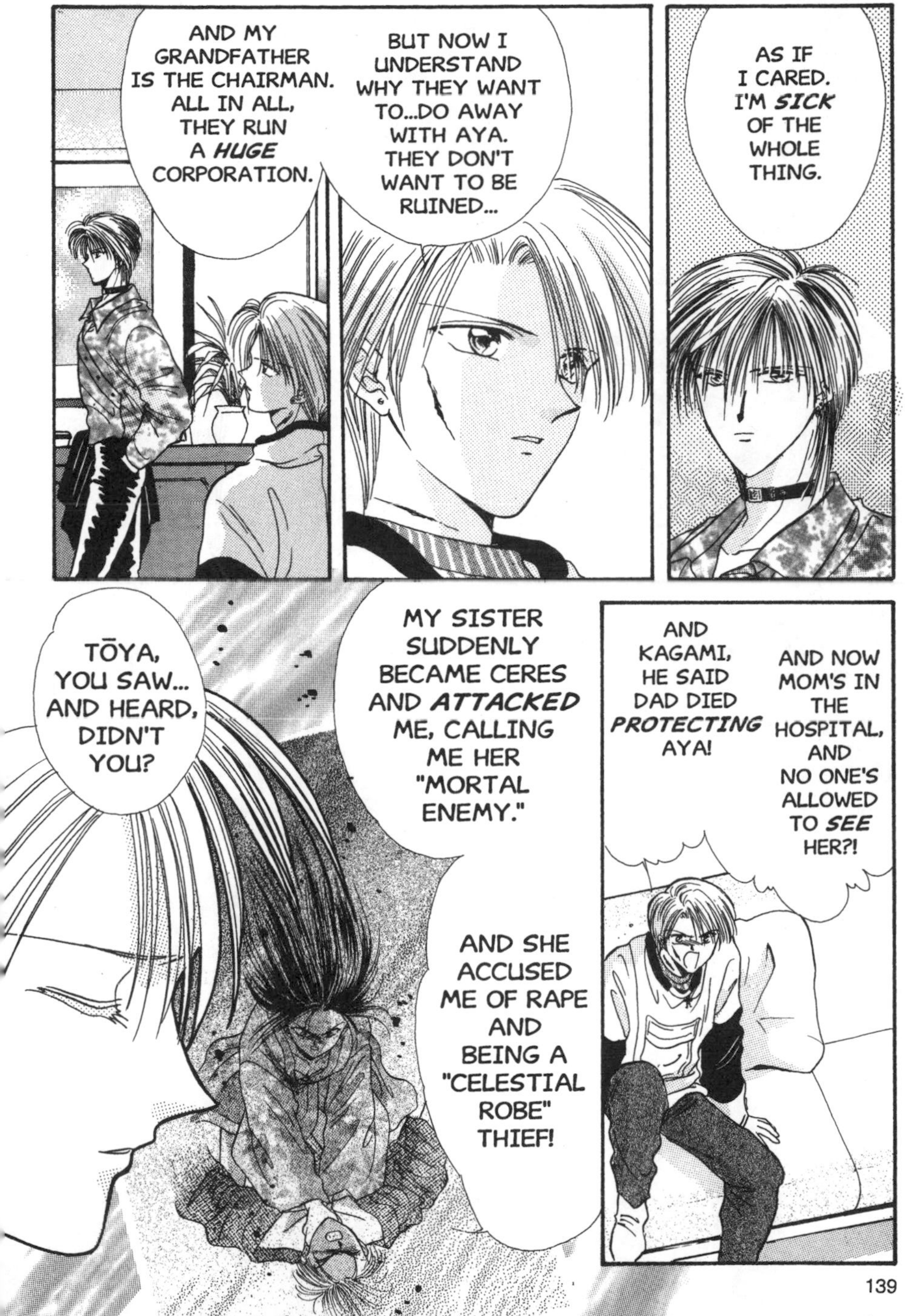
AND MY GRANDFATHER IS THE CHAIRMAN. ALL IN ALL, THEY RUN A *HUGE* CORPORATION.
BUT NOW I UNDERSTAND WHY THEY WANT TO...DO AWAY WITH AYA. THEY DON'T WANT TO BE RUINED...
AS IF I CARED. I'M *SICK* OF THE WHOLE THING.
TŌYA, YOU SAW... AND HEARD, DIDN'T YOU?
MY SISTER SUDDENLY BECAME CERES AND *ATTACKED* ME, CALLING ME HER "MORTAL ENEMY."
AND SHE ACCUSED ME OF RAPE AND BEING A "CELESTIAL ROBE" THIEF!
AND KAGAMI, HE SAID DAD DIED *PROTECTING* AYA!
AND NOW MOM'S IN THE HOSPITAL, AND NO ONE'S ALLOWED TO *SEE* HER?!

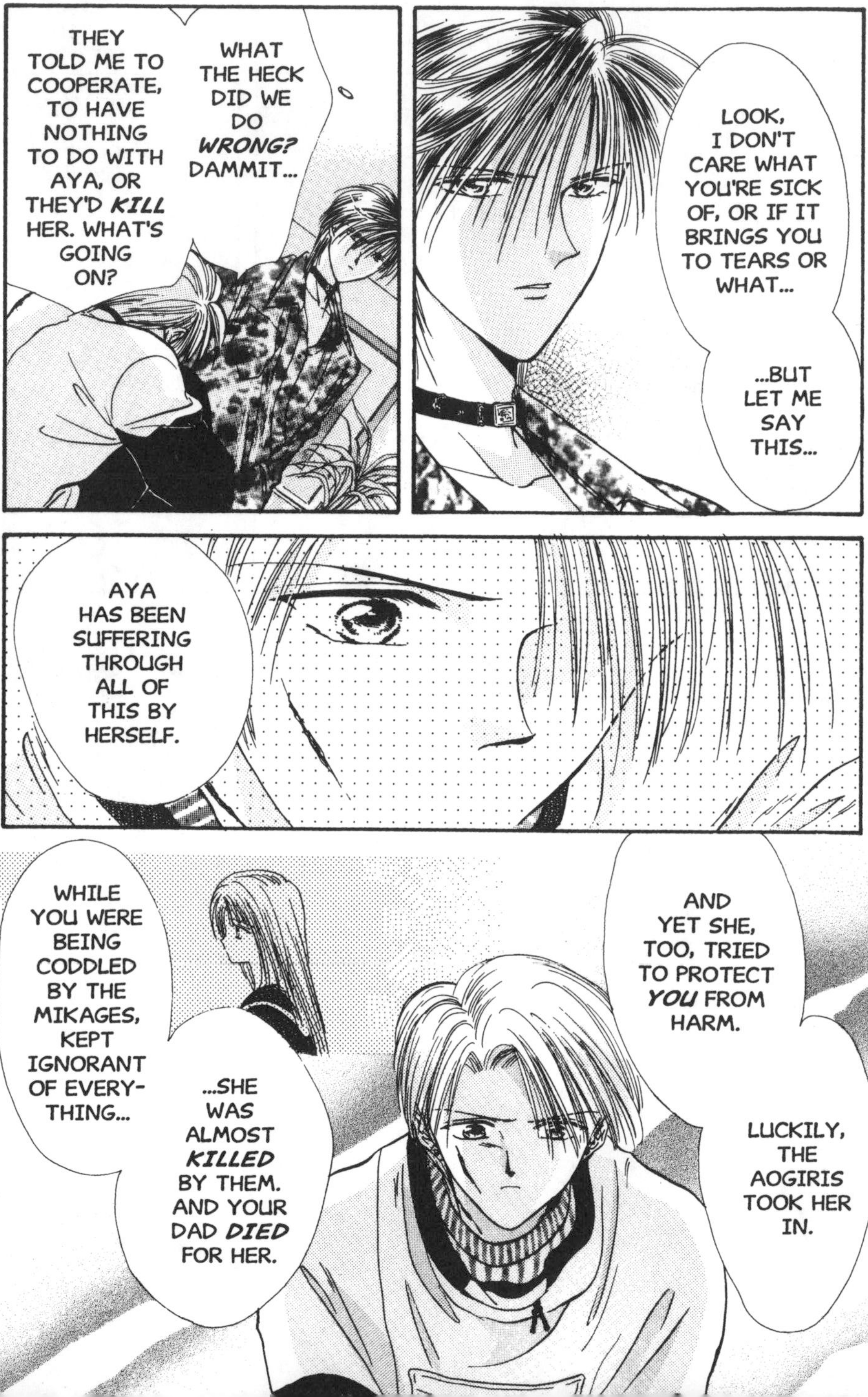
THEY TOLD ME TO COOPERATE, TO HAVE NOTHING TO DO WITH AYA, OR THEY'D *KILL* HER. WHAT'S GOING ON?
WHAT THE HECK DID WE DO *WRONG?* DAMMIT...
LOOK, I DON'T CARE WHAT YOU'RE SICK OF, OR IF IT BRINGS YOU TO TEARS OR WHAT...
...BUT LET ME SAY THIS...
AYA HAS BEEN SUFFERING THROUGH ALL OF THIS BY HERSELF.
WHILE YOU WERE BEING CODDLED BY THE MIKAGES, KEPT IGNORANT OF EVERY-THING...
...SHE WAS ALMOST *KILLED* BY THEM. AND YOUR DAD *DIED* FOR HER.
AND YET SHE, TOO, TRIED TO PROTECT *YOU* FROM HARM.
LUCKILY, THE AOGIRIS TOOK HER IN.

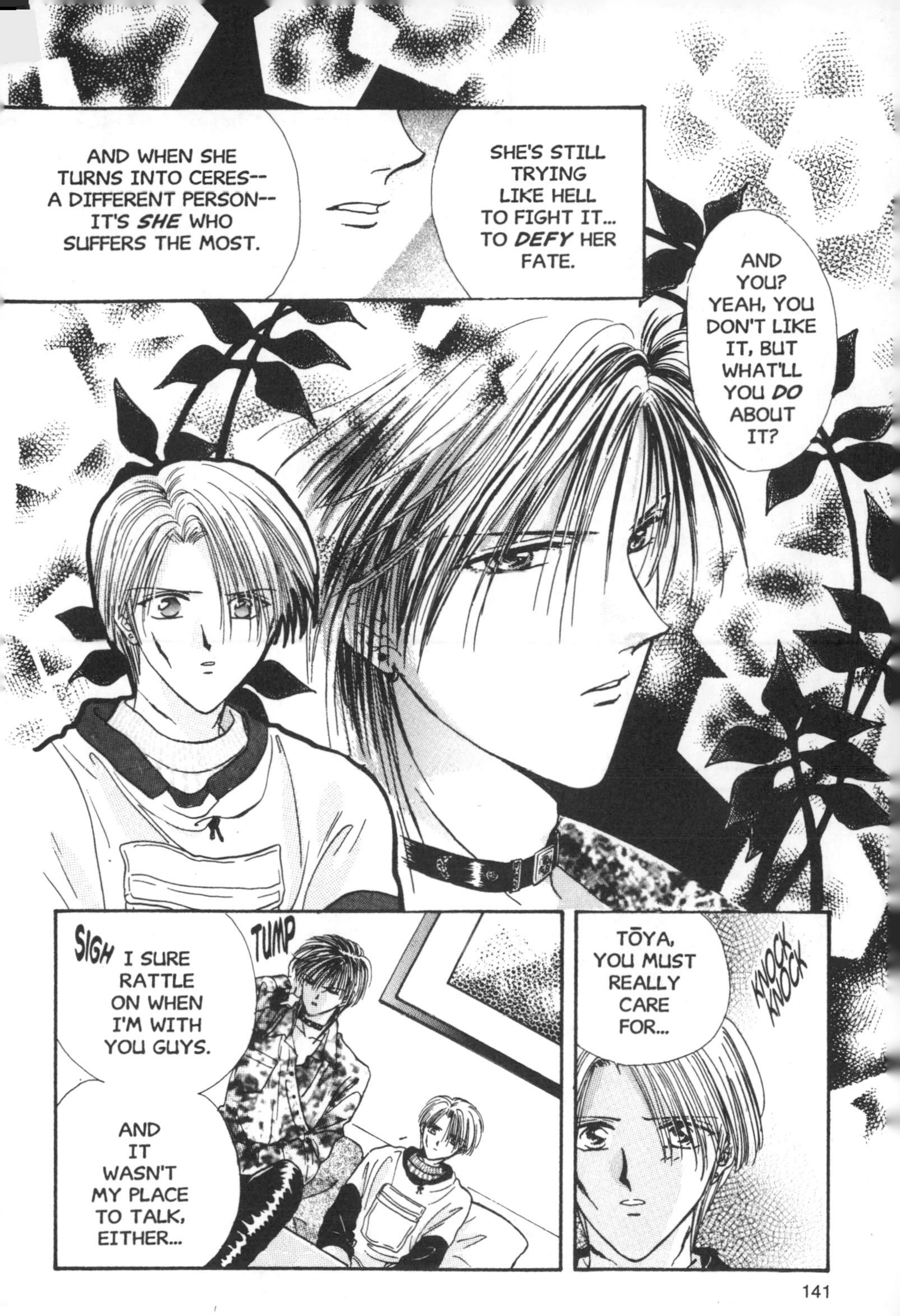
AND WHEN SHE TURNS INTO CERES-- A DIFFERENT PERSON-- IT'S *SHE* WHO SUFFERS THE MOST.
SHE'S STILL TRYING LIKE HELL TO FIGHT IT... TO *DEFY* HER FATE.
AND YOU? YEAH, YOU DON'T LIKE IT, BUT WHAT'LL YOU *DO* ABOUT IT?
SIGH
TUMP
I SURE RATTLE ON WHEN I'M WITH YOU GUYS.
AND IT WASN'T MY PLACE TO TALK, EITHER...
TŌYA, YOU MUST REALLY CARE FOR...
KNOCK KNOCK

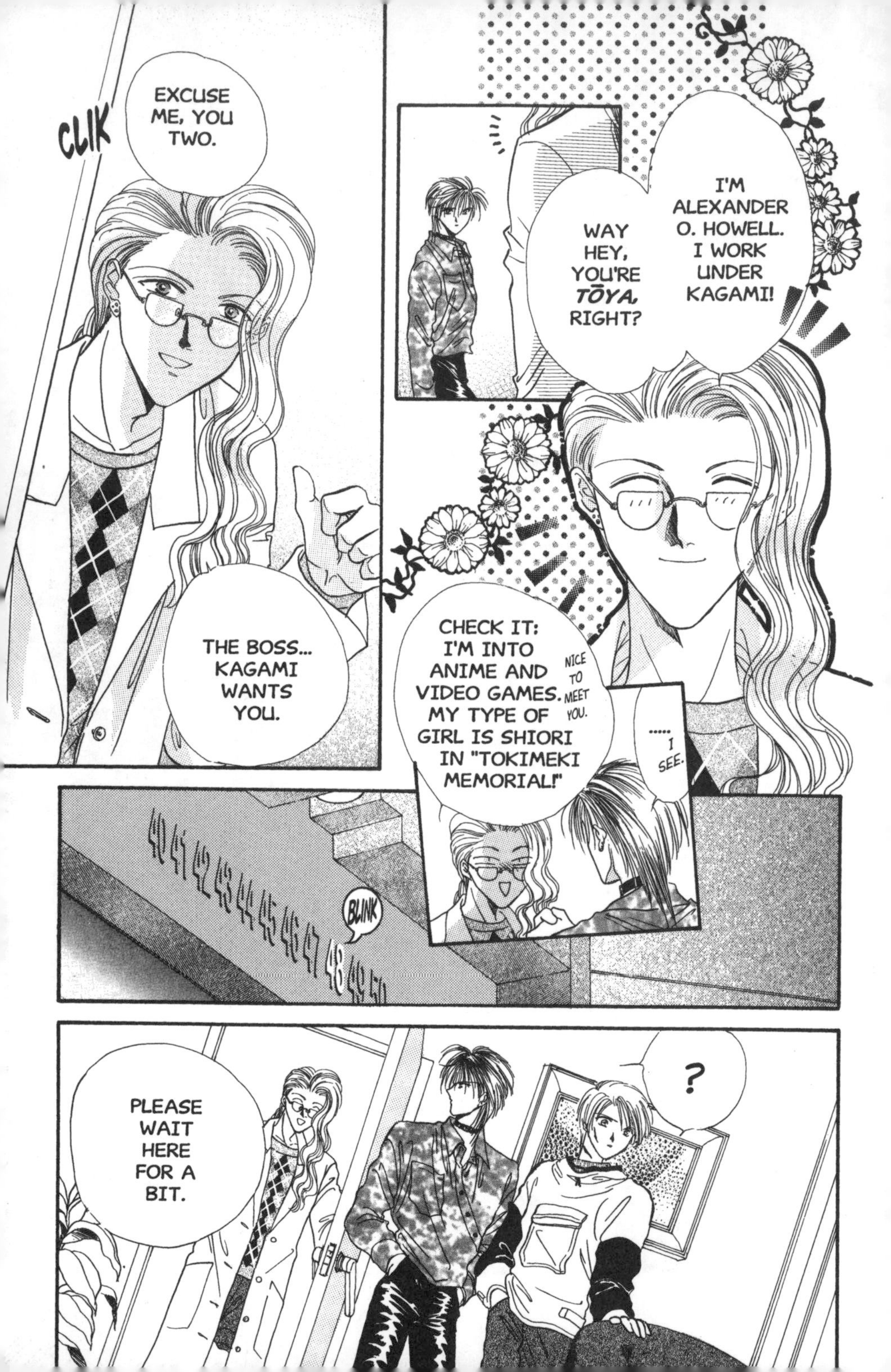
CLIK
EXCUSE ME, YOU TWO.
THE BOSS... KAGAMI WANTS YOU.
WAY HEY, YOU'RE *TŌYA,* RIGHT?
I'M ALEXANDER O. HOWELL. I WORK UNDER KAGAMI!
CHECK IT: I'M INTO ANIME AND VIDEO GAMES. MY TYPE OF GIRL IS SHIORI IN "TOKIMEKI MEMORIAL!"
NICE TO MEET YOU.
...... I SEE.
40 41 42 43 44 45 46 47 48 49 50
BLINK
PLEASE WAIT HERE FOR A BIT.
?

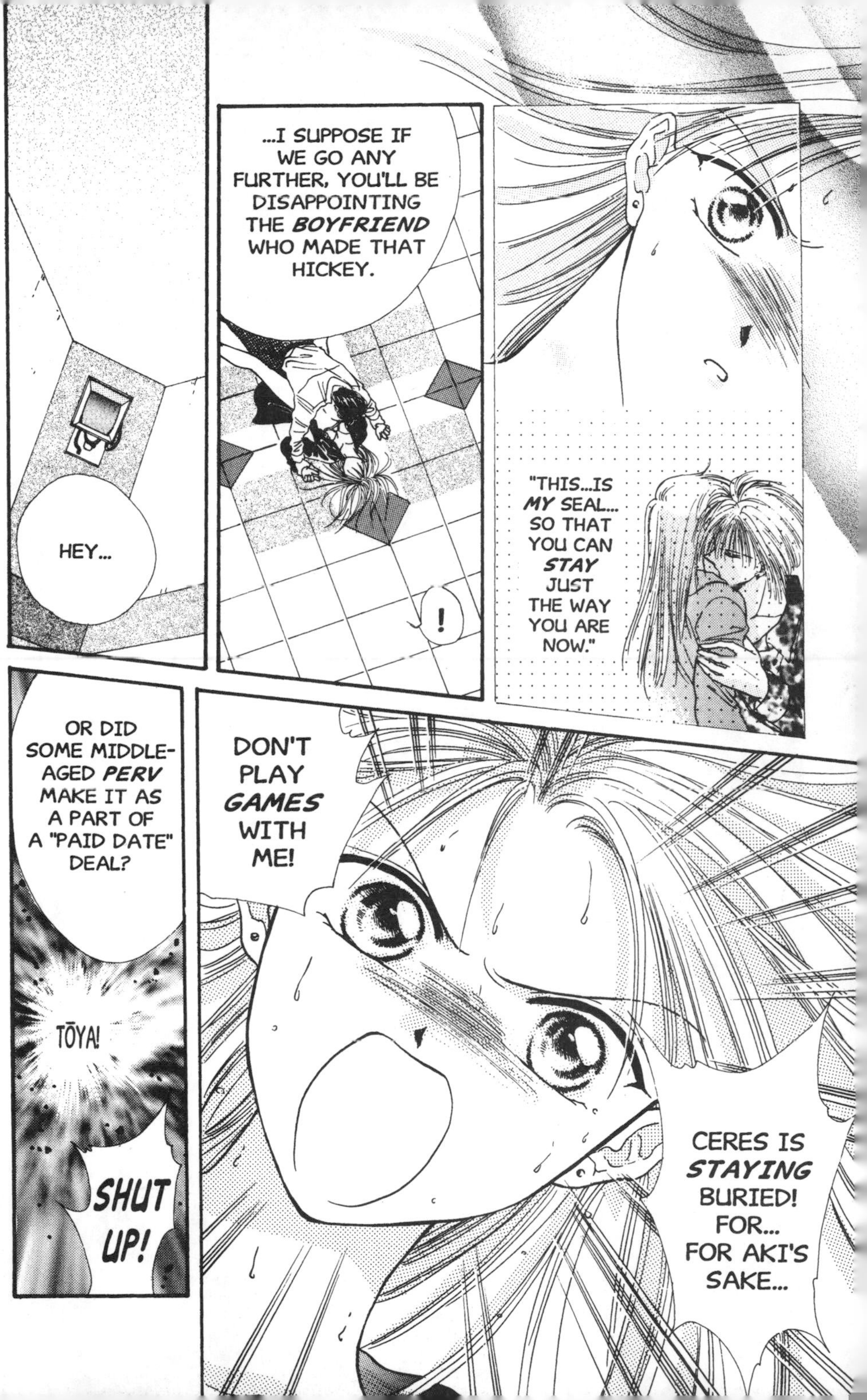
"THIS...IS MY SEAL... SO THAT YOU CAN STAY JUST THE WAY YOU ARE NOW."
...I SUPPOSE IF WE GO ANY FURTHER, YOU'LL BE DISAPPOINTING THE BOYFRIEND WHO MADE THAT HICKEY.
!
HEY...
DON'T PLAY GAMES WITH ME!
CERES IS STAYING BURIED! FOR... FOR AKI'S SAKE...
OR DID SOME MIDDLE-AGED PERV MAKE IT AS A PART OF A "PAID DATE" DEAL?
TŌYA!
SHUT UP!

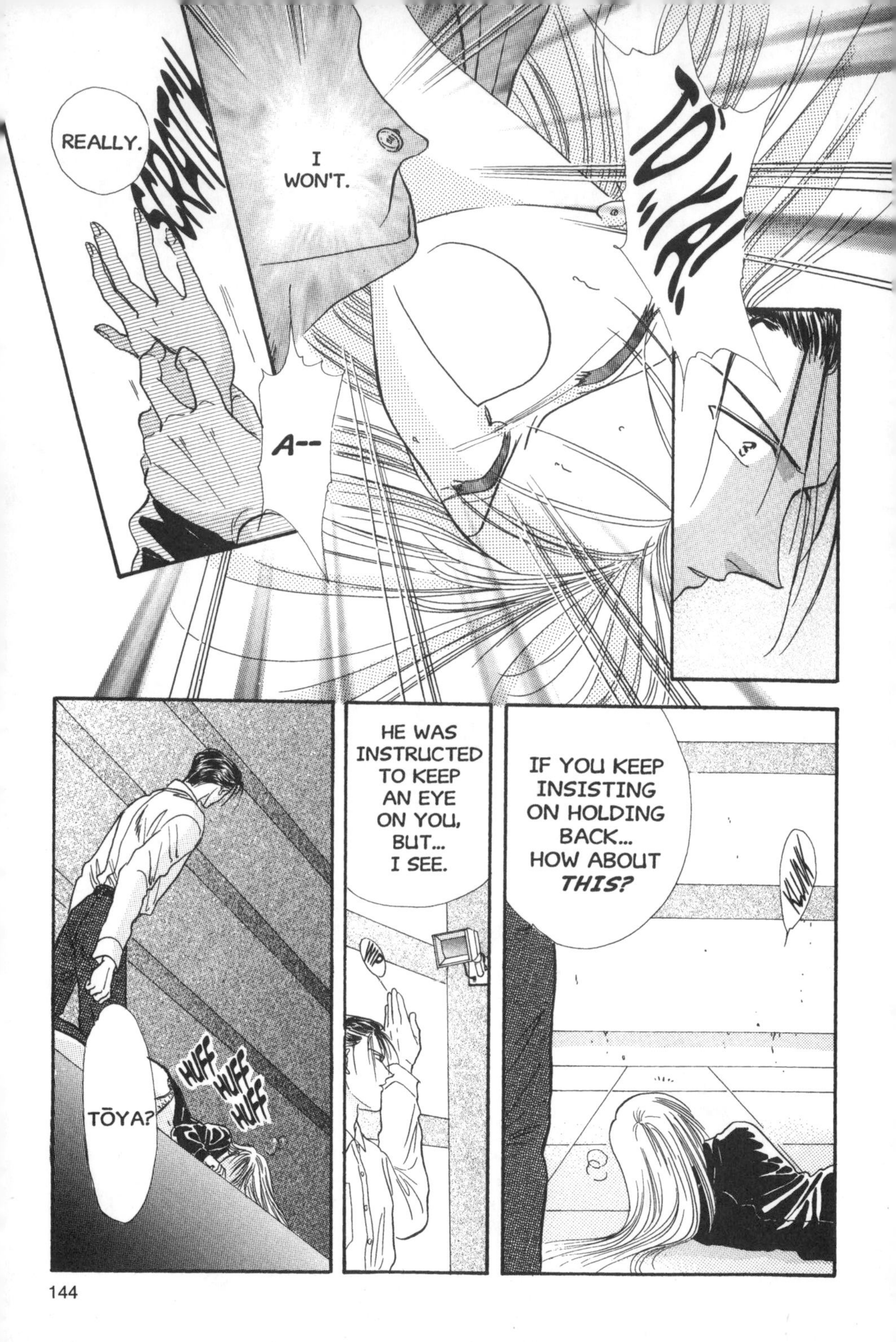
TŌYA!!
I WON'T.
REALLY.
SCRATCH
A--
IF YOU KEEP INSISTING ON HOLDING BACK... HOW ABOUT *THIS?*
KLINK
HE WAS INSTRUCTED TO KEEP AN EYE ON YOU, BUT... I SEE.
WIP
HUFF HUFF HUFF
TŌYA?

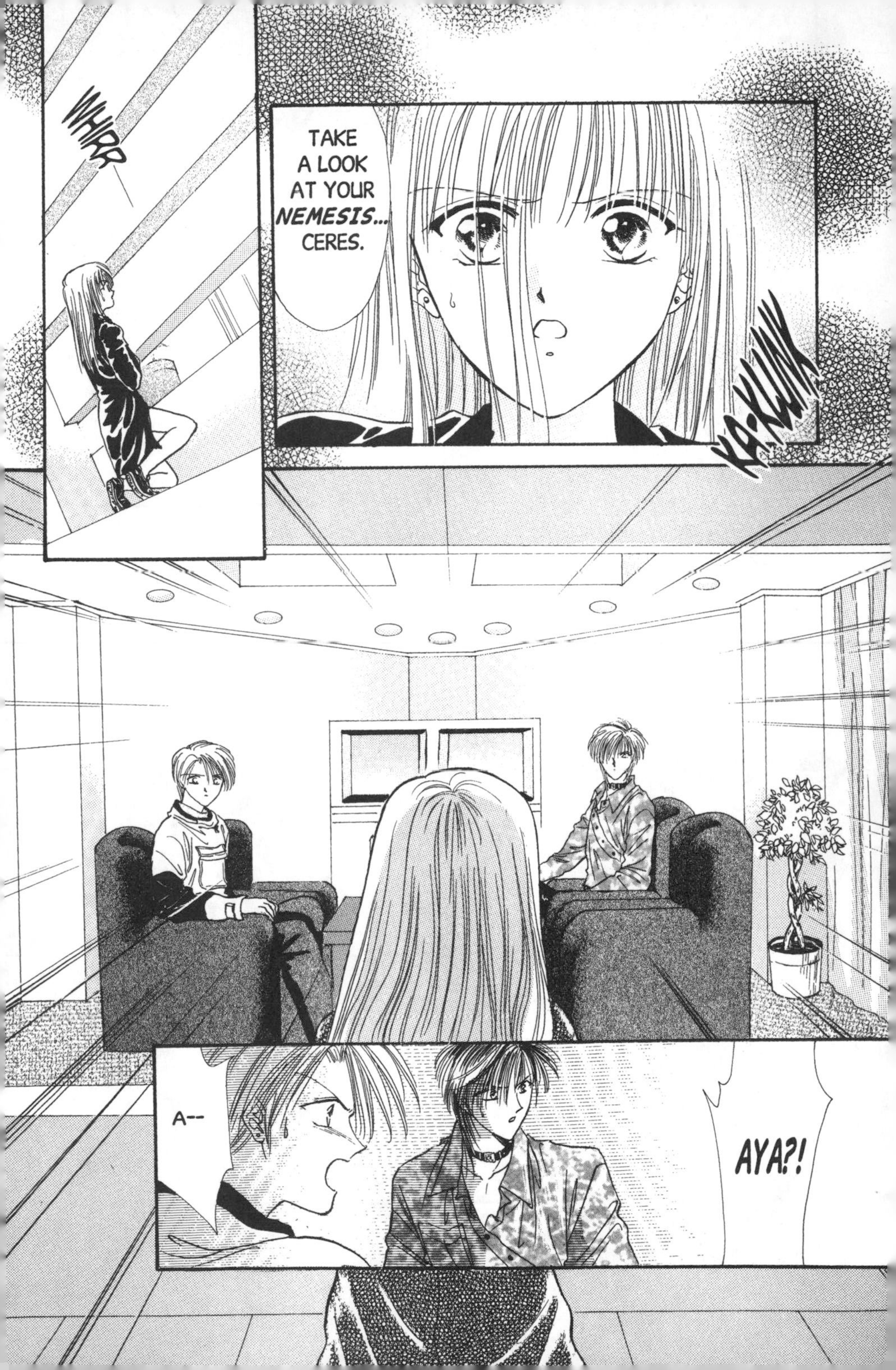
TAKE A LOOK AT YOUR NEMESIS... CERES.
KA-KUNK
WHIRR
AYA?!
A--

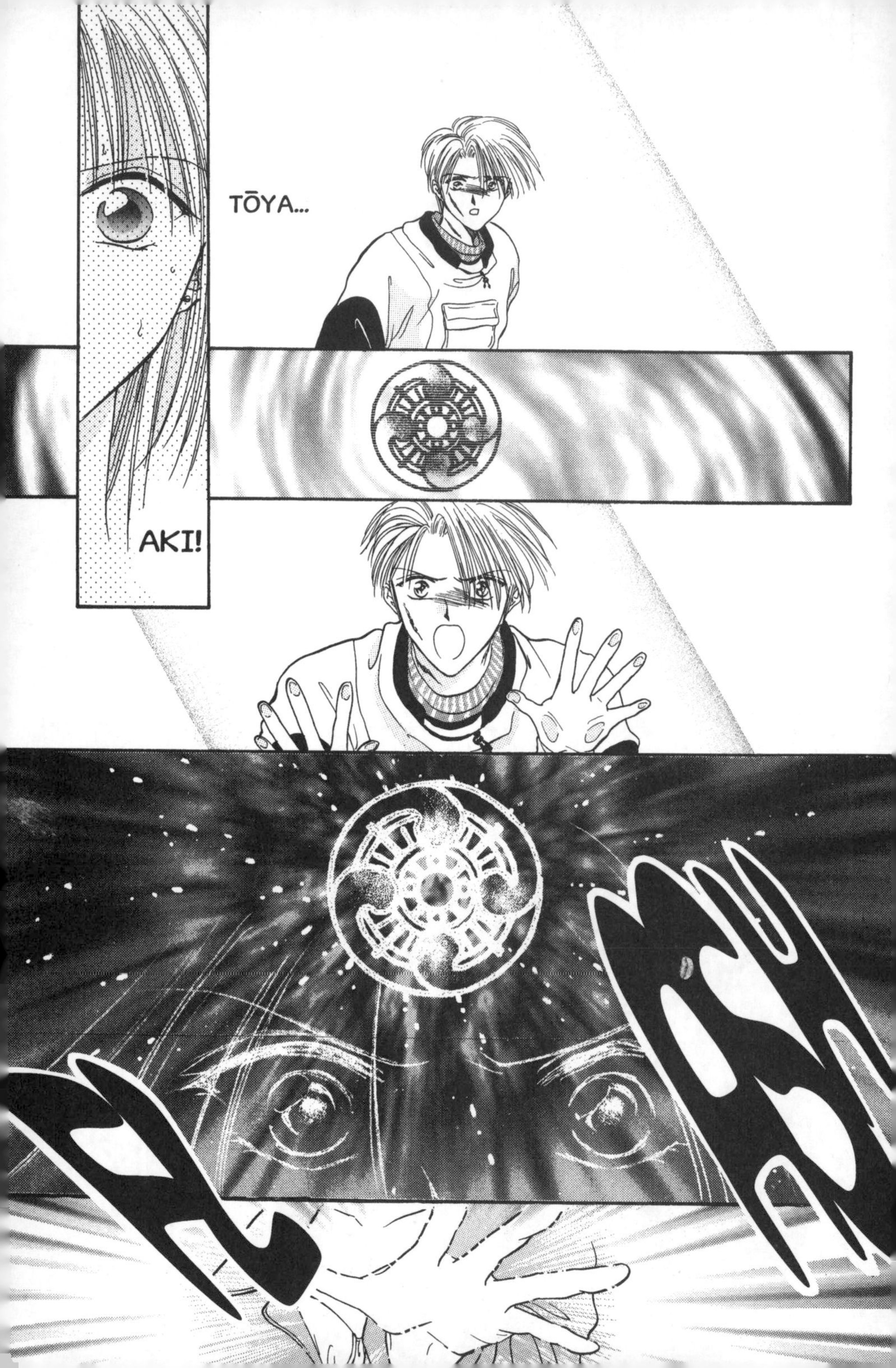
TŌYA...
AKI!

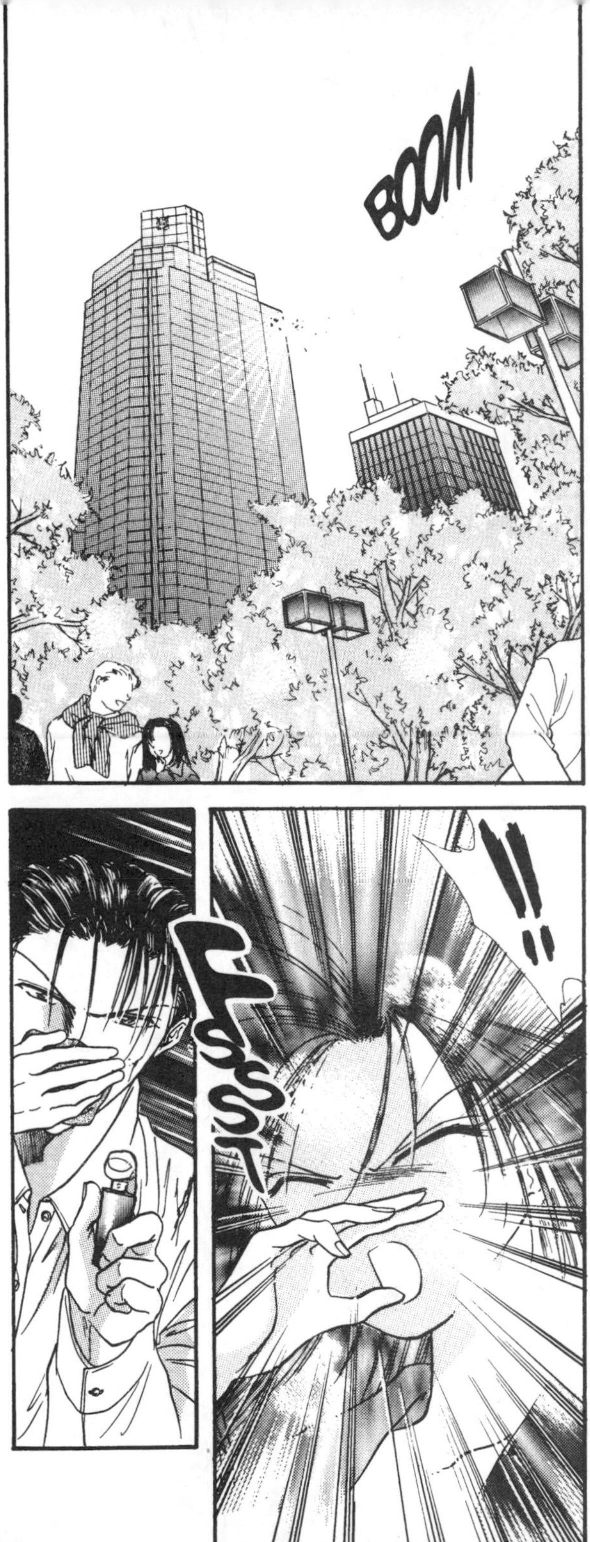
BOOM
!!

Ceres: 2

By the way, where I work, my assistants are whispering that Tōya is "a cyborg" or "an android." I guess that's a result of me trying not to make him very "human." I think a lot of people are thinking he's "aloof," but that's not quite right. It's just that he doesn't know how--or if he even has the capacity--to express his emotions. First of all, he doesn't know anything about himself, so it's not for other people to tell if he's kind, or cold... It's probably scary to not have any memories, and it would cause insecurity. So when Aya comes on to him so aggressively, does he really even know how to deal with it...? His memory will most likely serve as the crux of this story. (...Probably... um...) My assistants are saying, "I bet he's like a totally irrelevant delivery guy or something!" (Of course not!) Tōya is a favorite of Assistant M., but she likes Kagami the best. She's on the Mikages' side. To her, "Yūhi's like, not even!" She's not interested in younger men. (But she was a fan of Tasuki in FY...) Assistant H. says, "Tōya and Yūhi are both good, but I feel sorry for Yūhi because it looks like he doesn't have a chance" (of ending up with Aya). K. is all into "Aki!" I don't know about S., but she says, "Yūhi is cute, kind of like an Akita." My editor says, "Alec is good," but I wonder what he thinks is good about him. And why didn't he choose a girl?

Well anyway... (I get distracted by X-Files on TV) ... (still distracted)... This genre is so interesting. What else--oh, Tokumei Research 200x ("Hot Topic Research 200X") is good too! And Takeshi no Banbutsu Soseiki ("Takeshi's Book of All Things Genesis")... I don't watch much typical family drama these days... But Odoru Daisōsasen ("The Dancing Line of Criminal Investigation") is good too. Yeah. Oh!

I also watch Stalkers: Nigekirenu Ai ("Stalkers: Inescapable Love")! ...It's scary though... The acting is so good.

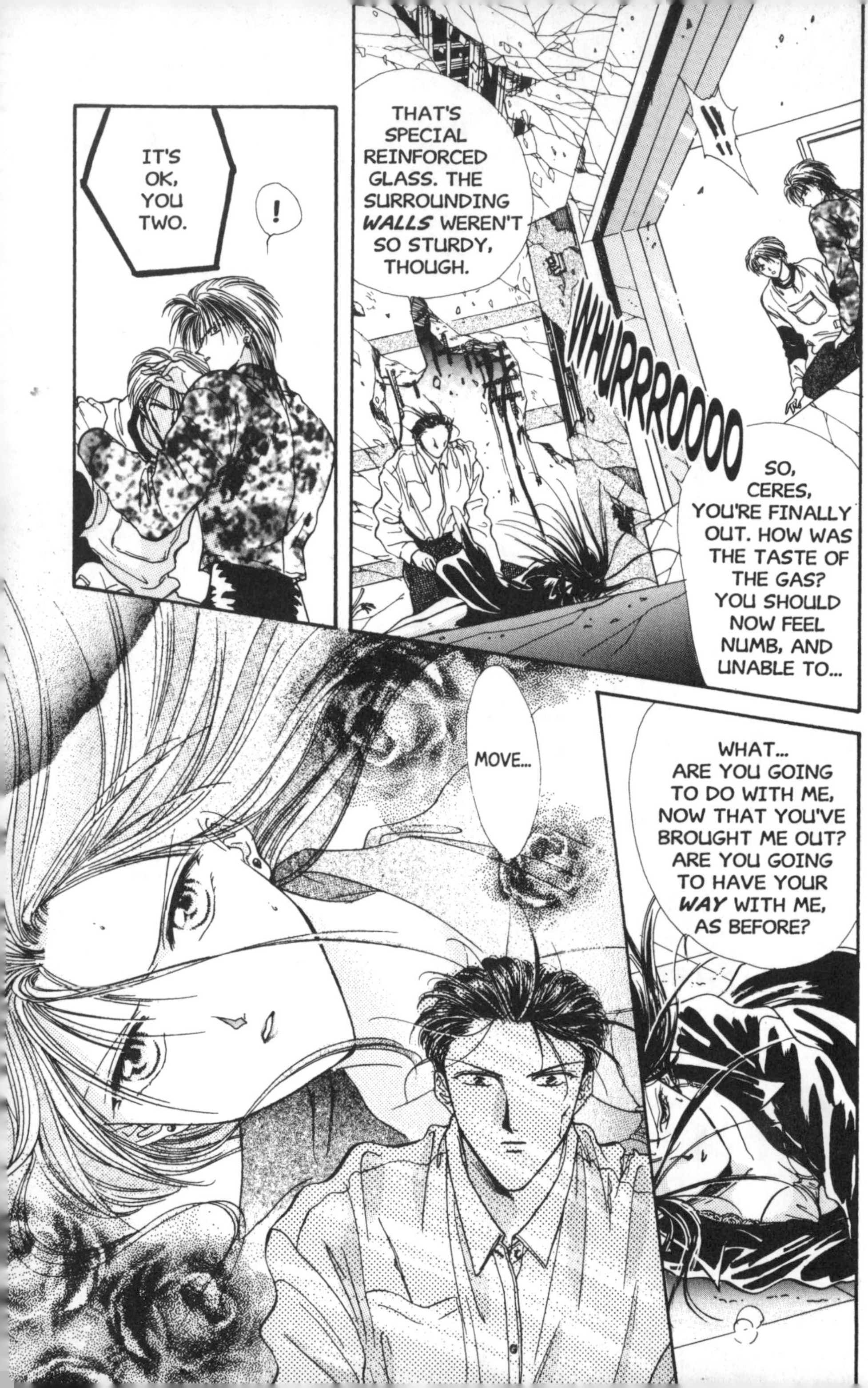
!!
THAT'S SPECIAL REINFORCED GLASS. THE SURROUNDING WALLS WEREN'T SO STURDY, THOUGH.
WHURRROOOO
SO, CERES, YOU'RE FINALLY OUT. HOW WAS THE TASTE OF THE GAS? YOU SHOULD NOW FEEL NUMB, AND UNABLE TO...
IT'S OK, YOU TWO.
!
MOVE...
WHAT... ARE YOU GOING TO DO WITH ME, NOW THAT YOU'VE BROUGHT ME OUT? ARE YOU GOING TO HAVE YOUR WAY WITH ME, AS BEFORE?

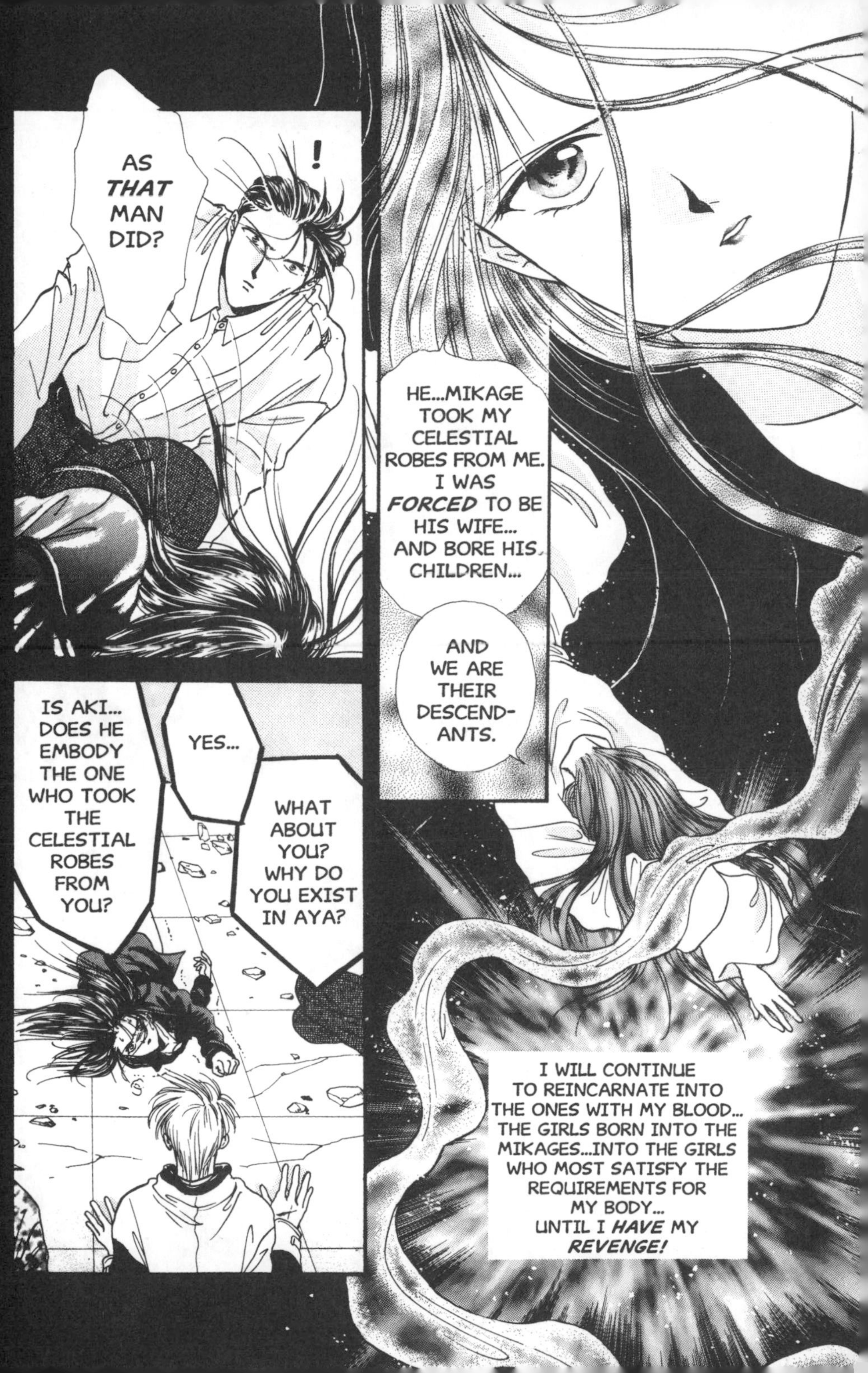
AS *THAT* MAN DID?
!
HE...MIKAGE TOOK MY CELESTIAL ROBES FROM ME. I WAS *FORCED* TO BE HIS WIFE... AND BORE HIS CHILDREN...
AND WE ARE THEIR DESCEND-ANTS.
IS AKI... DOES HE EMBODY THE ONE WHO TOOK THE CELESTIAL ROBES FROM YOU?
YES...
WHAT ABOUT YOU? WHY DO YOU EXIST IN AYA?
I WILL CONTINUE TO REINCARNATE INTO THE ONES WITH MY BLOOD... THE GIRLS BORN INTO THE MIKAGES...INTO THE GIRLS WHO MOST SATISFY THE REQUIREMENTS FOR MY BODY... UNTIL I *HAVE* MY ***REVENGE!***

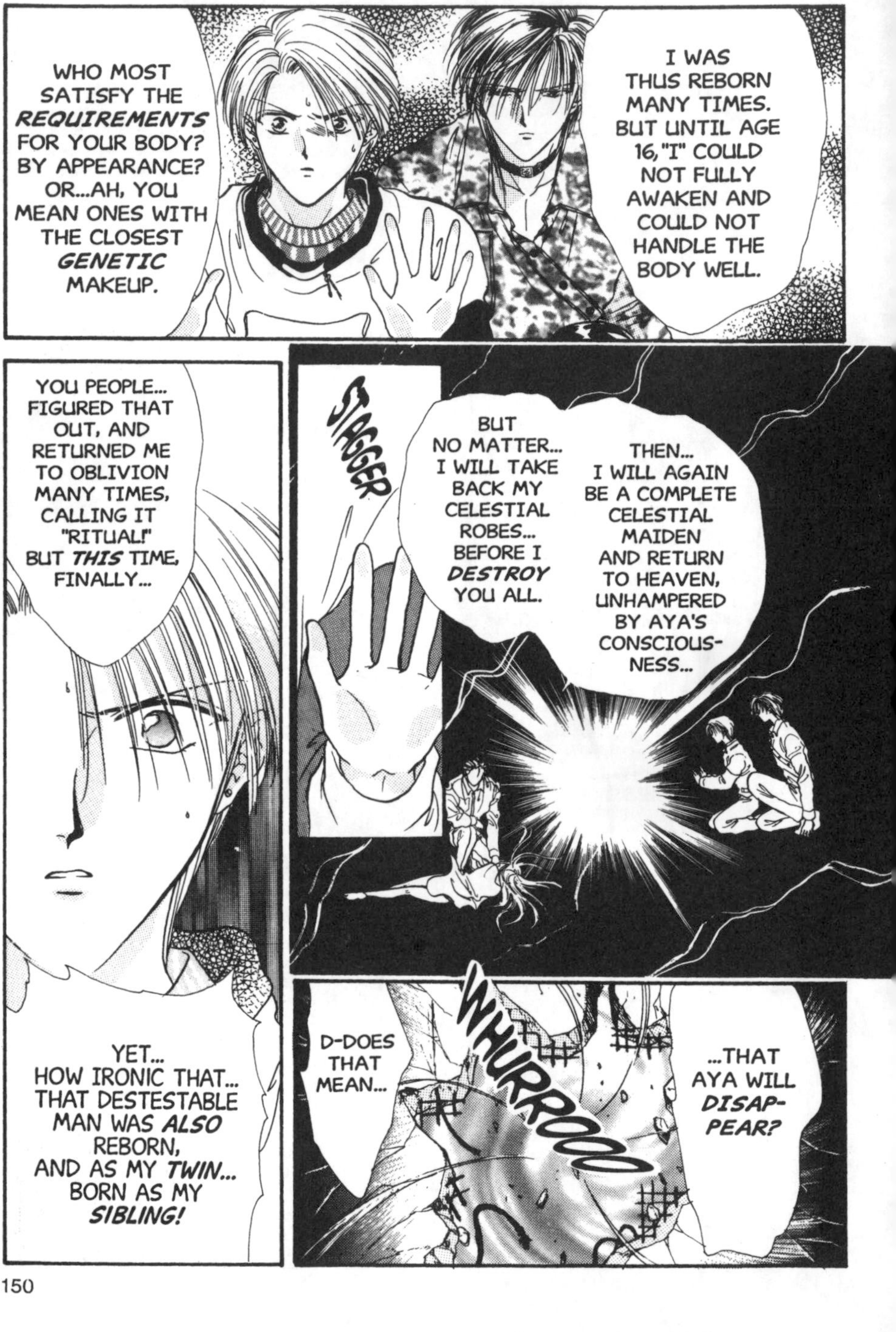
I WAS THUS REBORN MANY TIMES. BUT UNTIL AGE 16,"I" COULD NOT FULLY AWAKEN AND COULD NOT HANDLE THE BODY WELL.
WHO MOST SATISFY THE *REQUIREMENTS* FOR YOUR BODY? BY APPEARANCE? OR...AH, YOU MEAN ONES WITH THE CLOSEST *GENETIC* MAKEUP.
THEN... I WILL AGAIN BE A COMPLETE CELESTIAL MAIDEN AND RETURN TO HEAVEN, UNHAMPERED BY AYA'S CONSCIOUS-NESS...
BUT NO MATTER... I WILL TAKE BACK MY CELESTIAL ROBES... BEFORE I *DESTROY* YOU ALL.
STAGGER
WHURROOO
D-DOES THAT MEAN...
...THAT AYA WILL *DISAP-PEAR?*
YOU PEOPLE... FIGURED THAT OUT, AND RETURNED ME TO OBLIVION MANY TIMES, CALLING IT "RITUAL!" BUT *THIS* TIME, FINALLY...
YET... HOW IRONIC THAT... THAT DESTESTABLE MAN WAS *ALSO* REBORN, AND AS MY *TWIN*... BORN AS MY *SIBLING!*

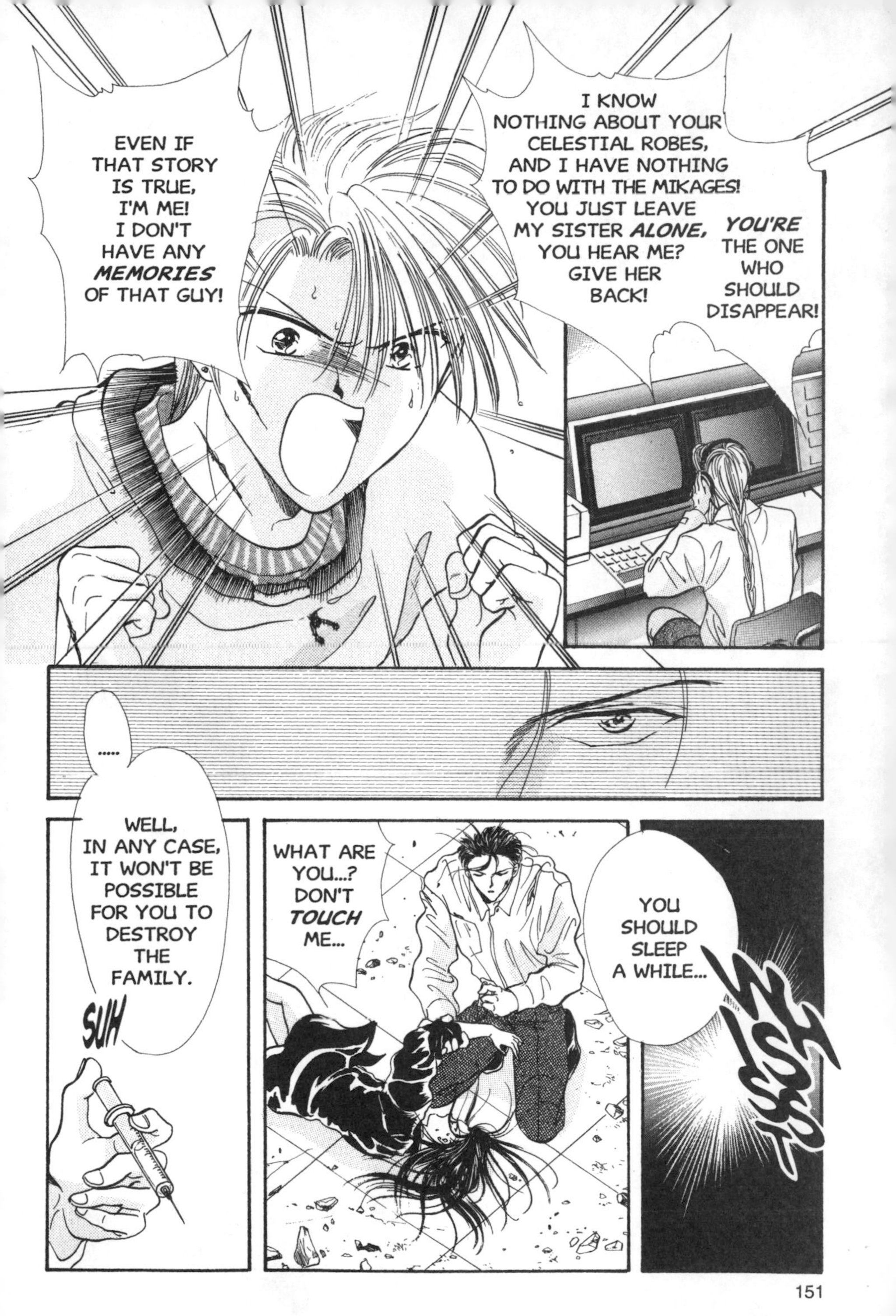
EVEN IF THAT STORY IS TRUE, I'M ME! I DON'T HAVE ANY *MEMORIES* OF THAT GUY!
I KNOW NOTHING ABOUT YOUR CELESTIAL ROBES, AND I HAVE NOTHING TO DO WITH THE MIKAGES! YOU JUST LEAVE MY SISTER *ALONE,* YOU HEAR ME? GIVE HER BACK!
YOU'RE THE ONE WHO SHOULD DISAPPEAR!
.....
WELL, IN ANY CASE, IT WON'T BE POSSIBLE FOR YOU TO DESTROY THE FAMILY.
SUH
WHAT ARE YOU...? DON'T *TOUCH* ME...
YOU SHOULD SLEEP A WHILE...

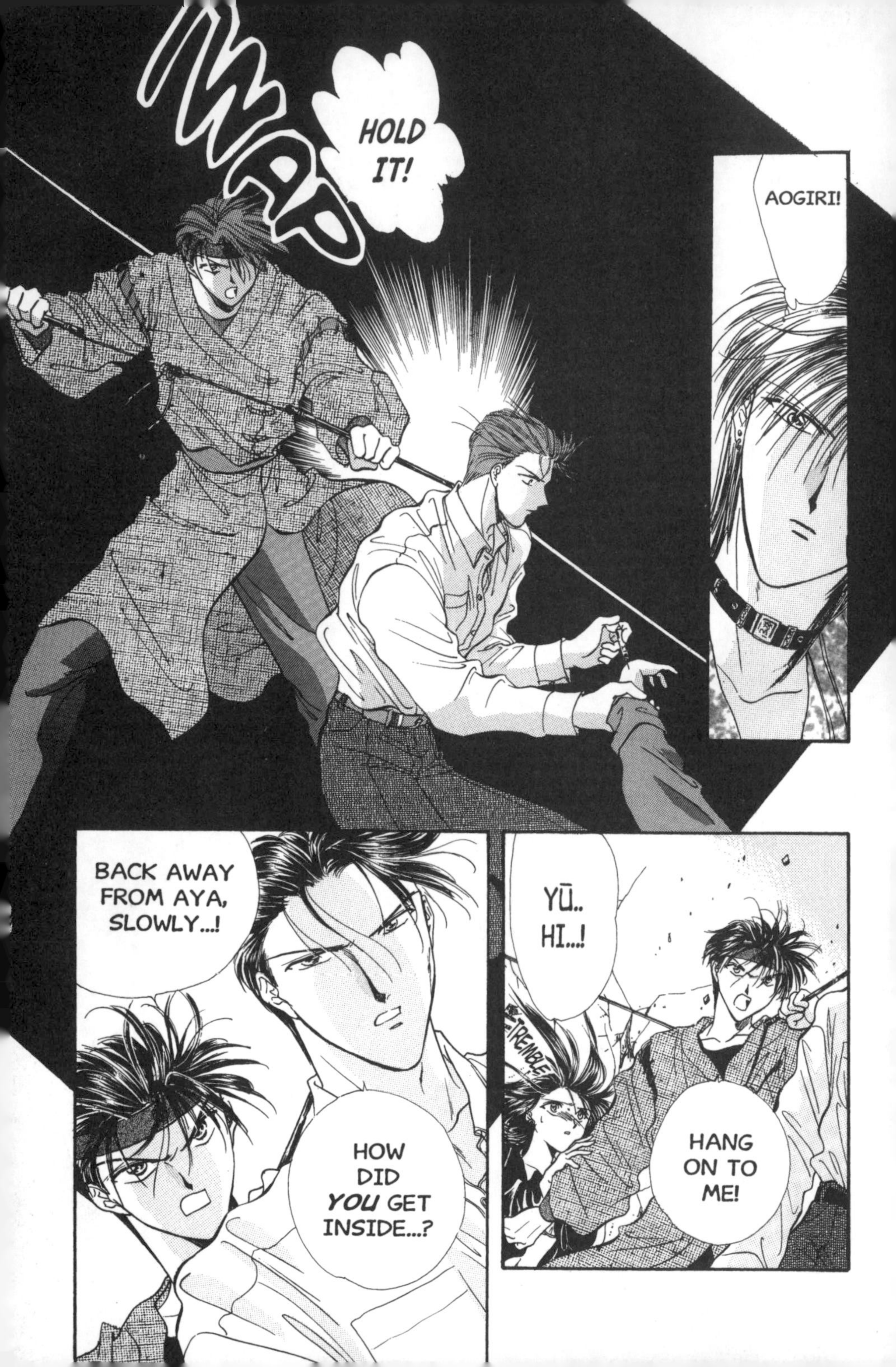
WAP
HOLD IT!
AOGIRI!
YŪ.. HI...!
TREMBLE
HANG ON TO ME!
BACK AWAY FROM AYA, SLOWLY...!
HOW DID *YOU* GET INSIDE...?

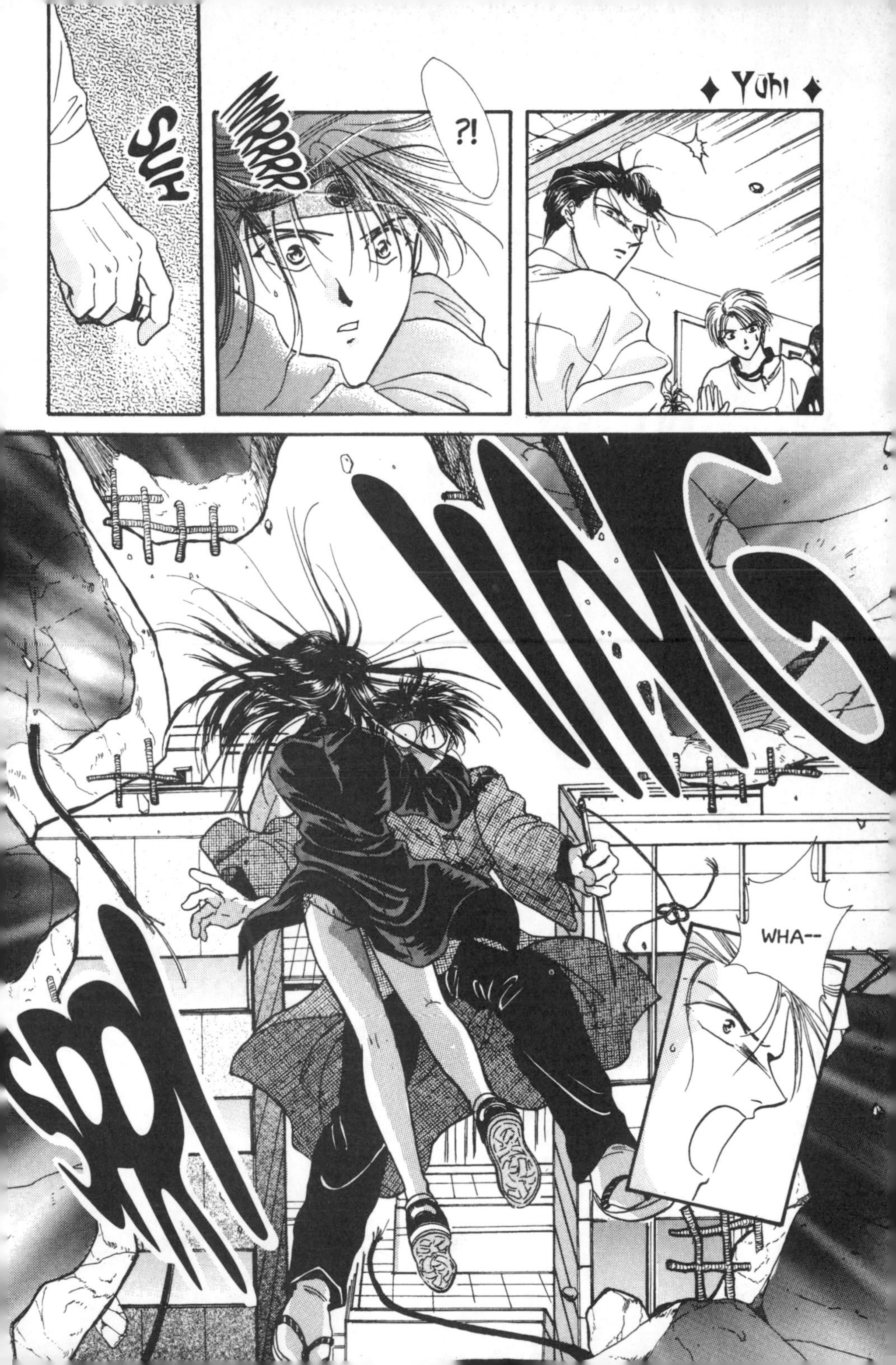
?!
MMRRRR
SUH
WHA--

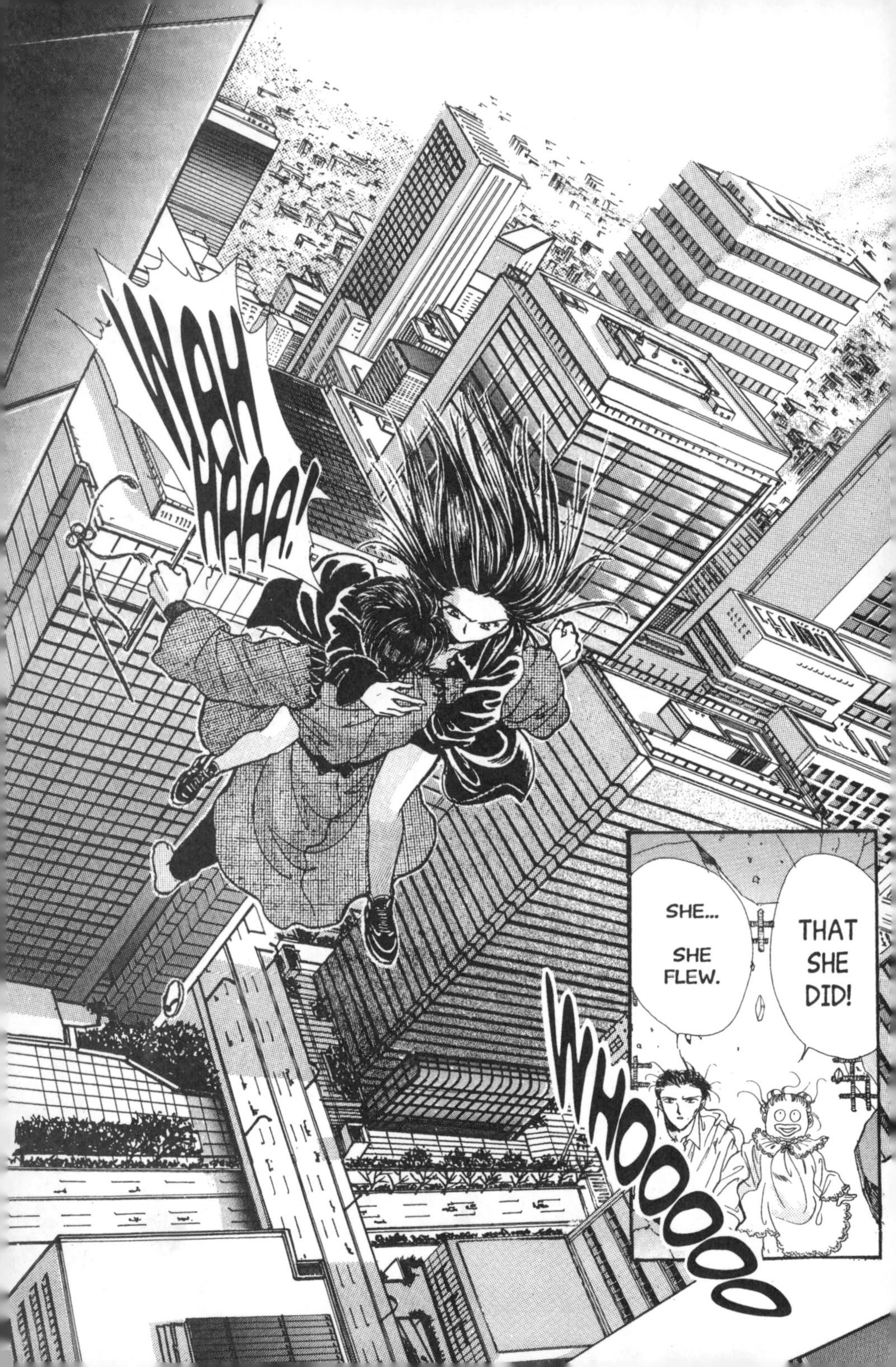
WAH HAAA!
THAT SHE DID!
SHE... SHE FLEW.
WHOOOOOO

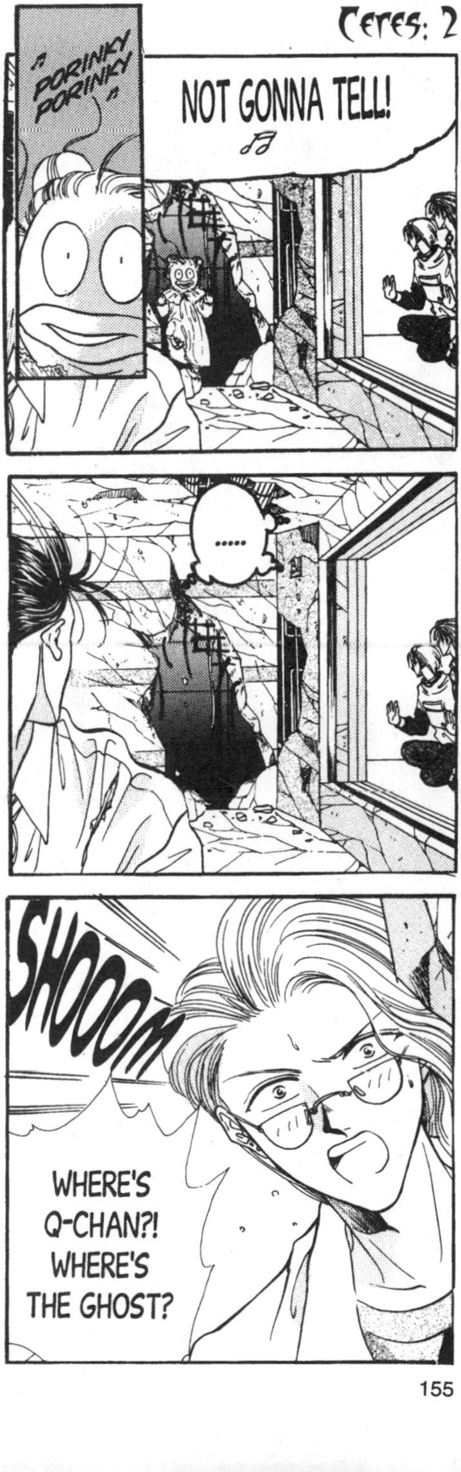
PORINKY PORINKY
NOT GONNA TELL!
......
SHOOOM
WHERE'S Q-CHAN?! WHERE'S THE GHOST?

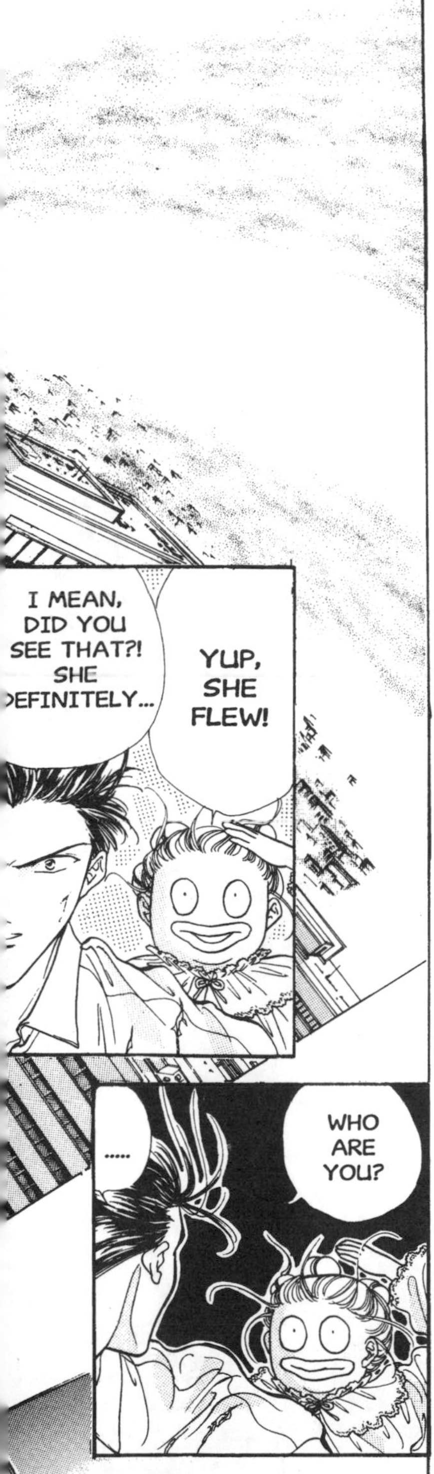
I MEAN, DID YOU SEE THAT?! SHE DEFINITELY...
YUP, SHE FLEW!
WHO ARE YOU?
......

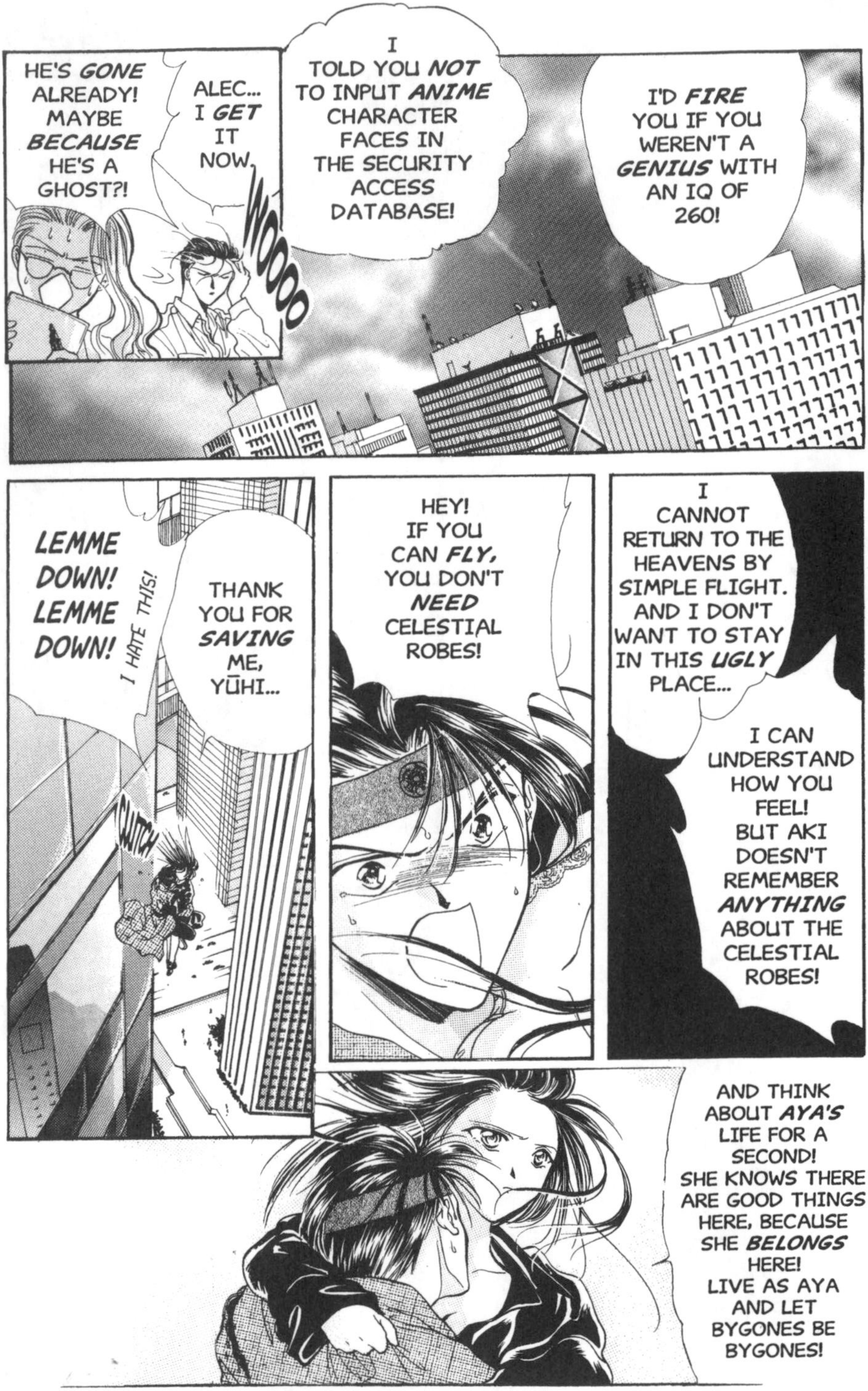
HE'S GONE ALREADY! MAYBE BECAUSE HE'S A GHOST?!
ALEC... I GET IT NOW.
WOOOO
I TOLD YOU NOT TO INPUT ANIME CHARACTER FACES IN THE SECURITY ACCESS DATABASE!
I'D FIRE YOU IF YOU WEREN'T A GENIUS WITH AN IQ OF 260!
LEMME DOWN! LEMME DOWN!
I HATE THIS!
CLUTCH
THANK YOU FOR SAVING ME, YŪHI...
HEY! IF YOU CAN FLY, YOU DON'T NEED CELESTIAL ROBES!
I CANNOT RETURN TO THE HEAVENS BY SIMPLE FLIGHT. AND I DON'T WANT TO STAY IN THIS UGLY PLACE...
I CAN UNDERSTAND HOW YOU FEEL! BUT AKI DOESN'T REMEMBER ANYTHING ABOUT THE CELESTIAL ROBES!
AND THINK ABOUT AYA'S LIFE FOR A SECOND! SHE KNOWS THERE ARE GOOD THINGS HERE, BECAUSE SHE BELONGS HERE! LIVE AS AYA AND LET BYGONES BE BYGONES!

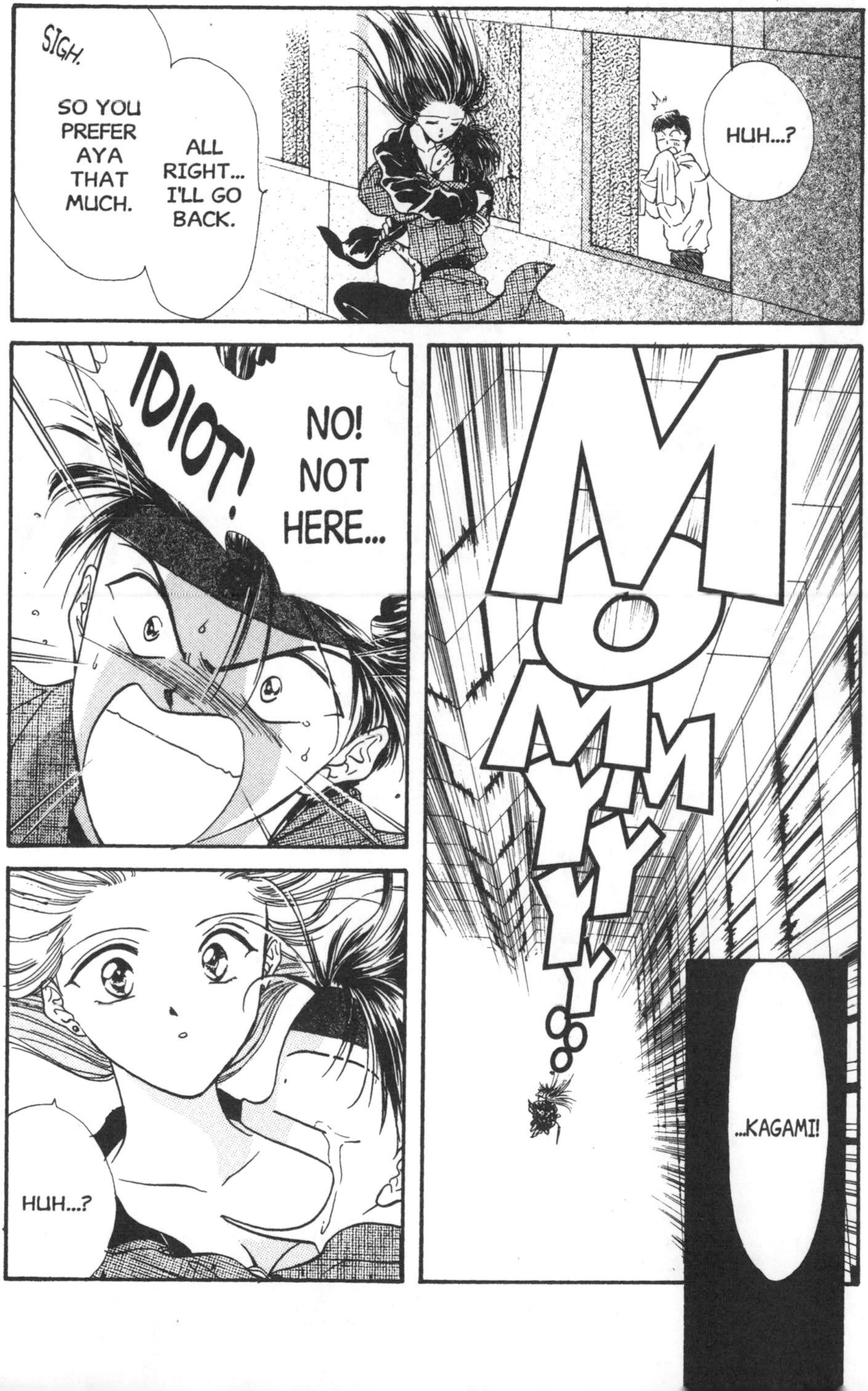
HUH...?
SIGH.
SO YOU PREFER AYA THAT MUCH.
ALL RIGHT... I'LL GO BACK.
MOMMYYYOOO
IDIOT!
NO! NOT HERE...
HUH...?
...KAGAMI!

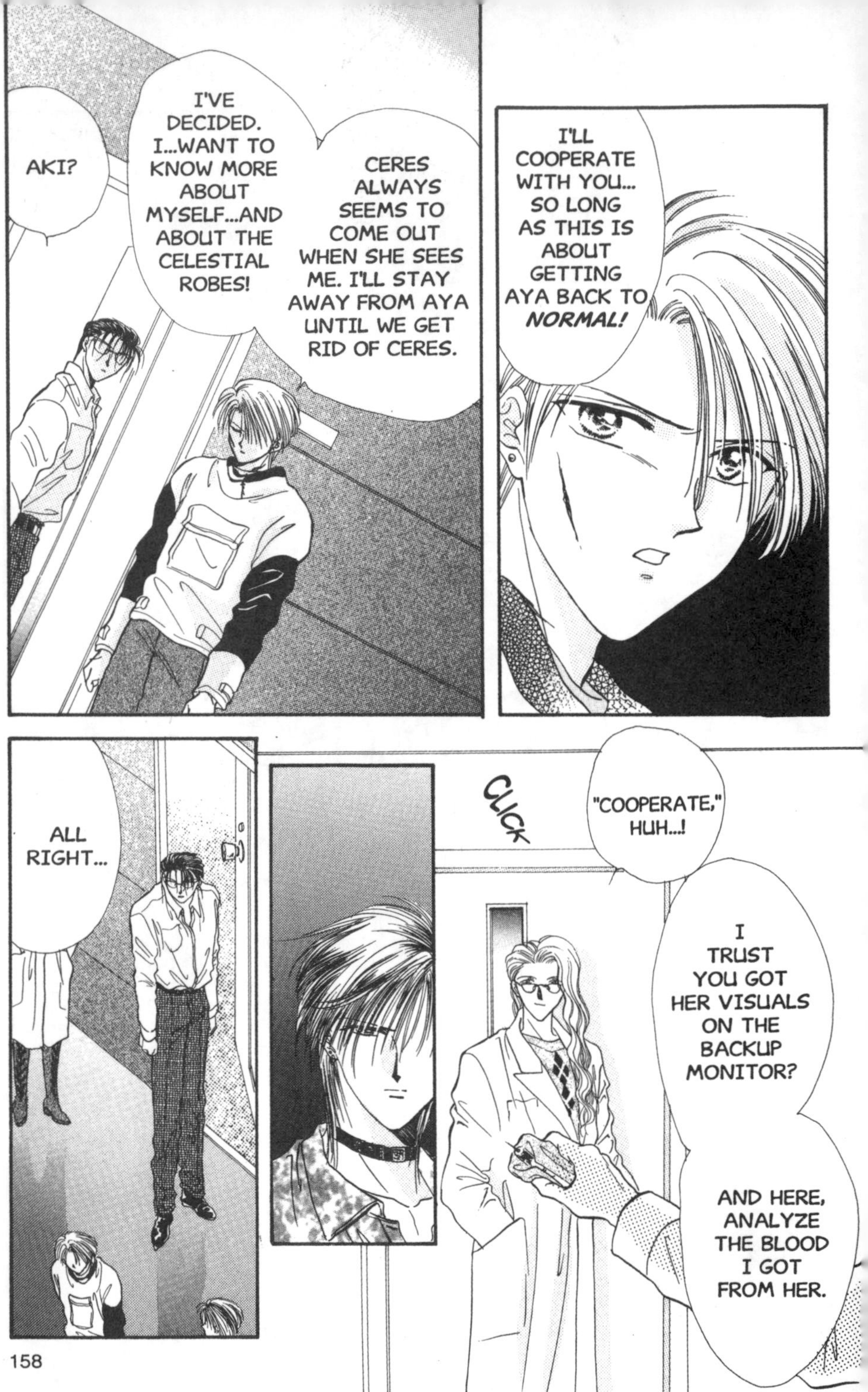
AKI?
I'VE DECIDED. I...WANT TO KNOW MORE ABOUT MYSELF...AND ABOUT THE CELESTIAL ROBES!
CERES ALWAYS SEEMS TO COME OUT WHEN SHE SEES ME. I'LL STAY AWAY FROM AYA UNTIL WE GET RID OF CERES.
I'LL COOPERATE WITH YOU... SO LONG AS THIS IS ABOUT GETTING AYA BACK TO *NORMAL!*
ALL RIGHT...
CLICK
"COOPERATE," HUH...!
I TRUST YOU GOT HER VISUALS ON THE BACKUP MONITOR?
AND HERE, ANALYZE THE BLOOD I GOT FROM HER.

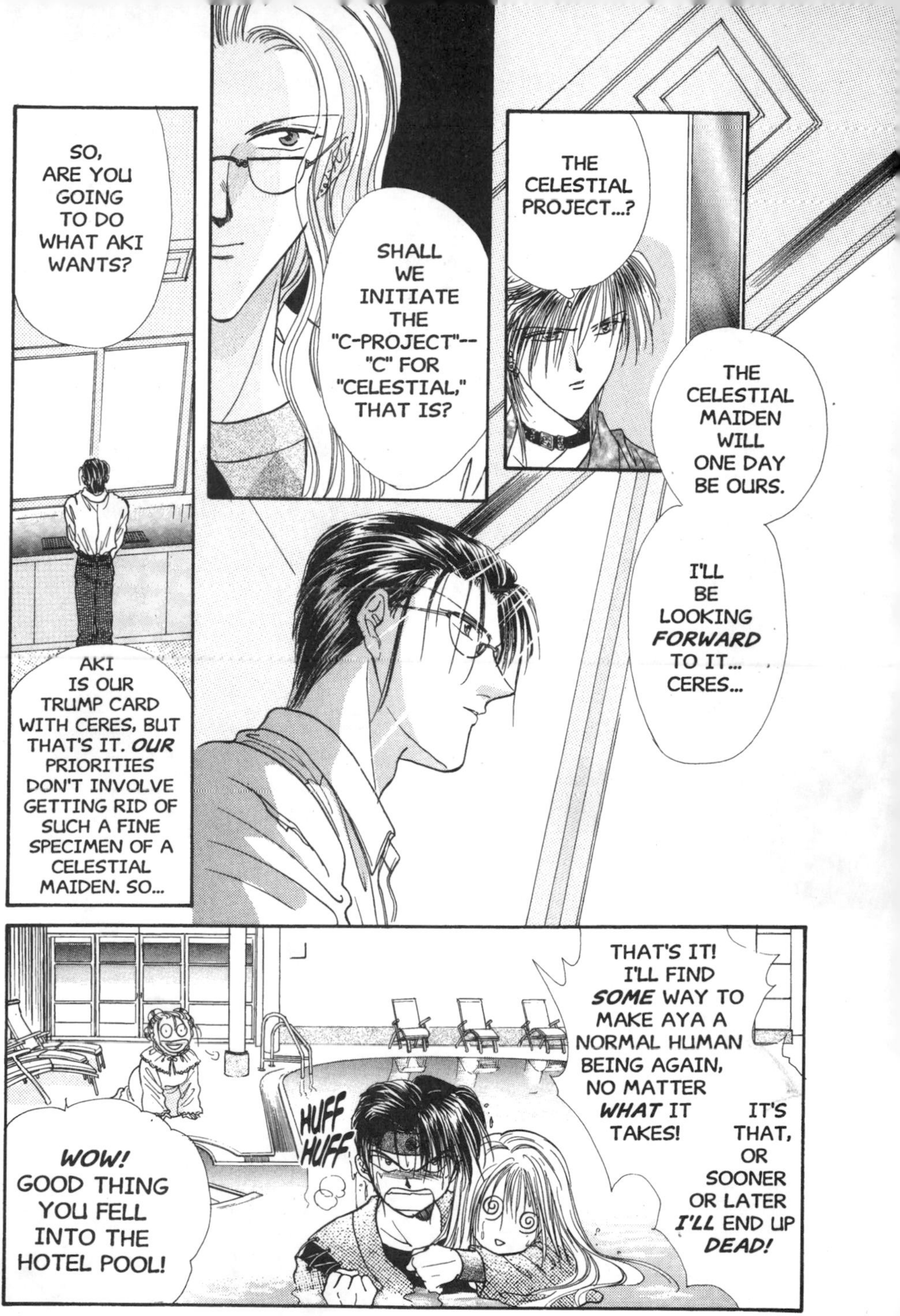
SO, ARE YOU GOING TO DO WHAT AKI WANTS?
AKI IS OUR TRUMP CARD WITH CERES, BUT THAT'S IT. ***OUR*** PRIORITIES DON'T INVOLVE GETTING RID OF SUCH A FINE SPECIMEN OF A CELESTIAL MAIDEN. SO...
SHALL WE INITIATE THE "C-PROJECT"-- "C" FOR "CELESTIAL," THAT IS?
THE CELESTIAL PROJECT...?
THE CELESTIAL MAIDEN WILL ONE DAY BE OURS.
I'LL BE LOOKING ***FORWARD*** TO IT... CERES...
WOW! GOOD THING YOU FELL INTO THE HOTEL POOL!
HUFF HUFF
THAT'S IT! I'LL FIND ***SOME*** WAY TO MAKE AYA A NORMAL HUMAN BEING AGAIN, NO MATTER ***WHAT*** IT TAKES!
IT'S THAT, OR SOONER OR LATER ***I'LL*** END UP ***DEAD!***

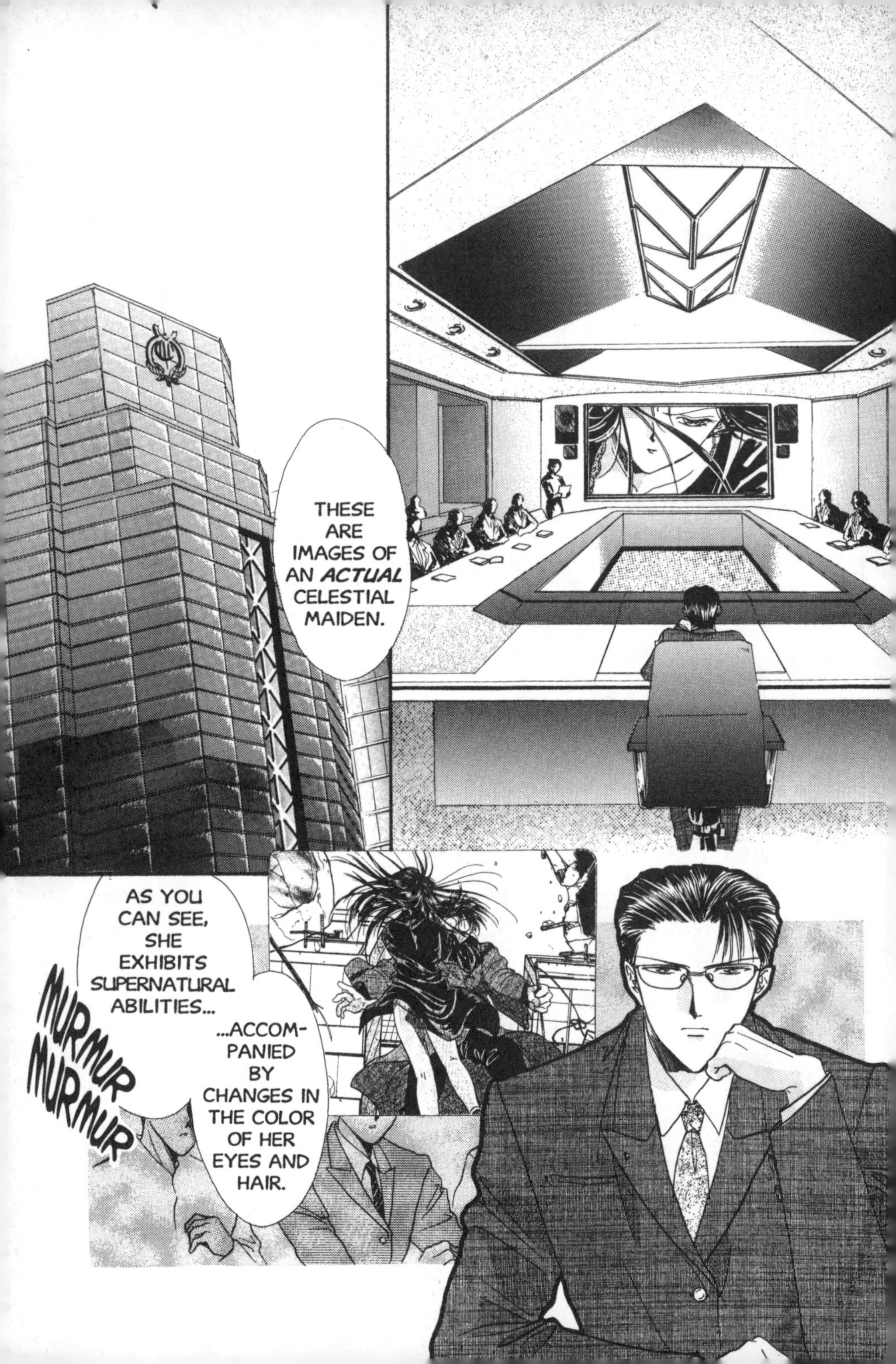
THESE ARE IMAGES OF AN *ACTUAL* CELESTIAL MAIDEN.
AS YOU CAN SEE, SHE EXHIBITS SUPERNATURAL ABILITIES...
...ACCOMPANIED BY CHANGES IN THE COLOR OF HER EYES AND HAIR.
MURMUR MURMUR

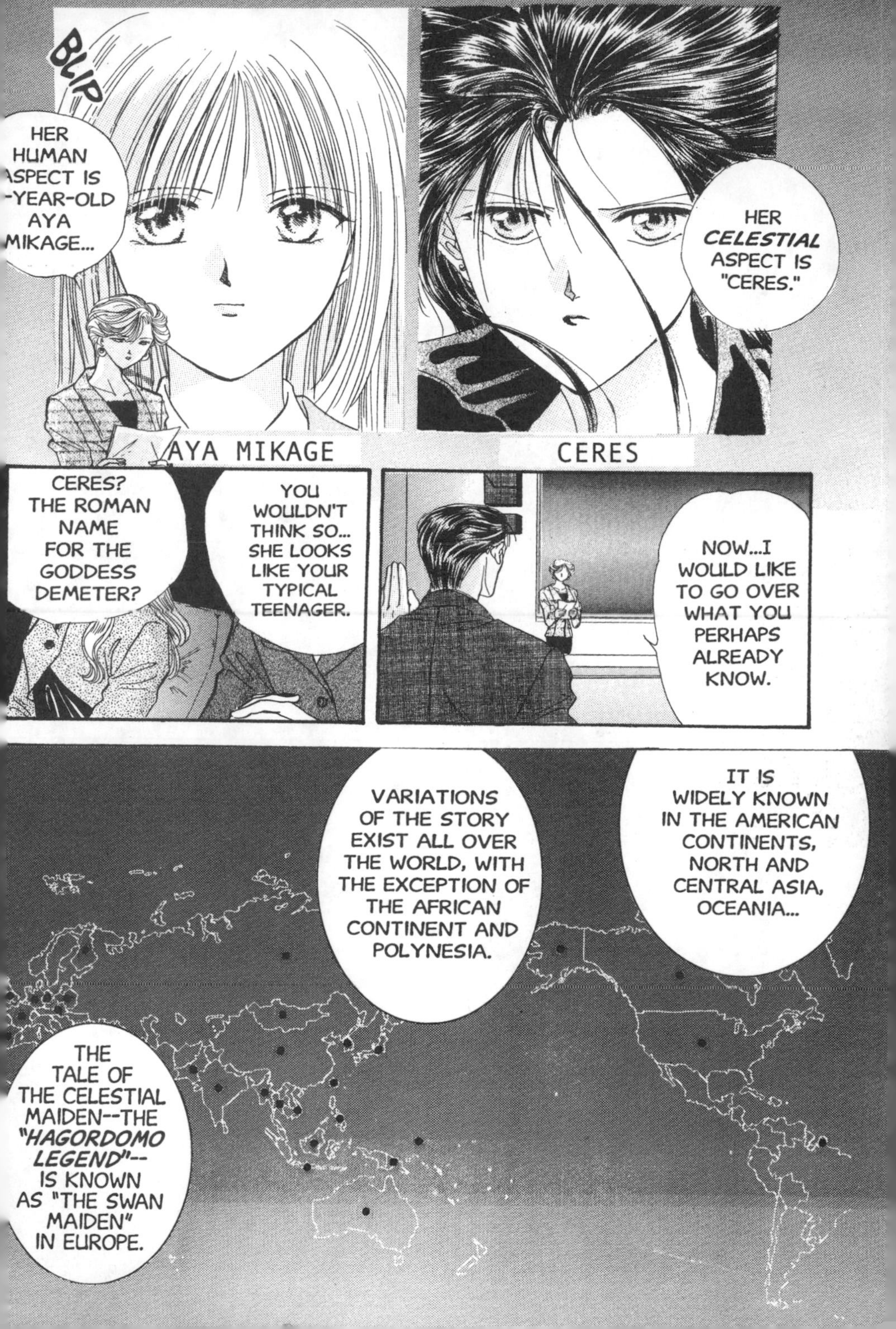
BLIP
HER HUMAN ASPECT IS -YEAR-OLD AYA MIKAGE...
AYA MIKAGE
HER *CELESTIAL* ASPECT IS "CERES."
CERES
CERES? THE ROMAN NAME FOR THE GODDESS DEMETER?
YOU WOULDN'T THINK SO... SHE LOOKS LIKE YOUR TYPICAL TEENAGER.
NOW...I WOULD LIKE TO GO OVER WHAT YOU PERHAPS ALREADY KNOW.
THE TALE OF THE CELESTIAL MAIDEN--THE *"HAGORDOMO LEGEND"*-- IS KNOWN AS "THE SWAN MAIDEN" IN EUROPE.
VARIATIONS OF THE STORY EXIST ALL OVER THE WORLD, WITH THE EXCEPTION OF THE AFRICAN CONTINENT AND POLYNESIA.
IT IS WIDELY KNOWN IN THE AMERICAN CONTINENTS, NORTH AND CENTRAL ASIA, OCEANIA...

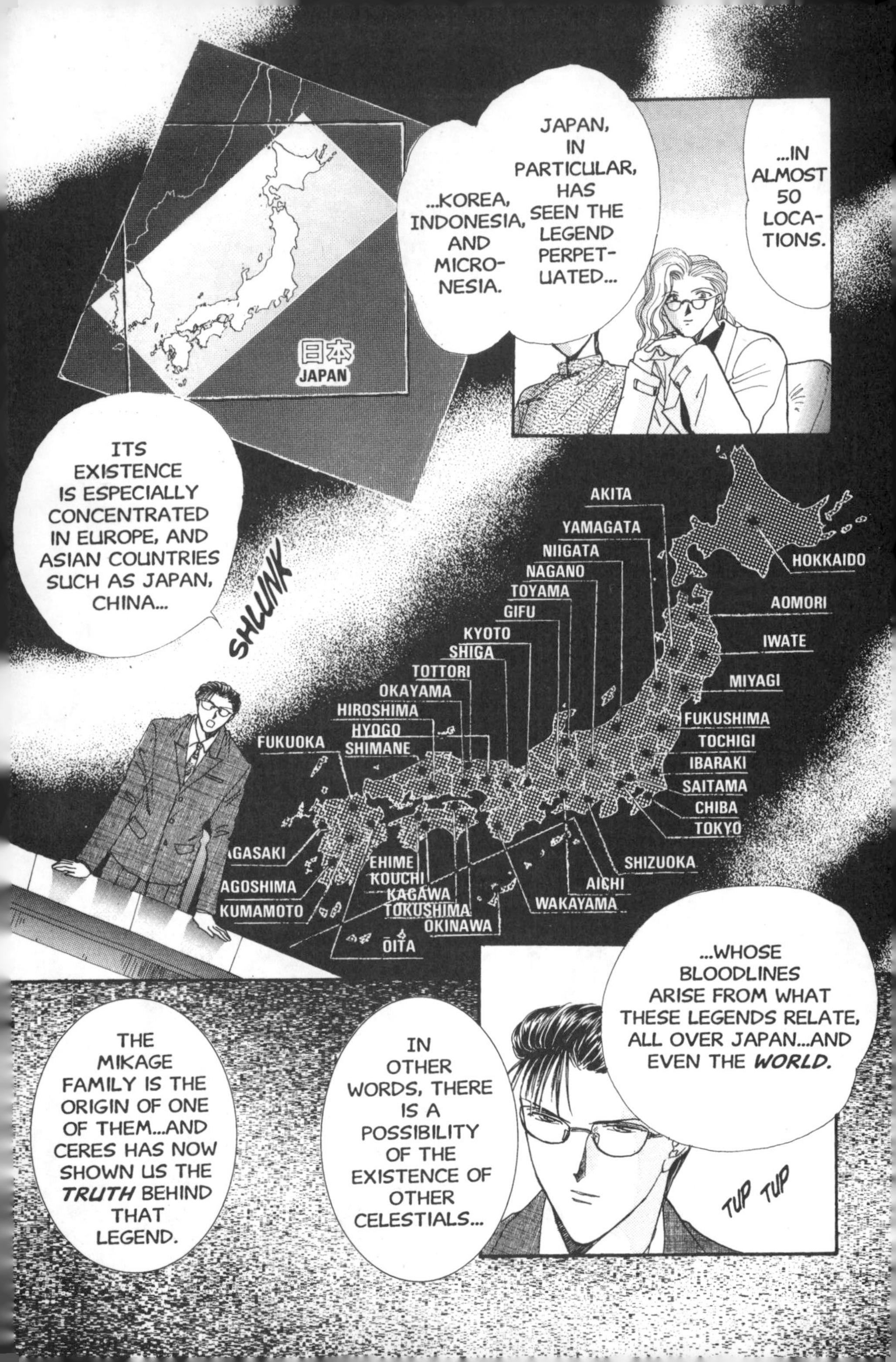
ITS EXISTENCE IS ESPECIALLY CONCENTRATED IN EUROPE, AND ASIAN COUNTRIES SUCH AS JAPAN, CHINA...
...KOREA, INDONESIA, AND MICRO-NESIA.
JAPAN, IN PARTICULAR, HAS SEEN THE LEGEND PERPET-UATED...
...IN ALMOST 50 LOCA-TIONS.
日本
JAPAN
SHUNK
AKITA
YAMAGATA
NIIGATA
NAGANO
TOYAMA
GIFU
KYOTO
SHIGA
TOTTORI
OKAYAMA
HIROSHIMA
HYOGO
SHIMANE
FUKUOKA
AGASAKI
AGOSHIMA
KUMAMOTO
EHIME
KOUCHI
KAGAWA
TOKUSHIMA
OKINAWA
ŌITA
WAKAYAMA
AICHI
SHIZUOKA
TOKYO
CHIBA
SAITAMA
IBARAKI
TOCHIGI
FUKUSHIMA
MIYAGI
IWATE
AOMORI
HOKKAIDO
THE MIKAGE FAMILY IS THE ORIGIN OF ONE OF THEM...AND CERES HAS NOW SHOWN US THE TRUTH BEHIND THAT LEGEND.
IN OTHER WORDS, THERE IS A POSSIBILITY OF THE EXISTENCE OF OTHER CELESTIALS...
...WHOSE BLOODLINES ARISE FROM WHAT THESE LEGENDS RELATE, ALL OVER JAPAN...AND EVEN THE WORLD.
TUP TUP

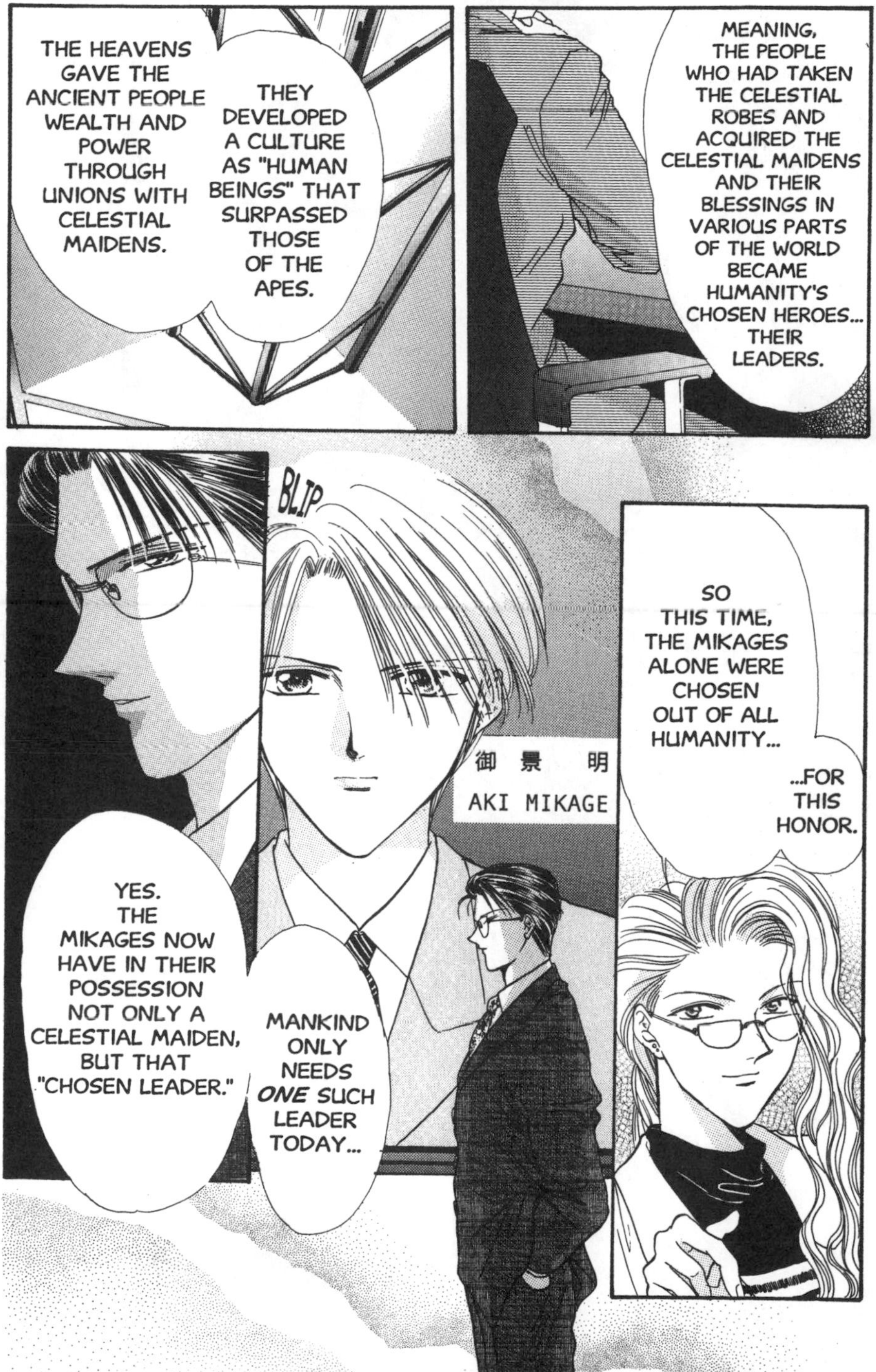
THE HEAVENS GAVE THE ANCIENT PEOPLE WEALTH AND POWER THROUGH UNIONS WITH CELESTIAL MAIDENS.
THEY DEVELOPED A CULTURE AS "HUMAN BEINGS" THAT SURPASSED THOSE OF THE APES.
MEANING, THE PEOPLE WHO HAD TAKEN THE CELESTIAL ROBES AND ACQUIRED THE CELESTIAL MAIDENS AND THEIR BLESSINGS IN VARIOUS PARTS OF THE WORLD BECAME HUMANITY'S CHOSEN HEROES... THEIR LEADERS.
BLIP
御景　明
AKI MIKAGE
YES. THE MIKAGES NOW HAVE IN THEIR POSSESSION NOT ONLY A CELESTIAL MAIDEN, BUT THAT "CHOSEN LEADER."
MANKIND ONLY NEEDS *ONE* SUCH LEADER TODAY...
SO THIS TIME, THE MIKAGES ALONE WERE CHOSEN OUT OF ALL HUMANITY...
...FOR THIS HONOR.

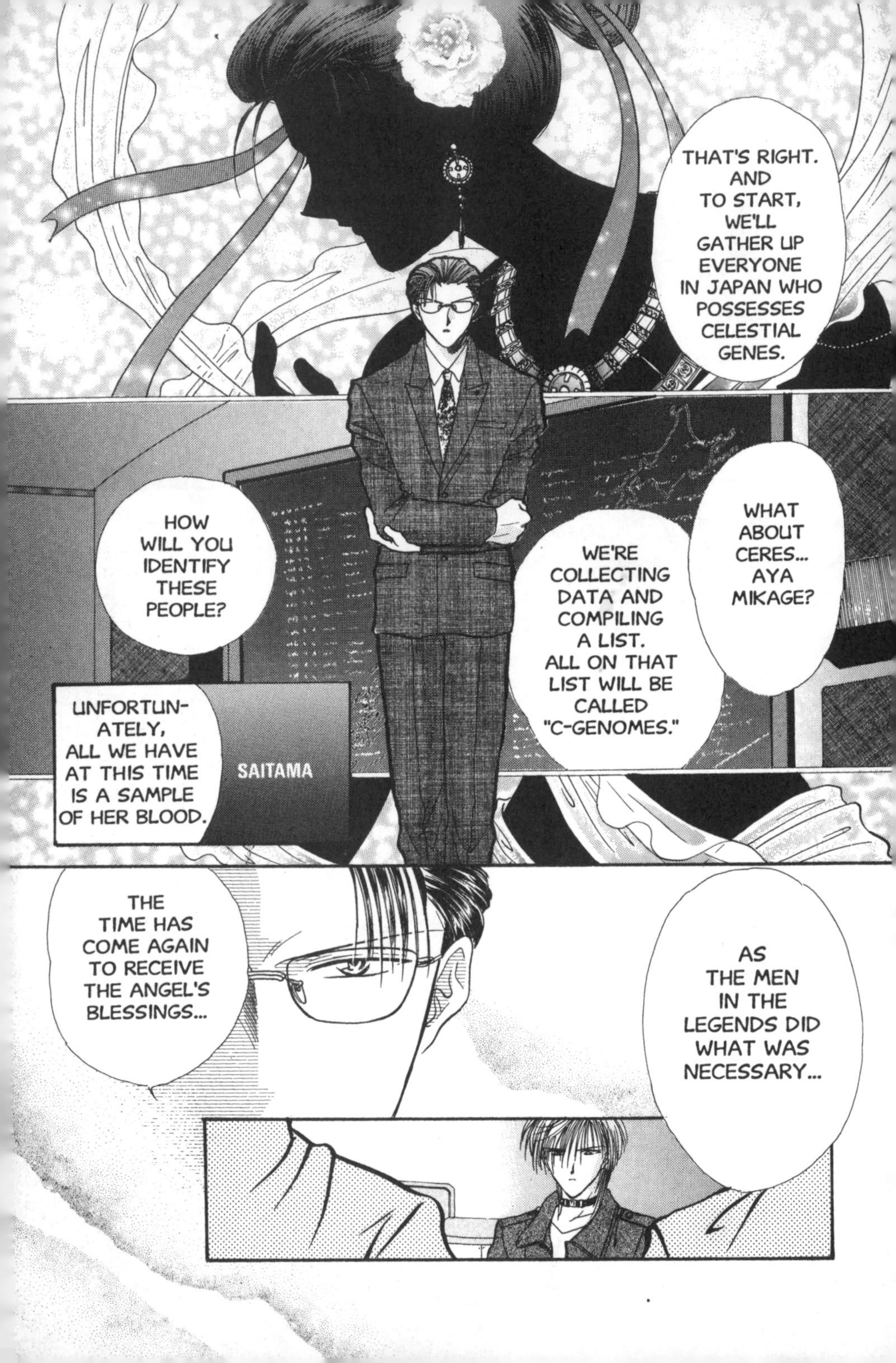
THAT'S RIGHT. AND TO START, WE'LL GATHER UP EVERYONE IN JAPAN WHO POSSESSES CELESTIAL GENES.
HOW WILL YOU IDENTIFY THESE PEOPLE?
WE'RE COLLECTING DATA AND COMPILING A LIST. ALL ON THAT LIST WILL BE CALLED "C-GENOMES."
WHAT ABOUT CERES... AYA MIKAGE?
UNFORTUN-ATELY, ALL WE HAVE AT THIS TIME IS A SAMPLE OF HER BLOOD.
SAITAMA
AS THE MEN IN THE LEGENDS DID WHAT WAS NECESSARY...
THE TIME HAS COME AGAIN TO RECEIVE THE ANGEL'S BLESSINGS...

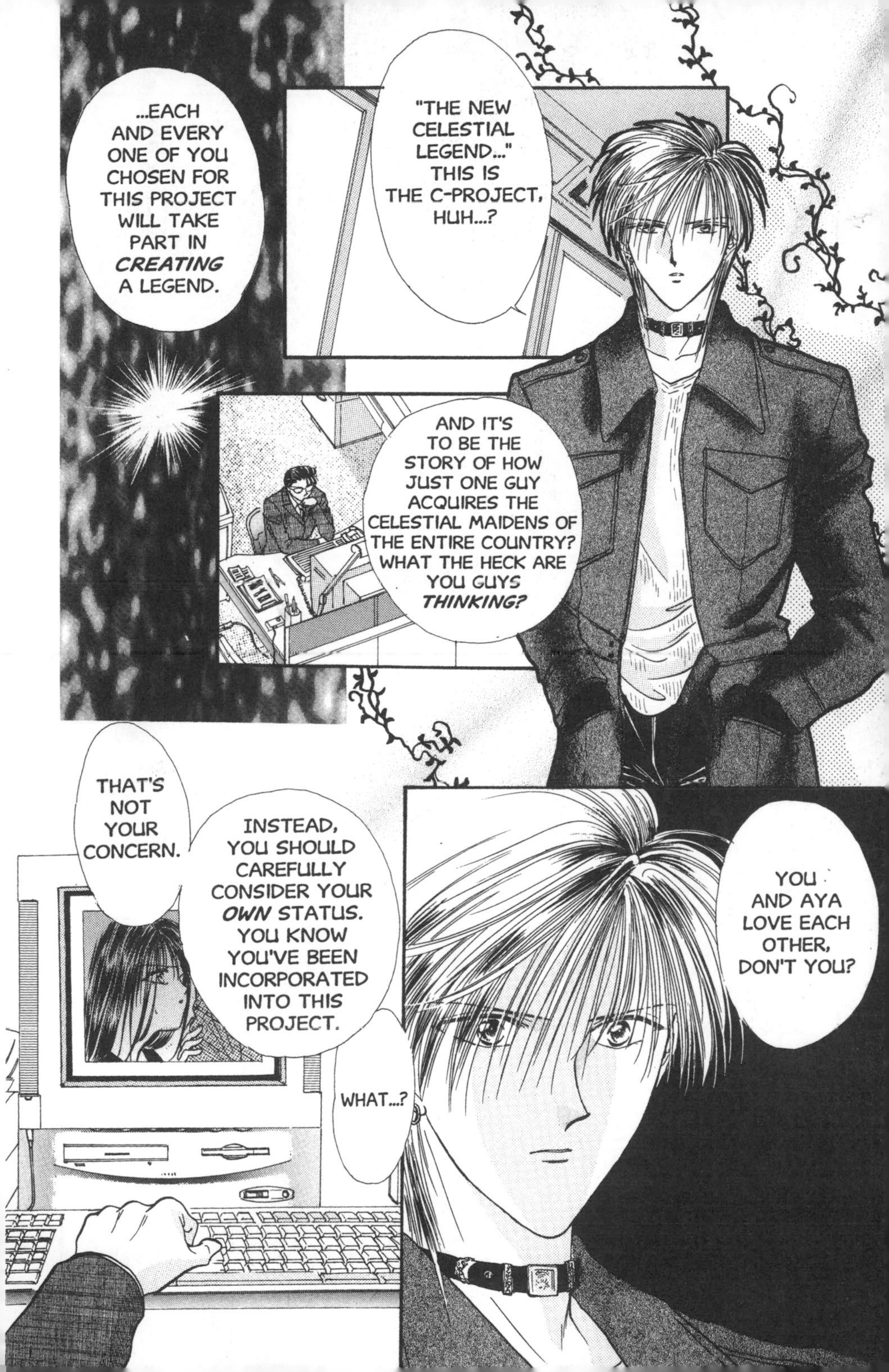
...EACH AND EVERY ONE OF YOU CHOSEN FOR THIS PROJECT WILL TAKE PART IN *CREATING* A LEGEND.
"THE NEW CELESTIAL LEGEND..." THIS IS THE C-PROJECT, HUH...?
AND IT'S TO BE THE STORY OF HOW JUST ONE GUY ACQUIRES THE CELESTIAL MAIDENS OF THE ENTIRE COUNTRY? WHAT THE HECK ARE YOU GUYS *THINKING?*
THAT'S NOT YOUR CONCERN.
INSTEAD, YOU SHOULD CAREFULLY CONSIDER YOUR *OWN* STATUS. YOU KNOW YOU'VE BEEN INCORPORATED INTO THIS PROJECT.
WHAT...?
YOU AND AYA LOVE EACH OTHER, DON'T YOU?

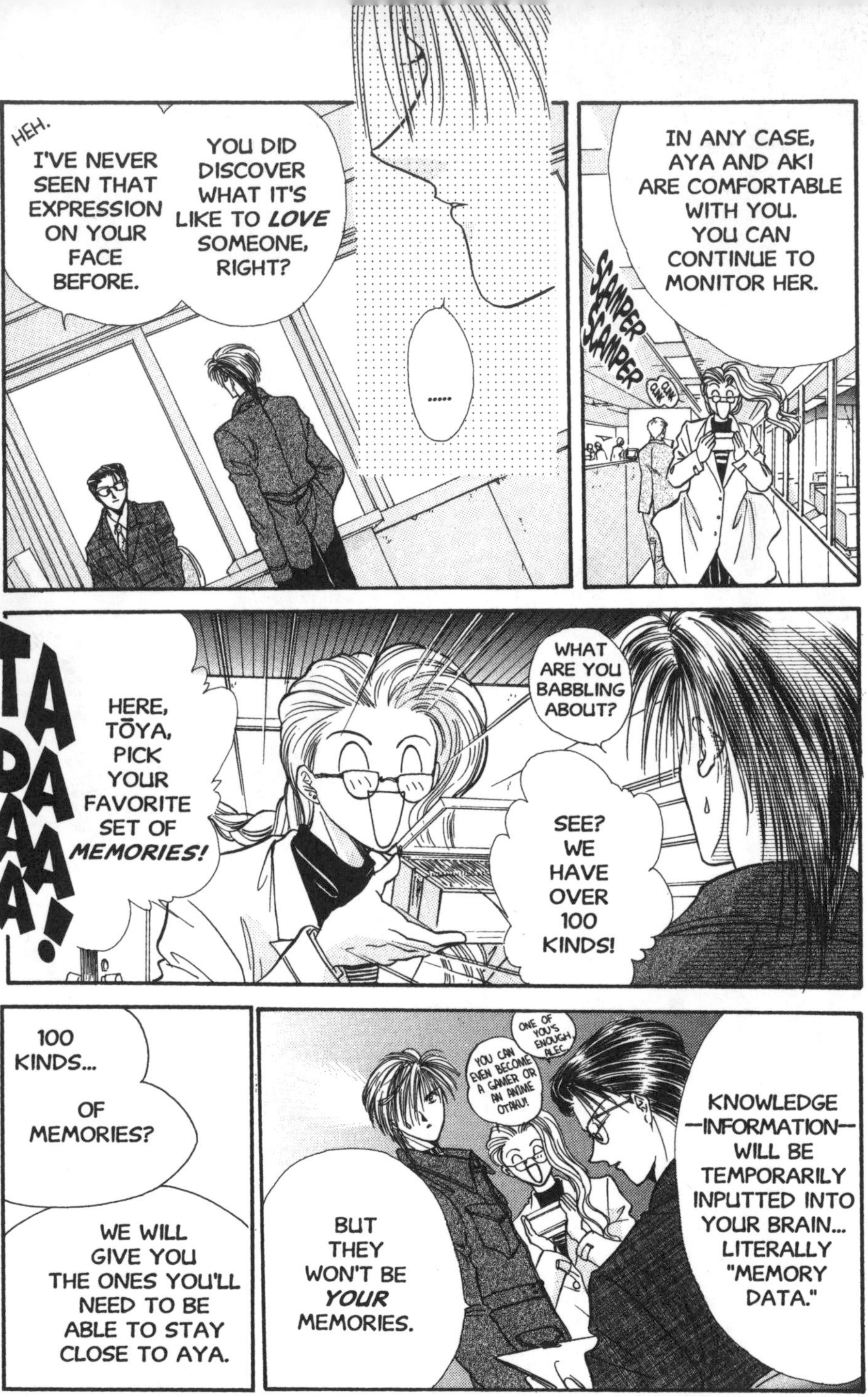
HEH.
I'VE NEVER SEEN THAT EXPRESSION ON YOUR FACE BEFORE.
YOU DID DISCOVER WHAT IT'S LIKE TO *LOVE* SOMEONE, RIGHT?
......
IN ANY CASE, AYA AND AKI ARE COMFORTABLE WITH YOU. YOU CAN CONTINUE TO MONITOR HER.
SCAMPER SCAMPER
CLINK CLINK
TADAAAA!
HERE, TŌYA, PICK YOUR FAVORITE SET OF *MEMORIES!*
WHAT ARE YOU BABBLING ABOUT?
SEE? WE HAVE OVER 100 KINDS!
100 KINDS...
OF MEMORIES?
WE WILL GIVE YOU THE ONES YOU'LL NEED TO BE ABLE TO STAY CLOSE TO AYA.
KNOWLEDGE —INFORMATION— WILL BE TEMPORARILY INPUTTED INTO YOUR BRAIN... LITERALLY "MEMORY DATA."
YOU CAN EVEN BECOME A GAMER OR AN ANIME OTAKU!
ONE OF YOU'S ENOUGH, ALEC.
BUT THEY WON'T BE *YOUR* MEMORIES.

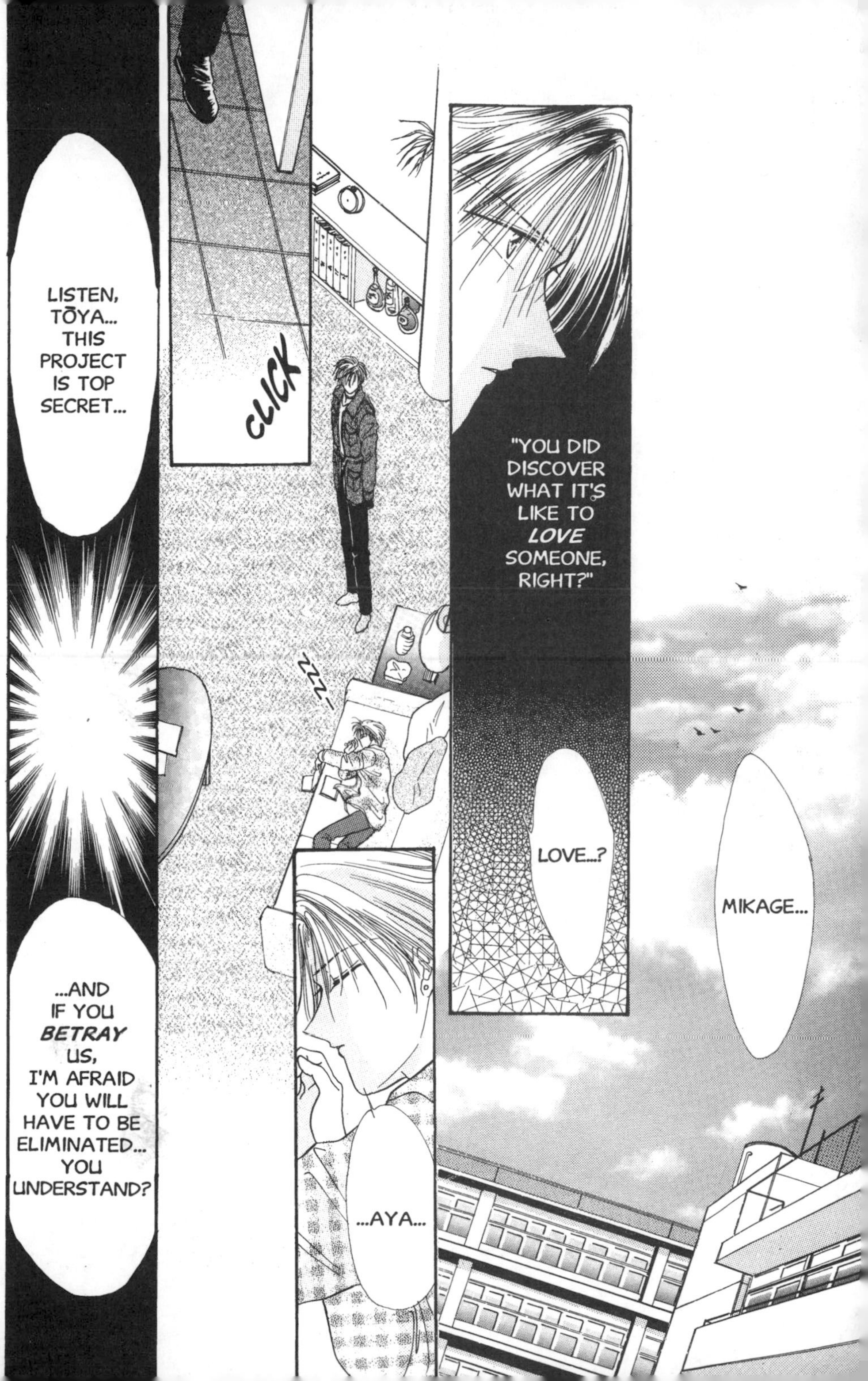
"YOU DID DISCOVER WHAT IT'S LIKE TO *LOVE* SOMEONE, RIGHT?"
LOVE...?
MIKAGE...
...AYA...
CLICK
ZZZ
LISTEN, TŌYA... THIS PROJECT IS TOP SECRET...
...AND IF YOU *BETRAY* US, I'M AFRAID YOU WILL HAVE TO BE ELIMINATED... YOU UNDERSTAND?

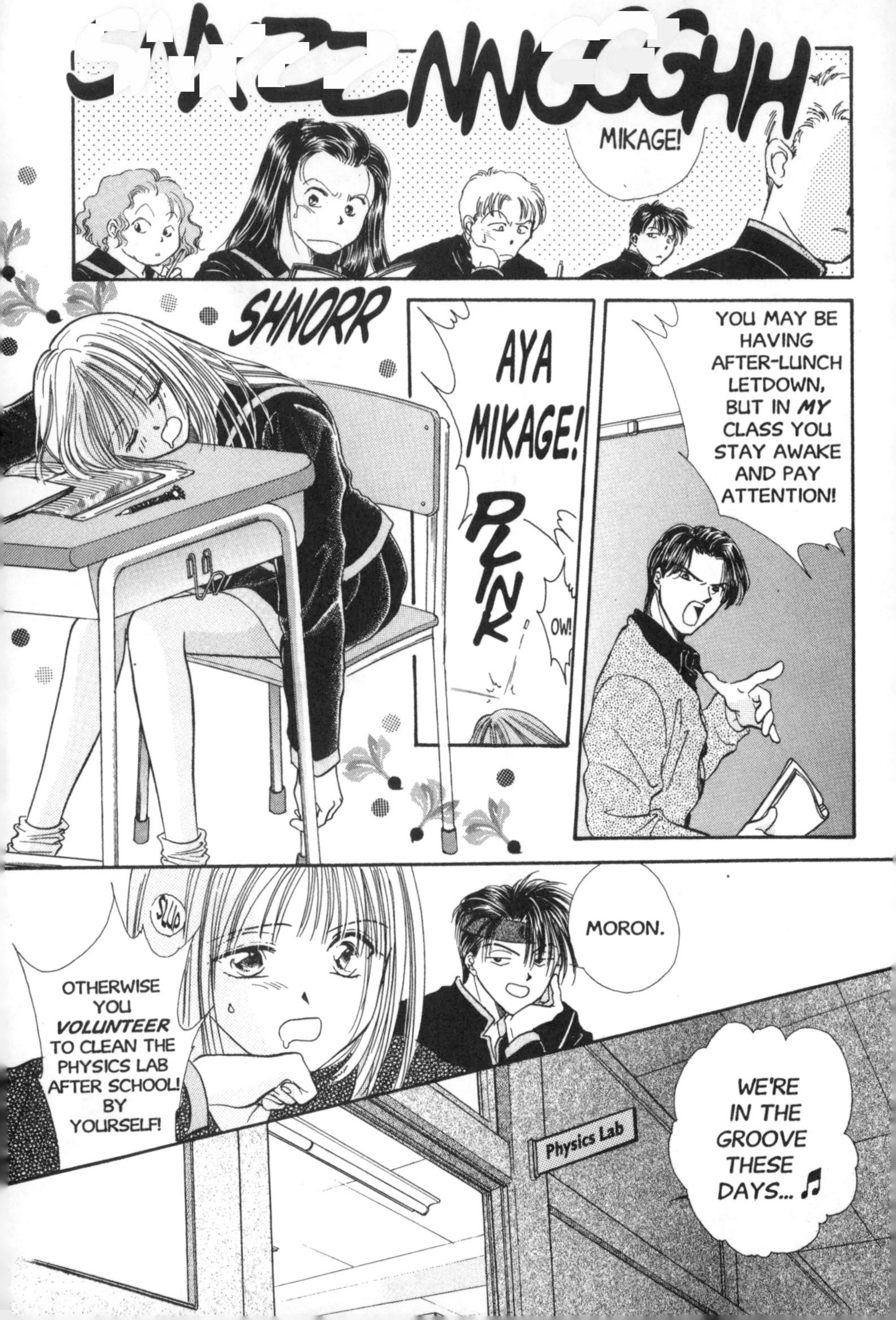
MIKAGE!
YOU MAY BE HAVING AFTER-LUNCH LETDOWN, BUT IN *MY* CLASS YOU STAY AWAKE AND PAY ATTENTION!
AYA MIKAGE!
PLINK
OW!
SHNORR
MORON.
SLUP
OTHERWISE YOU ***VOLUNTEER*** TO CLEAN THE PHYSICS LAB AFTER SCHOOL! BY YOURSELF!
Physics Lab
WE'RE IN THE GROOVE THESE DAYS... ♫

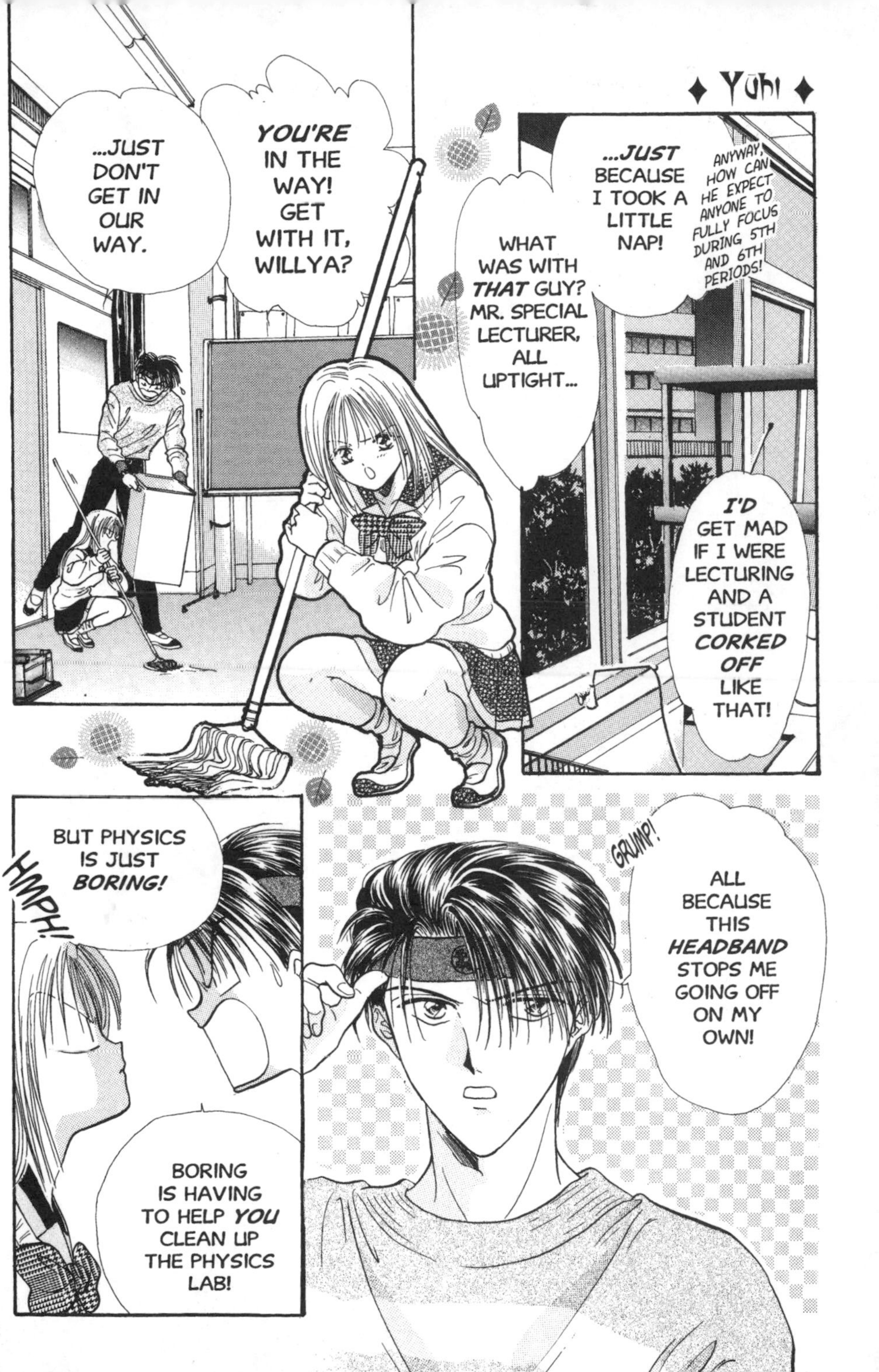
WHAT WAS WITH *THAT* GUY? MR. SPECIAL LECTURER, ALL UPTIGHT...
...*JUST* BECAUSE I TOOK A LITTLE NAP!
ANYWAY, HOW CAN HE EXPECT ANYONE TO FULLY FOCUS DURING 5TH AND 6TH PERIODS!
I'D GET MAD IF I WERE LECTURING AND A STUDENT *CORKED OFF* LIKE THAT!
YOU'RE IN THE WAY! GET WITH IT, WILLYA?
...JUST DON'T GET IN OUR WAY.
GRUMP!
ALL BECAUSE THIS *HEADBAND* STOPS ME GOING OFF ON MY OWN!
BUT PHYSICS IS JUST *BORING!*
HMPH!
BORING IS HAVING TO HELP *YOU* CLEAN UP THE PHYSICS LAB!

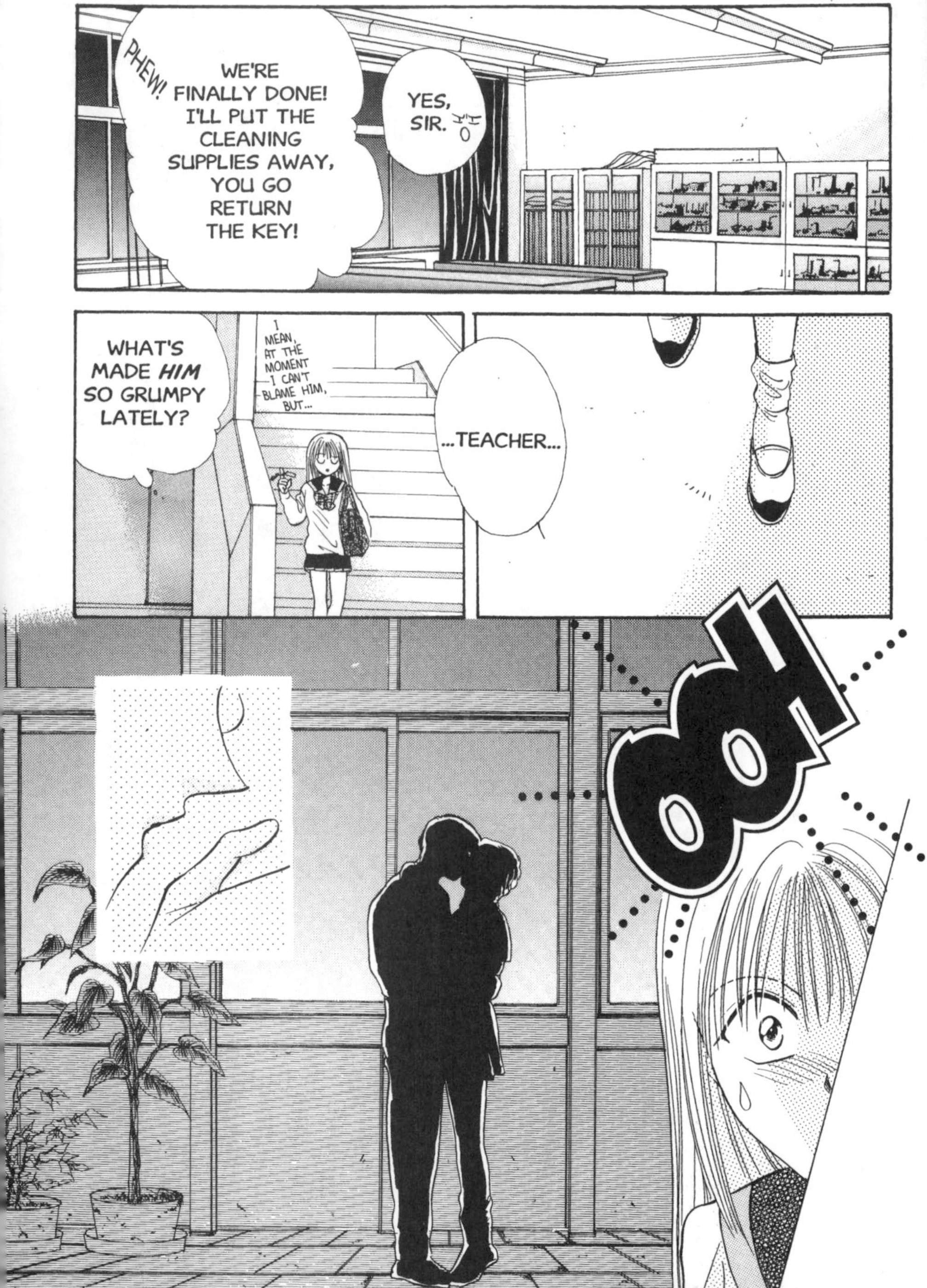
YES, SIR.
PHEW!
WE'RE FINALLY DONE! I'LL PUT THE CLEANING SUPPLIES AWAY, YOU GO RETURN THE KEY!
...TEACHER...
I MEAN, AT THE MOMENT I CAN'T BLAME HIM, BUT...
WHAT'S MADE *HIM* SO GRUMPY LATELY?
OO!

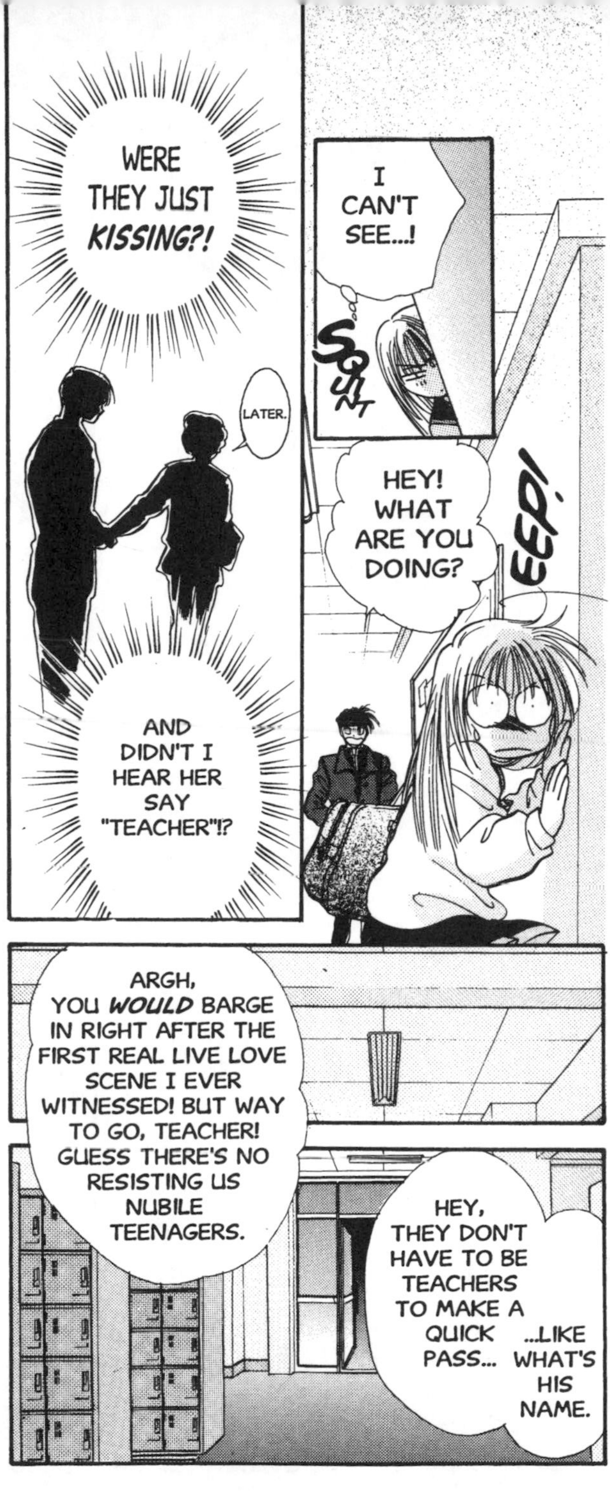
LATER.
WERE THEY JUST *KISSING?!*
AND DIDN'T I HEAR HER SAY "TEACHER"!?
I CAN'T SEE...!
SQUNT
HEY! WHAT ARE YOU DOING?
EEP!
ARGH, YOU *WOULD* BARGE IN RIGHT AFTER THE FIRST REAL LIVE LOVE SCENE I EVER WITNESSED! BUT WAY TO GO, TEACHER! GUESS THERE'S NO RESISTING US NUBILE TEENAGERS.
HEY, THEY DON'T HAVE TO BE TEACHERS TO MAKE A QUICK PASS...
...LIKE WHAT'S HIS NAME.

PRODUCTION DIARY

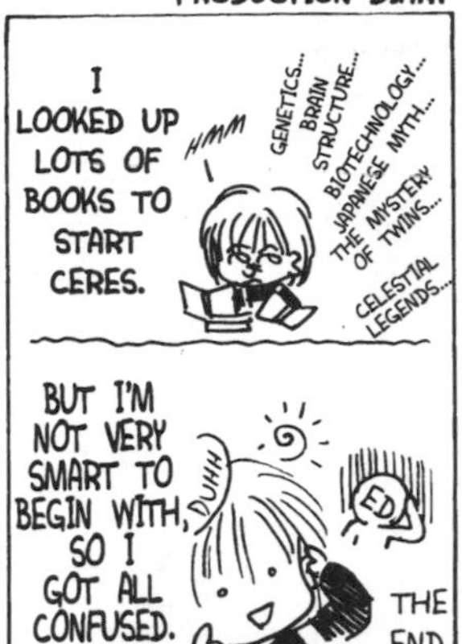
I LOOKED UP LOTS OF BOOKS TO START CERES.
HMM
GENETICS... BRAIN STRUCTURE... BIOTECHNOLOGY... JAPANESE MYTH... THE MYSTERY OF TWINS... CELESTIAL LEGENDS...
BUT I'M NOT VERY SMART TO BEGIN WITH, SO I GOT ALL CONFUSED.
DUHH
ED
THE END.

...Anyway, all you elementary and Jr. high schoolers who don't know about genetics, don't worry! You'll learn about it in high school bio. But there will be a lot of applications (?!) for genetics in the coming age, so I think it's good to know about it. ◡̈ Besides, it's more realistic than talking about "the blood of so-and-so."

It's incredible that all life is created from a blueprint that consists of just **four** nucleotides. This blueprint is called DNA (not the CD single by Makoto Kawamoto)... So even human beings take their shape according to the information encoded in DNA...

Oh! On another note, what's with the comment "Your self portraits (on the "about the author" page in vol.1) have gotten cuter"...? That's **Aya!** ◡̈

Also, **Aya's picture** somehow ended up in the profile page in Yutopia Collections vol.1 "Delicious Studies" due to an editing error! I'm not so stupid that I would beautify my self portrait that much! ◡̈ It was a mistake! Besides, I have short hair now. Sheesh!

Well, not much room left. See you in the next volume. Oh, about "the title illustrations being left out"--that's because *Ceres* doesn't have chapter titles. So there won't be any. I'll try to clump them in the extra pages at the end of the graphic novels.

Bye.

I just heard from my editor that Datahouse is coming out with a book called "Fushigi Yûgi's Mysterious Secrets"!

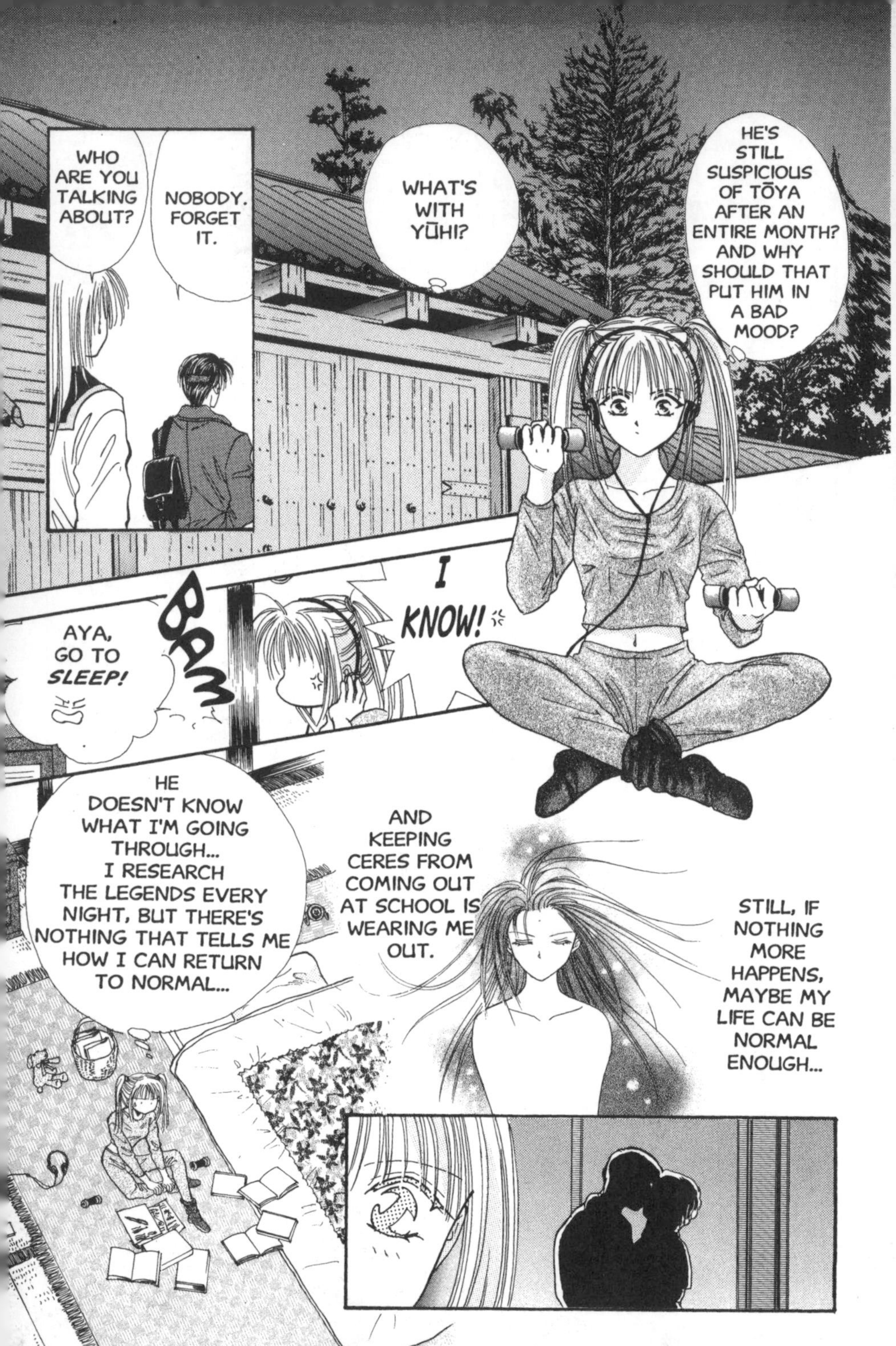
WHAT'S WITH YŪHI?
HE'S STILL SUSPICIOUS OF TŌYA AFTER AN ENTIRE MONTH? AND WHY SHOULD THAT PUT HIM IN A BAD MOOD?
WHO ARE YOU TALKING ABOUT?
NOBODY. FORGET IT.
AYA, GO TO SLEEP!
BAM
I KNOW!
HE DOESN'T KNOW WHAT I'M GOING THROUGH... I RESEARCH THE LEGENDS EVERY NIGHT, BUT THERE'S NOTHING THAT TELLS ME HOW I CAN RETURN TO NORMAL...
AND KEEPING CERES FROM COMING OUT AT SCHOOL IS WEARING ME OUT.
STILL, IF NOTHING MORE HAPPENS, MAYBE MY LIFE CAN BE NORMAL ENOUGH...

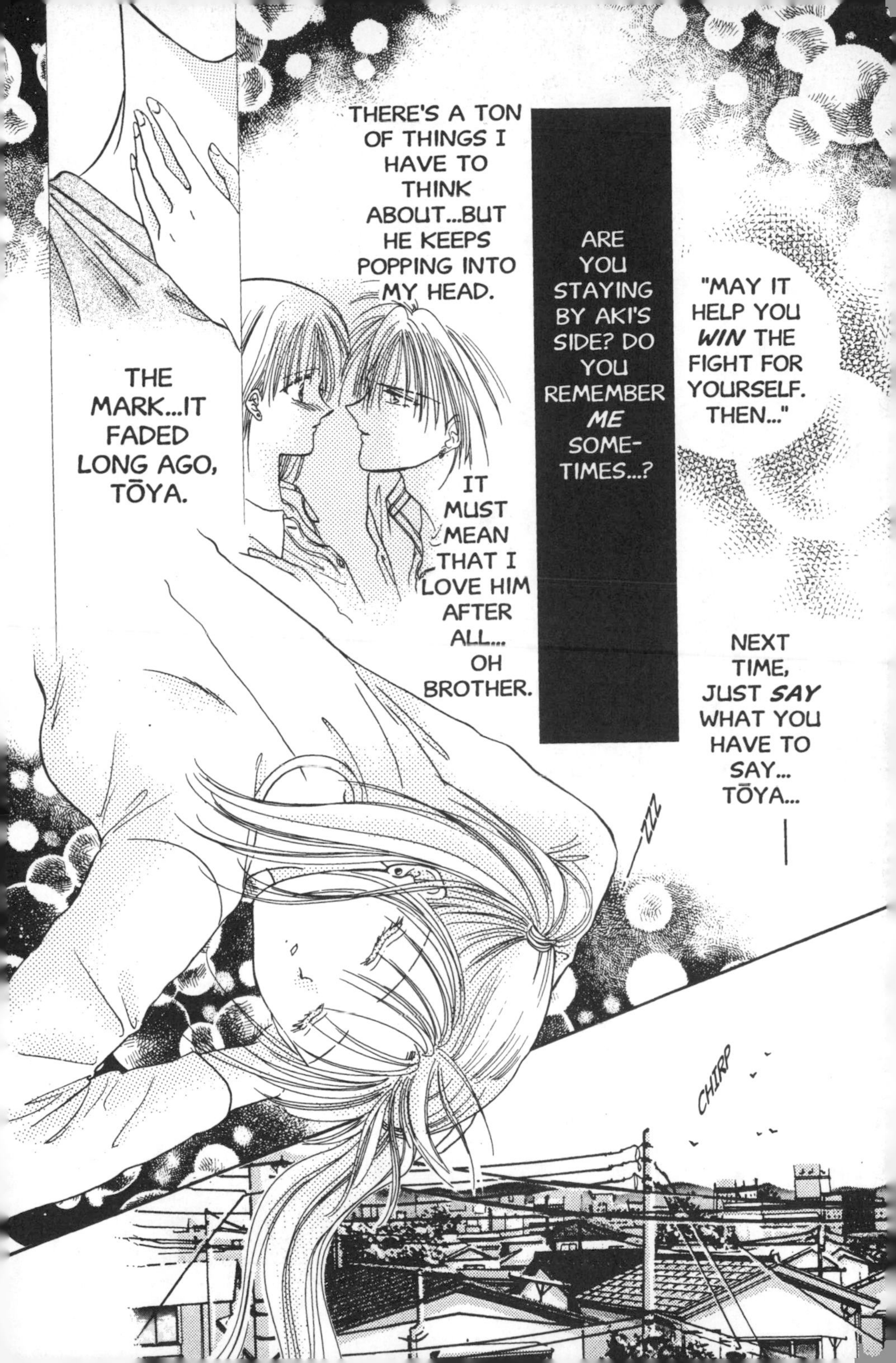
"MAY IT HELP YOU WIN THE FIGHT FOR YOURSELF. THEN..."
NEXT TIME, JUST SAY WHAT YOU HAVE TO SAY... TŌYA...
ARE YOU STAYING BY AKI'S SIDE? DO YOU REMEMBER ME SOMETIMES...?
THERE'S A TON OF THINGS I HAVE TO THINK ABOUT...BUT HE KEEPS POPPING INTO MY HEAD.
IT MUST MEAN THAT I LOVE HIM AFTER ALL... OH BROTHER.
THE MARK...IT FADED LONG AGO, TŌYA.
ZZZ
CHIRP

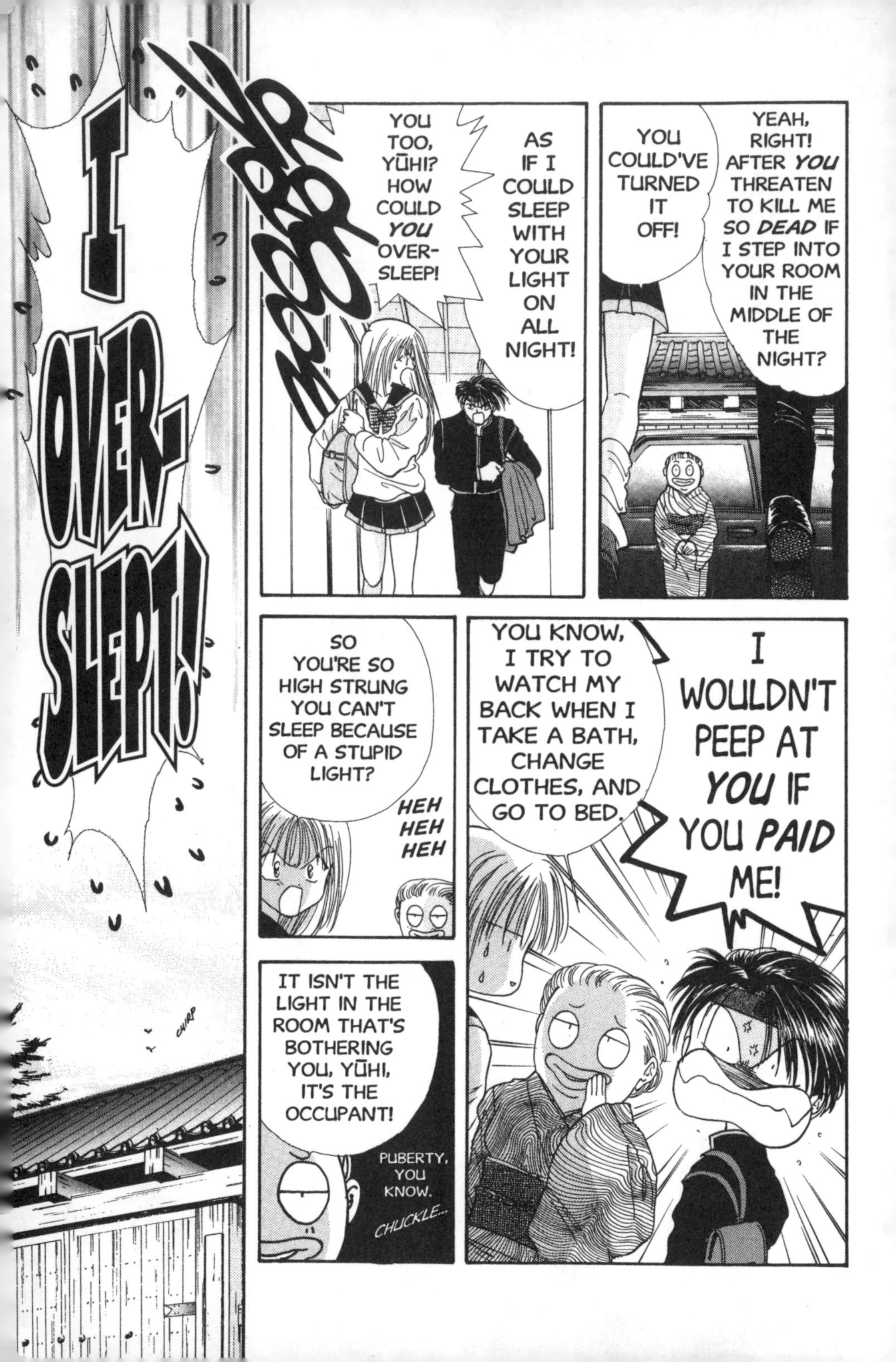
I OVERSLEPT!
CHIRP
YOU TOO, YŪHI? HOW COULD YOU OVERSLEEP!
AS IF I COULD SLEEP WITH YOUR LIGHT ON ALL NIGHT!
YOU COULD'VE TURNED IT OFF!
YEAH, RIGHT! AFTER YOU THREATEN TO KILL ME SO DEAD IF I STEP INTO YOUR ROOM IN THE MIDDLE OF THE NIGHT?
SO YOU'RE SO HIGH STRUNG YOU CAN'T SLEEP BECAUSE OF A STUPID LIGHT?
HEH HEH HEH
YOU KNOW, I TRY TO WATCH MY BACK WHEN I TAKE A BATH, CHANGE CLOTHES, AND GO TO BED.
I WOULDN'T PEEP AT YOU IF YOU PAID ME!
IT ISN'T THE LIGHT IN THE ROOM THAT'S BOTHERING YOU, YŪHI, IT'S THE OCCUPANT!
PUBERTY, YOU KNOW.
CHUCKLE...

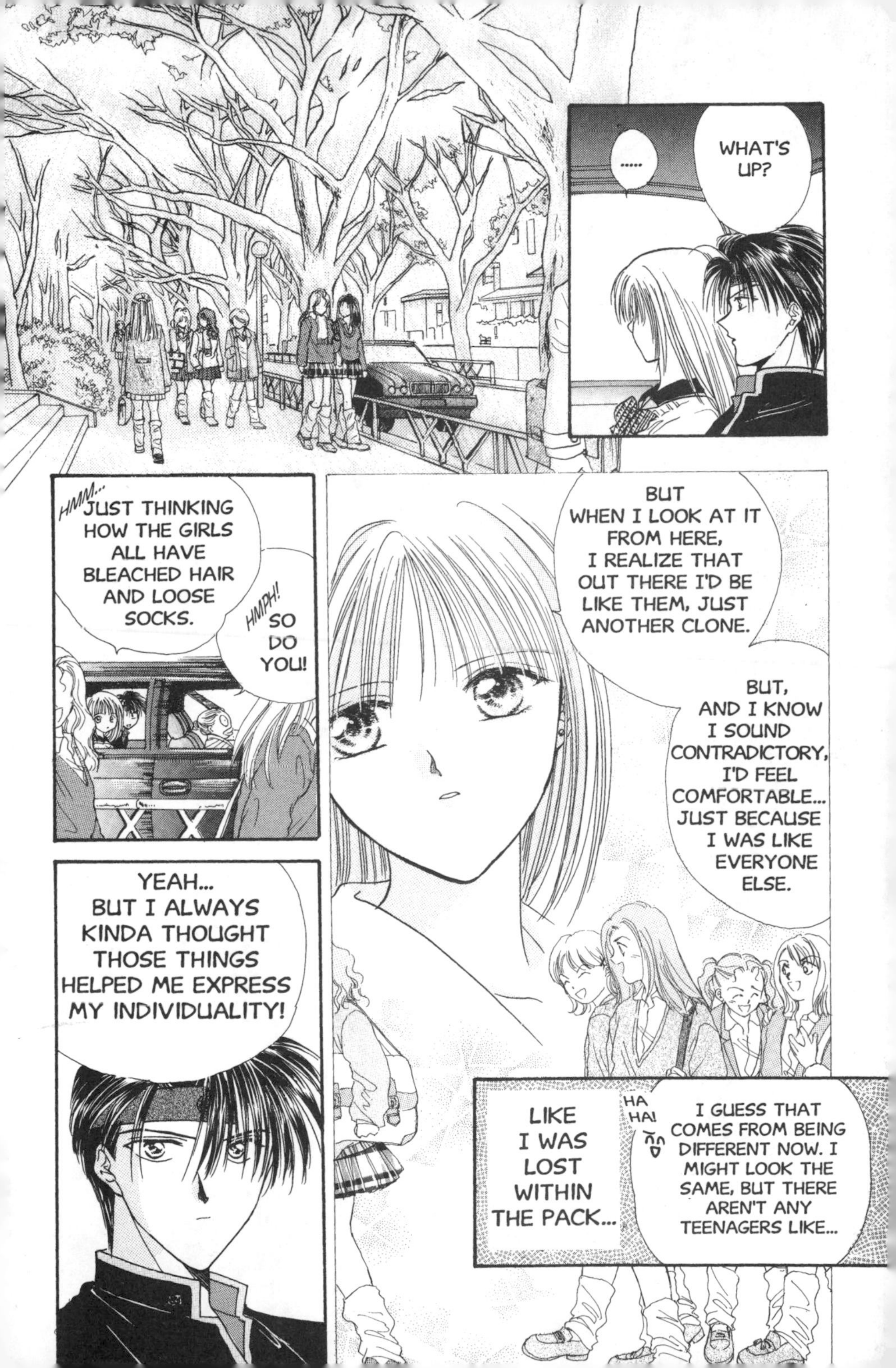
WHAT'S UP?
.....
HMM...
JUST THINKING HOW THE GIRLS ALL HAVE BLEACHED HAIR AND LOOSE SOCKS.
HMPH!
SO DO YOU!
YEAH... BUT I ALWAYS KINDA THOUGHT THOSE THINGS HELPED ME EXPRESS MY INDIVIDUALITY!
BUT WHEN I LOOK AT IT FROM HERE, I REALIZE THAT OUT THERE I'D BE LIKE THEM, JUST ANOTHER CLONE.
BUT, AND I KNOW I SOUND CONTRADICTORY, I'D FEEL COMFORTABLE... JUST BECAUSE I WAS LIKE EVERYONE ELSE.
HA HA!
I GUESS THAT COMES FROM BEING DIFFERENT NOW. I MIGHT LOOK THE SAME, BUT THERE AREN'T ANY TEENAGERS LIKE...
LIKE I WAS LOST WITHIN THE PACK...

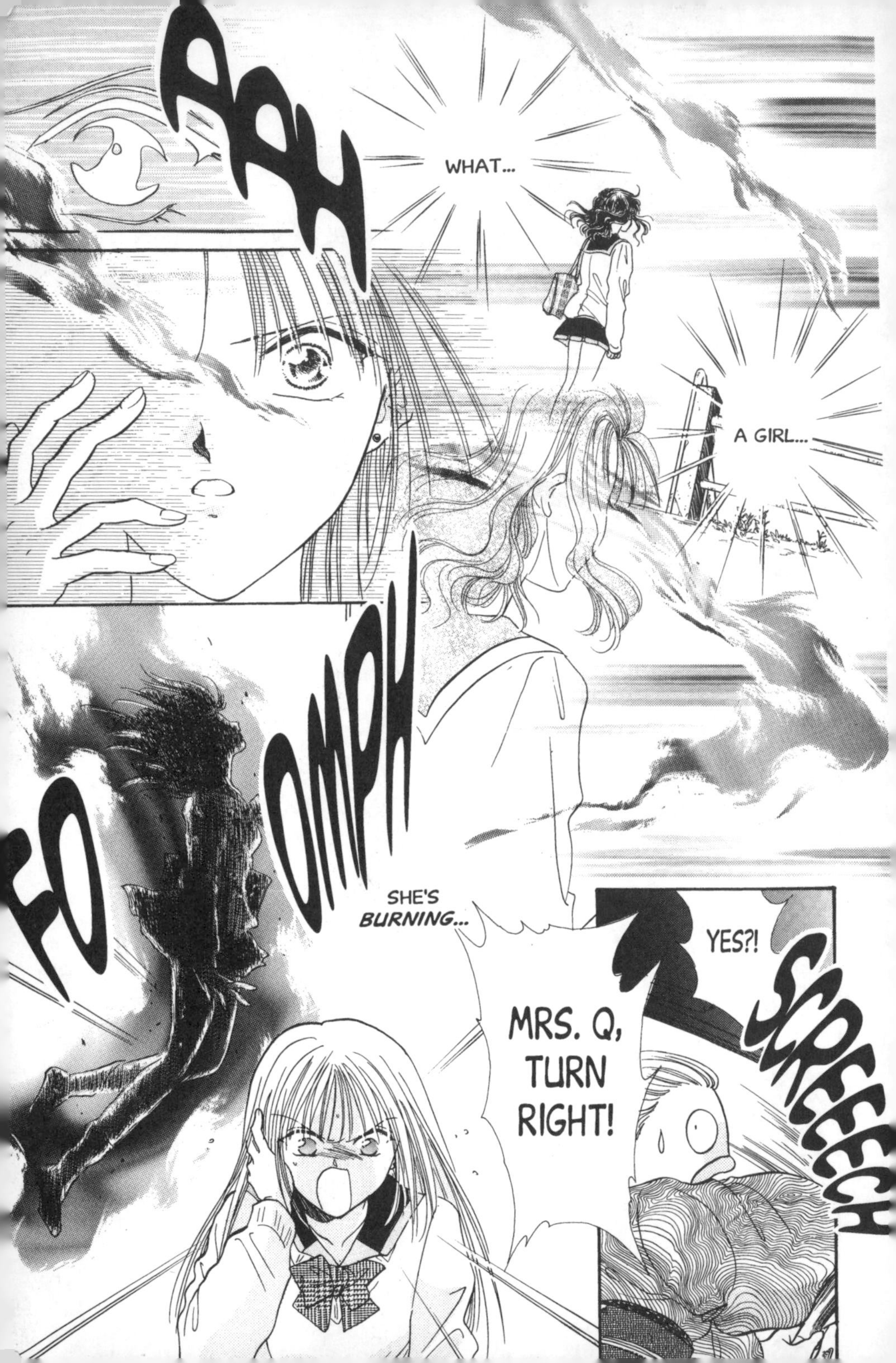
AAAH
WHAT...
A GIRL...
FOOMPH
SHE'S *BURNING...*
YES?!
SCREEECH
MRS. Q, TURN RIGHT!

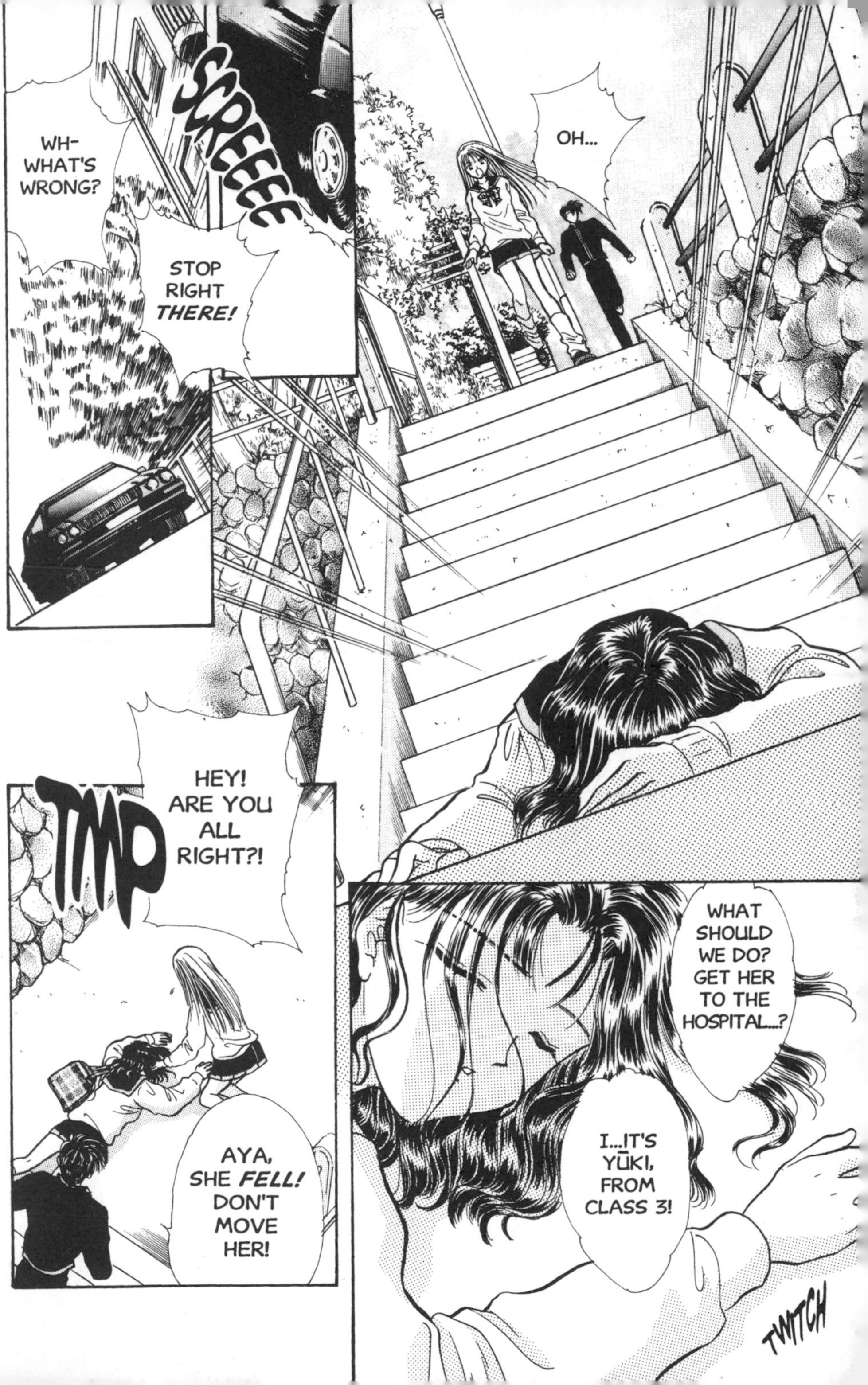
OH...
SCREEEE
WH- WHAT'S WRONG?
STOP RIGHT *THERE!*
HEY! ARE YOU ALL RIGHT?!
TMP
AYA, SHE *FELL!* DON'T MOVE HER!
WHAT SHOULD WE DO? GET HER TO THE HOSPITAL...?
I...IT'S YŪKI, FROM CLASS 3!
TWITCH

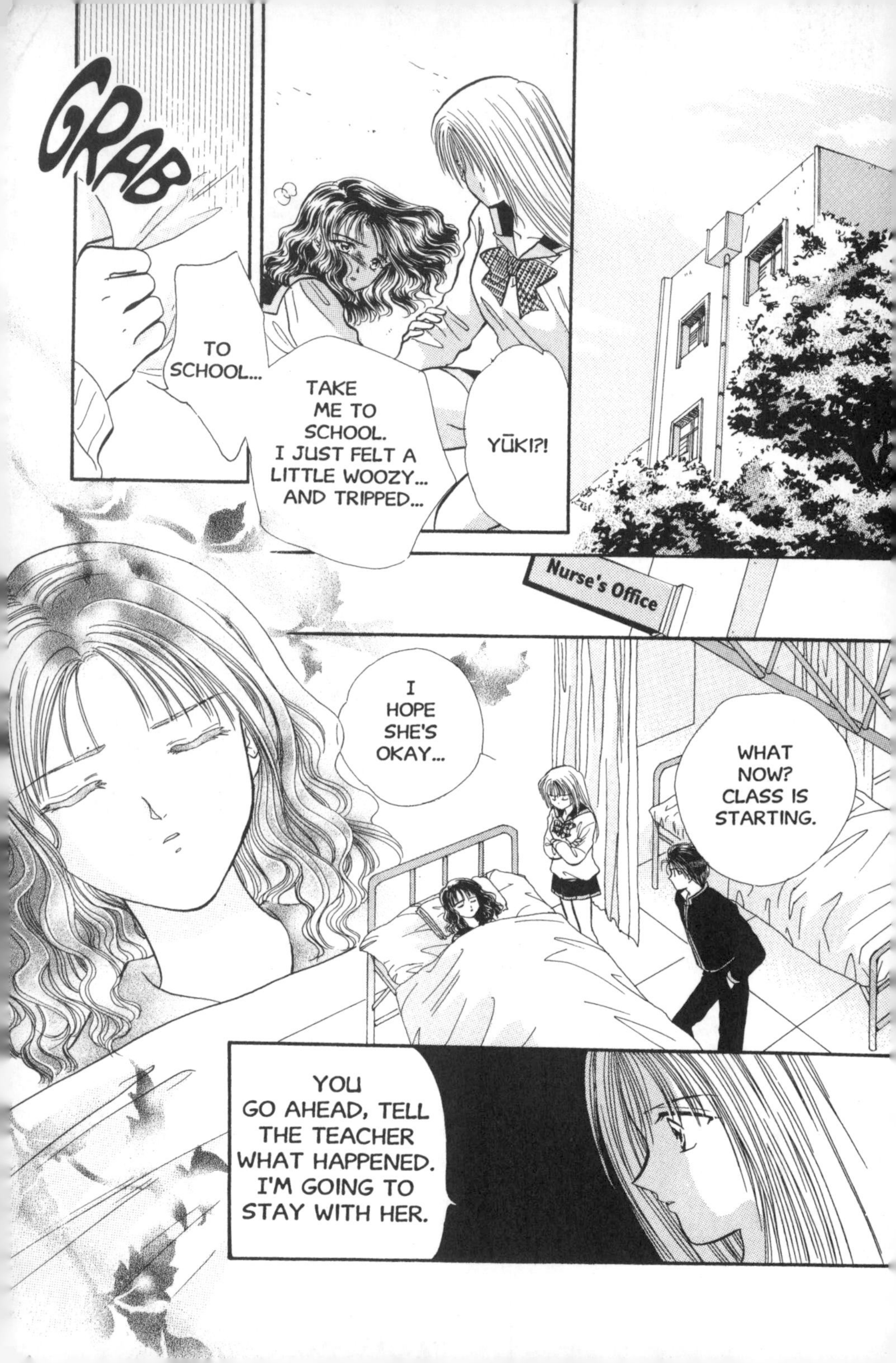
YŪKI?!
TAKE ME TO SCHOOL. I JUST FELT A LITTLE WOOZY... AND TRIPPED...
TO SCHOOL...
GRAB
Nurse's Office
WHAT NOW? CLASS IS STARTING.
I HOPE SHE'S OKAY...
YOU GO AHEAD, TELL THE TEACHER WHAT HAPPENED. I'M GOING TO STAY WITH HER.

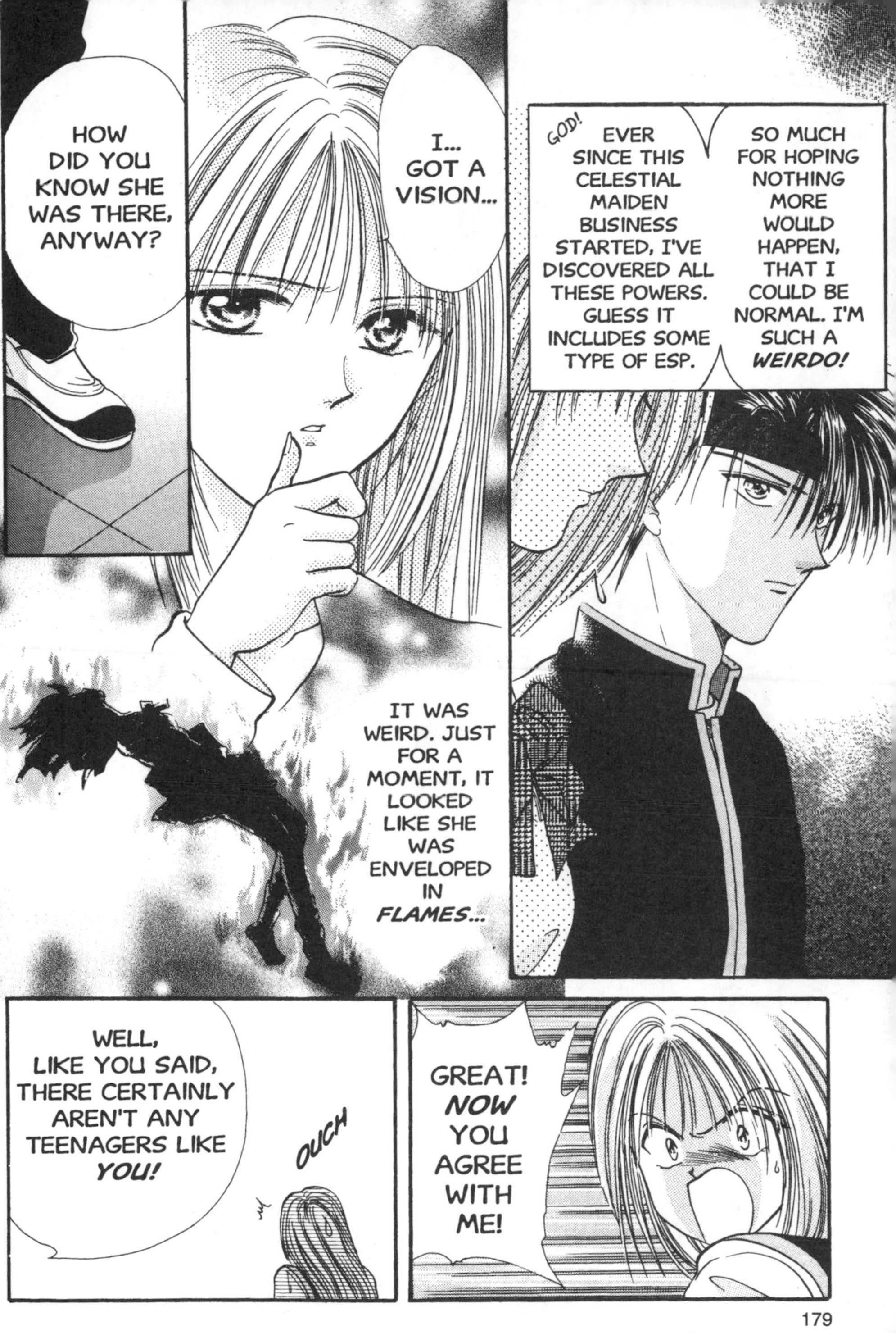
HOW DID YOU KNOW SHE WAS THERE, ANYWAY?
I... GOT A VISION...
IT WAS WEIRD. JUST FOR A MOMENT, IT LOOKED LIKE SHE WAS ENVELOPED IN *FLAMES...*
GOD!
EVER SINCE THIS CELESTIAL MAIDEN BUSINESS STARTED, I'VE DISCOVERED ALL THESE POWERS. GUESS IT INCLUDES SOME TYPE OF ESP.
SO MUCH FOR HOPING NOTHING MORE WOULD HAPPEN, THAT I COULD BE NORMAL. I'M SUCH A *WEIRDO!*
WELL, LIKE YOU SAID, THERE CERTAINLY AREN'T ANY TEENAGERS LIKE *YOU!*
OUCH
GREAT! *NOW* YOU AGREE WITH ME!

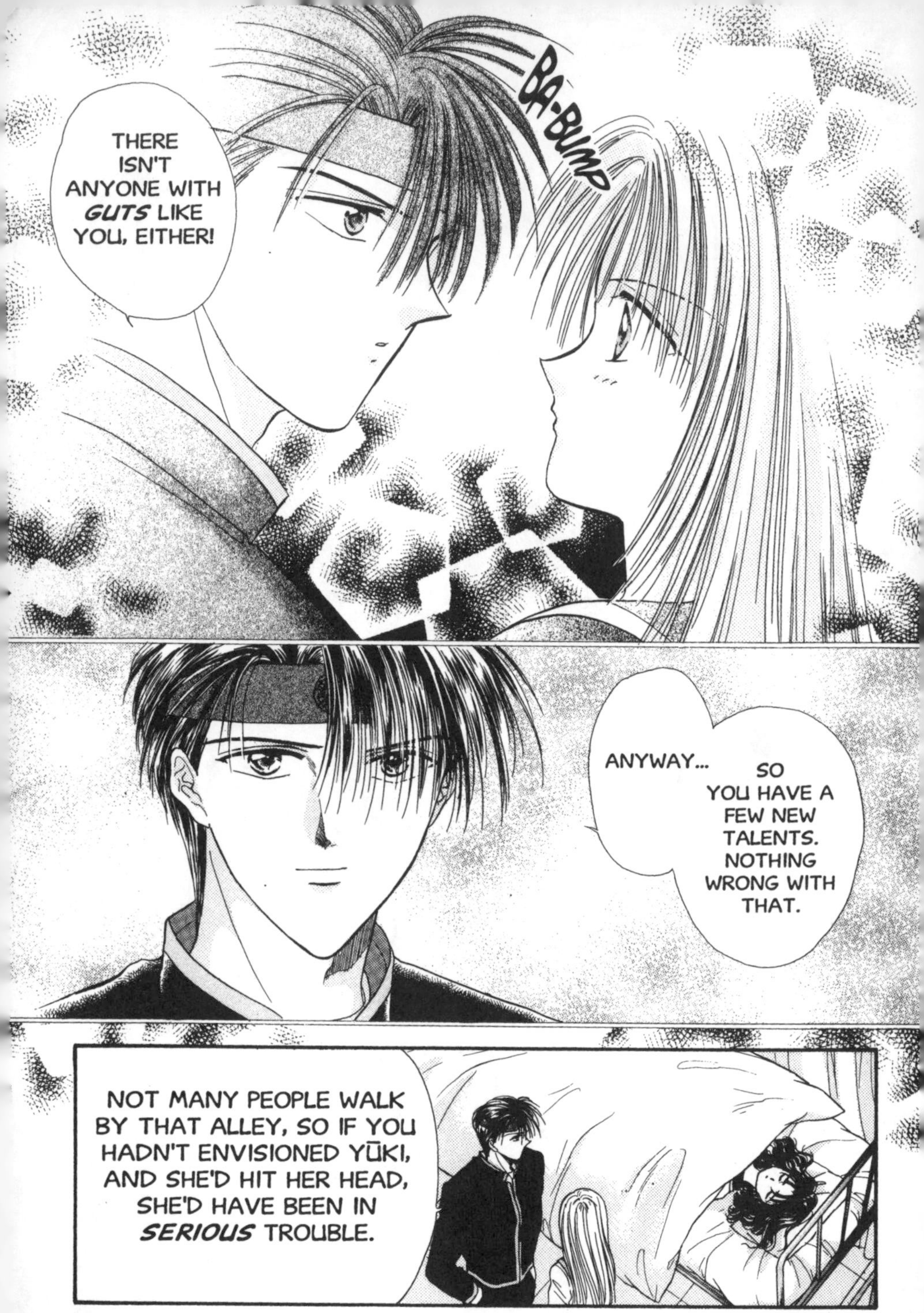
BA-BUMP
THERE ISN'T ANYONE WITH GUTS LIKE YOU, EITHER!
ANYWAY...
SO YOU HAVE A FEW NEW TALENTS. NOTHING WRONG WITH THAT.
NOT MANY PEOPLE WALK BY THAT ALLEY, SO IF YOU HADN'T ENVISIONED YŪKI, AND SHE'D HIT HER HEAD, SHE'D HAVE BEEN IN SERIOUS TROUBLE.

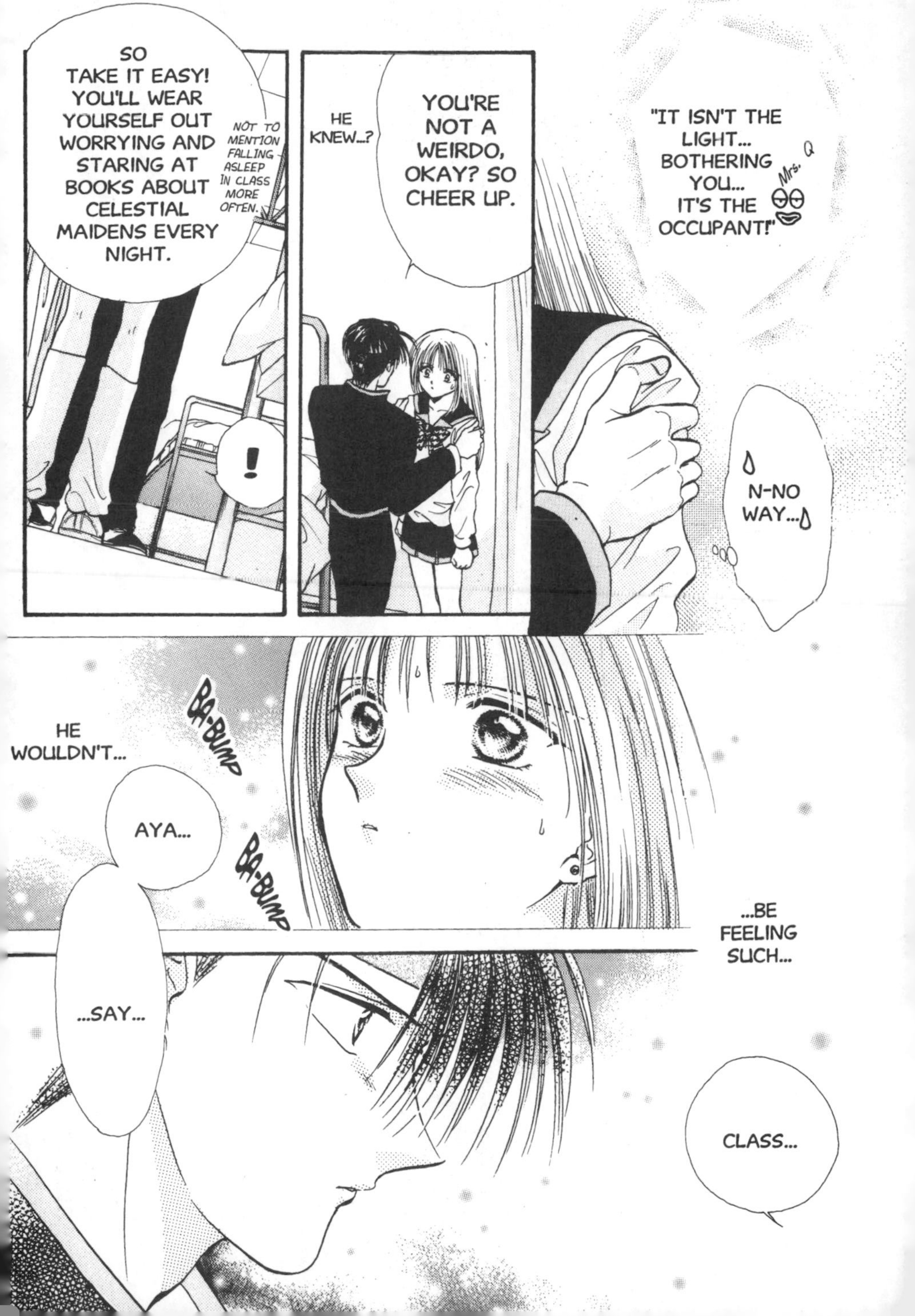
"IT ISN'T THE LIGHT... BOTHERING YOU... IT'S THE OCCUPANT!"
Mrs. Q
N-NO WAY...
YOU'RE NOT A WEIRDO, OKAY? SO CHEER UP.
HE KNEW...?
SO TAKE IT EASY! YOU'LL WEAR YOURSELF OUT WORRYING AND STARING AT BOOKS ABOUT CELESTIAL MAIDENS EVERY NIGHT.
NOT TO MENTION FALLING ASLEEP IN CLASS MORE OFTEN.
!
HE WOULDN'T...
BA-BUMP
BA-BUMP
...BE FEELING SUCH...
AYA...
...SAY...
CLASS...

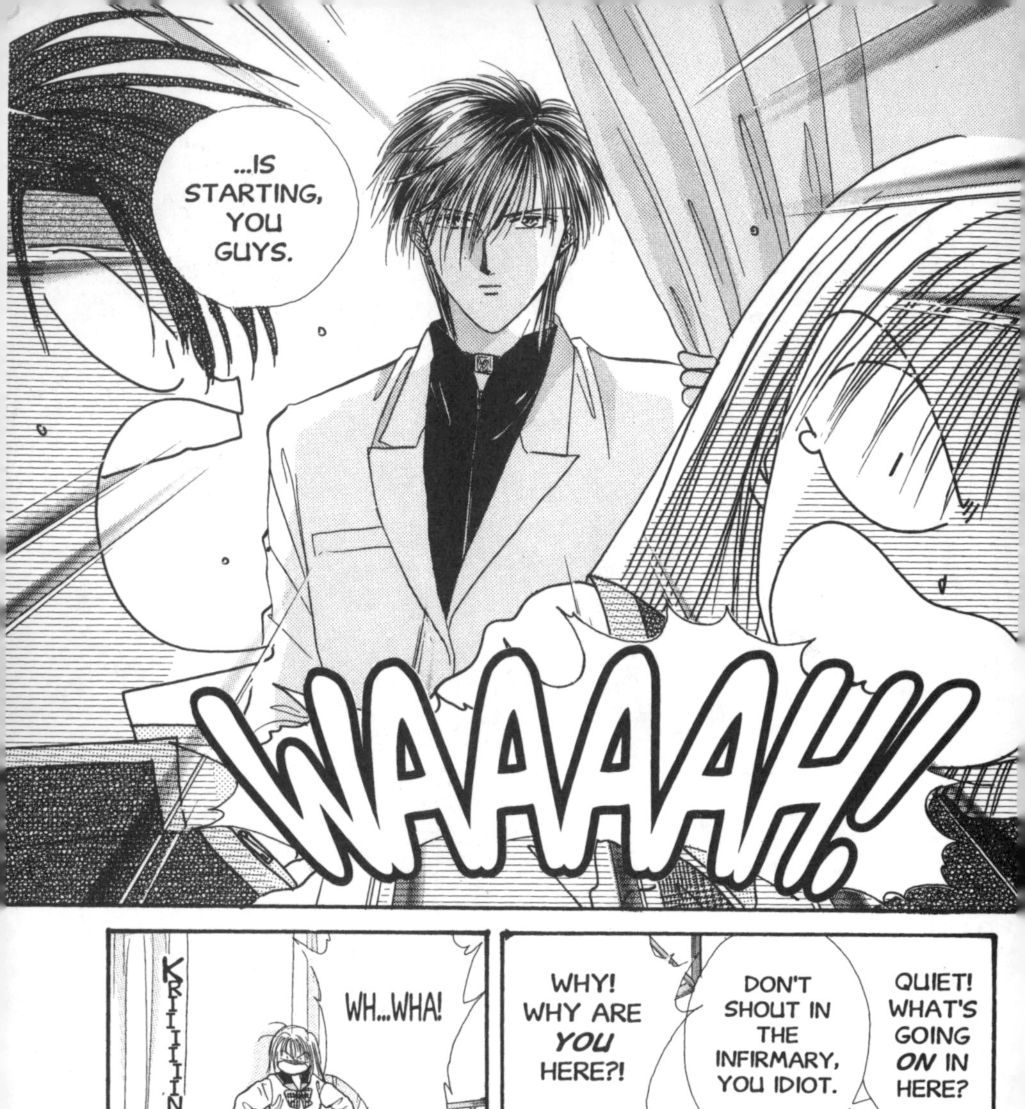
...IS STARTING, YOU GUYS.
WAAAAH!
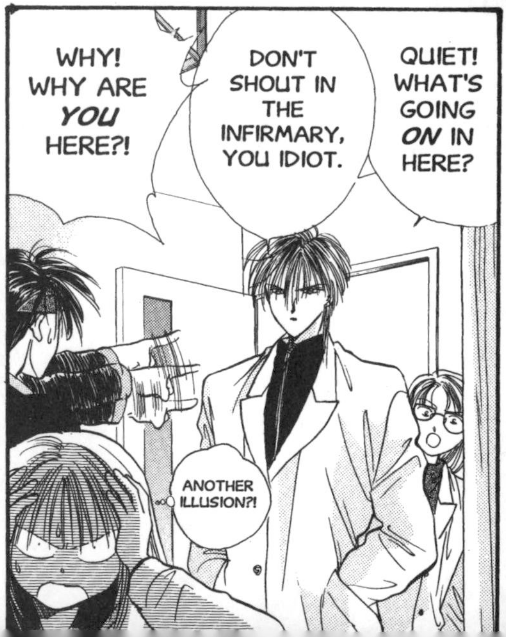
QUIET! WHAT'S GOING *ON* IN HERE?
DON'T SHOUT IN THE INFIRMARY, YOU IDIOT.
WHY! WHY ARE *YOU* HERE?!
ANOTHER ILLUSION?!
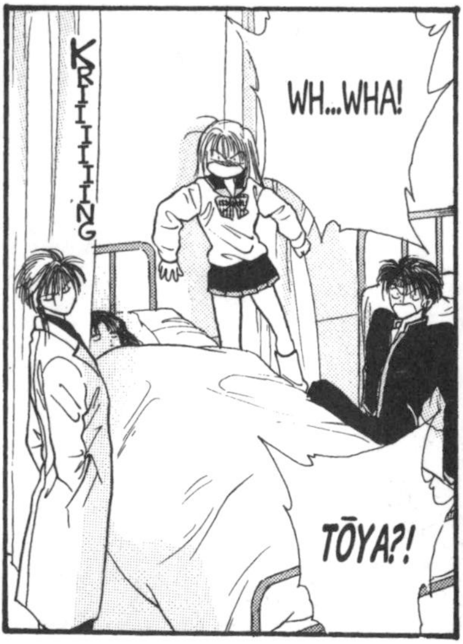
KRIIIIIING
WH...WHA!
TŌYA?!

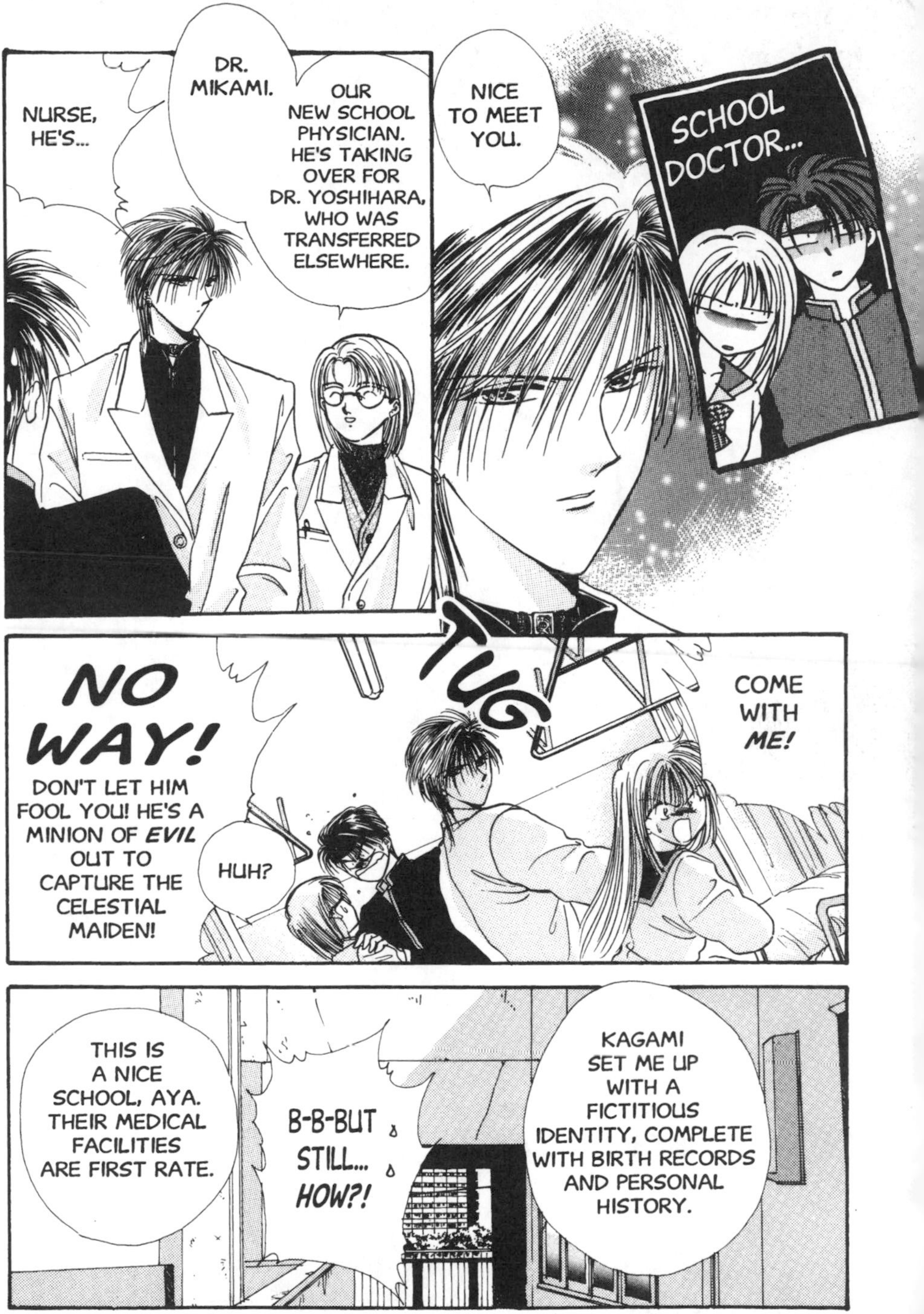
NURSE, HE'S...
DR. MIKAMI.
OUR NEW SCHOOL PHYSICIAN. HE'S TAKING OVER FOR DR. YOSHIHARA, WHO WAS TRANSFERRED ELSEWHERE.
NICE TO MEET YOU.
SCHOOL DOCTOR...
NO WAY!
DON'T LET HIM FOOL YOU! HE'S A MINION OF EVIL OUT TO CAPTURE THE CELESTIAL MAIDEN!
HUH?
TUG
COME WITH ME!
THIS IS A NICE SCHOOL, AYA. THEIR MEDICAL FACILITIES ARE FIRST RATE.
B-B-BUT STILL... HOW?!
KAGAMI SET ME UP WITH A FICTITIOUS IDENTITY, COMPLETE WITH BIRTH RECORDS AND PERSONAL HISTORY.

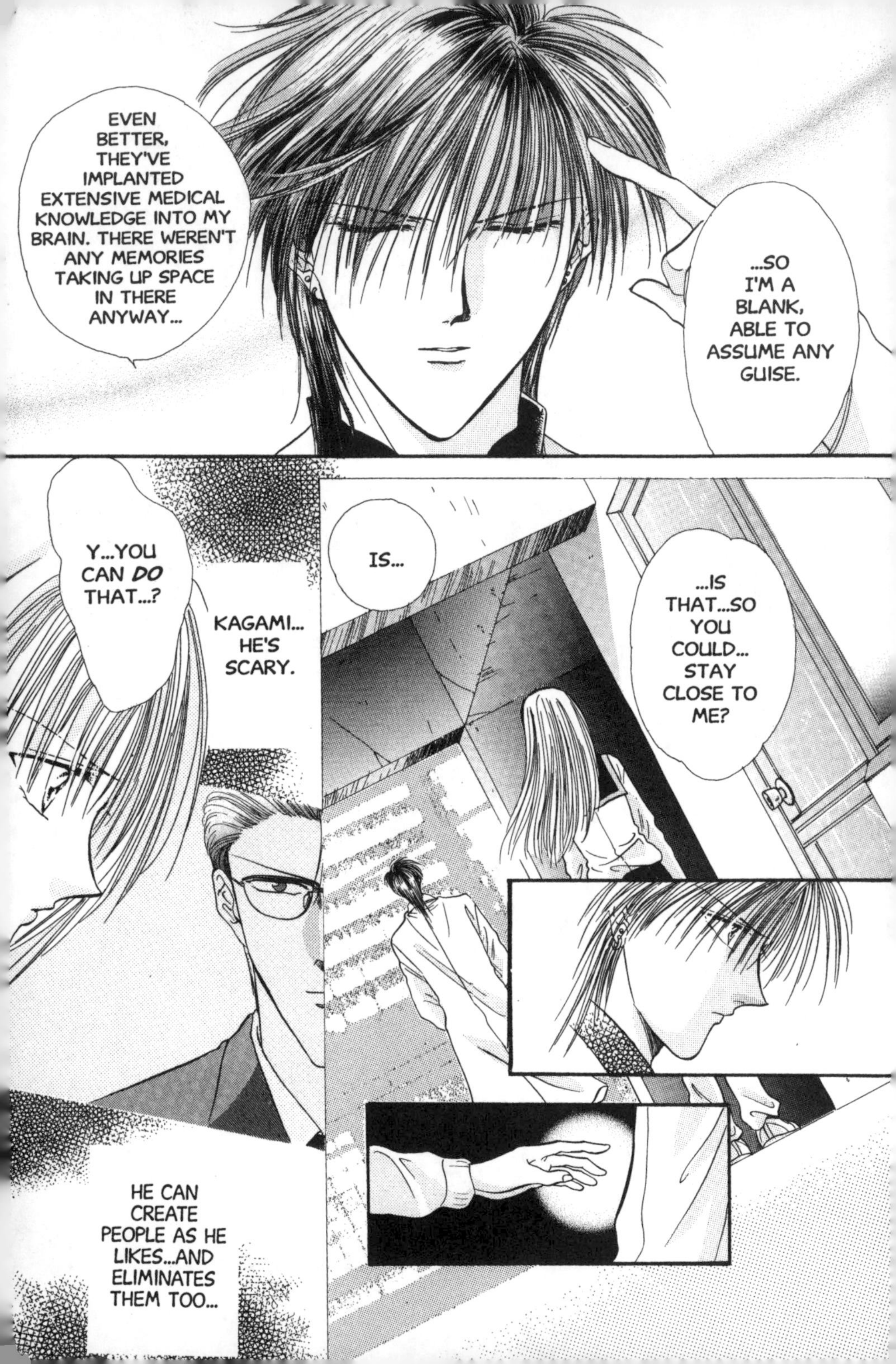
EVEN BETTER, THEY'VE IMPLANTED EXTENSIVE MEDICAL KNOWLEDGE INTO MY BRAIN. THERE WEREN'T ANY MEMORIES TAKING UP SPACE IN THERE ANYWAY...
...SO I'M A BLANK, ABLE TO ASSUME ANY GUISE.
Y...YOU CAN *DO* THAT...?
KAGAMI... HE'S SCARY.
HE CAN CREATE PEOPLE AS HE LIKES...AND ELIMINATES THEM TOO...
IS...
...IS THAT...SO YOU COULD... STAY CLOSE TO ME?

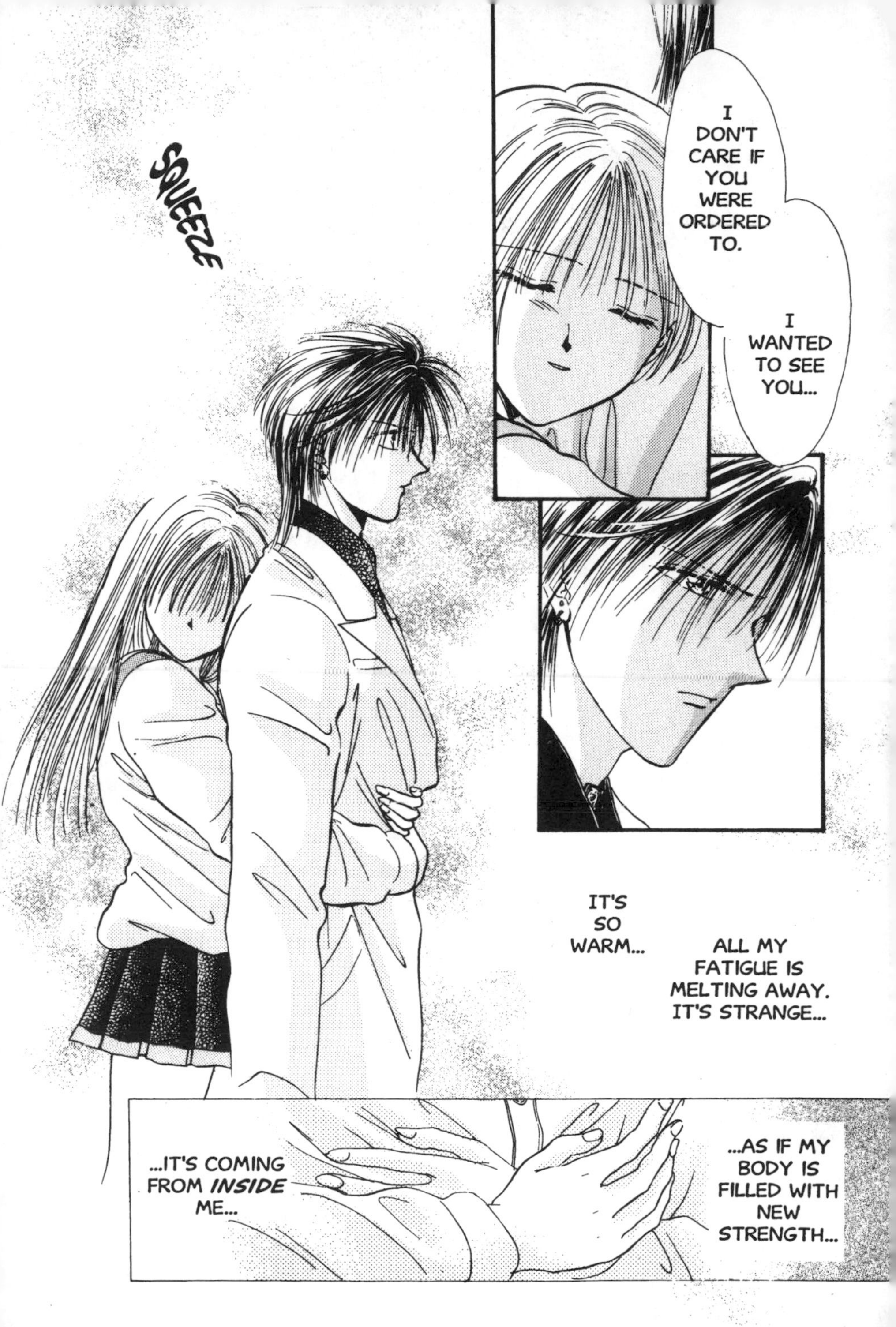

I DON'T CARE IF YOU WERE ORDERED TO.
I WANTED TO SEE YOU...
SQUEEZE
IT'S SO WARM...
ALL MY FATIGUE IS MELTING AWAY. IT'S STRANGE...
...AS IF MY BODY IS FILLED WITH NEW STRENGTH...
...IT'S COMING FROM *INSIDE* ME...

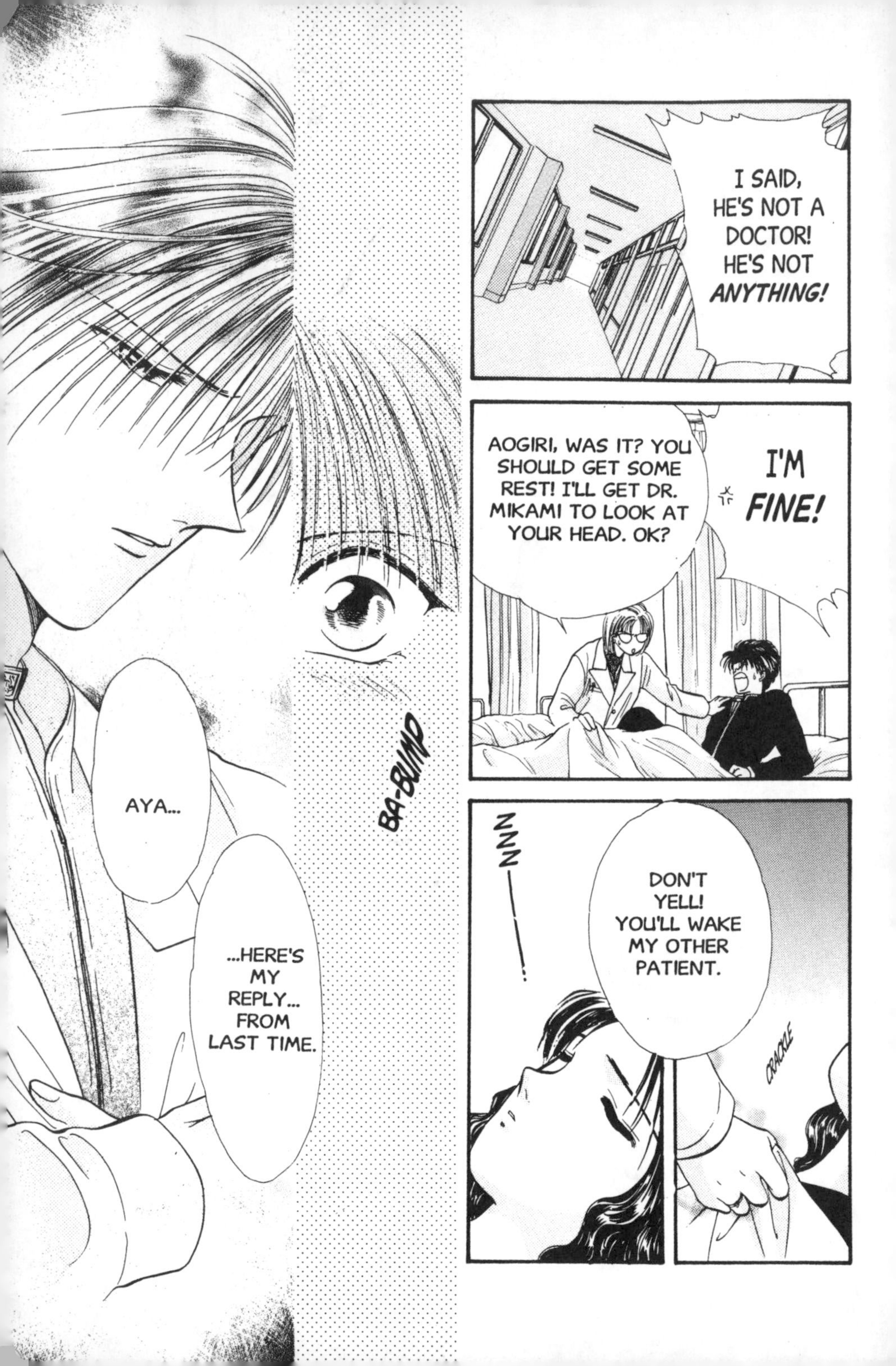
I SAID, HE'S NOT A DOCTOR! HE'S NOT ANYTHING!
AOGIRI, WAS IT? YOU SHOULD GET SOME REST! I'LL GET DR. MIKAMI TO LOOK AT YOUR HEAD. OK?
I'M FINE!
NNN—!
DON'T YELL! YOU'LL WAKE MY OTHER PATIENT.
CRACKLE
BA-BUMP
AYA...
...HERE'S MY REPLY... FROM LAST TIME.

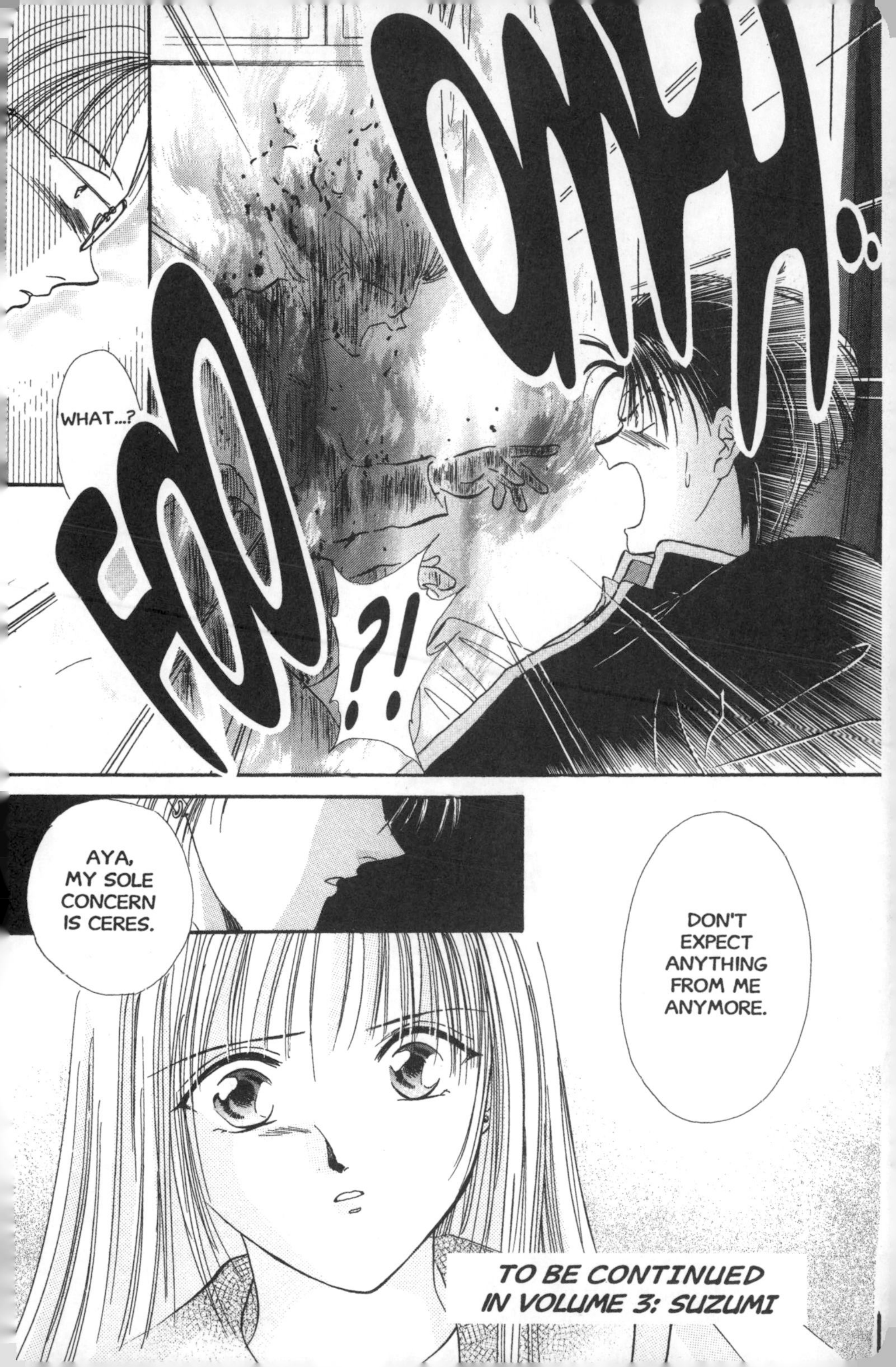
WHAT...?
?!
AYA, MY SOLE CONCERN IS CERES.
DON'T EXPECT ANYTHING FROM ME ANYMORE.
TO BE CONTINUED IN VOLUME 3: SUZUMI

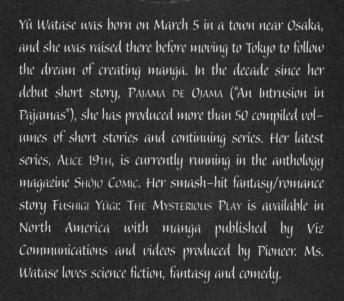

Yû Watase was born on March 5 in a town near Osaka, and she was raised there before moving to Tokyo to follow the dream of creating manga. In the decade since her debut short story, PAJAMA DE OJAMA ("An Intrusion in Pajamas"), she has produced more than 50 compiled volumes of short stories and continuing series. Her latest series, ALICE 19TH, is currently running in the anthology magazine SHŌJO COMIC. Her smash-hit fantasy/romance story FUSHIGI YÛGI: THE MYSTERIOUS PLAY is available in North America with manga published by Viz Communications and videos produced by Pioneer. Ms. Watase loves science fiction, fantasy and comedy.

MANGA FOR EVERYONE FROM ANIMERICA EXTRA

the anime fan's comic magazine

FUSHIGI YÛGI

"Thoroughly fun and almost impossible to put down." —Comics Buyer's Guide

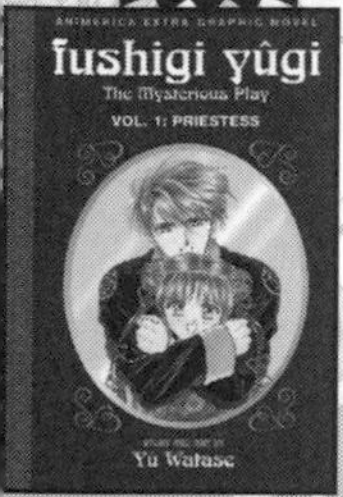

ANIMERICA EXTRA GRAPHIC NOVEL
fushigi yûgi
The Mysterious Play
VOL. 1: PRIESTESS
Yû Watase

Stranded inside the pages of a magic book, schoolgirl Miaka becomes the Priestess of Suzaku, destined to save a kingdom and find true love!

story & art by
Yû Watase
192-200 pages each

VOLUME	PRICE
Priestess	$15.95
Oracle	$15.95
Disciple	

VIDEO GIRL AI

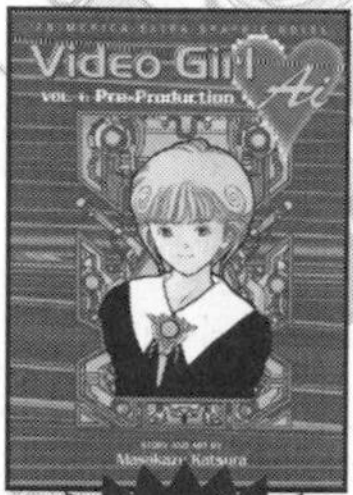

Video Girl Ai
VOL. 1: Pre-Production
Masakazu Katsura

"Katsura's artwork is first-rate. His layouts move the story along well, his characters are distinctive, and his girls are to die for." —Tony Isabella

When Ai emerged from Yota's VCR, she was supposed to be the girl of his dreams…but Yota will never trust video-box hype again!

story & art by
Masakazu Katsura
192-200 pages each

VOLUME	PRICE
Preproduction	$15.95
Mix Down	

X/1999

From the creators of MAGIC KNIGHT RAYEARTH and CARD CAPTOR SAKURA!

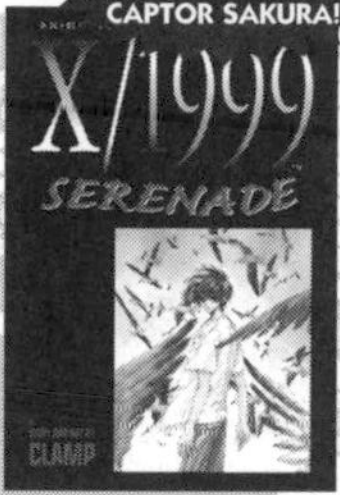

X/1999
SERENADE
CLAMP

In the city which is a blueprint for the Earth, the Seven Seals and Seven Harbingors fight for salvation or destruction…but the ultimate fate of the world rests on the young shoulders of super-psychic Kamui!

story & art by CLAMP
184 pages each

VOLUME	PRICE
Prelude	$15.95
Overture	$15.95
Sonata	$15.95
Intermezzo	$15.95

STEAM DETECTIVES

From the creator of SILENT MÖBIUS and MARTIAN SUCCESSOR NADESICO!

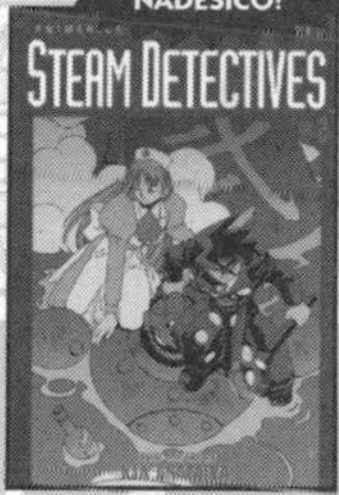

STEAM DETECTIVES

Start the engine! Stoke the fires! A young detective, a pretty nurse, and a giant robot fight crime in the Age of Steam!

story & art by
Kia Asamiya
192-208 pages each

VOLUME	PRICE
1	$15.95
2	

SHORT PROGRAM

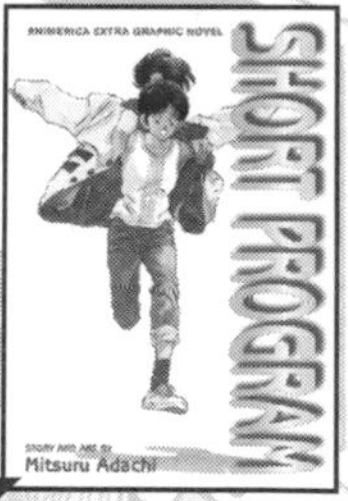

ANIMERICA EXTRA GRAPHIC NOVEL
SHORT PROGRAM
Mitsuru Adachi

A collection of eight sensitive and surprising short stories from a master of manga storytelling.

story & art by Mitsuru Adachi
256 pages
$16.95

"His pacing may be smooth as silk, but he can still knock you for a loop with the conclusions to his tales…" —Tony Isabella

MARIONETTE GENERATION

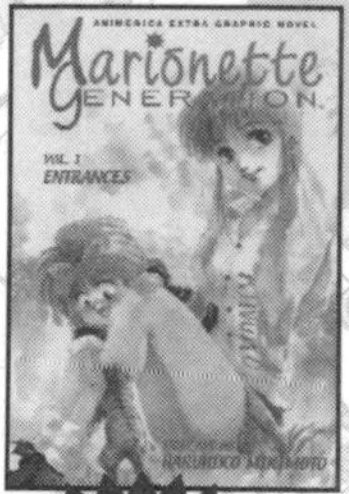

ANIMERICA EXTRA GRAPHIC NOVEL
Marionette Generation
VOL. 1
ENTRANCES

The odd love story of a befuddled artist, his cute-but-demanding assistant, and a living doll by one of Japan's most respected character designers.

story & art by
Haruhiko Mikimoto
184 pages

VOLUME	PRICE
Entrances	

From the character designer of MACROSS, ORGUSS, and GUNDAM 0080: WAR IN THE POCKET!

VIZ COMICS

Viz Comics
P.O. Box 77010
San Francisco, CA 94107

Phone: (800) 394-3042
Fax: (415) 348-8936

www.j-pop.com
www.animerica-mag.com
www.viz.com